# New Philosophies of Sex and Love

## Thinking Through Desire

# New Philosophies of Sex and Love

## Thinking Through Desire

EDITED BY
Sarah LaChance Adams,
Christopher M. Davidson,
and Caroline R. Lundquist

ROWMAN & LITTLEFIELD
INTERNATIONAL
London • New York

Published by Rowman & Littlefield International Ltd
Unit A, Whitacre Mews, 26-34 Stannary Street, London SE11 4AB
www.rowmaninternational.com

Rowman & Littlefield International Ltd.is an affiliate of Rowman & Littlefield
4501 Forbes Boulevard, Suite 200, Lanham, Maryland 20706, USA
With additional offices in Boulder, New York, Toronto (Canada), and Plymouth (UK)
www.rowman.com

**British Library Cataloguing in Publication Data**

A catalogue record for this book is available from the British Library
ISBN: HB 978-1-7866-0221-3
      PB 978-1-7866-0222-0

**Library of Congress Cataloging-in-Publication Data**

Names: LaChance Adams, Sarah, editor. | Davidson, Christopher M., 1980–
    editor. | Lundquist, Caroline R., editor.
Title: New philosophies of sex and love : thinking through desire / edited by
    Sarah Lachance Adams, Christopher M. Davidson, and Caroline Lundquist.
Description: London; Lanham, Maryland : Rowman & Littlefield International,
    Ltd, [2016] | Includes bibliographical references and index.
Identifiers: LCCN 2016037535 (print) | LCCN 2016043879 (ebook) |
    ISBN 9781786602213 (cloth : alk. paper) | ISBN 9781786602220
    (pbk. : alk. paper) | ISBN 9781786602237 (Electronic)
Subjects: LCSH: Love. | Sex.
Classification: LCC BD436 .N49 2016 (print) | LCC BD436 (ebook) |
    DDC 128/.46–dc23
LC record available at https://lccn.loc.gov/2016037535

⊖™ The paper used in this publication meets the minimum requirements of American
National Standard for Information Sciences—Permanence of Paper for Printed Library
Materials, ANSI/NISO Z39.48-1992.

Printed in the United States of America

For Robert Dewitt Adams, with whom I flourish.

—SLA

To K and to E for frank discussions regarding sex and love, and to M & D, D & L, and R & N for extending love through hospitality.

—CD

To the love-bruises on all of our hearts, and to the acts of love that help to heal them.

—CL

# Contents

# Acknowledgments

We would like to thank the following people who made this book possible: the University of Wisconsin, Superior for a Faculty Development Grant; members of the Society for the Philosophy of Sex and Love; student research assistants Xuan Chen and Yasmina Antcliff; students in the University of Wisconsin, Superior's Philosophy of Love and Sex course in Fall 2014 who read, presented on, and critiqued an early version of the manuscript (Brooke Collins, Calla Hodgkinson, Ceasyn Chaffe, Cecelia Preston, Claire Johnson, Codi Gleesing, James Braden, John Staine, Joseph Maxwell, Joseph Olson, Kristina Mencel, Mariah McDonald, Marisa Soliz, Olivia Miller, Stephanie Eastvold, Theresa Johnson and Xuan Chen); and numerous anonymous reviewers.

*Part I*

# DESIRE'S DISSONANCE

*Chapter One*

# Introduction

## *Desire's Dissonance*

### Sarah LaChance Adams, Christopher M. Davidson, and Caroline R. Lundquist

There are moments when the world feels out of joint, when our familiar patterns of thinking and acting are disrupted. They arise, more often than not, when our accustomed ways of organizing, interpreting, and valuing are at odds with something else, something *new*. These moments of dissonance are unsettling, but we ought not to take refuge in the familiar on that account; for although we find dissonance uncomfortable, it overflows with philosophical promise. Dissonance alerts us to theoretically rich contradictions, indicating spaces of conceptual ambiguity in what had previously seemed to be plain truths or common sense. Hence, when we choose to dwell with—and think through—the unfamiliar, we can become conscious of, and begin to explore the deep significance of our intuitions and our pre-reflective experience in all their chaotic dynamism. There is no end to the insights that can arise as a result of the choice to go down these untrodden pathways of thought, where the familiar can become strange, and the strange, strangely familiar.

The chapters in this volume *dwell* with desire's dissonance, and in so doing they uncover insights that are as intriguing as they are unsettling. Desire is the location of mystifying and invigorating tensions, the shifting nexus of apparent oppositions: deliberative reason and unformulated experience, power and resistance, one's present becoming and one's past being, cultural "knowledge" and embodiment, yearning and explicitly held values, deception and love of truth, exploitation and friendship, spontaneity and premeditated design, and so on. Seeming opposition often indicates a unique and vital relation.

The philosophical *modus operandi* of these chapters is to engage with lived experience, to embrace conceptual fluidity and ambiguity, and to think via the hermeneutic circle. For example, while some people might seek to distinguish between perverted sexuality and typical or "normal" sexuality, we explore how abject bodies can become objects of mainstream desire precisely because they are transgressive. While others seek to find a strong conceptual divide between consent and coercion, we wonder about the phenomenon of seduction as simultaneously deceiving and disclosing. We are especially interested in the way that marginalized experiences may expand, lend nuance to, or even undermine our previous understanding of the phenomena in question.

The authors in this anthology understand that any *one* method of revealing a phenomenon may conceal the truths that would arise via others. They recognize, for instance, that although medical narratives will have much to tell us about erectile dysfunction and intersexed embodiment, relying on these narratives alone risks overshadowing the sociocultural context that codetermines the meaning of these phenomena. Seeking a diagnosis, for example, may bar us from asking whether certain types of nonnormativity should be pathologized to begin with. Diagnosis, like many forms of judgment or meaning-making, arises in a particular setting that may have a role in *constructing* the precise condition that practitioners only intend to *delineate*. When we contextualize a diagnosis—or any other judgment—by noting how it assumes a certain conceptual framework, we can better see both its value and its limitations. Hence, the chapters in this volume reflect the belief that a dialogical engagement between disciplines with apparently different epistemological assumptions is critical to the most dynamic and robust inquiry. By going beyond any single approach to sex and love, such as cognitive science, classical phenomenology, first-person narrative, medical science, analytic logic, or social construction, these chapters travel *around* a phenomenon, marking and then exploring its convergent and divergent aspects.

These chapters are unique in that they place more emphasis on examining the *workings* of our normative assumptions than on arguing for positions of right and wrong. We wonder what certain ethical imperatives reveal about a worldview. For example, we ask what the cultural status of monogamy discloses regarding our beliefs about "real" love and fidelity. The authors of these chapters do not dictate the *outcomes* of ethical inquiry. Instead, they ask what perspectives and prejudices are hidden within our predominant cultural mores.

Sex and love are inherently risky. Among their hazards is the productive undermining of our most cherished certainties. For this reason, we hope this anthology will be more provocative than conciliatory. The authors here share the spirit of daring by examining the established pathways for sex and love, observing the grooves established by experience, and reading from them the etchings of conformity and resistance. They explicate both common and non-normative experiences—demonstrating that ignored, misrepresented and disciplined bodies may reveal unfamiliar, but exciting, new options. Our desires are reflective of where we have been; who we want to be; our self-betrayals, self-restraint, and self-discoveries; our powers to create and deceive; and our political and vocational investments. Desire is elusive, conflicted, shifting, fleeting, and nonlinear. It can be manipulated, corrupted, faked, and medicated, but it also can be a source of power, creativity, compassion, and wisdom. As philosophically minded thinkers, it behooves us to attend to desire's dissonance, to esteem an attitude of humble and respectful curiosity, and to recognize that if we are not risking what we think we know, then we are not venturing enough.

The chapters in part II go beyond traditional taxonomies of love and desire to explore inclusive descriptions that can account for the variety of their manifestations. The authors entertain questions such as: What is love's essential character? What is its scope? Are its boundaries clear or ambiguous? What qualities are held in common between diverse kinds of love? What distinguishes "real" love from false loves that dominate or distort?

In chapter 2, Louis A. Ruprecht Jr. revives the myth of Eros as a self-contradictory creature created through the drunken copulation of *Poros* (resource or "a way") and *Penia* (poverty). Eros yearns because he is always in need like his mother, but like his father, he also has the ability to stretch for what is outside of his grasp. Drawing on the Ancient emphasis on process, Ruprecht questions the contemporary subject-seeking focus on sexual identity as substance. Eros, he claims, is not focused on the self, but rather on the space between self and the other. It is a *reaching*-beyond-oneself toward another, unsettling the very effort toward *grasping* self-definition. Desire is about what one does *not* have. If desire were viewed as the having-of-an-object, then it would always be a failure since objects ultimately fade, dissipate and die. The successful "end" of desire can only be natality (procreation and/or creation), but this finale is really an overture that is, hopefully, destined to exceed one's own existence. Thus, for Ruprecht, desire seeks infinity.

In the *Symposium*, Socrates blends the myth regarding the origin of Eros with a description of philosophy. Philosophizing starts in response to the confusion of an *aporia* (the absence of a way, *a-poros*), when one comes to know that one does not know. Philosophy, a la Socràtes, is knowledge of ignorance. Similarly, Ruprecht's vision of philosophy is in between having and not having, and pulses with the dynamic push–pull of *eros*: "Greek philosophy is tragicomic thinking, the attempt to think the unthinkable by thinking in the middle, attempting to join what has been separated far too casually: love and sex, Eros and Aphrodite, the thinking of desiring thought itself." The process that animates both love and love of wisdom never comes to rest in a fixed object; it is in between beginning and finishing.

The meaning of love has changed quite radically over time, which makes engagement with the philosophical questions to which it gives rise notoriously difficult. An even more fundamental issue is that it is not clear what kind of definition we ought to seek. Rather than seeking a strict normative definition of love, which might exclude important experiences, or a minimal definition that would leave the concept thin on meaningful content, Chiara Piazzesi argues in chapter 3 that we ought to fashion a description of love that is both pliable and robust. As she explains, to minimally define a living room only by a floor, a ceiling, and some number of walls may work—but a similarly minimal definition of love would tell us very little.

Piazzesi notes that our definition will need to analyze discourse and social roles. The emotions of love require an understanding of our contemporary discourse because they do not occur in a purely subjective immediate intuition. We do not experience "love as such" and then try to talk about it. Discursive ways of making meaning are inseparable from a feeling of love itself. Situating how love feels within the ways we find ourselves talking about love gives us a much firmer grasp on the phenomena. Moreover, discourse analysis allows for a wide range of "loves," both good and bad, to be understood and sorted without forcing normative claims into the definition itself. Approaching love's meaning in this fashion highlights the implicit structures of the wide range of understandings of love operating in our culture today.

Like Piazzesi, Michael Kim in chapter 4 emphasizes both the difficulty and the importance of thinking about love, reminding us that while love is simultaneously among the hardest things to think about philosophically, it is also one of the most critical. Instead of asking what the definition of love would be, Kim asks "how is love possible at all?" What are the conditions of possibility for the emergence of love? Whereas Piazzesi emphasizes the social and discursively contextualized contexts of love's historical, shifting nature, Kim links the difficulty in defining love to its ontological status: at the limit or crossing of self and other, and life-world transformation.

In a desperate but common move, many lovers try to realize their love as a fixed, discrete *thing*: the intimately offered body reduced to a brute proof, or the declaration of "I love you" as an externalized self. However, following Sartre, Kim claims that love cannot be reduced to an object; it is not an act, a feeling, or a simple state of affairs. In fact, there is a double difficulty preceding the emergence of love: not only must we let our beloveds be who (not what) they are, we also must not make ourselves into an object. Nevertheless, if the central focus of love was respect for individual autonomy, then it could be reduced to a relatively distant, contractual affair. Each lover would remain largely unchanged by the other. Marion, with his concept of the "crossing" of two subjects, provides the corrective. The changes that come to us in love are not the kind that can be chosen by a single self; they are much more radical than what can be achieved by two free existents' coinciding wills. Love gives birth to a new world and is, therefore, the most radical of changes. Love surpasses drawing closer to another, interchanging ideas, or sharing experiences. Love is an emergence that does not arise in a *place*, Kim argues, but rather in the *displacement* of oneself.

Monogamy exerts such a strong normative hegemony that for many it seems like the only possible configuration of "real love." In chapter 5, Erik Jansson Boström elucidates monogamy as embedded in a particular world-view in the manner of Max Weber. In the course of his analysis, Boström shows that there are distinct types of monogamy and polyamory, giving us a detailed taxonomy for understanding diverse ways of loving. Each has a unique internal logic, making sense of desire and love in wholly different ways. As Boström shows, sketching these ideal versions of each worldview lies somewhere between description and evaluation, revealing what makes a set of values "tick" by explicating some of its key features. Describing a worldview neither invalidates it nor justifies it, but making its premises explicit would be a propaedeutic to either end. Such a method of explication is especially important for monogamy, whose ubiquity has made it difficult to see. In the end, polyamory is understood as an alternate worldview, just as comprehensible and authentic as monogamy. Polyamorism clearly indicates new possibilities not only in terms of the *quantity* of relationships, but more notably, it opens up wider variety in the *qualities* that legitimate relationships may have.

Love, particularly as envisioned as something that one "falls" into or as something that occurs "naturally" between parents and children, is often posited as the antithesis of agency. Sex is frequently portrayed as either impulsive and risky, or as habitual and stale. Heteronormative gender dynamics are regarded as mere manifestations of biological and cultural programming. The chapters in part III challenge these unimaginative ideas. In their place, the authors offer friendship and comradeship, as manifested both in familial and romantic relationships, as ways of reclaiming agency.

In chapter 6, Elena Cuffari considers models of heterosexual relationships that depict men as immature boneheads who will pursue sex with as many women as possible at almost any cost, and that represent women as obsessed with fidelity, spending much of their time in desperate attempts to prevent, delay, and deal with the after-effects of male cheating. Moreover, Cuffari notes that in such stock accounts, female behavior is defined inversely, as a reaction against male tendencies. This makes cheating by females seem nearly impossible. But perhaps even more damaging is the fact that female friendships are imperiled as other women are construed as enemies to one's romantic relationship. Although these images of female and male genders are quite different, they share the feature of being gender-based disavowals of agency.

Cuffari critiques spurious appropriations of scientific research that lend an air of authority to popular culture's truisms about heterosexual relationships.

She raises doubts about popularly accepted economic cost-benefit calculations, biological accounts, and universally enforced social norms. Turning to cognitive science, she gives a grounded philosophical account that avoids reductionism and makes sense of a biologically sensible freedom. As deployed by Cuffari, cognitive science undermines the false dichotomy of an unfettered, individualistic freedom versus strict determination that is emblematic of many pop-biological, sociological, and economic accounts. Ultimately, Cuffari asserts that couples together make a space where commitment can emerge, a process that shapes their agency without eliminating all sense of freedom.

Pussy Riot's famous 2012 performance of musical protest in a Moscow cathedral embodied anger. But as Fulden Ibrahimhakkioglu notes in chapter 7, this anger was misconstrued as hatred by the court, by members of the Russian government, and by various popular media pundits. The case of Pussy Riot is a variation on an all-too-familiar theme: the misrepresentation of the complex emotions motivating feminist activism as baseless and impulsive "rage" or blind "hatred." This distortion of feminist activism has all but absorbed the concept "feminist" in the popular imagination. The story of Pussy Riot illuminates a truth that has been covered over by the notion of the "angry feminist": that feminist rage can be and often is motivated by love and solidarity.

Before we can correct such misconceptions, Ibrahimhakkioglu argues that we must begin by recognizing that in the political realm, love, anger, and action are often intertwined. In the context of the ACT UP movement, for example, anger functioned to mobilize those who had lost loved ones to AIDS. Here, as in so many cases of activism, anger was instrumentally effective and arose initially out of love. Anger may not sustain a movement, but anger *and* love may. If we attend to the overwhelmingly positive reception of Pussy Riot by the global community, then we will perhaps suspect that the old image of the bitter feminist may eventually be eclipsed by that of the socially aware "holy fool," whose fury is born of love, who rages and rocks for justice, and whose ethos is infectious.

In chapter 8, Christine Overall examines a form of love rarely analyzed by philosophers: the love between parents and adult children. The dependency that comes with the status of child must be attenuated once the child becomes an adult, but numerous questions surround the relation. Are dependency and autonomy at all compatible? Exactly when does the child become an adult? Does the parent have a better understanding of their offspring (having known the child their whole life) or perhaps does the parent know less than friends and lovers once the child leaves the parent's home?

Distinguishing between its ontological features (what a parent is, what a child is, what relations they necessarily have) and its epistemological features (what the parent knows of the child in early childhood and does not know in later life, what the child knows of himself through the parent, and so on), Overall considers themes related to love in general: identity, maintaining relationships through significant life changes, and dependency and autonomy. Indeed, today this particular bond is often of a longer duration and perhaps greater intensity, as parents live longer and as adult children more often continue to live with their parents. The specific difficulties of this relation hold lessons for us regarding love more generally.

Part IV brings our attention to nonnormative bodies and how they are excluded from or marginalized by popular and medical narratives of sex and love. Making sense of one's own body can be painfully difficult if one does not have a narrative to serve as a guide. As Phoebe Hart explains in her largely autobiographical chapter 9, her intersexed body does have a medical narrative, but that narrative does little to help her communicate the sense that her body makes to her lovers. In certain nonmedical narratives, others with her condition were spoken of as having a charming, elf-like appearance, and of holding a powerful allure over people. Hence, Hart asks whether or to what extent the medicalization of the intersexed body has reduced it to a mere medical "condition" rather than a rare and beautiful body, a source of erotic wonder.

While Hart is not hostile to the medical description of herself, she responds to its thinness by developing her own self-narrative through a documentary film. For Hart, it is not a matter of selecting existing narratives and then identifying with them; hers is a more challenging and creative task. Her identity is an original work, the result of heartfelt explorations of her family history, her body's capabilities, and her romantic relationships. This project of weaving her own self-narrative may act as an inspiration for defying gender normativity more broadly.

In chapter 10, Rebecca Kukla tackles the difficulties the pharmaceutical industry has had in addressing female sexual dysfunction. Those involved in researching the issue have moved from asking how to fix the problem, to realizing that they cannot agree on a foundational question: what exactly is the nature of the problem? As Kukla explains, attempts to understand problems in the expression of female desire struggle from the start because there is no agreement on what female desire *is*—therefore, there is no agreement on when that desire functions properly or when it does not. This is difficult to reconcile with the fact that roughly half of women report sexual dysfunction. Thus, while women's sexual dysfunction appears to be statistically normal, its precise nature is unknown.

Despite the fact that women report sexual frustration and low levels of enjoyment at higher proportions than do men, there have been multiple pills to treat erectile dysfunction for some time, while only one recent (and controversial) female libido drug has been approved. As Kukla points out, men's sexuality is treated as fundamentally biological and simple, whereas the "mystery" of women's sexuality is consistently explained through nonbiological, psycho-social emotional grounds: her partner, her social life (family, job), and her nonsexual emotional life (stress, depression). It seems the pharmaceutical industry has not found a way to improve on Freud's observation that psychology had no grasp on the so-called dark continent of adult female sexuality. Female sexuality remains a mystery—*the* mystery, perhaps, of sexuality.

In chapter 11, Amy E. Taylor explores the surprising ways in which one's bodily and sexual identity can be challenged, expanded and ameliorated through the use of artificial objects. The object that here takes on an unexpected role is the strap-on dildo used by "Michael," whose cancer treatments left him incapable of achieving an erection. The "impotence" of his sex organ made Michael feel like a failure as a person, and understandably so; the link between body and self-image is painfully familiar to most of us. Michael initially resisted sexual play and experimentation involving objects, since such play may seem to suggest, submissiveness and risk the loss of important elements of previous body schema.

As Taylor explains, the eventual incorporation of artificial objects into his bodily consciousness reveals the malleability of that consciousness and of our ways of moving through the world. Referring to Merleau-Ponty, Taylor shows how Michael's sexual experience resembles the case of a blind person whose habitual ways of walking have come to incorporate the presence of a cane. As Michael discovered, there are multiple paths to some of our most valued and cherished bodily experiences, and some of them are most unexpected. Taylor's subtle understanding of embodiment reminds us that some forms of "artificial" modification can become absolutely central to who we "really" are. One consequence of this is that we can think about our body's limits, its possibilities and the nonnatural means we might use to expand it, without denying our embodied "nature" in any way.

The chapters in part V navigate the unnerving interplay between, on the one hand, manipulation and deception, and on the other hand, love of truth in romance and friendship. In chapter 12, Alain Beauclair examines the desire-producing activity of seduction in order to question its character and legitimacy as a mode of discourse. Since seduction aims to produce new desires and since desire is intrinsically linked with personal identity, to seduce another would be to change them. Must we then cede, he wonders, that to be seduced is to be subjugated? Beauclair claims that the answer to this question hinges on another: "What is the relationship between seduction and truth?"

Turning to Plato's dialogue *Phaedrus*, Beauclair finds that much of persuasion relies on the ability to make what is false appear to be true. Rhetoric separated from the truth is little more than clever deception; rhetoric that aims to persuade by way *of* the truth is another matter entirely. In Beauclair, s view, Socratic persuasion can be distinguished from persuasion in the pejorative sense in that Socrates approaches his interlocutors in a mode of friendship, seeking to discover the truth through dialogue. The end is not laid out in advance but is to be determined through discourse between friends who are lovers of wisdom. "This," Beauclair concludes, "is the seductive character of Socratic speech—his is a playful mode of self-discovery, where one engages the other not as a subordinate, combatant or authority, but as an ally." If Beauclair is right, then seduction has a transformative power capable of either corrupting or expanding oneself.

Drawing from recent empirical research, phenomenology, and feminist theory, in chapter 13, Hildur Kalman explores the reasons why people fake orgasms, including the values attached to orgasms and the cultural norms that seem to encourage faking. Among her observations are that men, as well as women, often fake orgasms. In addition, many women report faking orgasms in order to end painful sex. They are willing both to endure pain and to forego orgasm in order to give their partner the satisfaction of sexual "success" that comes with "giving" someone an orgasm. In cultural contexts in which "both men and women are expected to be interested in having sex at times when they actually are not," partners fake orgasm to avoid openly acknowledging their lack of desire. This reveals the common assumption that orgasm is the *telos* of sex; once it is done, sex is done.

Kalman is concerned that the habit of faking orgasm can deleteriously affect the sexual lives of the people who engage in it, harming their sexual creativity and flourishing. When faking becomes routine, she argues, it undermines the possibility of what might be a more authentic erotic encounter, in which "the sexual acts are ends in themselves" and genuine closeness is accompanied by the possibility of play. Kalman claims that this is an ideal toward popular conceptions of orgasm and sexuality ought to move. But such movement is possible only when we communicate our desires and experiences to our partners honestly and recognize that when it comes to sex, "there does not need to be a script with a self-evident end."

*Part II*

# DEFINING DESIRE

## Chapter Two

# Finding and Then Losing Your Way

## *Eros and the Other in Greek Literature and Philosophy*

### Louis A. Ruprecht Jr.

There are many ways to begin a philosophical meditation on sex and desire and, as we will see again shortly, one of the most common ways is to begin "mythically," with a myth that is not one's own—as I will here. If such a beginning is good enough for Plato, then it should be good enough for us. While this is primarily a meditation on ancient erotic reflection, the moderns lie in the background, and will come into the foreground later on. But my beginning, as it were, is spoken in a modern, mixed philosophical and poetic idiom—much like Plato's own. In *Eros the Bittersweet: An Chapter*, Anne Carson writes:

> Eros is an issue of boundaries. He exists because certain boundaries do. In the interval between reach and grasp, between glance and counterglance, between "I love you" and "I love you too," the absent presence of desire comes alive. But the boundaries of time and glance and I love you are only aftershocks of the main, inevitable boundary that creates Eros: the boundary of flesh and self between you and me. And it is only, suddenly, at the moment when I would dissolve that boundary, I realize I never can … If we follow the trajectory of eros we consistently find it tracing this same route: it moves out from the lover toward the beloved, then ricochets back to the lover himself and the hole in him, unnoticed before. Who is the real subject of most love poems? Not the beloved. It is that hole.[1]

Carson's reflection is inspired by Sappho's famous Fragment #31, articulating a strange and elusive lover's triangle. But Plato's *Phaedrus* lies in the background. And back of the *Phaedrus* lies the *Symposium*, to which I turn first.

## THE MYTH

I begin with one of the loveliest and most memorable of all the stories that Socrates ever told, one that appears in the *Symposium*, assuredly one of Plato's loveliest and most memorable dialogues.[2]

In fact, even this deceptively simple beginning needs substantial qualification. Plato himself never appears at this party, nor in this dialogue; he appears only three times in all the dialogues assigned to him.[3] In the fertile space his absence helps to create, Plato hints that Socrates told this story to Aristodemus, who told it to Phoinix and to Apollodorus. Phoinix told it to someone else, who told it to Glaukon, who got it all mixed up. Apollodorus is telling it now to an unnamed person who appears to be one of the two main interlocutors, one of our conduits into this dialogue, the man through whom everyone else's story will be related to us. Clear enough? Quite literally, nearly every sentence in this dialogue has the same awkward, clunky cadence, each sentence and each story prefaced with the same telltale phrases: "he said" and "she said" and "they said." Philosophy, Plato seems to be warning us—challenging us to remember this, and to keep it carefully in mind—is one-half hearsay. "Not mine, this myth."[4] It is a lot like love in that way, so we should be on our guard … especially when the topic before us is *eros*.

Someone said that Socrates told this story at a party, but in fact, he was simply relating a story that had previously been told to him by a mysterious woman from Mantineia, which was an important and contested city well to the south of Athens. The woman was an erotic seer of sorts, named Diotima. "She taught me *erotica*," Socrates told his assembled guests,[5] with a wink and a smile. It will take some time to learn what kind of teaching this entails.

This is a very serious matter in what is otherwise a most whimsical dialogue, the idea that our most precious words are often not our own. At the outset of the dialogue, we are informed that we are hearing nothing more than the jumbled second-hand report of various men's jumbled memories, the recollection of events from a party that took place a very long time ago. No one's memories are very clear anymore (doubly so, since everyone except Socrates nodded off in a stupor before the party ended near dawn the next day), but some versions of events are clearly *more* unreliable than others.

Everyone seems to agree on how it started, though. The tragic poet, Agathon, was throwing himself a dinner party to celebrate his first victory in the City Dionysia, the spring festival held in honor of the god Dionysus, at which three tragic poets took turns presenting four plays each on a day dedicated exclusively to their stagecraft. On the last day of the festival, a winner was declared and the feasting commenced. Hungover from the previous day's revels, a smaller circle of Athenian elites, mostly friends of Agathon, had gathered to toast his success. Sensing the mellower mood of this second celebration, a rather self-important medical doctor named Eryximachus made the proposal that, in turn, made the party: that they dismiss the flute girls; that each symposiast drink as much or as little as he saw fit; and that they would offer up, each man in his turn, a speech in honor of Eros, the muted and mysterious god of Love.

To make his case, the good doctor quoted the tragic poet, Euripides, from a play we no longer possess, the *Melanippe*. The line Eryximachus quoted, however, seems especially apt, especially well-suited to the purpose: οὐ γὰρ ἐμὸς ὁ μῦθος [*ou gar emos ho mythos*], "the myth is not my own" (or more literally, "not mine, the myth").[6] The doctor confesses that the idea for this altogether novel topic for a symposium was not his but rather belonged to Phaedrus, the shining young man to his right who will eventually speak first in honor of the god. Phaedrus observes that *Eros*, alone of all the gods, has never had hymns offered up to him; he proposes correcting this blasphemous oversight now. It is a very curious observation, and surely Plato's audience knew that it was not true.[7] No matter, the delicious round of inspired and inspiring speeches that Phaedrus's falsifying claim inspires culminates in Socrates's, who also offers up words of wisdom that are allegedly not his own. His story, like the ideas they will inspire, was Diotima's before it became his.

With surprising effortlessness born of high literary art, Plato has etched several important philosophical matters into memorable, high relief. First, *eros* comes into subtle focus when the normal rules are suspended, and each speaker is permitted to go his or her own way. Second, *eros* comes to this party borne on the wings of a gross mischaracterization: the very foundation of the symposium and our memory of it is uncertain. Third, and more to the present point, no one can speak of love on his or her own. This is not plagiarism; it is poetry. We need the words of others to bring our own-most passions into the light. What is the purpose of lyric and other love poetry, after all? It is to provide us with such words, and such novel glimpses of the self through its desire for another. "Not mine, this myth"... when *eros* is the topic, apparently, it never is. For *eros* is not about the self; it is about some other, as well as the charged, if unbridgeable, space separating the two.

## THE STORY

The story that is planted subtly within Plato's story is about a party, and that story about a party is repeated at this party, now. Diotima told it to Socrates, who relayed it to his friends, and whose retelling we have overheard. That mythic earlier party was organized to celebrate, not a tragedy such as

Agathon's, but rather the birth of Aphrodite. And all the gods came. More to Diotima's point, two lesser-known divinities were present at this party. The first of them was Resource (*Poros*), who according to the myth was the son of Cleverness (*Mêtis*). These were both charged names for a Greek audience; we should recall that the word for "name" and "noun" was identical in ancient Greek (*onoma*). These names suggest that Socrates (or Diotima, or Plato—we will never know for sure) is deliberately playing with a philosophical and literary vocabulary, all to make an important point about the generation of love.

A *poros* is literally "a way," as in our English idiom of "finding your way" or "making your way." As far as Plato was concerned, Socrates's special genius lay in his unique ability to make us lose our way, with words. The give-and-take of the Socratic question-and-answer known as an *elenchus* was designed to force one's philosophical interlocutors to realize that they did not know what they thought they knew. The end result of such Socratic interrogation was an *aporia*, literally a "no-way," the kind of philosophical dead end where the speaker and the thinker alike are forced to admit that there is no way out of their current conundrum. Admitting that this is the necessary first step along a path of inquiry makes fresh thinking and new insight possible. There is a *poiêsis*, a poetic creativity, to any such new way of thinking.

As to this last point, Aristotle appears to agree. "The way out [*lysis*] of an *aporia*," he observes, "is a discovery [*heuresis*]." That line comes from the *Nicomachean Ethics*, in the important Seventh Book, devoted to the complex topics of moral psychology and moral failure.[8] It is important to recall that Aristotle's lecture notes on "ethics" concern the world of *human*, not divine, philosophy (in fact, Aristotle mentions this *anthropina philosophia* at the very end of this lecture course[9]). For a human being, as opposed to a god, what may come after an *aporia* is a discovery. Not the discovery of a new truth, necessarily (that is how this phrase has been translated by some modern interpreters—misleadingly in my judgment), just that "ah-ha" moment in which real wonder—in art and philosophy and religion—tends to be born. Aristotle insists that philosophy itself is born out of this feeling of astonishment that things exist, and wonder from whence they have come[10]; Heidegger will agree and describe this originary philosophical mood as "wonderment."[11] Anne Carson builds upon this Greek lexical arrangement and eroticizes it, describing the philosopher as "one whose profession is to *delight* in understanding."[12] Plato, at least in the text of the *Symposium*, is attempting to place us, as readers, somewhere in between the mood of wonderment and the delight in understanding. Reflection upon that "space between" is a highly significant feature of this dialogue.[13]

In fact, just after Socrates's intriguing suggestion that Diotima "taught [him] *erotica*," and shortly before the presentation of the heterodox myth of Eros's birth to which I have already alluded, Socrates reports a dazzling exchange with Diotima that first inspired him to aporetic wonderment, and thus to the brink of new understanding. Diotima has asserted that Eros is neither good nor beautiful; Socrates is shocked and objects strenuously.

> "How can you say that, Diotima?" I demanded. "Can Eros then be evil ... or ugly?"

> But she said, "Stop it! Do you really think that whatever isn't beautiful must then necessarily be ugly?"

> "Of course."

> "And that anyone who isn't wise is ignorant? Don't you realize that there is something in between [*metaxu*] wisdom and ignorance?"

> "Like what?"

> "Do you still not see it?" she asked. "Having correct opinions without having the words for them. That isn't knowledge for how can something without reasons be knowledge? But it's not ignorance either—how can it be ignorance, if it happens to be true? Correct opinions are just this way—they're in between [*metaxu*] understanding and ignorance.

> "What you've said is true," I admitted.

> "Then don't insist on the thing which isn't beautiful being ugly, or the thing which isn't good being evil. And when you can bring yourself to agree that Eros is neither good nor beautiful, then it won't be necessary for him to be ugly and evil anymore. Rather, he is something in between [*metaxu*] the two."[14]

The vocabulary deployed here is fascinating; it is designed to bring us from *eros* to the brink of philosophy, and then ricochets back upon love again. The words Diotima uses for "knowledge" are *epistêmê* and *phronêsis*, ideas that Aristotle will render canonically as "theoretical" and "practical" wisdom in his *Nicomachean Ethics*.[15] The word she uses for "ignorance" is *amathia*, which carries the subtle sense of being poorly trained or poorly schooled. In between the two stands *orthê doxa*, a "straight seeming," and hence an "orthodoxy" of sorts. Correct and straight opinions cannot claim the status of either theoretical or practical wisdom, since they cannot yet produce a satisfying account of themselves, a *logos*, which would fully entitle us to claim them. But they are not wrong, and they are not strictly speaking ignorant either, since they happen upon a truth. Much of human life, Diotima suggests, is lived in this middling terrain; all lovers know that space very well, a place beyond or beneath their words. "Not mine, the myth."

This brings us to *mêtis*, the same word, and the same kind of cleverness, that made Odysseus and his wife Penelope such fascinating mainstays of the mythic Greek imagination. In Homeric epic, love, *erotic* love, requires great cleverness, graced with acts of subtlety and suppleness in equal measure. It needed *mêtis* for Odysseus to find his way home. It needed *mêtis* for Penelope to hold off her over-eager suitors for a decade. It needed *mêtis* for Odysseus to figure out how to ambush them all in his own home while disguised as a beggar; and it wanted a very special kind of *mêtis* for Odysseus and Penelope to find their way back to each other's hearts after twenty years apart.[16] A lot of words and stories stood in their way. In short, for the philosopher and for the lover alike, when you find your way blocked, when there is literally no way out (nor forward), then it is *eros* that offers a special sort of cleverness … the discernment and discovery born of wonder, showing us how to proceed, obliquely, side-to-side, and thus to find some other way.

Which brings us back to Socrates's (or Diotima's) little myth, the story that follows fast upon this philosophical rumination on the "in between." Resource (*Poros*) had drunk deeply at the nectar bowls that evening, and so he wandered out into Zeus's little pleasure garden, where he promptly fell into a stupor, then to sleep. Another immortal, Poverty (*Penia*), spied him there, and since she had no other way, no means of her own, to make a child, she decided to make her way, to make *a* way, to *Poros*. The wording in this story is striking. Diotima literally says that "due to her child aporia [*dia tên hautês aporian paidion*], she made it [*poiêsasthai*] to Poros… She lay with him," Diotima smiles, "and thus she conceived Eros."[17] That, we can now see, is all a kind of lover's *mêtis*.

This mythical lover's genealogy explains why Eros serves as Aphrodite's servant and confidante: first, because he was conceived on Aphrodite's birthday; and second, since he is by nature a lover of beauty, he is forever drawn to the most beautiful of all divinities, Aphrodite herself. Notice that I just said "forever"; I will need to come back to that important idea in a moment. For the introduction of time to erotic reflection implicates us in a shift from myth and poetry to philosophy.

## ANGELS AND DEMONS

Diotima's point, or Socrates's if you will, in relating this delightful little story is to emphasize two things about Eros that are important for the views he will go on to defend later in a more philosophical way and with his own distinctive words and images. Gradually, we will see this myth become his own. First and foremost, Eros is not one of those blithely content and effortless Olympians, a god who has everything (and everyone) at his fingertips. This god is anything but that. Eros must *work* at his desires. As a child of *Poverty*, he restlessly strives to get what he does not have and cannot hold. He is, in a word, *pure* desire: unquenchable thirst; insatiable hunger; desire for the beautiful that constantly pursues, constantly overreaches itself, and hence can never really possess. He embodies the erotics of reaching, not grasping. Such restless erotic energy comes from Poverty, the mother of the boy. But Resource is his father, and so for every outrageous desire, Eros manages to find a way. The machinations of this god are endless, playful, and serious by turns. Hence, this mythological portrait—of restless, clever, *creative* desire and the new discoveries it enables—is fundamental to Socrates's (and to Plato's, and to Diotima's) picture of the erotic life among human beings. It is not just an art of living;[18] it is the very soul of art.

But Socrates also retells this story to emphasize the surprising and heterodox idea that Eros is not a god. Neither mortal nor immortal, Eros in this story is one of those middling creatures who play such a pivotal role in the Homeric and the Platonic universe (here is another resonant register for the all-important word, *metaxu*, I suggest). Socrates calls them *daimôn* or *daimones*, and we are meant to recall that his own personal *daimôn* speaks to him periodically, always in the negative, to warn him off of something he has just done, or something he is about to do. In a related dialogical reflection on *eros*, the *Phaedrus*, Socrates's *daimôn* actually orders him to compose another speech in honor of this god, when the first one he offered up for Phaedrus's pleasure involved him in an unwitting blasphemy.[19] Socrates's second speech (literally called a *palinode* in Greek, a "once again song") is one of the finest and most inspired speeches we will ever hear him make. He appears to have been inspired negatively by his *daimôn*, and positively by his passionate desire for Phaedrus. He is, in short, caught between the two.

So Eros in Diotima's story is a *daimôn*, not a divinity, one who exists forever in between grinding poverty and infinite resources, a being who has and does not have, who runs and dances and flies and pursues, yet who is oriented always toward the beauty he does not possess but in which he finds his inspiration. Here is Diotima's rousing conclusion to her myth, prompting still more confusion in her wide-eyed young apprentice:

"And so he is by nature neither mortal nor immortal. In one day, then, when he is happy, he will spring into life, but then he dies, only to be brought back to life again through his father's nature! But his power is always ebbing away, so that Eros is never utterly at a loss [*aporei*] nor ever completely fulfilled [*ploutei*]. He exists in the middle [*en mesôi*], in between wisdom [*sophias*] and ignorance [*amathias*]…"

"Then who, Diotima, are the philosophers," I asked, "if it's neither the wise nor the ignorant ones?"

"That would be obvious even to a child," she answered. "They are the ones who are in between [*metaxu*] the two: and Eros is one of them."[20]

Now, in some ways, this is a very controversial—certainly heterodox, and perhaps even heretical—portrait of the god. We should recall that the proposal to praise Eros was initiated in a falsehood; it culminates now in a blasphemy ... or else something in between a blasphemy and a truism. In more traditional Greek mythology, Eros was thought to be the son of Aphrodite herself, and the two are often depicted together, in a stunning iconic counterpoint to later Christian imagery of the Virgin and her Child. We are all probably familiar, at least vaguely, with that image of the naked or scantily clad goddess, playfully engaged with her mischievous son, who is threatening constantly to fire off his little bow and arrows. Homer famously spoke of "wingéd words"; later, he added a wingéd god and his wingéd darts to the mischievous mixture of human creativity and human desire.

But Socrates hides his heresy.[21] He goes out of his way to emphasize the *continuities* of this new and very different story with more traditional Greek myths (he does much the same thing at the beginning of the *Phaedrus*[22] with his artful avoidance of de-mythology). If he was a *religious* renegade (and we should recall that he was put to death in Athens in large measure based on the belief that he was[23]), then he was not so in any aggressive sense. Socrates, in Plato's opinion, went out of his way consistently to emphasize the continuities of his thought with more traditional Athenian myths, even when he was breaking most dramatically from their traditional meaning. The god of the philosophers need not cause religious people to lose their way, just to slow down in their journeying, taking a moment for wonder, in which to ponder their myths afresh.

"Not mine, this myth"; it never is. So too here. Diotima's and Socrates's delightful little story about *Poros* and *Penia* results in a fairly traditional portrait of the young and powerful *daimôn* who is linked forever-after to Aphrodite.

## SEX AND SEXUALITY

The Greek language itself toyed artfully with this simultaneous connection-and-separation. Eros is not Aphrodite, but he never strays very far from her side. The "things associated with *eros*" (*ta erotika*) and the "things associated with Aphrodite" (*ta aphrodisia*) were also intimately related but lexically distinct. In modern English, the distinction between "erotica" and "aphrodisiacs" is harder to draw since we have so thoroughly sexualized them both. But it was a very clear distinction in ancient Greek. If you wished to pose a *sexual* question, then you would ask about *aphrodisia*. Have you had sex recently? In Greek you would ask how it stands "with the things of Aphrodite?"[24] But *eros* was another matter, in Classical Greek.

While this is perhaps too simple a way to put a very complicated distinction, we might begin by observing the following: *Sex*, viewed biologically, is a matter of friction and synapses; *Sexuality*, by contrast, involves urgent and pressing matters of personal identity. Sex is simple; desire is not. Our modern conception of "sexuality" owes much to emerging psychological discourses of the late nineteenth and early twentieth centuries in Europe, of course; it is instructive to recall that most of these early psychologists, and not just Freud, drank deeply at the well of Greek mythology. The modern conception hinges in fact on an ancient Greek philosophical distinction: that between being and doing. "Sex" involves something one *does*, whereas "sexuality" involves *who one is*—thereby fundamentally upping the ethical and moral stakes, as we witness in a variety of vehement and volatile debates around the world today concerning sexual practices, sexual identities and even the increasingly cloudy canons of monogamous marriage. Religion and mythology play as large a role in these debates as politics does. The Greeks would find such modern quarrels perplexing, to say the least, the source of yet one more *aporia*.

The central point to hold in view is this: *sexuality* is modern; *sex* is not. We owe our modern discourse of "sexuality" and "sexual identity" (or "orientation") to psychology and, with it, the enormously influential taxonomy of heterosexuality versus homosexuality, a taxonomy whose very universality resulted in a "sudden, radical condensation of sexual categories" around the turn of the twentieth century.[25] If the term "homosexuality" was created in or around 1870,[26] then by 1905 it was so thoroughly established that Freud could use it as a virtual starting point for his attempt to develop a theory of human sexuality. At the outset of his *Three Contributions to a Theory of Sexuality*, Freud attempts to distinguish as clearly as he can between the psychological and the biological perspective on human sexuality. Biologists, who think of human and animal [*bei Mensch und Tier*] sexual needs together, focus on what they call "sexual instinct" [*Geschlechtstriebes*]. By contrast, psychologists (who appear to view human sexuality as quite different from that of other animals) will do well to distinguish between a "sexual object" [*Sexualobjekt*] and a "sexual aim" [or "sexual goal," *Sexualziel*]; doing so will help to clarify how an aberrant organization-and-socialization of the libidinal energy of the child may come to have large adult consequences.[27]

It is striking how uncharitable, and often how distorting, contemporary readings have been of this, Freud's most clinical and oft-revised and really quite imaginative little book. Freud sought to overturn any number of false assumptions we owe to Romantic myth and Judaeo-Christian religion: that sexual impulses are absent in infancy; that they emerge quite suddenly and for the first time at puberty; that they are exclusively heterosexual; and that their aim is strictly procreation. Freud is willing to speak of deviations in sexual object and aim, but not "sexual deviants." He suspects that all humans possess "originally bisexual predispositions" [*ursprünglichen bisexuellen Veranlagung*],[28] and are thus all, technically speaking, "perverse" [*den Perversen*].[29] And while his scientific ambition to construct a biology of the human brain never wavered, he concluded these three essays with the admittedly "unsatisfactory conclusion" [*unbefriedigende Schluß*] that a theory of human sexuality eluded him, because human biology is inseparable from culture and society.[30] He simply could not isolate the necessary variables in creatures such as ourselves.

Buried in a footnote in the middle of the first chapter on "Sexual Aberrations" [*Die sexuellen Abirrungen*], we find what is one of the most insightful moments in Freud's comparative use of ancient texts, such as Plato's *Symposium* (and we should recall that in the Fourth Preface to the book, written in May 1920, Freud concluded that "the extended sexuality [*die erweiterte Sexualität*] of psychoanalysis corresponds [closely] with the Eros of the divine Plato [*dem Eros der göttlichen Plato*])."[31] "The most profound difference between the love-life [*Liebesleben*] of the ancient world and our own is likely to be found here: that the ancients placed the emphasis [*Akzent*] on the impulse itself [*auf den Trieb selbst*], whereas we place it on the object [*auf dessen Objekt*]."[32] In other words, we moderns are concerned with taxonomies of sexual identity; Plato was concerned with sexual desire. Or, to revise my earlier claim: Sexuality is modern; *eros* is not.

Here we come to the crux of Foucault's remarkable and extensive engagement with Freud's "Theory of Sexuality," and what Foucault coyly refers to as the "repressive hypothesis" that played such an important role in the twentieth century's greatest feat of alchemy: "turning sex into discourse." Foucault's most significant revisions to traditional Freudian theory are well known. First and foremost, he rejects the crude scientism that aspires to a scientific *theory* of sexuality. There can be no such theory, Foucault cautions (Freud seemed to agree, if unhappily); all we can hope to achieve is a *history of the concept* of sexuality.[33] Second, Foucault observes that same-sex sexuality had been a significant part of the human psychological terrain at least since ancient Greek times, and it is worthy of our continued reflection as something more than a "symptom." Here again, I do not think Foucault is very far from Freud: Freud too views what he admits should better be called "homoeroticism" than "homosexuality"[34] as much more than a symptom, especially for "the divine Plato." To these important revisions from the first volume of Foucault's *History of Sexuality*, I would add several more that are implicit in the stunning Preface to the second volume.[35] It will not do to write off religion as Freud seems to do in his most reductive studies, like his 1920 *The Future of an Illusion*. Especially in a world, like the Greek world, where the line between philosophy and religion is devilishly difficult to draw, religion is a significant source of ethical reflection; it is treated as such in Volume Two of Foucault's *Histoire*. If that is true of Greek religion (Eros was a god, after all), then it is equally true of the Greek conception of romantic love. This, too, ought not be written off as mere illusion, symptom, or what have you. It was taken to possess deep philosophical significance, as the *Symposium* amply attests. Foucault, of course, was hesitant to speak of selves or souls, preferring to speak of *subjects*. What concerned him were the modern *institutions* that help form our moral imaginations as *patient*, as *criminal*, as *student*, as *citizen* ...

And yet when Foucault came to an historical exploration of Greek reflection on the moral imagination of the lover, everything changed, including his understanding of his own work. To be sure, the *sexual* subject was modern, and quite novel. But the *desiring* subject was perennial, Foucault now saw, and various Greek conceptions of this subject's essential practices—what he calls "arts of existence" [*arts de l'existence*] and "techniques of the self" [*techniques de soi*], arts and techniques that placed diet and exercise on an equal footing with sexual activity[36]—seemed to possess rich potential for contemporary reflection outside of the repressive hypothesis and its regimes of discourse.

Foucault published the first volume of his *Histoire de la sexualité* in 1976; the second volume appeared in 1984. It is worth recalling that Sir Kenneth Dover published his ground-breaking study of Greek homosexuality in 1979,[37] and John Boswell published his ground-breaking study of the medieval emergence of new anti-gay theology and legislation in 1981.[38] Sedgwick took up Foucault's challenge to "think differently" [*penser autrement*], by performing her artful reinterpretation of this history of sexual taxonomies in 1990. The political question of whether sex could be turned into anything other than discourse was acute at this time.

Anne Carson, with whose work I begin and end this chapter, published *Eros the Bittersweet* in the midst of this frenzied new thinking, in 1986.[39] In it, she would use two Greek works, Sappho's poetic fragments and Plato's *Phaedrus*, to undertake a provisional "essays" of her own. There is not one word about "lesbianism" in relation to Sappho, and not one word about "homoeroticism" in relation to Plato. The work, in short, shows us rather than tells us what else can be done with these same texts—so much, then, for sex and sexuality. That myth is not mine; rather, eros is the central matter. *Eros* involves neither sex nor sexuality, not directly. Rather, *Eros* involves that great literary imponderable, the shoal upon which each and every moral philosophy eventually shipwrecks. *Ta erôtika* is what Diotima taught, not *ta aphrodisia*. She was speaking, of course, of love. And she spoke of it in highly dramatic ways.

## TRAGEDY AND COMEDY

Plato and Socrates both saw themselves in an agonistic relationship to drama; two of the most famous people at this symposium were a comic poet named Aristophanes, and a tragic poet named Agathon, who was also the host to his own victory celebration. Surely then, it bears reflecting for a moment on the role of *eros* in Greek drama.

To put it very plainly: *eros is tragic, not comic.* Sex can be a cruel joke; love cannot be. Sex in Greek comedy is exaggerated, objectified, bodily, buffo and hopelessly, even desperately, funny. It is also often cruel and unsympathetic.[40] By contrast, there is precious little sex in Greek tragedy. What there is, is erotic attachment, desperate and passionate and unreasoning … and often violent. Until the modern period, people did not die for sex (nor, tragically *of* sex either), but the Greeks were very well aware of how many people died for love. The tragic stage is littered with their corpses and haunted by their murders—of self and other. It was a part of Plato's bold new philosophical task to trump and even to surpass Greek drama.[41] Greek philosophy is tragicomic thinking,[42] the attempt to think the unthinkable by thinking in the middle, attempting to join what has been separated far too casually: love and sex, Eros and Aphrodite, the thinking of desiring thought itself. By the time Socrates has finished relating Diotima's little story to his friends, some novel and important distinctions have become clearer to us, who are still Plato's quiet collaborators today.

The first and perhaps foremost of them is the power of insight born from being in the middle, the attempt to occupy the middle ground that joins separate elements that are threatening to fly apart. Socrates learns *erôtika* from Diotima, and then he teaches this middling sort of wisdom to his fellow symposiasts. Socrates's infamous irony comes into subtle focus precisely here: he is subtly mocking the view that if you *desire* beauty, then you do not *have* beauty, and that if you desire wisdom you likely do not have that either. Surely, he winks at us, you realize by now that there is something in between beautiful things and ugly things, wise people and ignorant people, lovers and their beloveds: that something constitutes the essentially human way of being in the world. And to be in *that* world, the world where human beings desire, is to inhabit time in an excruciating way.

## MORTALS AND IMMORTALS

The really decisive shift in Socrates's and Diotima's playful "love chat" comes when she performs a sort of phenomenology of the lover in love.

When I desire you in all of your beauty, it is not that I do not think myself beautiful; rather I am responding to a beauty *different* than my own, desiring a form of beauty I do not possess. Then what happens when I *do* have it? In an instant, she suggests, I discover a new desire: now I want to have this beauty, forever. I want the other, forever; in Anne Carson's lyrical phrasing, I want the space between reach and grasp to disappear.[43] Here is the paradox that the Greek verb, which is also a noun, names very well: *erôs, as noun or verb,*[44] *is the desire of a finite being for infinity.*

We know that possessing forever is impossible, for a human being. There is no way out of time; temporality just is our mode, as well as the ultimate human *aporia*. Suddenly we recall that the first time Socrates introduced us to his "philosophy of the middle," it was not in relation to beauty or goodness or wisdom—it was in relation to time. *Eros*, he informed us to our mingled surprise and delight, is neither mortal nor immortal, but something *in between* the two. How can such a being be?

I would like to offer a casual thought-experiment by way of a preliminary answer, with proper thanks to St. Valentine. What do lovers give each other as love gifts? Flowers, gems, and food (especially chocolate).[45] It is an instructive list of gifts. Flowers are beautiful because they are mortal; their evanescent beauty lasts but a day. "Diamonds," by contrast, "are forever"; so the advertising industry would have us believe (inviting the forgetting, I suppose, that any such precious item may be lost or stolen). A gem's beauty derives from its hardness, its stubborn refusal to age or change in any way. In short, flowers are mortal, diamonds are immortal, and both are fundamentally associated with erotic, desiring beings. As for chocolate ... well, chocolate is a different and more sensual matter, something that must be consumed to be enjoyed. There is a kind of poetry, and a dizzying logic, in that love-gift, too.

We seem to find ourselves in the presence of a deep erotic intuition, this whimsical introduction of time and change into the very center of the lover's universe. Among the Greeks, and certainly still today in the industrialized west, physical beauty was most often associated with youthfulness. The Greek word for a beloved was commonly the word for youth (*pais*)[46]; when the beautiful youth began to grow a beard, then it was considered the time for him to depart from that social role and to become a lover in his turn.[47] As such, the beautiful object of desire will not, and cannot, last. But we want it to last, forever. Why desire what we know to be impossible? Why concentrate upon desires that can only end in frustration or failure or heartbreak? Was there break-up built in to the Athenians' pederastic paradigm? And if so, was this the paradoxical fruit born of the drunken wedding-embrace of *Poros* and *Penia*, a self-contradictory creature who cannot ever stop wanting, in time?

Diotima, of course, was a woman, and as such, she is depicted as gravitating toward images of childbearing to make her meaning plain. "All humans are pregnant," she tells Socrates, "whether in body [*kata to sôma*] or in spirit [*kata tên psychên*], and when we come of age, our nature desires to give birth."[48] Souls aiming at the physical body create children, and souls aiming at other souls create virtue. Both kinds of offspring have singular value and importance in a properly managed Greek city.

> In this way everything mortal is preserved—not by its being utterly the same forever, like the divine, but by what is old withdrawing and leaving something else behind, something new, something similar to [*hoion*] itself. This is the way, Socrates, that the mortal partakes of immortality, bodily and in all ways.[49]

Diotima explicitly calls this "a divine thing," since "pregnancy and birth impart immortality to a living being who is mortal."[50] Procreation, in all its forms, just *is* creation, for those mortal artists and lovers who are locked in time.

In sum, *Eros* finds a way past mortality by making something new to leave behind. The finite desire for infinity fuels the greatest arts of which human beings are capable: poetry and philosophy, piety and grace. Small wonder that even the most rabidly aggressive of later scriptural monotheists could never quite shake free of Plato's desirous grip … though goodness knows, some tried. It has something to do with finding your way to the middle, finessing the fractures borne of time. We may call this philosophy, or theology, or art; it scarcely matters in a Socratic register. The man made myths at least as often as he made philosophical meaning, after all. What appears to matter is the passion and the generosity of the lover's gesture.

In a period we may quite appropriately refer to as his "middle period,"[51] Plato penned his most lyrical and most memorable dialogues: *Republic*, *Symposium*, *Phaedrus*, and *Phaedo*. The topics vary (ranging from justice and the ideal city, to passionate desire and beauty, to the quest for effective and truthful writing, and the immortality of the soul), but all four dialogues pay close attention to mortality and immortality, the weird linkage between pleasure and pain, to the vague longing the human soul feels for a realm beyond the realm of flux and change. Not content to desire, the human soul desires *forever*. Not content to possess for one day, the human soul desires to possess for *all* its days. And that simply is not possible.

We can see the central Socratic point more clearly now: It is actually the fact of finitude that makes *eros* possible to begin with. As Anne Carson puts it, "No difference: no movement. No eros."[52] Finite possibility slams up against its inevitable limitations. Then Poverty finds her way to Resource, and *eros* is born. *This finite desire for infinity* has tormented many mortal spirits and severed countless embodied souls, but it has also inspired much to which human beings seem to attach special, and even sacred,[53] value. Thus

Plato's startling, rousing and rhapsodic conclusion is this: *Eros* is not sex, it is not identity, it is not substance and it is not god. Socrates observed that it would require a god to say what the soul actually *is*, but that human beings are especially adept at saying what such things *are like*. *Eros*, then, is the metaphor we live by.[54]

## NOTES

1. Anne Carson, *Eros the Bittersweet: An Essays* (Princeton: Princeton University Press, 1986), 32–33.

2. The passage appears at *Symposium* 203a–204a. For the Greek text of the *Symposium*, I am using Sir Kenneth Dover, ed., *Plato: Symposium,* (New York: Cambridge University Press, 1980). While translations from the Greek are my own, I have profited enormously from a number of marvelously creative and sometimes lyrical English versions, including Suzy Q. Groden, *The Symposium of Plato* (Amherst: University of Massachusetts Press, 1970); Alexander Nehamas and Paul Woodruff, *Symposium* (Indianapolis: Hackett Publishing Company, 1989); Tom Griffith, *Symposium of Plato/ΠΛΑΤΩΝΟΣ ΣΥΜΠΟΣΙΟΝ* (Berkeley: University of California Press, 1990); Seth Benardete, *Plato's "Symposium,"* with commentary by Allan Bloom and Seth Benardete (Chicago: The University of Chicago Press, 1993, 2001); Avi Sharon, *Plato's Symposium* (Newburyport: Focus Publishing, 1998); and C.D.C. Reeve, ed., *Plato on Love* (Indianapolis: Hackett Publishing Company, 2006), 26–87.

3. These elusive references are at *Apology* 34a and 38b, and *Phaedo* 59b. In the first two, Plato is mentioned as one of Socrates's contemporary followers who was present at his trial; in the third, it is reported that Plato was too ill to appear in the prison cell on the day that Socrates drank the hemlock. Some illness ...

4. Plato, *Symposium*, 177a.

5. Ibid., 201d. For more on this fascinating phrasing, see Louis A. Ruprecht Jr., *Symposia: Plato, the Erotic and Moral Value* (Albany: State University of New York Press, 1999), 42ff.

6. Ibid., 177a.

7. While it is the case that the corpus of so-called Homeric Hymns do not include one specifically dedicated to *Eros*, Phaedrus begins his own speech of praise by citing the poetic works of Hesiod and Parmenides, and concludes with a significant invocation of Homer's *Iliad*.

8. Aristotle, *Nicomachean Ethics*, 1146 b8. The Nicomachean Ethics has a complex ten-book structure (one might also call it an "architecture") and a complex mode of presentation. There are long discussions of considerable depth and detail, but there are also pithy, short pronouncements such as here. One way of imagining this mode of presentation is that Aristotle used this text as a starting point for his lectures, and thus these pithy short statements would have been prompts for further discussion with his students. For the Greek text, I am using H. Rackham, ed. and trans., *Aristotle: The*

*Nicomachean Ethics* (Cambridge: Loeb Classical Library of Harvard University Press, 1926, 1975), 384–85. An excellent English translation is Martin Ostwald's *Nicomachean Ethics* (Indianapolis: The Bobbs-Merrill Company, Inc., 1962), though in this case his version extrapolates the passage considerably: "For the solution of a problem is the discovery of a truth" (179).

9. Aristotle, *Nicomachean Ethics*, 1181 b15.

10. Aristotle, *Metaphysics*, 981 a2–530 and 997 a25–30.

11. Martin Heidegger, *An Introduction to Metaphysics*, trans. Ralph Manheim. (New Haven: Yale University Press, 1959), 1–9 and 206. Heidegger was much pre-occupied with the question of philosophical moods: he mentions despair, rejoicing, boredom, and patience in short order here. "Wonder," I take it, is what these moods may become upon reflection.

12. Carson, *Eros the Bittersweet*, xii, italics mine. A new edition of this marvelously creative and important book is available as a Dalkey Archive edition published in 1998.

13. For more on the range of meanings associated with the Greek word *metaxu* in this dialogue, see Louis A. Ruprecht, *Symposia: Plato, the Erotic and Moral Value* (Albany: State University of New York Press, 1999), 55–57.

14. Plato, *Symposium,* 201e–202b.

15. Aristotle, *Nicomachean Ethics*, 1139 b15–35 and 1140 a25–1140 b30.

16. For a marvelous meditation on *mêtis* in the *Odyssey*, see John J. Winkler, "Penelope's Cunning and Homer's," in *Constraints of Desire: The Anthropology of Sex and Gender in Ancient Greece* (New York: Routledge, 1990), 129–61.

17. Plato, *Symposium,* 203b.

18. I borrow this phrase from Alexander Nehamas, *The Art of Living: Socratic Reflections from Plato to Foucault* (Berkeley: University of California Press, 1998); his analysis of Platonic (as distinct from Socratic) irony in the *Euthyphro* (19–45) is a dazzling exercise in close comparative reading. I also call sympathetic attention to his reading of the *Symposium* in *Virtues of Authenticity: Essays on Plato and Socrates* (Princeton: Princeton University Press, 1999), 303–15.

19. Plato, *Phaedrus,* 242c–243e.

20. Plato, *Symposium,* 203e–204a.

21. The same issue recurs in *Apology,* 21a–22a. Like Oedipus, Socrates receives a prophecy (that he is the wisest of all men). Like Oedipus, he tries to outrun it (by proving it wrong, with *elenchus*). And that attempt to elude the prophecy confirms it, resulting in his death.

22. Plato, *Phaedrus*, 229b–230a.

23. Plato, *Apology*, 24b; but compare the comic charge at 19b.

24. See Henry G. Liddell and Robert Scott, *A Greek-English Lexicon* (Oxford: Clarendon Press, 1940), 293.

25. This phrase comes from the introduction to Eve Kosofsky Sedgwick's *Epistemology of the Closet* (Berkeley: University of California Press, 1990), 9 (1–63). Sedgwick is identified as one of the foundational figures in that imprecise hodge-podge, Queer Theory, because she so clearly and so passionately underlined the necessary relation between sexuality, gender and the political. Her great insight,

one aimed at de-stabilizing this taxonomy (and perhaps all such taxonomies), was to show how many other taxonomies and assumptions were hidden in the hetero- versus homo binary: most notably *gender* (since a sexual identity is grounded exclusively in the gender of one's sexual object choice) and *culture* (since the nature versus nurture distinction is so ritualized and inexact). To these I would add *religion*, which is often seen at odds with an allegedly secular version of scientific reason. Foucault understood this very well, as we will see.

26. Traditionally, it is said that the first appearance was in Richard von Krafft-Ebing, *Psychopathia Sexualis* or else in Carl Westphal, *Archiv für Neurologie* (both roughly dated to 1870). In the twelfth and final edition revised by Krafft-Ebing himself shortly before his death in 1902—*Psychopathia Sexualis: A Medico-Forensic Study*, ed. Victor Robinson (New York: Pioneer Publications, 1939, 1953)—there is a long discussion of "Homo-sexual Individuals, or Urnings" (364–82), bookended by discussions of "Psychical Hermaphroditism" (352–64), "Effemination" (382–89), "Androgyny" (389–94), and "Congenital Sexual Inversion in Women" (395–443). While "Sodomy" was deemed an "Unnatural Abuse" (561) by Krafft-Ebing, and "pederasty" was in his view primarily a matter of *immissio penis in anum* (571), he was notably opposed to its legal interdiction (573–74). For more on this see Michel Foucault, *Histoire de la Sexualité I: La Volonté de Savoir* (Paris: Éditions Gallimard, 1976), 59; David Halperin, *One Hundred Years of Homosexuality* (New York: Routledge, 1989), 115n1 and 158–59n17; and Sedgwick, *Epistemology of the Closet*, 2.

27. This is laid out on the first page of *Drei Abhandlungen zur Sexualtheorie*, in *Sigmund Freud: Gesammelte Werke, Fünfter Band, Werke aus den Jahren 1904–1905* (Frankfurt an Main: S. Fischer Verlag, 1942) V: 33 (27–145).

28. Ibid., 40.

29. Ibid., 71.

30. Ibid., 145.

31. Ibid., 32.

32. Ibid., 48n1.

33. Michel Foucault's *Histoire de la Sexualité I: La Volonté de Savoir* was translated by Robert Hurley as *The History of Sexuality*, Volume I, *An Introduction* (New York: Vintage Books, 1978); the preface to that volume (3–13) lays out the revisions to the scientism of the repressive hypothesis with intellectual finesse and genuine humor.

34. Freud, *Drei Abhandlungen zur Sexualtheorie*, 45n1.

35. Michel Foucault's *Histoire de la Sexualité II: L'Usage des Plaisirs* (Paris: Éditions Gallimard, 1984) was translated by Robert Hurley as *The History of Sexuality*, Volume II, *The Use of Pleasure* (New York: Vintage Books, 1985); the preface to that volume (3–24) is among the most intellectually elegant things that Foucault ever wrote. By explaining how this more traditionally historical project was related to his earlier works of archaeology and genealogy, Foucault traced the way in which ancient Greek reflections on sexual practices, mores and desires might be made available to do contemporary philosophical work. I see this chapter as a small contribution to that same historical endeavor.

36. Foucault, *Histoire de la Sexualité* II, 18–19ff.

37. Sir Kenneth Dover, *Greek Homosexuality* (Cambridge: Harvard University Press, 1979).

38. John Boswell, *Christianity, Social Tolerance and Homosexuality: A History of Gay People from the Beginning of the Christian Era* (Chicago: University of Chicago Press, 1981). Few path-breaking works have been more cruelly maligned than this one; for a nice overview of the book's continuing importance and relevance, see Mathew Kuefler, ed., *The Boswell Thesis: Essays on Christianity, Social Tolerance and Homosexuality* (Chicago: University of Chicago Press, 2006).

39. Martha Nussbaum published *The Fragility of Goodness: Luck and Ethics in Greek Tragedy and Philosophy* (New York: Cambridge University Press, 1986) in that same year.

40. For a brilliant reflection on the meanness of comedy, in relation to the hopefulness of tragedy, see Walter Kerr, *Tragedy and Comedy* (New York: Simon and Shuster, 1967).

41. See Martha C. Nussbaum, *The Fragility of Goodness*, 87–88, 122–35.

42. This mingling of comedy and tragedy is very clearly marked at the conclusion of the *Symposium* (223d). For some excellent and probing reflection on the meaning of "tragicomic" thinking, see *The Cornel West Reader* (New York: Basic Civitas Books, 1999), 1–5, as well as Robert C. Pirro, *The Politics of Tragedy and Democratic Citizenship* (New York: Continuum, 2001), 74-97, and Louis A. Ruprecht Jr., "Muted Strains of Emersonian Perfection: Reflections on Cornel West's Tragic Pragmatism," *Soundings* 95.3 (2012): 309–32.

43. See Carson, *Eros the Bittersweet*, xi, 26–29.

44. It is one of Aristotle's more delightful observations to distinguish nouns from verbs by saying that a noun (*onoma*) is a vocalization without time (*aneu chronos*), whereas a verb (*rhêma*) is a vocalization with time (*meta chronos*): see *Poetics* 1457 a10–15. Perhaps it is not too much to observe that, in the *Symposium* at least, Plato is attempting to turn *erôs* from a noun into a verb in this very sense.

45. I owe this point to Nussbaum, *The Fragility of Goodness*, 1–8, 20–21, though she limits her analysis to gems and flowers.

46. This point is nicely developed by John Boswell in *Christianity, Social Tolerance and Homosexuality*, 28–31.

47. The so-called pederastic paradigm defining the social roles of male lover (*erastês*) and beloved (*erômenos*) was first enunciated by Sir Kenneth Dover in *Greek Homosexuality*. While his emphasis upon the non-penetrative "intercrural" nature of sexual activity between such age-differentiated couples (91–100) is not entirely borne out by the evidence he cites, the book remains a foundational resource. See also Jan N. Bremmer, "Adolescents, Symposion, and Pederasty," in Oswyn Murray, ed., *Sympotica: A Symposium on the Symposion* (Oxford: Clarendon Press, 1990), 135–48.

48. Plato, *Symposium,* 206c.

49. Ibid., 208b.

50. Ibid., 206c.

51. See Ruprecht, *Symposia*, 1 and 147n29.

52. Carson, *Eros the Bittersweet*, 66.

53. I am indebted to my friend and colleague, Gary Laderman, for the way he traces an emerging modern language of "sacrality" that may be investigated quite independently of the norms and nuances of traditional religiosity. See his *Sacred Matters: Celebrity Worship, Sexual Ecstasies, the Living Dead and Other Signs of Religious Life in the United States* (New York: The New Press, 2009), esp. 141–60 on "Sexuality."

54. Plato, *Phaedrus*, 246a. For more on the place of metaphor in philosophical reflection, see Ruprecht, *Symposia*, 20, 78–79, 125.

# BIBLIOGRAPHY

Aristotle. *Nicomachean Ethics*. Edited and translated by H. Rackham. Cambridge: Loeb Classical Library of Harvard University Press, 1975.

———. *Nichomachean Ethics*. Translated by Martin Ostwald. Indianoplis: The Bobbs-Merrill Company, Inc., 1962.

Boswell, John. *Christianity, Social Tolerance and Homosexuality: A History of Gay People from the Beginning of the Christian Era*. Chicago: University of Chicago Press, 1981.

Bremmer, Jan N. "Adolescents, Symposion, and Pederasty." In *Sympotica: A Symposium on the Symposion*, edited by Oswyn Murray, 135–148. Oxford: Clarendon Press, 1990.

Carson, Anne. *Eros the Bittersweet: An Essay*. Princeton: Princeton University Press, 1986.

Dover, Kenneth. *Greek Homosexuality*. Cambridge: Harvard University Press, 1979.

Foucault, Michel. *Histoire de la Sexualité I: La Volonté de Savoir*. Paris: Éditions Gallimard, 1976.

———. *Histoire de la Sexualité II: L'Usage des Plaisirs*. Paris: Éditions Gallimard, 1984.

———. *The History of Sexuality, Volume I, An Introduction*. Translated by Robert Hurley. New York: Vintage Books, 1978.

———. *The History of Sexuality, Volume II, The Use of Pleasure*. Translated by Robert Hurley. New York: Vintage Books, 1985.

Freud, Sigmund, *Drei Abhandlungen zur Sexualtheorie*, in *Gesammelte Werke, Fünfter Band, Werke aus den Jahren 1904-1905*. Frankfurt am Main: S. Fischer Verlag, 1942.

Halperin, David. *One Hundred Years of Homosexuality*. New York: Routledge, 1989.

Heidegger, Martin. *An Introduction to Metaphysics*. Translated by Ralph Manheim. New Haven: Yale University Press, 1959.

Kerr, Walter. *Tragedy and Comedy*. New York: Simon and Shuster, 1967.

Krafft-Ebing, Richard von. *Psychopathia Sexualis: A Medico-Forensic Study*. Edited by Victor Robinson. New York: Pioneer Publications, 1939, 1953.

Kuefler, Mathew, editor. *The Boswell Thesis: Chapter on Christianity, Social Tolerance and Homosexuality*. Chicago: University of Chicago Press, 2006.

Laderman, Gary. *Sacred Matters: Celebrity Worship, Sexual Ecstasies, the Living Dead and Other Signs of Religious Life in the United States.* New York: The New Press, 2009.

Liddell, Henry G., and Robert Scott. *A Greek-English Lexicon.* Oxford: Clarendon Press, 1940.

Nehamas, Alexander. *The Art of Living: Socratic Reflections from Plato to Foucault.* Berkeley: University of California Press, 1998.

Nussbaum, Martha. *The Fragility of Goodness: Luck and Ethics in Greek Tragedy and Philosophy.* New York: Cambridge University Press, 1986.

Pirro, Robert C. *The Politics of Tragedy and Democratic Citizenship.* New York: Continuum, 2001.

Plato. *Apology.* Translated by Harold North Fowler. Cambridge: Harvard University Press, reprint edition, 1999.

———. *Phaedrus.* Translated by Harold North Fowler. Cambridge: Harvard University Press, reprint edition, 1999.

———. *Symposium.* Translated by Seth Benardete. Chicago: The University of Chicago Press, 2001.

———. *Symposium.* Translated by Kenneth Dover. New York: Cambridge University Press, 1980.

———. *Symposium.* Translated by Tom Griffith. Berkeley: University of California Press, 1990.

———. *Symposium.* Translated by Suzy Q. Groden. Amherst: University of Massachusetts Press, 1970.

———. *Symposium.* Translated by Alexander Nehamas and Paul Woodruff. Indianapolis: Hackett Publishing Company, 1989.

———. *Symposium.* Translated by Avi Sharon. Newburyport: Focus Publishing, 1998.

Reeve, C.D.C., editor. *Plato on Love.* Indianapolis: Hackett Publishing Company, 2006.

Ruprecht Jr., Louis A. "Muted Strains of Emersonian Perfection: Reflections on Cornel West's Tragic Pragmatism." *Soundings* 95, no. 3 (2012): 309–32.

———. *Symposia: Plato, the Erotic and Moral Value.* Albany: State University of New York Press, 1999.

Sedgwick, Eve Kosofsky. *Epistemology of the Closet.* Berkeley: University of California Press, 1990.

West, Cornell. *The Cornel West Reader.* New York: Basic Civitas Books, 1999.

Winkler, John J. "Penelope's Cunning and Homer's." In *Constraints of Desire: The Anthropology of Sex and Gender in Ancient Greece*, 129–61. New York: Routledge, 1990.

## Chapter Three

# Love, and a Romantic Living Room

## *Remarks for an Inquiry on Ordinary Love Today*

### Chiara Piazzesi

Knowledge means everything to you. Even your animalism, you want it
in your head. You don't want to *be* an animal, you want to observe your
own animal functions, to get a mental thrill out of them ... What is it but
the worst and last form of intellectualism, this love of yours for passion
and the animal instincts?

—D. H. Lawrence, *Women in Love*

When we enter a living room, be it ours or someone else's, an entire, consistent world of possible activities, conversations, states of minds, feelings, and
thoughts unfolds for us.[1] We can admire someone else's taste in decorating,
or we can relax among familiar objects. We can lead a serious discussion with
friends or strangers about global environmental policies, or we can finally
start reading the book that has been waiting so long on the coffee table (or on
the floor, depending on the living room).

How do we know, though, that we find ourselves in a "living room?"—mostly
just by doing, thinking, and feeling what we usually do, think, and feel in a
living room. Notwithstanding this immediacy, we can still imagine questioning that we actually are in a living room, for instance, while visiting a very
big or a very eccentric house, in order to make sure that the room we arrived
in is indeed the one our host wants us to sojourn in for a pre-dinner cocktail.
Wittgenstein has shown us that, in order to relieve our uncertainty, we do not
need a method for generating abstract definitions like those often demanded
by mainstream philosophy. In other words, we seem to know (or to learn)
what a living room is just by knowing (or by practically learning) it: our
familiarity feels natural, grounded in what we are, and—except for disruptive
events—it recovers rapidly after having being shaken.

This self-referentiality is not at all a dead-end.[2] On the contrary, epistemo-logical analysis of our seemingly natural knowledge of love provides a rich ground to improve our understanding of who we are. The circular structure of our way of knowing and experiencing something familiar provides the self-transparency that allows us to mostly avoid problematizing our ordinary world and life. This self-transparency sometimes lures us into thinking that we have a privileged access to the "truth" of experience, a truth that we can achieve just by "thinking harder" or "trying harder" to unveil what is essential to universal human experience. These remarks are particularly relevant when it comes to an inquiry on ordinary love experience today. As in the case of many other experiences, perceptions, and emotions, we are inclined to regard love as a natural feature of human beings that "naturally" occurs in specific contexts and interactions. Exactly as in the living room example, we likely take our experi-ence for granted. This disposition of ours, though, does not constitute evidence that our apparently immediate experiences are indeed natural and immediate.

According to a mainstream philosophical understanding, the first require-ment for an inquiry on love would be a general definition of the object of inquiry, that is to say, of "romantic" love.[3] In other words, it requires that we look for the general theory that we do not require while immersed in ordi-nary experience. I will argue that this approach leads to a twofold misunder-standing. On the one hand, it perpetuates the "loop" of self-transparency by pretending that "thinking harder" would spread out the essence of our experi-ence, liberate it from the trappings of common sense, and reveal the "truth" at its core. On the other hand, though, this approach does not take common sense and self-transparency as seriously as it should. By treating common sense as something that should be dissolved in order to grasp the essence of things, this approach throws the baby out with the bathwater: it jettisons the historical diversity, the social character, and the semantic richness of ordinary experience. The twofold misunderstanding, thus, concerns the general episte-mological framework and the specific object of inquiry.

I will suggest an alternative way of addressing the question, one that con-siders historicity and diversity as indispensable to the endeavor: indeed, they allow the appraisal of the complexity of what makes our simplest and most self-evident experiences possible. Taking history and cultural variety into consideration would enable both epistemological and existential reflexivity, a double gesture that, as I will argue, can be carried out by paying attention to the discursive, practical, and commonsensical dimensions of love experience.

## UNDERSTANDING AN UNDERSTANDING OF LOVE

While attempting to understand love today, we must first ask what kind of object we seek to understand. We must also bring to light and critically discuss our implicit theory of love, the one that, to paraphrase Max Weber, is already involved in the "fact" (sources, materials) and frames it from the start.[4] In order to appraise the salience of an object or a value, Weber claims that we must share the cultural values and meanings that allow us to isolate such an object or value as legitimate source of scientific knowledge (thus to "extract" knowledge from it). The current mainstream philosophical approach, for instance, is inclined to gather its conceptual tools and its evidence about love from philosophers and thinkers of any possible historical era, fortified by the epistemological presupposition (often implicit) that they are all talking about the same thing. This is tantamount to assuming that love is a universal human experience and that its importance lies in its transhistorical and transcultural continuity. Consequently, according to this same approach, the nature of the investigated object allows for normative definitions, which distinguish what love is from what it is not. Love is this one thing that we define through its features *a*, *b* and *c*; hence, the rest isn't truly love (rather perversion, anomaly, self-delusion, etc.), despite the fact that our culture, trivialized discourse, or media mistakenly call it such.

Such an approach takes a strong stance that difference, variety, and historical change are considered to be unessential to the object, as merely accessory: a sort of white, surrounding noise that prevents us from seeing and embracing what is really important. If Nietzsche's claim that "only something which has no history can be defined" is right, then giving a straightforward definition of love implies not taking historical variation, and differentiation within the same cultural framework, into account.[5] In particular, whereas historical change is manifested by linguistic variation, that is to say by the multiplication of possible uses of the word "love" to denote manifold feelings, attitudes, behavioral patterns, relationships and so on, the typical normative strategy consists in reducing the difference and discontinuity by reducing what is seen as mere linguistic "confusion." Consider the following excerpt by Harry Frankfurt:[6]

> It is important to avoid confusing love—as circumscribed by the concept that I am defining—with infatuation, lust, obsession, possessiveness, and dependency in their various forms. In particular, relationships that are primarily romantic or sexual do not provide very authentic or illuminating paradigms of love as I am construing it. Relationships of those kinds typically include a number of vividly distracting elements, which do not belong to the essential nature of love as a mode of disinterested concern, but that are so confusing that they make it nearly impossible for anyone to be clear about just what is going on. Among relationships between humans, the love of parents for their infants or small children is the species of caring that comes closest to offering recognizably pure instances of love.[7]

It could be argued, from a psychoanalytic perspective for instance, that parental love also involves some of the major "distracting elements" that

Frankfurt is referring to.[8] Aside from this, though, even a common competent speaker could wonder why most of the intense and meaningful experiences and situations that she labels with the word "love" should instead be excluded from the latter's essential definition.[9] Does this exclusion provide clarity for the speaker, or for the researcher? Whereas such a prescriptive definition is useful as long as ethical matters are at stake (in order to make us aware of what a good life could or should be according to a certain theory), discarding multiplicity, variation, and difference—some of the main sources of cultural differentiation—is too high of an epistemological price for an inquiry seeking to grasp the categories of contemporary love experience, the current paradigm(s) of romantic love in Western societies.[10] The quest for a generally valid definition of love satisfies the need for order by assuming that there is a derivative (and therefore axiological) relation between love as a universal good or feature on the one hand, and the confusion of its manifestations in everyday life and language on the other. Such an approach, together with the philosophical "needs" from which it springs, has been masterfully criticized by Wittgenstein in his *Philosophical Investigations.*

Without the sense for discontinuity and historical change, moreover, such an approach also sacrifices a reflexive critical insight into its own theoretical premises, that is to say it sacrifices epistemological awareness.[11] It could be observed, for instance, that the feeling of confusion, puzzlement, together with semantic indetermination (allowing one to say everything and its opposite about love), characterized Western love discourse—in poetry, philosophy, literature and so on—from its very beginning. As Luhmann points out, the opposition between love and reason (also in the sense of instrumental rationality), hence of (romantic) love and social order, is one of the *topoi* of Western love semantics that most contributed to love's social integration and differentiation.[12] Thus, the game of looking for an appropriate definition of love, and of bringing a rational order in its realm, was one of the constant and main blueprints of love discourse in the West. Moreover, this orientation in Western love discourse is the structural underpinning for the rationalization process that love underwent since the late eighteenth century, with the proliferation of self-help books and columns that were meant to provide individuals with the right know-how to integrate love into a more and more rationally organized emotional existence.[13] All these cultural products are indeed contributions to love's semantics that keep love discourse going and provide the necessary room for the definitional game: they perform different uses of the grammar of love discourse, the structural features of which allow the concrete variety that some mainstream definitions regard as confusion, nevertheless "contributing" to its proliferation.

There is another way by which a definitional and normative approach sacrifices its own epistemological awareness. By comparing scholarly and philosophical assertions about love as if they were steps to providing a consistent theory of what love is, such an approach treats science, as Feyerabend would argue, "*sub specie aeternitatis.*" In other words, it assumes "that the elements of our knowledge—the theories, the observations, the principles of our arguments—are timeless entities that share the same degree of perfection, are all equally accessible, and are related to each other in a way that is independent of the events that produced them."[14]

Since the historicity of knowledge is not part of such an epistemological framework, if we want to preserve and appraise the relevance of changes in ideas, subjectivities, and relationship forms, that is, the historical shifts in a yet uninterrupted "talking" about love and experiencing love in the West, we must provide a different epistemological framework. By assuming that contemporary patterns can be isolated and described, I assume that, within Western love experience, something is continuous, and something is not. The discontinuities relate to an open possibility for attachment, emotional experience, and desire to unfold, a possibility which seems to be universal,[15] yet "love" is a universally open domain of experience precisely *inasmuch* as it is subject to historical, cultural, and social change. We could thus replace an inappropriate leading question (*what is love?*) by paraphrasing the title of a well-known short story by Raymond Carver: *What are we talking about when we are talking about love?* The accent is put on the talking and on its link to place and time. "Love" is the placeholder for all the ways in which, here and now, we make sense of experience (perceptions, emotions, judgments, contexts, stages of the construction of our identities, relationships, attitudes) and we embrace tradition by referring them to the horizon of meaning that we understand as that of love. This cannot be described as the act of subsuming empirical occurrences under a general definition: Our folk theory of love already includes the possible, legitimate uses of the notion.

There is a two-way dynamic connecting what is generally said about love to individual experiences of love. The general discourse sets and articulates patterns of legitimacy: it establishes a *grammar*. In other words, it provides individuals, couples, and groups with frameworks or "scripts" for the definition (for "making sense") of their experience.[16] Conversely, individuals, according to their respective competences, use this grammar to identify, acknowledge, state, present, and share (creative) definitions of their emotional experiences, of their relationships, of their identities. Thus, they shift the discourse and the grammar, either slightly or significantly, and open up room for further attributions, that is, discursive legitimacies.[17] The spiral movement, which takes place in time and has a history, unfolds through creative mimesis, projection, reflexivity, and generalization. The "what" of Carver's formulation, thus, seeks an insight in our stories, psychosocial dispositions, values, and history.

A general definition of love can be relevant within the inquiry that I have described inasmuch as it refers to the acquired, shared, and consistently updated sensibility for a multiplicity of meanings, contexts, attitudes, behavioral patterns, claims, and relationships that can be denoted and qualified through the idea "love." It is a heuristic possibility within a complex grammar that is historically and culturally produced. I will illustrate this with an example.

## WHAT IS A LIVING ROOM? PROS AND CONS OF A MINIMAL DEFINITION

"(Romantic) love" seems not to be a concept such as "chair" or "fork," for which a minimal definition (e.g., "an eating tool consisting in a handle and some tines") would be thorough enough to allow for the subsuming of a certain object under the corresponding concept. It is more of a concept such as that of "living room."

"Living room" denotes a room, a space, just as "love" can denote an emotion, a way of feeling. But "living room" also denotes a quality of such a room, which cannot be described in an exhaustive way by making a list of "do/do not" with regard to furniture, decoration, accessories, or even activities fitting the "living room." "Living room," though, gives us criteria to provide meaningful examples of what a living room can and cannot look like, of what can and cannot be done in it, and so forth. If someone were to say that she has a shower in her living room, this could be at odds with my standard representation of a living room, but I would not necessarily deny that it is a living room. Instead of rejecting the new situation according to a general standard definition of "living room," I would probably reflect on my pre-comprehension and integrate the new situation into it, as a fancy and ironic use of the concept that I share with the person—a new use that I feel the grammar of "living room" allows. This is a good example of why no definition could with full reliability distinguish between love and not love within actual love experience—unless in a very general way or in a case-by-case subjective assessment.

As previously mentioned, a prescriptive definition (what love ought to be in order to be "love") would be meaningful for normative purposes: no living room without a couch, an armchair, without a TV, without someone smoking a pipe, and so on; accordingly, love cannot be love if it is selfish and self-centered, love must selflessly care for the other, and so forth. Yet we know that style, fashion, and taste for furniture change in time: Schopenhauer, Nietzsche, Freud, D.H. Lawrence, and Proust acquaint us with notions of love as self-deceptive generosity, sublimated selfishness, jealousy and possessiveness, self-destruction and destruction of the other, and so on. Further, in the Western history of love, erotic love has been initially excluded from marriage as a threat, later included into the spousal bond as its very basis[18]; once limited to heterosexual couples, then redefined in an inclusive way as love between (two) people.[19] Historical and cultural variation, thus, recommends caution: A prescriptive definition misses the richness of variations and nuances that are still alive in our sense for the "grammar"[20] of love.

What about a minimal definition? We could say that a living room should at least have a ground, a ceiling, and some walls, and that romantic love is an affective involvement with another person, expressing, in time and space, some form of proximity or desire for proximity to that person, implying a certain positive value of that person to the subject, as well as a reference to sexuality. Unfortunately, every term of this definition would require further clarification.[21] It really seems that we have only a ceiling and a ground, not even an armchair, and we don't even know how many walls are required. The definition is meaningless, because nobody (except perhaps a philosopher) would recognize from the ceiling and the ground that "living room" is the case here. The minimal definition is, in Wittgenstein's words, an attempt to find "the real artichoke by stripping it of its leaves."[22]

Thus, our living room is not a living room yet, unless we *do* something to provide it with elements allowing us to recognize that it is a living room (put a couch, a rug, a TV, or just some pillows on the ground in a circular form). This gesture of bestowing meaning refers to a range of possibilities (activities, thoughts, interactions, connections, feelings) that are linked to the idea "living room" on the one hand, and to the actual specification of this idea in space and time on the other. The grammar of "living room" establishes boundaries for legitimate uses and practices connected to the notion, where "legitimate" means that other people can understand them as successfully relating to the idea "living room." Such legitimacies are not "inferred" from or necessarily implied by a previous, thorough definition of a living room, which would float in our minds waiting to be applied to real states of affairs. On the contrary, every possible minimal definition is already the outcome of a competence, since I ought to master the grammar in order to find my way into the uses of the concept.

Thus, in order to understand our current understanding of "love," a minimal definition can serve as a preliminary and provisional orientation, which ought to be kept flexible and open to the possibility that someone has a shower in her living room, and that our minimal definition would not have been able to predict in what sense and why this still fits to the grammar of "living room." This kind of theoretical surprise awaits us as soon as we look into actual forms of self-understanding and of the understanding of others, practices, values, and normative attributions linked to something such as love in current Western societies.

Instead of defining what a romantic living room should be, we could instead examine how people arrange their living rooms to get the feeling of being in a romantic living room, thus expecting others to appraise them as such and to share their experience. We could also pay attention to the fact that, up to a certain threshold of extravagancy, we are already able to under-stand and, depending on our social abilities, to undertake specific activities by simply approaching to someone's living room, and to fine-tune our attitude and our posture according to its atmosphere (romantic, elegant, cozy, formal, etc.). If we were confronted simply with a ground, a ceiling, and a certain amount of walls, we probably would not express the same ability.

## THE IMPORTANCE OF BEING ORDINARY

Now that the traditional definitional approach has been discarded, we need to provide another conceptual and methodological framework allowing us to grasp the continuity as well as the diversity of patterns of love experience. My suggestion is that we build on the concept of discourse, on the analysis of practices, and on the idea of emotion work.

Borrowing from Roland Barthes, we can use the notion of "discourse" to indicate all of the symbols, patterns, ideas, *topoi*, literary figures and plots, mottos and proverbs, or in a word the paradigms of love that have contributed and still contribute to our present understanding.[23] Such paradigms result from historical and sociocultural processes of articulation, interpretation and re-interpretation, transmission, and generalization. "Love discourse," there-fore, is a theoretical abstraction to represent the condensation of cultural and social history into conceptions, dispositions, and attitudes that make up the skeleton of a sociocultural environment as well as of the mind-frames of the individuals that have been socialized in it. As J.-C. Kaufmann puts it, socio-cultural and historical inquiries introduce us to the "social factory" that pro-duces the categories of our love experience.[24] These categories converge into the "grammar" of love discourse and love practices. In addition to the com-monsense understanding and to "what people say about love," "discourse" means the tradition lying behind every symbol and *topos* that we are able to use while talking (and thinking) about love. Crystallization of paradigms and paradigm variation go hand in hand.

As the result of the long and consistent work of the "categories factory," love discourse (narrative patterns, symbols, folk psychology, common sense attributions, evaluations, etc.)[25] is *one* part of the inquiry on the ordinary discourse of love. Complementary to discourse, as Kaufmann observes, are actual individual practices connecting contexts to available symbols and frames of meaning. These two dimensions—availability of discourse and individual appropriations of it—imply a third one: emotional experience, that is, feelings together with the thoughts and the "toward" that are associated to them[26]. We do not have any direct knowledge of another person's emotional experience unless the subject describes, represents, and interprets it: Here, knowledge comes through *sharing* emotional or affective experience.

This brings us back to the availability of a grammar of understanding, interpreting, performing, and sharing affective dispositions on the one hand; to the interactional and individual patterns of acquaintance with it on the other. Experience in social contexts not only offers a chance for universal behavioral systems to unfold: it also *molds* them into meaningful practices, thoughts, and feelings. Since, within the framework of social performances, discursive patterns and symbolic structures shape our relational and interactional experience with others (take for example, the influence of gendered affective styles in Western civilization), they consequently shape: our emotional dispositions (dispositions to certain patterns of "feeling towards," that is, to feelings and thoughts/evaluations connected to them); our reflexivity with regard to emotional and affective experience; finally, the reasoning and valuing which are the basis of what we could call, with A. R. Hochschild, "emotion work."[27] I would like to examine each.

Individual emotional dispositions are the first aspect of the interaction between individual capacity to have feelings and the symbolic-normative frameworks that social life establishes. Though these dispositions are to a certain extent personal and singular, a great part of them is molded by cultural and social patterns. Such patterns contain ideas and beliefs regarding not only emotions themselves, but more largely what it is like to be a person, to be a person in a certain social position, to be a person of a certain gender, and so on.[28] Hence, distinct emotional dispositions are shaped by different ideas about the nature of love and about the moral and biological connection between love and gender, different understandings of intimate attachment and forms of attachment during infancy and childhood specific to a certain society or culture, different ideas and norms about the relation between (passionate) love and institutionalized forms of relationships, such as marriage or partnership, and different legitimacies concerning the connection of sex and love, and so on. This system of beliefs is indeed a system of rules for emotional expression that draws normative boundaries for the performance and the recognition of personal identities (which also means *gendered* identities) in love intimacy.

Let us address the second area, that of the reflexivity on emotional and affective experience. "Reflexivity" means here the capability for acts of perception, cognition, understanding, and appraisal, in which the self is at the same time subject and object of such acts, as well as the qualitative link (awareness plus reference to value commitments or beliefs) between subjective and objective in the apperception. In one of his studies on sexuality and love in the Western world, J.-L. Flandrin observes that for the historian as well as for the man on the street, "no understanding of what another feels is possible unless one understands his awareness of his feelings,"[29] since "the psychological reality of human behaviour can only be approached via the subject's inner awareness of the same." Despite the "unquestionable" originality of "all individual behaviour," "the outward manifestations of our drives can only be shaped by the conventions of a specific culture; our feelings become apparent to us when expressed in the words and images which this culture offers us." Flandrin's study seeks to appraise the differences between sixteenth- and twentieth-century conceptions of love by examining book titles that refer to love or to a web of concepts connected to it: book titles "give us the value of words accepted in a chronologically and geographically defined society"; however, they "indicate only those ideas which a civilization dares to display."[30] In order to "truly understand the significance of this display,"[31] we must combine it with, and integrate it through, an inquiry on individual expressions of feeling (for instance, in private correspondence and printed texts): we want to grasp the way in which individuals "bargain" with emotional rules that norm social space. We want to grasp what it is to be a "subject" of love experience.

With regard to emotional dispositions, there can be two patterns of reflexive "negotiation," which display rules and structures of recognition. First, there can be a purely emotional pattern, meaning an emotion about an emotion, which is also part of emotional dispositions. Second, there can be a more genuinely reflexive pattern,[32] that is, a discursive reflection on or about an emotion, according to the model of the internal conversation. There is no sharp *qualitative* distinction between pure emotional and pure cognitive self-appraisal: they are interwoven, and activated in different combinations and reciprocal "proportions." Among the main variables regulating the combination, we find the depth of the embodiment of specific (and even clashing) emotion rules and structures of recognition and the complexity and unfamiliarity of a certain context of experience or interaction. A further variable is the occasional uncertainty about the most appropriate emotion in a certain situation, which requires a deeper reflexive examination than the emotional appraisal could allow. This can also entail an oscillation between the appraised emotion and the appraising emotion within the first pattern of reflexivity. Finally, we can mention the specific balance of rationality and emotions distinguishing a sociocultural framework and the corresponding individual *habitus* (plural).

The specific work that we carry out in order to conform our emotions to the standards and norms of appropriateness regulating interactions in our society has been defined as *emotion management* or *emotion work*. This is the third aspect of emotional experience as regulated by social patterns. The very idea of emotion work implies that this regulation is not passive, but rather requires individual agency to be carried out in an appropriate, adaptive, and personal way. In A. Hochschild's theoretical framework, emotion work is not an external adjustment; rather it is involved in the "private emotion system."[33] As E. Goffmann had already observed, experience and "deep" memory of socially shared "feeling rules" mold the expression of feelings and emotions. But, Hochschild adds, they also inform emotions and emotional dispositions themselves through a self-monitoring and self-shaping work of emotion management, that Hochschild calls "deep acting." Moved by dynamics of social acceptance and rejection, or by other social and professional constraints[34] connected to role performances, individuals conform to feeling rules and "bargain" with them. As Hochschild explains, a "social role—such as that of bride, wife, or mother—is partly a way of describing what feelings people think are owed and are owing. A role establishes a baseline for what feelings seem appropriate to a certain series of events. When roles change, so do rules for how to feel and interpret events."[35] The conformity involves outer expression as well as inner experience, since individuals are reflexively confronted with the awareness of how they feel *and* with the awareness of how they should be, could be, or are expected to feel in a certain context. Struggling to harmonize actual with expected emotions, individuals make up their "heads" and manage their "hearts." Emotion work is a pattern of reflexivity that involves an *active* effort ("strategy") to harmonize actual emotion experience and emotional or "conversational" reflexive feedback. By focusing on reflexivity toward experience of emotions and intimacy, we can examine how individuals are committed to emotion rules, and through them, give love a place in the understanding of their lives. Since individual emotional life, reflexive patterns and discourse are intrinsically connected, combining the reconstruction of discursive patterns with the analysis of forms of reflexivity and emotion work affords a rich epistemological framework for the investigation of ordinary love experience. Indeed discourse (sociocultural legitimacies, values, norms, narratives, etc.) is not external, but rather, discourse lives in the heads and in the (managed) hearts of individuals: it is a space for regulated subjectivation.

## CONTEMPORARY PATTERNS: SOME INTRODUCTORY REMARKS

With these remarks on the discursivity and reflexivity of love experience in mind, let us now turn to contemporary patterns of love in order to briefly test the theoretical and methodological framework that we have sketched so far. Although this test would clearly require a more extensive argument to be adequately carried out, I will nevertheless provide an outline of what an inquiry on ordinary love would look like when conducted by means of this epistemological and conceptual apparatus.

As soon as we take a closer look at those patterns, it becomes clear that there are additional reasons for focusing on the constellation of discursive and reflexive dispositions within emotional experience. We can summarize them by pointing out two major tendencies of the twentieth and twenty-first centuries: the increasing importance, specification and inclusiveness of love discourse on the one hand; the corresponding increasing importance, specification and inclusiveness of reflexive practices toward love experience on the other. These two tendencies are linked by mutual influence. Love discourse undergoes massification and "therapeutization," hence affecting individual awareness and anxiety with regard to the management of one's emotional life and "personality," as well as one's relationships. Conversely, the increasing demand for advice and orientation, arising from the "duty" of self-determination and individualization, fosters the parceling and the detailing of discourse, its pervasiveness, and its omnipresence. Self-aware emotion management (in the form of self-help, therapeutic attitude, emancipation, etc.) has become a major *modus* of emotional experience, a consistent and careful monitoring of emotional "spontaneity," which canalizes it into patterns of meaningfulness.

A fundamental impulsion to self-reflection within love experience arises from the revolutionary configuration of the romantic love ideal, forged and developed as of the end of the eighteenth and throughout the nineteenth centuries. A love relationship as a life-long or at least long-term emotional and existential commitment, that is, the marital relationship as the unity of institutional commitment and passionate (erotic) love that imposed itself in the nineteenth century[36], is more likely than traditional marriage to be the source of conflicts in which emotional and psychological issues are at stake.[37] An additional instability factor lies in the fact that passionate love (i.e., emotional intensity) progressively became *the* fundamental criterion not only for committing to a marital union but also for appraising and maintaining it. Erotic love is now considered the fundamental source of meaningfulness for a relationship, such that every alternative reason for commitment (even those that have been at the very core of Western marriage for centuries, such as money and material advantages, social protection, immigration, social reproduction *à la* Bourdieu, etc.) is regarded and dismissed as morally dubious. Emotional intensity, which is uncertain and precarious, is expected to serve as the basis for commitment. Hence, the instability of unions based on love gradually becomes a social issue, and consequently, a major object for social reflection (and discourse). Attempts to contain the impact of the romantic revolution and to reframe individual freedom are made through an ideology of the gendered moral psychology of love,[38] as well as through the conservative appeal to reasonable love or *amour conjugal*,[39] both of which seem to be back in fashion today.[40] The general trend shows intensification and a multiplication of social reflexivity on love bonds, as well as an insistence on individual responsibility for awareness and control concerning emotional life and relationships. Supported and in a certain sense "obliged" by knowledge and information deriving from morals, psychology and later psychoanalysis, physiology and now neurobiology, individuals are increasingly expected to relate in a self-reflexive way to love (emotional experience), marriage (ethical bonds), sexuality[41] (physiology, nature, morality), and so forth—all this, of course, according to and depending on their gender, as well as, more recently, to their sexual orientation. The reflexive pattern, to which romantic love ideology gave birth, persists throughout the twentieth century,[42] and by virtue of its very structure, becomes increasingly complex, unfolding its specificities along some major lines of normativity and meaningfulness, and embracing a large variety of themes and issues. This is the kind of love that A. Giddens conceptualizes as "confluent love," and which serves as basis to the form of partnership that he defines as "pure relationship."[43]

The first group of themes that contribute to make reflexivity on love relationships more complex originates from both the process and the movement of women's emancipation. This self-aware process and the connected claims have specifically raised self-awareness—among women *and* among men—with regard to affective styles, effects of embodied gender biases, corresponding emotional dispositions and behavioral patterns in intimacy.[44] Since at least M. Wollstonecraft's *Vindication*, the experience of heterosexual (romantic) love can be deeply tainted by the awareness of inequality, domination and violence between men and women.[45]

A second thematic axis, which is also related with women's emancipation and gender issues, is the one that reproduces and reinforces the nineteenth-century tendency to naturalize or psychologize behavioral patterns and triggers for conflicts by tracing them back to the essential character of gender differences. Trivialized discourse and advice literature consistently disseminate a wide range of beliefs connected to the allegedly *gendered* moral psychology of love, that is, to assumptions regarding what men and women in love naturally feel, think, do, hope for, want, and so on.[46] This pattern attributes conflicts to the nature of gendered characters and insists on the awareness of gender differences as a way to solve such conflicts. Thus, it is clearly at odds with those versions of the emancipatory discourse that stress the constructed nature of gender differences and biases. Although gender differences are among the major themes of contemporary reflexivity on love experience, their value and meaning with regard to the functionality of love itself are highly ambiguous.[47]

Partly by virtue of women's increasing self-awareness, independence, and emancipation, as well as the corresponding social and political changes throughout the twentieth century, and partly on the basis of a more general, consumer-oriented discourse concerning individuality, self-fulfillment, and individualistic well-being standards, a third reflexive trend revolves around the axiological clash of criteria for individual self-fulfillment and satisfaction with criteria for happiness and harmony in love relationships. Love is certainly still regarded as the key to a fulfilled and happy life, and long-term commitment is generally considered, in the different forms that relationships can assume, as the ideal framework for such happiness.[48] Yet men *and* women are "expected" to consider themselves as the most important, longest, most consistent and meaningful individual project. If, in the heterosexual sphere, instability and unreliability of love (relationships) spring from major social changes that mostly depend on women's emancipation, the reaction to such jeopardizing factors expresses an even stronger shift of the balance of individual commitment toward the "duty" of self-fulfillment (social and professional self-development, but also the whole rhetoric of finding one's "true" self). Where two analogous styles of individual self-definition conflict with one another, the irritation is unlikely to be relieved by having recourse to traditional roles, tools, and emotional rules—at least not in an overt, explicit, and discursive way.[49] Thus, the need for direction grows, whereas reflexivity gains the additional meaning of self-commitment, of "care of oneself," that is, of an emotional investment on the value of a consistent, self-centered self-reference. On the one hand, a self-reference of this sort is clearly at odds with one of the main traditional definitions of love, according to which the latter would imply a form of self-forgetfulness, a priority of love over self-love (*at least* from one side of the love bond).[50] On the other hand, it generates a broader clash of prescriptions, based on a new articulation of the old opposition of passionate love and love as commitment, an opposition that Western love discourse still reiterates and reproduces. With regard to this second point, emotional intensity, which is part of the experience of passionate love and not necessarily of long-term relationships, is increasingly loaded with a positive moral value inasmuch as it is associated with self-fulfillment and self-satisfaction. For social actors confronted with the difficulty of finding reliable criteria for measuring or assessing their happiness and satisfaction, consumer culture offers a ready-to-use solution through the connection of emotional intensity and "thickness" in individual life.[51] Since intense emotional experience is typically transitory and episodic within love relationships—depending, for instance, on the phase of the love bond—it provides no base for long-term, stable individual production of meaningfulness. Whereas frustration and routine were traditionally accepted as belonging to the ordinary marital pattern,[52] the over-idealized romantic quest for personal fulfillment *through* love bonds leads one to interpret frustration as a potential good reason (or at least a strong indicator) to reconsider and revise one's commitments.

Regarding this scenario, scholars such as J. C. Kaufmann observe that the disenchantment involving current love experience is only one side of the problem: the paradoxical responses to it also deserve consideration.[53] Like our predecessors, we are aware of the possibility (probability) for passionate love to end, or to fail. Unlike them, we are also aware of the fact that a *love relationship* can fail for all sorts of reasons other than a lack of love: This is why we search for information, advice, counseling and so on. These reflective forms undoubtedly provide us with a deeper insight into the clockwork mechanics of love relationships (communicational patterns, emotional dispositions, conflicts, etc.). At the same time, though, this contributes to the disenchantment that taints contemporary love experience: as P. Watzlawick would put it, the solution to the problem is, to a certain extent, the problem itself.[54] Current love experience is generally made sense of both through a stronger idealization of love (in accordance to the romantic ideology), and through the rationalization that responds to the disillusionment with the possibility of a happy love life (often measured through emotional intensity). Insight, meant to respond to uncertainty, can instead lead to stronger skepticism and emotional detachment: the sense of disillusionment cannot be dissolved through rational assessment and calculation, which are extremely unlikely to foster the demanded emotional intensity.

## CONCLUDING REMARKS

"Cheshire Puss," she began ... "Would you tell me, please, which way I ought to go from here?" "That depends a good deal on where you want to get to," said the Cat.

—Lewis Carroll, *Alice's Adventures in Wonderland*

This short exploration of some major features of current love experience is not meant to provide an exhaustive description of contemporary love patterns. It is rather aimed at supporting the opening plea in favor of epistemological awareness, and at giving an example of the inquiry that I have in mind.

I shall briefly return to the main point that is at stake here. In an inquiry focusing on understanding love and its conditions of possibility, attention to historicity and variation do not prevent a fundamental comprehension of love as a universal experience. On the contrary, the focus on historicity, specificity, and difference can bring to light the continuity of issues and themes that seem to generally belong to the way love is experienced and understood in Western civilization. The history of "our" current love experience is the history of a constellation of emotions and desires; corresponding social bonds and forms of attachment; corresponding (or competing) institutions; *plus* the crucial function of all this with regard to individual self-constitution and self-understanding, to learning to encounter the other through desire and respect, and to turning this into a project of identity and life. It is the history of an emotion-based pattern of meaningfulness for human life, which has been shaped and developed through an uninterrupted hermeneutical attention for emotional experience, for its meaning, and for the conditions of possibility of a totalizing intimacy with the other. Thus, discursivity—as a reflective disposition toward the *modi* of socializing emotional experience (intimacy, attachment, bonds, gender roles and identities, frames and contexts for emotions, meaning of emotions, interactional patterns)—is not accessory: it is the medium allowing all these different dimensions to communicate and interface with each other. It is interesting to point out that the same argument could be made with regards to the understanding of other phenomena, such as friendship or justice.

The approach that I have sketched avoids the reduction of love to a specific cultural program, to an abstract universal, or to a subjective experience. All these reductions would miss at least one side of the story: They would miss the multidimensionality of the collective and individual production of meaning as a perceptive, emotional, and discursive performance in space and time. Thus, there is a way in which my living room here and now does not just say something about what a living room generally is and about myself as a living-room owner but also something about how individuals emotionally connect to ideas, share them, and *live* with them. We have to provide the right perspective to make it *visible*. The first epistemological step, I believe, is to problematize our self-transparency.

## NOTES

1. I would like to express my gratitude to Emily Hartz, Martin Breaugh, Maria Cristina Fornari, Antonella Balestra, Sarah LaChance Adams, Christopher Davidson and to the participants of the Committee on Social Thought Colloquium at the University of Chicago for their stimulating remarks. My research was made possible by the Käthe Kluth Postdoctoral Fellowship at the University of Greifswald (Germany).

2. In addition to Wittgenstein, see Clifford Geertz on common sense, "Common Sense as a Cultural System," in *Local Knowledge: Further Essays in Interpretive Anthropology* (New York: Basic Books, 1983), 73–93, and Michel de Certeau on

practical knowledge *L'Invention du quotidien. 1. Arts de faire.* (Paris: Gallimard-Folio, 1990).

3. Although the phrase "romantic love" is historically loaded—exactly in the same way as "erotic love"—I allow myself to use it to distinguish the form of intimacy I am focusing on from, say, parental love, religious love and so on. In the following, "love" refers to this form of love.

4. Max Weber, "Kritische Studien auf dem Gebiet der Kulturwissenschaftlichen Logik," *Archiv für Sozialwissenschaft und Sozialpolitik* 22 (1906).

5. Friedrich Nietzsche, *On the Genealogy of Morality*, ed. Keith Ansell-Pearson (Cambridge: Cambridge University Press, 2007), II, 13.

6. Harry G. Frankfurt, *The Reason of Love* (Princeton: Princeton University Press, 2004), 43.

7. Similarly, French philosopher Corinne Pelluchon stated in a recent publication that "there are […] forms of love that are more or less blurred, but there is only one essence of love, that is fulfilled when we suffer for what the other person suffers for and when we are capable of self-sacrifice for the other person" L'Unicité et le sens de l'amour, in *Amour toujours*, ed. Jean Birnbaum [Paris: Gallimard-Folio, 2013], 48).

8. See, for example, the Freudian and Kleinian theories of infantile sexuality and of the eroticization of breast-feeding: Sigmund Freud, "The Infantile Sexuality," in *Three Essays on the Theory of Sexuality*, trans. James Strachey (New York: Basic Books, 2000); Melanie Klein, *The Psychoanalysis of Children* (New York: Grove Press, 1960). For a discussion of the psychoanalytic complexity of mother–child relationship during breastfeeding, see also Edith Frampton, "Fluid Objects: Kleinian Psychoanalytic Theory and Breastfeeding Narratives," *Australian Feminist Studies* 19 (2004): 357–68.

9. Further examples of normative and exclusive definitions of love can be found in bell hooks, *All about Love: New Visions* (London: The Women's Press, 2000). Trivialized versions of this philosophical stance are legion in blogs, magazines, and columns: as a specimen, see Sheryl Paul, "The Truth about Love," *The Huffington Post* (August 6, 2012).

10. Let alone the fact that mainstream philosophical definitions of love, by working with an implicit theory of love the underpinnings of which are in commonsensical reduction of difference and variation, create a standard, a "normality" (thus a norm) that excludes. For instance, Flavia Monceri—see especially "L'amore di chi? Decostruzioni e ricostruzioni di un'istituzione sociale," in *Eros e discorso amoroso*, eds. Antonella Balestra and Chiara Piazzesi. [Pisa: Edizioni ETS, 2015], but also Flavia Monceri, "Queer Loves: Restating Bodies, Genders, and Sexualities," *Teoria*, 29, no. 2 (2009): 177–95—argues against mainstream philosophical accounts of romantic love that exclude same-sex love and desire as well as people with disabilities from the very framework of "functional" love, or, when they happen to take them into consideration, they almost invariably do it through the reference to the heterosexual paradigm.

11. See Mike Featherstone on the importance of taking into account the link between a philosophy of love and "a particular set of social, intellectual and moral circumstances" from which it arises: "Love and Eroticism. An Introduction," *Theory, Culture & Society* 15, nos. 3–4 (1998): 1–18.

12. Niklas Luhmann, *Love as Passion* (Cambridge: Harvard University Press, 1986).

13. Regina Mahlmann, *Was Verstehst du unter Liebe? Ideale und Konflikte von der Frühromantik bis Heute* (Darmstadt: Primus Verlag, 2003); Regina Mahlmann, *Psychologisierung des "Alltagsbewußtseins." Die Verwissenschaftlicung des Diskurses über Ehe* (Opladen: Westdeutscher Verlag, 1991); Cas Wouters, *Sex and Manners: Female Emancipation in the West, 1890–2000* (London: Sage, 2002).

14. Paul Feyerabend, *Against Method* (London: Verso, 1993), 106.

15. The biological anthropologist Helen Fisher pleads for a vision of romantic love as intercultural universal based on an evolutionary disposition to attachment and serial monogamy: see, for example, "The Nature of Romantic Love," *The Journal of NIH Research* 6 (1994): 59–64. See also John Bowlby *Attachment and Loss. Vol. 1: Attachment* (New York: Basic Books, 1999); 2nd edition. *Attachment and Loss. Vol. 2: Separation: Anxiety and Anger.* (New York: Basic Books, 1973); *Attachment and Loss. Vol. 3: Loss: Sadness and Depression.* (New York: Basic Books, 1980) Cindy Hazan and Phillip Shaver's application of Bowlby's theoretical framework to romantic relationships, ("Romantic Love Conceptualized as an Attachment Process," *Journal of Personality and Social Psychology* 52 (1987): 511–24), and an overview of attachment theory and love in Mario Mikulincer, "Attachment, Caregiving, and Sex within Romantic Relationships: A Behavioral Systems Perspective," in *Dynamics of Romantic Love: Attachment, Caregiving, and Sex*, eds. Mario Mikulincer and Gail S. Goodman (New York: The Guilford Press, 2006), 23–44.

16. William Simon and John H. Gagnon, "Sexual Scripts: Origins, Influences and Changes," *Qualitative Sociology* 26, no. 4 (2003): 491–97.

17. These dynamics between social frameworks, individual dispositions, and the social room for creativity are accurately described by Pierre Bourdieu's theory of habitus; see his *Pascalian Meditations*, (Stanford: Stanford University Press, 2000).

18. See Jean-Claude Kaufman, *The Curious History of Love*, (Cambridge: Polity Press, 2011) and Niklas Luhmann, *Love as Passion*.

19. See President Barack Obama's statement on the U.S. Supreme Court's ruling of June 26th, 2013 declaring the unconstitutionality of Defense of Marriage Act for "writing inequality into the entire United States Code" by denying federal benefits to legally married same-sex couples (*United States v. Windsor*, 570 U.S. [2013]). Obama stated that "we are a people who declared that we are all created equal—and the love we commit to one another must be equal as well."

20. As Alan Soble puts it, "If a claim or a theory about love implies that many cases of what we ordinarily call love aren't love, that is a reason (not necessarily decisive) for denying the claim of the theory." Alan Soble, *The Philosophy of Sex and Love* (St. Paul: Paragon House, 2008), 129.

21. We could take "involvement" in a psychological, physiological, or metaphorical sense, and we would have three different theories of love; the same thing occurs if we interpret "imply" and "value" as meaning "value bestowal" or "value appraisal" (see Bennett Helm, "Love," *Stanford Encyclopedia of Philosophy*, 2009), or if we take "value" as moral, real, economical, functional, psychological and so on.

22. Ludwig Wittgenstein, *Philosophische Untersuchungen*, in *Werkausgabe*, Band 1 (Frankfurt am Main: Suhrkamp 1984); *Philosophical Investigations* (Oxford: Blackwell, 1953), § 164.

23. Roland Barthes Barthes, *A Lover's Discourse: Fragments* (New York: Hill and Wang, 1978).

24. Kauffman, *The Curious History of Love*, 7.

25. Take for instance the fact that a symbolic pattern such as "blind love" or "passionate love," which also means a love that does not respect social boundaries and ethical legitimacies, is perfectly understandable in our current practice, and that, beyond any possible moral censure, it is surrounded by an aura of social indulgence.

26. Here I refer mainly to Peter Goldie's definition of emotion as "feeling towards" or "thinking of with feeling." See, for instance, *The Emotions: A Philosophical Exploration* (Oxford: Clarendon Press, 2000), 58.

27. Arlie R. Hochschild, *The Managed Heart: Commercialization of Human Feeling* (Berkeley: University of California Press, 1983).

28. See, for instance, Charles Taylor, *Sources of the Self: The Making of Modern Identity* (Cambridge: Harvard University Press, 1992), on the ways moral commitments and value appraisals shape identity and subjectivity; Elias' studies on the process of civilization (*The Civilizing Process*) and on the link between social regulation of emotions and the increasing sense of one's individuality and individual subjectivity in Western Europe (*The Society of Individuals*); and Bourdieu's idea of individual "*habitus*" (e.g., *Pascalian Meditations*) as a set of individual cognitive, perceptive, and affective dispositions linking personality to a structured social space.

29. It could be argued that it is possible to notice that someone else is in love (angry, depressed, or sad) without the person being aware of her feelings: we would thus understand her feelings without having access to her awareness of them. However, what we do in this case is imagine how someone who is unaware of her feelings *would* understand them if she were (to become) aware of them. Further, we project or propose an understanding that is based on categories of appraisal, interpretation, and attribution that we suppose to share with the concerned person, so that our understanding would make sense for her too. Hence, we would replace her defective reflexivity through ours, but we would nevertheless draw our categories from the same common patterns of understanding of feelings that would allow us to understand another's awareness of her feelings.

30. Jean-Louis Flandrin, *Sex in the Western World: The Development of Attitudes and Behaviour*, trans. Sue Collins (Chur: Harwood Academic Publishers, 1991), 13 f.

31. Flandrin, *Sex in the Western World*, 32.

32. I am inclined to claim that the emotional pattern *is* a reflexive pattern, inasmuch as it draws a cognitive and affective connection between the awareness of an emotional state and its appraisal with regard to the specific situation of the subject of the emotion: in this sense, an emotion on an emotion is a global self-appraisal, and not only an appraisal of the emotion itself, disconnected from the *hic et nunc* of the subject of both emotions.

33. Hochschild, *The Managed Heart*.

34. In addition to the patterns of emotion work within intimate life, Hochschild has also analyzed those connected to the requirements of professions such as flight attendant (*The Managed Hart*). In this respect emotional work, as "emotional labor," becomes part of labor and is commercialized as such (e.g., the market value of a flight attendant's smile).

35. Hochschild, *The Managed Heart*, 74 f. "A rising divorce rate, a rising remarriage rate, a declining birthrate, a rising number of worker women, and a greater legitimation of homosexuality are the outer signs of changing roles. ... If periods of rapid change induce status anxiety, they also lead to anxiety about what, after all, the feeling rules are."

36. Prior to late eighteenth century, love was mainly considered either as "passion" or as "marital love," the latter being the fulfillment of marital commitment to (gendered) respect, care, and material support, closer to *amicitia* than to erotic love; the former being the opposite, disruptive power of appetites and desires, mostly immoral, irrational, and antisocial. The reflection on the moral and aesthetic tension between these two opposite movements in the human soul gave birth to most of the finest masterworks in arts, music, and literature from the Middle Ages on.

37. Luhmann, *Love as Passion*; Mahlmann, *Was Verstehst du unter Liebe?*

38. See Mahlmann, *Psychologisierung des "Alltagsbewußtseins."* for an analysis, through marriage advice books, of the nineteenth-century ideology attributing different duties and responsibilities to men and women within passionate love and marital unions. By ascribing to women "the service of love," the "job" of "human relations," nineteenth-century gendered ideology of love actually assigns to women the duty of managing conflicts within marital communication *because* they are expected to be more sensitive and capable of empathy. This assignment progressively implies for women the moral responsibility for *raising* conflicts that they "produce" inasmuch as they can address them and meta-communicate about them (90 ff.). Hence, nineteenth-century moral psychology of love and marriage "solves" the issue of instability by tying women into a double bind. It is not difficult to see the link between this trend and the "hysterization of women's bodies" that Foucault (*The History of Sexuality Vol. 3: The Care of Self* [London: Penguin, 1990]) highlights in his nineteenth-century discourse on sexuality.

39. See, for example, Jean-Jacques Rousseau's conception of *amour conjugal* as solution to the clash of passionate love—as self-centered and selfish—and marriage in *La Nouvelle Héloïse* (in *Œuvres complètes*, vol. 2. [Paris: Bibliothèque de la Pléiade, 1964]), together with Elena Pulcini's excellent analysis of the question: *Amour-passion et amour conjugal. rousseau à l'origine d'un conflit moderne* (Paris: Editions Honore Champion, 1998), but also Honoré de Balzac's *Physiologie du mariage* (Paris: Levavasseur et Urbain Canel, 1829.).

40. Very different examples of the revival of the ideology of *amour conjugal* can be found in Sven Hillenkamp's *Das Ende der Liebe. Gefühle im Zeitalter Unendlicher Freiheit* (Stuttgart: Klett-Cotta, 2009), Arnold Retzer's *Lob der Vernunftehe: Eine Streitschrift für Mehr Realismus in der Liebe* (Frankfurt am Main: Fischer, 2009), Lori Gottlieb's *Marry Him: The Case for Settling for Mr. Good Enough* (London: Dutton, 2010), and Pascal Bruckner's *Le mariage d'amour a-t-il échoué?* (Paris: Grasset, 2010).

41. On the construction of sexuality as self-awareness of desire, where monitoring, management, and micro-definition of desire foster the intensification and the parceling of control, see Foucault (*History of Sexuality*, Vols. 1–3).

42. Mahlmann, *Psychologisierung des "Alltagsbewußtseins."*

43. Anthony Giddens, *The Transformation of Intimacy: Sexuality, Love and Eroticism in Modern Societies* (Cambridge: Polity Press, 1992).

44. Raewyn W. Connell, *Masculinities*, 2nd edition (Berkeley: University of California Press, 2005).

45. Mary Wollstonecraft, *A Vindication of the Rights of Woman* (Cambridge: Cambridge University Press, 1995).

46. John Gray's *Mars and Venus* series provides a very telling example of these attributions and to its link to problem-solving strategies within heterosexual relationships.

47. Regarding the first axis, analogous patterns of inequality and domination are experienced and discussed within same-sex relationships, although not necessarily with reference to a gendered dynamics, but they can also "parodied" in the framework of homosexual encounters (through an imagery that uses categorical oppositions such as top and bottom, active and passive, etc.). See Leo Bersani and Adam Phillips, *Intimacies* (Chicago: Chicago University Press, 2008), and chapter 2 in particular. Regarding the second axis, ambiguity is also true with regard to same-sex relationships, as well as to the recent and less recent discourse that opposes same-sex marriage by contesting the legitimacy of the legal recognition of an allegedly "unnatural" bond.

48. This is one of the aspects of current love experience that Anthony Giddens' model of a "pure relationship," according to Stevi Jackson, fails to grasp. See also Mahlmann, *Was Verstehst du unter Liebe?*

49. There has been quite a lot of empirical work showing a persistent gap between what people say and what people do in terms of producing gender equality within intimate relationships, especially with regards to the division of non-remunerated work. For a discussion, see Lynn Jamieson, "Intimacy Transformed? A Critical Look at the 'Pure Relationship,'" *Sociology* 33, no. 3 (1999): 477–94, and Stephanie Coontz, "Gender Equality and Economic Inequality: Impact on Marriage," in *Gender and Couple Relationships*, eds. Susan M. McHale et al., 79–90 (Springer, 2016).

50. That is, mostly from the woman or from the feminine-identified part (although the *ideology* prescribes double-sided self-forgetfulness). A role swap, which implies switching emotional rules as well, can only occasionally serve as a solution to this kind of gender impasse within love relationships, since it seems not to be open (yet) to systematization or generalization in current Western social structure. See Arlie Hochschild on the question of care labor: *The Commercialization of Intimate Life: Notes from Home and Work* (Berkeley: University of California Press, 2003).

51. As Wouters points out, the individual "quest for an exciting and satisfying lust-balance," avoiding both "emotional wildness" and "emotional numbness," refers to a landscape where "the increased demands on emotion management will have intensified both the fantasies and the longing for (romantic) relationships characterized by greater intimacy, as well as the longing for easier (sexual) relationships in which the

pressure of these demands is negligible" (Sex and Manners, 160)—and which, I would add, provide a low(er)-cost emotional intensity. See also "Balancing Sex and Love since the 1960s Sexual Revolution," *Theory, Culture and Society* 15, nos. 3–4 (1998): 187–214). Kaufmann dramatizes the opposition of the two patterns: in addition to two concurring forms of emotional involvement, they draw two concurring "regimes" of decision, agency, assessment, and two clashing patterns for happiness (*The Curious History of Love*).

    52. See Balzac, *Physiologie du mariage*, for a portrait.

    53. Kaufman, *The Curious History of Love*.

    54. Paul Watzlawick et al., *Change: Principles of Problem Formation and Problem Resolution* (New York: Norton, 1974).

## BIBLIOGRAPHY

Alexander, Jeffrey C. "The Strong Program in Cultural Sociology." In *The Meanings of Social Life*, edited by Jeffrey C. Alexander, 11–26. New York: Oxford University Press, 2003.

de Balzac, Honoré. *Physiologie du mariage*. Paris: Levavasseur et Urbain Canel, 1829.

Barthes, Roland. *A Lover's Discourse: Fragments*. New York: Hill and Wang, 1978.

Bersani, Leo, and Adam Phillips. *Intimacies*. Chicago: Chicago University Press, 2008.

Bourdieu, Pierre. *Pascalian Meditations*. Stanford: Stanford University Press, 2000.

Bowlby, John. *Attachment and Loss. Vol. 1, 2nd edition. Attachment*. New York: Basic Books, 1999.

———. *Attachment and Loss. Vol. 2: Separation: Anxiety and Anger*. New York: Basic Books, 1973.

———. *Attachment and Loss. Vol. 3: Loss: Sadness and Depression*. New York: Basic Books, 1980.

Bruckner, Pascal. *Le mariage d'amour a-t-il échoué?* Paris: Grasset, 2010.

Burkart, Günter. "Auf dem Weg zu einer Soziologie der Liebe." In *Liebe am Ende des 20. Jahrhunderts. Studien zur Soziologie Intimer Beziehungen*, edited by Kornelia Hahn and Günter Burkart, 16–49. Wiesbaden: Springer Fachmedien, 1998.

de Certeau, Michel. *L'Invention du quotidien. 1. Arts de faire*. Paris: Gallimard-Folio, 1990.

Connell, Raewyn W. *Masculinities*, 2nd edition, Berkeley: University of California Press, 2005.

Coontz, Stephanie. "Gender Equality and Economic Inequality: Impact on Marriage." In *Gender and Couple Relationships*, edited by Susan M. McHale et al., 79–90. Springer, 2016.

Duncombe, Jean, and Dennis Marsden. "Love and Intimacy: the Gender Division of Emotion and 'Emotion Work.'" *Sociology* 27, no. 2 (1993): 221–41.

Elias, Norbert. *The Society of Individuals*. Oxford: Blackwell, 1991.

———. *The Civilizing Process: Sociogenetic and Psychogenetic Investigations*, revised edition. Oxford: Blackwell, 2000.

Featherstone, Mike. "Love and Eroticism. An Introduction." *Theory, Culture & Society* 15, nos. 3–4 (1998): 1–18.

Feyerabend, Paul. *Against Method.* London: Verso, 1993.

Fisher, Helen. "The Nature of Romantic Love." *The Journal of NIH Research* 6 (1994): 59–64.

Flandrin, Jean-Louis. *Sex in the Western World*: *The Development of Attitudes and Behaviour*, translated by Sue Collins. Chur: Harwood Academic Publishers, 1991.

Foucault, Michel. *History of Sexuality, Vol. 1: The Will to Knowledge.* London: Penguin, 1998.

———. *The History of Sexuality, Vol. 2: The Use of Pleasure.* London: Penguin, 1992.

———. *The History of Sexuality, Vol. 3: The Care of Self.* London: Penguin, 1990.

Frampton, Edith. "Fluid Objects: Kleinian Psychoanalytic Theory and Breastfeeding Narratives." *Australian Feminist Studies* 19 (2004): 357–68.

Frankfurt, Harry G. *The Reason of Love.* Princeton: Princeton University Press, 2004.

Freud, Sigmund. "The Infantile Sexuality." In *Three Essays on the Theory of Sexuality.* Translated by James Strachey. New York: Basic Books, 2000.

Geertz, Clifford. "Common Sense as a Cultural System." In *Local Knowledge: Further Essays in Interpretive Anthropology*, 73–93. New York: Basic Books, 1983.

Giddens, Anthony. *The Transformation of Intimacy: Sexuality, Love and Eroticism in Modern Societies.* Cambridge: Polity Press, 1992.

Goldie, Peter. *The Emotions*: *A Philosophical Exploration.* Oxford: Clarendon Press, 2000.

Gottlieb, Lori. *Marry Him*: *The Case for Settling for Mr. Good Enough.* London: Dutton, 2010.

Gray, John. *Men Are from Mars, Women Are from Venus*: *The Classic Guide to Understanding the Opposite Sex.* New York: Quill, 2004.

Hazan, Cindy, and Phillip Shaver. "Romantic Love Conceptualized as an Attachment Process." *Journal of Personality and Social Psychology* 52 (1987): 511–24.

Helm, Bennett. "Love." *Stanford Encyclopedia of Philosophy.* 2009. http://plato.stanford.edu/entries/love/ (accessed July 1, 2013).

Hillenkamp, Sven. *Das Ende der Liebe. Gefühle im Zeitalter Unendlicher Freiheit.* Stuttgart: Klett-Cotta, 2009.

Hochschild, Arlie R. *The Commercialization of Intimate Life*: *Notes from Home And Work.* Berkeley: University of California Press, 2003.

———. *The Managed Heart*: *Commercialization of Human Feeling.* Berkeley: University of California Press, 1983.

hooks, bell. *All about Love*: *New Visions.* London: The Women's Press, 2000.

Jackson, Stevi. "Families, Domesticity and Intimacy." In *Introducing Gender and Women's Studies*, 3rd edition, edited by Diane Richardson and Victoria Robinson, 125–43. New York: Macmillan, 2008.

Jamieson, Lynn. "Intimacy Transformed? A Critical Look at the 'Pure Relationship.'" *Sociology* 33, no. 3 (1999): 477–94.

Kaufman, Jean-Claude. *The Curious History of Love.* Cambridge: Polity Press 2011.

Klein, Melanie. *Envy and Gratitude and Other Works, 1946–1963*. London: Hogarth Press, 1984.

———. *The Psychoanalysis of Children*. New York: Grove Press, 1960.

Luhmann, Niklas. *Love as Passion*. Cambridge: Harvard University Press, 1986.

Mahlmann, Regina. *Psychologisierung des "Alltagsbewußtseins." Die Verwissenschaftlicung des Diskurses über Ehe*. Opladen: Westdeutscher Verlag, 1991.

———. *Was Verstehst du unter Liebe? Ideale und Konflikte von der Frühromantik bis Heute*. Darmstadt: Primus Verlag, 2003.

Mikulincer, Mario. "Attachment, Caregiving, and Sex within Romantic Relationships. A Behavioral Systems Perspective." In *Dynamics of Romantic Love: Attachment, Caregiving, and Sex*, edited by Mario Mikulincer and Gail S. Goodman, 23–44. New York: The Guilford Press, 2006.

Monceri, Flavia. "L'Amore di chi? Decostruzioni e ricostruzioni di un'istituzione sociale." In *Eros e Discorso Amoroso*, edited by Antonella Balestra and Chiara Piazzesi, 185–204. Pisa: Edizioni ETS, 2015.

———. "Queer Loves: Restating Bodies, Genders, and Sexualities." *Teoria*, 29, no. 2 (2009): 177–95.

Nietzsche, Friedrich. *On the Genealogy of Morality*, edited by Keith Ansell-Pearson. Cambridge: Cambridge University Press, 2007.

Obama, Barack. "Statement by the President on the Supreme Court Ruling on the Defense of Marriage Act." http://www.whitehouse.gov/doma-statement (accessed on July 1st, 2013).

Paul, Sheryl. "The Truth about Love." *Huff Post Weddings, the Blog*. Posted on Aug. 6, 2012. http://www.huffingtonpost.com/sheryl-paul/love-is-loss-and-other-li_b_1614066.html (accessed July 1, 2013).

Pelluchon, Corinne. "L'Unicité et le Sens de l'Amour." In *Amour Toujours?*, edited by Jean Birnbaum, 45–64. Paris: Gallimard-Folio, 2013.

Pulcini, Elena. *Amour-Passion et Amour Conjugal. Rousseau à l'Origine d'un Conflit Moderne*. Paris: Editions Honore Champion, 1998.

Retzer, Arnold. *Lob der Vernunftehe: Eine Streitschrift für Mehr Realismus in der Liebe*. Frankfurt am Main: Fischer, 2009.

Ricoeur, Paul. *Amour et Justice*. Paris: Points Essais 2008.

Rousseau, Jean-Jacques. *La nouvelle Héloïse. In Œuvres complètes*, vol. 2. Paris: Bibliothèque de la Pléiade, 1964.

Shaver, Phillip, and Cindy Hazan. "A Biased Overview of the Study of Love." *Journal of Social and Personal Relationships* 5 (1998): 473–501.

Simon, William, and John H. Gagnon. *Sexual Conduct*. 2nd edition. New Brunswick: Aldine Transaction, 2005.

———. "Sexual Scripts: Origins, Influences and Changes." *Qualitative Sociology* 26, no. 4 (2003): 491–97.

Soble, Alan. *The Philosophy of Sex and Love*. St. Paul: Paragon House, 2008.

Tanner, Klaus. *'Liebe' im Wandel der Zeiten. Kulturwissenschaftliche Perspektiven*. Leipzig: Evangelische Verlagsanstalt, 2005.

Taylor, Charles. *Sources of the Self: The Making of Modern Identity*. Cambridge: Harvard University Press, 1992.

Watzlawick, Paul, John H. Weakland, and Richard Fisch. *Change: Principles of Problem Formation and Problem Resolution*. New York: Norton, 1974.

Wittgenstein, Ludwig. *On Certainty*. Oxford: Basil Blackwell, 1969.

———. *Philosophical Investigations*, Oxford: Blackwell, 1953.

Weber, Max. 'Kritische Studien auf dem Gebiet der Kulturwissenschaftlichen Logik.' *Archiv für Sozialwissenschaft und Sozialpolitik* 22 (1906): 143–207.

Wollstonecraft, Mary. *A Vindication of the Rights of Woman*. Cambridge: Cambridge University Press, 1995.

Wouters, Cas. "Balancing Sex and Love since the 1960s Sexual Revolution." *Theory, Culture and Society* 15, nos. 3–4 (1998): 187–214.

———. *Sex and Manners: Female Emancipation in the West*, 1890–2000. London: Sage, 2002.

*Chapter Four*

# Love at the Limit of Phenomenology (à la Sartre and Marion)

Yong Dou (Michael) Kim

Freely drawing from Sartre and Marion, I argue that the demand of transcendental philosophy for thought to think its own conditions also functions as a reflection on the conditions of possibility for the appearance of love. Part I discusses the difficulty of thinking love not as a thing but as an event. Instead of asking, "what is love?," I ask, "what makes love possible?" I then turn, in part II, to Sartre's analysis of the non-appearance of the self to itself in phenomenological reflection. The "I" allows one to think but, as transcendental, is not accessible to simple reflection. Then, in part III, I look to Marion's notion of "crossing" to describe a way of speaking of self and Other that does not depend on an essential idea of the "self." I then conclude, in part IV, with some indications of how the formal structure of love—not as the union of self and Other but the "crossing" of Two—constitutes a new, unique, and singular subject such that the appearance of love itself becomes a condition of possibility for encountering a world.

## I. THE TRANSCENDENTAL QUESTION: HOW DOES LOVE APPEAR?

At the start of his discussion of Stendhal's famous study *De l'amour*, Ortega y Gasset observes that "the theoretician arrives at a philosophic conclusion due to an exasperated desire to concur with reality. With this end in mind, he takes infinite precautions, one of which is to maintain the multitude of his ideas in strict unity and cohesion. He is aware that what is real is remarkably singular. ... In contrast to the real, our minds and our sensibilities are disjointed, contradictory and multiform."[1]

To theorize about love courts the temptation (just as our desperate pursuits of it often do) of confusing the idealizations, myths, and solipsistic counterfeits of love for its reality. To speak of love, however, has been a favorite conceit of philosophy since Socrates who, in one of the important exceptions to his usual claims of ignorance, professed that "the only thing I say I understand is the art of love."[2] The importance of love as an ethical concept has found new life in contemporary philosophy, but perhaps it is possible to rescue the Platonic spirit that inscribed love into the very meaning and task of philosophy as love of wisdom. Among the lessons of the elenctic dialogues is that we mistake the nature of wisdom if we expect an answer to the famous "what is X?" question to look like a proposition that would halt or "complete" its pursuit. Similarly, perhaps the relevant philosophical question is not merely "what is love?" but "how is love possible?" In this spirit, following clues in the series[3] formed by Sartre[4] and Marion,[5] we will find that love reveals itself not only as the consort of the good (i.e., as an ethical concept) but as a nodal point between thought and world. On the one hand, reflection on the conditions necessary for love's appearance offers thought a site to thematize its conditions; at the same time, the appearance of love is itself the condition for the construction of a world. In short, at the limit of phenomenology—at the limit of thought's attempt to interrogate itself—in love we find the possibility of encountering not the world that was left behind under the *epoché* of phenomenological method but, rather, a new world that appears precisely in the interruption and division of the knowing subject.

This dehiscence is not merely the trauma incurred at the dissolution or even destruction of love—when we find ourselves shattered against the shores of a world emptied of vibrancy—but the spontaneous irruption of a new existence. Much like a work of art, the appearance of love is in each instance singular. But, unlike the work of art, love remains outside historical time and its absolute singularity renders it unrepresentable and non-substitutable. In other words, love cannot be captured conceptually by reference to its historical moments, even as the experience of love has in various ways been distorted by culture and ideology. Among the virtues of an account of love's transcendental, rather than merely historically specific, conditions is to avoid falling victim to the misogynist[6] and heteronormative idealizations of beauty and romantic (viz., sexual) love extant in the historical record.[7] On the one hand, there is a real(ity) of love that is not merely the product of history, social institutions, or even libidinal drives; on the other, however, it is not possible to deduce an ideal of love *a priori* without reference to actual amorous encounters.

What is at stake in the following account of love is a particular relationship between the transcendental and the empirical. If love were merely reducible to (pre-reflective) experiences, then a philosophical account of love would be limited to an account of its empirical (social, cultural, historical) conditions and limitations or to a genealogy of the deformations to which love has been subjected. To insist that there is a real(ity) of love, however, necessitates a conception of love that is not reducible to its experience in the desires produced by culture or capital but also is more than what can be discovered by armchair reflection; this "more" is what is called below a "world." The capacity to reflect on our experiences of love itself requires an act of love, which then is the condition that makes possible the love that has been experienced. This apparent circularity is both constitutive of love itself but is also indicative of its fecundity for philosophical reflection.

If, as Plato and Aristotle suggested, philosophy begins in wonder, then a philosophical reflection on love might begin with the astonishment that love exists at all. Love is, after all, perhaps the most contingent and elusive of all phenomena. No act of thought can deduce it *a priori* and of it no one can legitimately claim entitlement or desert. Just as love appears to the lover as a gift, appearing without necessity or merit, so too love offers to philosophy more than the opportunity for mere eulogy and lament. Instead, reflection at the limits of thought on the structure of love reveals what it means, in love, to encounter a world. Therefore, rather than bowing to the ineffable mystery of love as that which cannot be grasped by thought, perhaps we might ask instead what the possibilities are for thinking that holds itself open to love. What conditions must obtain for love to appear? That place, so we shall discover, is not that of a "center" (viz., of an ego or an "I") but of a de-centered subject. The moment and locus (the "event") of decentering, however, is nothing other than the appearance of love. *Prima facie*, it seems that we are caught in a vicious circle insofar as the appearance of love (the de-centering of the subject) is that place from which love appears. The logic of this appearance is that of a repetition, which is the only possible form love might take if we do not want to think of love as an object, a possession, or as presence. It is precisely these attempts to posit the being of love that betray it,[8] which is manifested even in banal cases, for example, when I take my lover for granted: I have already declared my love (e.g., in a marriage vow) and so my love "is there," obvious, ready-at-hand, present if only the beloved would see it. Or, as Sartre has shown in his analyses of bad faith in *Being and Nothingness*, I say that my love "is present" in my body that I offer to the Other, in the Other's body that I take for myself, or in the oath ("I love you"). An authentic love, on the other hand, Sartre suggests, is one that is not entangled in the presence of love or, in other words, in the "desire to be."

Yet as various existential analyses of anxiety have demonstrated, nothing is more difficult than what Sartre calls "conversion" of the subject away from itself and its bad faith. Just as in *Being and Nothingness* Sartre described the necessity of a kind of "existential psychoanalysis" to sublimate our tendencies of being in bad faith so that we can live our freedom without ultimately denying it, the motive of conversion is "the impossibility of recovering oneself ... to give a foundation to one's being by creating something *outside oneself*."[9] We will remain viciously ensnared in inauthentic and impossible attempts to grasp the being of the self so long as we insist on the one who loves and, consequently, consumed by the economy of lover and beloved or of libido and object love.

Instead, in love, what is in question is the limit between oneself and another. Naively speaking, we think of a limit as an extrinsic determination: to be limited is to be limited by something else. Yet a thing is defined precisely by its limit insofar as any thing without limit is paradoxically "everywhere and nowhere." In one sense, a limit is the principle of identity, that is, as that which determines some thing as that particular thing and not something else. Although the limit is not only a spatial principle, we might describe it as the boundary between the inside and the outside. But the boundary itself is neither inside nor outside; its structure is the double movement of in/exclusion. To love means to tarry at the limit[10] between subject and object or, more accurately, between self and Other (since to treat another as an object is prohibited by any loving relationship). Love appears only at this limit, since that which manifests as the property of a subject (defined through its willing choices) does not seem to be love at all (e.g., nothing is more absurd than the attempt to will myself to love and it is not clear that an unrequited love is anything more than infatuation).

What does it mean for thinking to tarry at the limit between oneself and another without either reducing the Other into an object apprehended by the possessive gaze or seeing in the Other only the mirror of my own intentions? "Intentions" here should be understood in a double sense: both in the usual sense of my desires, perspectives, and ends but also in the phenomenological sense of the direction of my conscious acts. It is in the structure of intentionality that Sartre would find the resources to find a "hole in being" or what in *Being in Nothingness* is called *néant*, i.e., the non-coincidence of the subject not only with its (intentional) objects but even with itself. It is to this sense of the *cogito* that we must now turn, for it is here that thinking will encounter its limit in the act of thinking itself, encountering that which, strictly speaking, cannot be thought.[11]

## II. DECENTERING REFLECTION: FROM BEING TO EVENT

> Love is the perception of individuals. Love is the extremely difficult realisation that something other than oneself is real. Love ... is the discovery of reality.[13]

Sartre's analyses of bad faith in *Being and Nothingness, Nausea,* and several of his other literary works indicate ways in which the ambiguity of the limit of non/being gets forgotten or obscured (willfully or not) by projects of being, particularly insofar as being is conceived as presence to self. What, Sartre asks, is this "self?" In an early essay soon after his discovery of Husserl, Sartre argues that

> if, impossible though it be, you could enter "into" a consciousness you would be seized by a whirlwind and thrown back outside ... for consciousness has no "inside." It is just this being beyond itself, this absolute flight, *this refusal to be a substance*, which makes it a consciousness. ... To be is to fly out into the world, to spring from the nothingness of the world and of consciousness suddenly to burst out as consciousness-in-the-world. When consciousness tries to recoup itself, to coincide with itself once and for all, closeted off all warm and cosy, it destroys itself.[13]

Sartre finds in the structure of intentionality the possibility of a *cogitans* without a *res*: when consciousness attempts to intend itself and take itself for an object, consciousness never finds itself but always something else (even if it is another act of consciousness, which then becomes objectified into a "state").

This insight is developed further in the *Transcendence of the Ego* where Sartre distinguishes between positional and non-positional consciousness in the reflective act. In pre-reflective consciousness, consciousness is positionally aware of its intended object and only nonpositionally aware of itself: "When I run after a streetcar, when I look at the time, when I am absorbed in contemplating a portrait, there is no I. There is consciousness *of the streetcar-having-to-be-overtaken*, etc., and non-positional consciousness of consciousness."[14] The "I" appears only on the act of reflection when the reflecting consciousness (positionally) directs itself toward the pre-reflective consciousness (and its intended object). At this point, the "I" appears neither on the level of the pre-reflective consciousness (as the intended object of reflection) nor as the subjectivity of the reflecting consciousness itself (which remains non-positional): "this transcendent object of the reflective act is the *I*."[15] The I appears *through* the act of reflection but not as its intended object:

> What radically prevents the acquisition of real cognitions of the ego is the very special way in which it is given to reflective consciousness. The ego never appears, in fact, except when one is not looking at it. The reflective gaze must be fixed on the *Erlebnis,* insofar as it emanates from the state. Then, behind the state, at the horizon, the ego appears. It is, therefore, never seen except "out of the corner of the eye." As soon as I turn my gaze toward it and try to reach it without passing through the *Erlebnis* and the state, it vanishes.[16]

The "I," Sartre finds, is never coincident with itself—the "I" can never be identical to its representation or, in other words, the "I" can never be the "me." As soon as an intentional consciousness intends itself, by that very act it turns itself into an object and my subjectivity (the consciousness that I am, that I live, intend, experience, etc.) slips away. This "I" that I am, Sartre says, is "transcendent to all the states which it unifies [which I can intend by reflection], but not as an abstract X whose mission is only to unify: rather, it is the infinite totality of states and of actions which is never reducible to *an* action or to *a* state"[17] or, more importantly, to a thing. Reflection reveals the radical ontological distinction between subjectivity and objectivity: "the transcendent *I* must fall before the stroke of the phenomenological reduction."[18]

What is revealed, for Sartre, is the transcendental sphere of consciousness as "*absolute* existence, that is to say, a sphere of pure spontaneities which are never objects and which determine their own existence."[19] "Spontaneity" here means self-determination, like the Leibnizian monad whose determinations are purely intrinsic as a result of its positive essence [*haecceitas*]. The "I" of consciousness, Sartre says, is not simply an "inside" but is always caught in the oscillation between in/outside. Spontaneity is nothing other than the operation of the limit: consciousness is "purified" by reflection insofar as it is always "clear as a strong wind. There is nothing in it but a movement of fleeing itself, a sliding beyond itself"[20] such that every movement "inside" toward subjectivity throws it back "outside" toward an object.

In reflection the "I" is consistently surpassed, transcended, yet it is only at this moment of transcendence that the "I" can appear (without ever being "present"). When I am reading, for example, the "I" does not appear—it is "tacit" or non-positional; when I say "I am reading," the "I" appears but only fleetingly so insofar as the object-I is no longer the "I" who is now reflecting and being aware of reading. Yet it is at this level of first-order reflecting, when the "I" first appears, that the ethical question emerges: who or what is this "I" that I both am and am not?

This question for Sartre is more than that of a *cogitans* without a *res*: it is that of an existence without being—an absolute, impersonal spontaneity: "Each instant of our conscious life reveals to us a creation *ex nihilo*. Not a new *arrangement,* but a new *existence*."[21] This is an existence more spontaneous than even Leibniz's monad, insofar as consciousness appears "as infinitely overflowing in its possibilities the *I* which ordinarily serves as its unity."[22] My possibilities are not contained "within" me (e.g., in my "complete concept," as Leibniz would say), if "I" am nothing other than this absolute existence of transcendence. Just as Leibniz had reduced freedom to the necessity of monadic spontaneity, however, so too this transcendence is "beyond" freedom and necessity. The "I" is not simply its future (that which it "is not"). The "I" is located between past and future, i.e., between what I am/not. As Sartre would say in *Being and Nothingness*, to identify with what I am not (thus denying my actualities) is just as much a moment of bad faith as the attempt to identify simply with what I am (thus denying my possibilities). When the "I" appears in transcendence, it is not only in the negation (in what I "am not") but also at the moment or the limit between and the ambiguity of what I am and what I am not.

This is the ethical moment in a dual sense. On the one hand, the moment of transcendence puts the "I" into question. How can I give an account of myself if "I" cannot simply be identified with what I "am"—with the history of my actions, my memories and representations of myself, desires, intentions, and so on? I must be both faithful to the "I" that I am (the "I" that I have been) while also and at the same time embracing the "I" that I am not yet (the possible "I" or the "I" that I am insofar as I am my freedom).

In addition to this first problem, Sartre also notes that

> this conception of the ego seems to us the only possible refutation of solipsism ... As long as the *I* remains a structure of consciousness, it will always remain possible to oppose consciousness, with its *I*, to all other existents. ... But if the *I* becomes a transcendent, it participates in all the vicissitudes of the world. ... It falls like all other existences at the stroke of the *epoché* ...[23]

Without a sufficient account of the "I" it would, at least initially, seem that we can neither give an account of the relation between myself and an Other, particularly insofar as an ethical relation to the Other involves the proper "spacing" of myself and an Other.

This problem would not be further addressed until *Being and Nothingness* where, amidst Sartre's analyses of bad faith—which are generally founded in the "desire to be" and the attempt to identify either with what I am or, negatively, in the denial of my being by the identification with what I am not—we find not only bad faith relations to ourselves (in the way we experience our past, present, and future, our bodies, etc.) but also bad faith relations to Others. In bad faith I am looked at by the Other:

> If the Other-as-object is defined in connection with the world as the object which sees what I see, then my fundamental connection with the Other-as-subject must be able to be referred back to my permanent possibility of *being seen* by the Other. ... With the Other's look the "situation" escapes me. ... I *am no longer master of the situation.*[24]

In short, I face the Other as a threat to my freedom. In being looked at by the Other, my freedom becomes an object—it becomes a "characteristic of my being" such that "the in-itself recaptures me ... and fixes me wholly in my very flight ... But this fixed flight is never the flight which I am for myself; it is fixed *outside*. ... I must [therefore] turn back toward it and assume *attitudes* with respect to it."[25] These are the attitudes of masochism, indifference, and sadism that are presented in the succeeding pages according to which either I deny my subjectivity and become an object for the Other or I reduce the Other's subjectivity into an object for me. The analysis of (inauthentic) love here attempts, unsuccessfully, to overcome these one-sided objectifications. I love the Other insofar as the Other is the one who "makes me be"[26]—it is not the objectivity of the Other that I value, since I cannot be loved by an object; yet at the same time, the lover cannot simply be satisfied by the oath "I love you," for "who would be content with a love given as pure loyalty to a sworn oath? Who would be satisfied with the words, 'I love you because I have freely engaged myself to love you and because I do not wish to go back on my word.'?"[27] What the lover demands is the impossible juxtaposition of transcendence and facticity: "He wants a freedom but demands that this freedom as freedom should no longer be free."[28] Insofar as the lover wants "to exist *a priori* as the objective limit of this freedom [of the Other]," the lover wants to be the Other's "whole world," thus putting himself "on the side of the world."[30]

It is at this point where the two aspects of the ethical problem converge: i.e., when the for-itself is revealed to be a relation, as "the upsurge of the Other touches the for-itself in its very heart."[31] What, in short, is an authentic relation in which I neither deny my subjectivity, nor assert my subjectivity at the expense of other subjectivities, nor, finally, assert a subjectivity in bad faith to myself by refusing the ambiguity of what I am/not by identifying with either side of this duality instead of tarrying at the limit?

> The authentic [person] perpetually surpasses the temptation Bataille has described for us: *to be* everything. … The relation of the For-itself to everything is different if the Me falls away. Henceforth it is: to exist as someone for whom *there is* everything. Instead of there being a fall, there is a surpassing. And the relation to contingency is similarly inverted: in being taken up it becomes *gratuitousness*, that is, the perpetual outbreak of the free decision *that there is* a world.[32]

What is Bataille's temptation? Bataille proposes an "inverted Platonism" of immanence according to which there is no "I" because the "I" is everything in the equivalence of sense, death, and *eros*. Instead, Sartre proposes that in immanence we need not posit the being of relation but that

> the consciousness of gratuitousness (or of generosity as the original structure of authentic existence) is indissolvably linked to the consciousness of Being as a fixed explosion. … This is not just to manifest pure Being, it is to make pure Being appear within a world, to *put it into relation*. … The For-itself *is Relatedness*. There is a relation [only] because the For-itself is a relation to itself and relates to being through its ontological structure.[33]

This structure is explicitly defined by Sartre as love: "The structure 'libera-tion/gratuity' is the internal core, the 'nonthetic consciousness (of) the gift.'"[34]

Relation is only possible at the limit between self and Other according to which the Other is not reduced to the intentions of a self. One solution might be to name the heteronomy of the Other the point of ethics, viz., in the injunction "Thou shalt not kill" as a "negative" transcendence that maintains a strict separation between oneself and another. For Sartre, however, the relation or limit between self and Other is double and not a simple partition, for he locates negativity already on the side of the self: *the being by which Nothingness comes to the world must be its own Nothingness.*[35] The limit is the ambiguity or duality of the am/not and, as such, is not only negative but *generous* insofar as relation does not simply provide external determina-tions but is the structure according to which the activity of multiple (intrin-sic) determinations—of intentional consciousnesses of two for-itselfs—are compossible:

> All desire posits truth and freedom. It is illegitimate and impure only secondar-ily if it is poisoned by the will *to be* (In-itself for-itself) and by the presence in it of the Other. ... Get rid of the I and the Me. In their place put subjectivity as a lived monadic totality [i.e., a purely intrinsic determination] that refers back to the self of consciousness by itself ... and the *Ego* (I reserve this name for the always open-ended Me which is referred to by the undertaking. Always open-ended, always deferred). ... The ego *exists to lose itself*—it is the Gift. Reconciliation with Destiny is generosity. ... Only a freedom can be a destiny for a freedom.[36]

Instead of merely "leaping ahead" of the Other or otherwise relating to the Other by "spacing" myself in relation to her, for Sartre, I ought to receive or "make room for" the Other by the gift. Generosity cannot simply be a with-drawal from the Other (this would amount to indifference) nor can I "give" so much that I smother the Other. Both of these attitudes of giving result from the failure to accept the anxiety that love might not be, i.e., that I need not *be* to love. Generosity is only possible when I love, i.e., when I tarry at the limit: the limit of self/Other, of non/being, according to which I neither retreat into my circle of immanence nor obscure the for-itself that presents itself to me as another (heteronomous) freedom.

In *Being and Nothingness*, in the analyses of bad faith, the Other was revealed or presented to me as a threat to my freedom in which "I surpass his ends with my own ... I transform his freedom into a given quality, I can do violence to him."[37] In encountering the Other by the Other's look, I fail to encounter this particular Other but only encounter another freedom "in general" against which I must be on guard by retreating into my circle of immanence.[38] In authentic love, on the other hand, "I love if I *create* the contingent finitude of the Other as being-within-the-world in assuming my own subjective finitude and in *willing* this subjective finitude."[39] It is the lover who has undergone "conversion" by purifying reflection whose being is called into question and who can "love without being." This is the one for whom the love may not be.[40] This anxiety of a love that might not be—that might not be returned, that might end, and so on—must itself also be willed.[41]

### III. CROSSING, OR: NOT ONE BUT TWO

[I]n absolute reality all the life of every self is, or is dependent on, love. ... All perceptions of other selves are states of love.[42]

For Sartre, however, love remains in the end a problem of will[43] and, there-fore, primarily a problem of ethics instead of, as suggested above, providing the basis for a transcendental philosophy or phenomenology, which thinks its own conditions of possibility according to the structure of an event rather than a persistent subject. While certain passages of the *Notebooks* suggest that Sartre ultimately moves toward thinking at the limit of subjectivity, the danger that lurks behind an ethics of authenticity is that such an opera-tion attempts to occupy the place from which appearance appears instead of holding this place open. Sartre had gestured toward the decentering of subjectivity in his analysis of phenomenological reflection, but what remains to be thought more explicitly is the constitution of the "subject" of love by the appearance of love itself, which can be described not only as a "relation" between lover and beloved but in the emergence of a figure of the Two.

Occasionally, Sartre would gesture toward the metaphysical implications of his ethics: ' "There is' being because the for-itself is such that there is being. The character of a *phenomenon* comes to being through the for-itself."[44] Here the concept of "phenomenon" follows from the famous section of *Being and Time* where Heidegger proposes the necessary relation between phenomenol-ogy and ontology and where he poses the problem of the "appearance of appearance":

The being of beings can least of all be something "behind which" something else stands, something that "does not appear." Essentially, nothing else stands "behind" the phenomena of phenomenology. *Nevertheless, what is to become a phenomenon can be concealed.* And precisely [it is] because phenomena are initially and for the most part *not given* [that] phenomenology is needed.[45]

Heidegger himself in his later work would reconsider the "givenness" of phe-nomena and, as Marion observes, "phenomenology does not break decisively

with metaphysics until the moment when and exactly in the degree to which
... it names and thinks the phenomenon (a) neither as object ... (b) nor as
being ...”[46] But, Marion continues, "what remains is to take the most perilous
step: to think this *self/itself* [*se/soi*]—which alone permits the phenomenon
to show *itself*.”[47] This "most perilous step" occurs at the limit of phenomenology, that is, when the task is not the thinking of the phenomenon (that
shows or gives itself to appearance) but the thinking of the "itself" or, in
other words, not "the *thing* itself" (*die Sache selbst*) of Husserl but, simply,
the "itself" given.

"To have done with the 'subject,'" Marion says, "it is ... necessary not to
destroy it, but to reverse it—to overturn it. ... At the center stands no 'subject,' but a gifted, he whose function consists in receiving what is immeas-
urably given to him, and whose privilege is confined to the fact that he is
himself received from what he receives.”[48] "I" receive the gift, but it is only
by so receiving that this "I" has sense. Just as I am the gifted who receives,
so too "I" am generous insofar as I tarry at the limit where "I" am called into
question by the excess and exteriority of the given. Just as Sartre had defined
the structure of the relatedness of the for-itself as love (*supra*), at the end of
*Being Given*, Marion invokes Heidegger's assertion that love is the fundamental "motive" for phenomenology[49] to suggest that only this notion of the
gifted can do justice to the appearance of love.

In *Prolegomena to Charity* and *The Erotic Phenomenon*, Marion introduces the pivotal notion of "crossing" as the operation of love. In §21 of *The
Erotic Phenomenon*, Marion begins with the ethical injunction "Thou shalt
not kill." This (negative) injunction, Marion claims, does not exhaust the
signification of the face:

> In hearing "Thou shalt not kill," I can and must, by virtue of being a lover, hear
> "Do not touch me"—do not advance here, where I arise, for you would tread
> ground that, in order for me to appear, must remain intact; the site where I am
> must remain untouchable, unassimilable, closed to you in order that my exterior-
> ity remain open to you ... The erotic phenomenon ... will only appear to you if
> you fix upon this intact signification the excess of your intuition to love loving.
> You will only receive this phenomenon by not taking hold of it, by not killing
> it, and thus first of all by not touching it.[50]

When we love, at the limit of self and Other, however, we are not simply
maintaining the duality of the un/touched. The lover offers the most subtle
touch: the touch of the caress, or the touch that barely touches, for a touch
that does not touch at all is absolutely separated (and thus remains an ethical
problem of "thou shalt not"). There is, rather, what Derrida calls a "law" of
tact [*la loi du tact*] or a "logic" of liminal touch, according to which touching

remains limitrophe; it touches what it does not touch; it does not touch; it
*abstains* from touching on what it touches … it in effect installs a kinship that
is at the same time *conjunctive* and *disjunctive*. … But what it thus brings into
contact … *partes extra partes,* is first of all contact *and* noncontact. And this
contact without contact, this *barely touching touch* [the "most subtle" touch] is
unlike any other, in the very place where all it touches is the other.[51]

The Other *qua* other remains an absolute exteriority, i.e., as the one I must
not touch and whom I must not transgress. As Sartre has shown, the Other
interrupts the dialectic of the in-itself and the for-itself: I cannot regard the
other as in-itself nor as for-itself (since in either case I must either regard the
Other as a threat to my freedom or abrogate my freedom to the Other). The
transformation of the Other into the beloved is the event of love in the caress
or the kiss.

This "most subtle touch" is possible through the operation of "crossing."
"Crossing" occurs as the result of a paradox: "[a signification] gives itself
while saying that it gives itself, *as if* it were giving itself and *as capable of
not giving itself,*"[52] which occurs through an oath or promise—not simply
"here I am!" but "here I am … and here I shall remain."[53] The oath has sense
only in the time of this unique event, i.e., in the repetition and fidelity to the
event necessitated by its excess and unrepresentability to presence (because
it *has not* happened).[54] As Sartre had already reminded us, the oath can never
be present lest the lover fall into bad faith.[55] In the oath I give myself, without
waiting for reciprocity or exchange, as an act of faith. The sense of the oath,
then, is a "crossing" insofar as it constitutes a "common" signification without reducing it to the same signification: "The two *egos* do not join together
in a common, directly visible intuition, but rather in a common signification
that is indirectly put into phenomenality by two irreducible intuitions."[56] The
oath, then, is not strictly speaking a simple statement of communication ("I
love you") but, rather, that which takes place only through a constant process
of attestation through material experience (e.g., in sexuality, cohabitation,
reproduction, speech, and so on; or, in short, what we might call a life).[57]

Immediately following the introduction of the crossed phenomenon,
Marion turns to the flesh as the site or scene of crossing. The flesh is more
than the body of extension or objective constitution that resists me; it is more
than a facticity to be surpassed (Sartre). At most, as both Sartre and Marion
have indicated, I can seduce the body but I cannot love the Other as body.[58]
The flesh is the "*there* where the elsewhere reaches me,"[59] insofar as it is my
facticity as it is lived and transcended by the in- and ex-tensions of an "I"
that touches and is touched by the world (by being-in-the-world). The flesh
is not only my being-*in*-the-world but it is my vulnerability *to* the world, that
is, my materiality.

And so, "if there is ever an other flesh, and thus an other's flesh, it must by definition behave the opposite of physical bodies [i.e., as things I can grasp, that are 'ready at hand' as equipment, etc.], which is to say, like my own flesh behaves as opposed to them ..."[60] The flesh is that which does *not* resist me the way that objects do but instead admits me. I am received by the flesh. I constitute myself in a world of objects but "I can only free myself and become myself by touching another flesh ... because only another flesh can make room for me, welcome me ... that is, comply with my flesh [*faire droit à ma chair*] and reveal it to me by providing it a place."[61] The English translation "comply" is eminently appropriate, as the most subtle touch is a com-plication—a folding-together or embrace—of flesh that is a touching-without-touching insofar as "even if only one flesh touches a body ... still one flesh never touches another flesh, because the one immediately draws back and fades away before the other, not even resisting enough to allow for an impact ..."[62] It is this responsiveness of flesh to flesh that leads Marion to say that the caress must be thought outside of or otherwise than contact and spatiality.[63] Instead, we must think of the com-plication of flesh as "the most subtle touch," i.e., the limit at which flesh yields to the advance,[64] offering itself in the form of this infinite responsiveness that permits us to tarry at this limit without economy or violence. Strictly speaking, here the Other does not "confront" me—I do not face the Other, even as another free-dom—nor am I merely "with" the Other (as in sociality where I am "with" others [*Mitdasein*]). In love I am helically entwined (the com-plication of flesh refers primarily, then, not to the physicality of the sexual act but to the encounter of and in the world that makes sexuality possible).

This responsiveness of flesh "provides a place" where the Other appears to the gifted as offered (given) in what Marion calls not "intersubjectivity" but "intergivenness" (*interdonation*).[65] The structure of the "inter-" is the duality of the limit that permits the compossiblity of the Two—i.e., that there are two (and not just One)—or the "crossing" of the two in an intimate relation as the singular site or scene of love's appearance. On the one hand, the numericity[66] of the Two is of a different order than a simple multiplicity if for no other reason than that indefinite substitutability (e.g., of bodies or of gazes) is the surest indication of love's absence. But just as the Other is non-substitutable, so too the "I" who is gifted in love is also non-substitutable insofar as I must recognize myself not just as the unique addressee of the Other's summons but that "I" am now a response to the Other, who could, as Sartre observed, potentially be lost in that response.

The various counterfeits of love, on the other hand, collapse the persistent duality of love into the economy of desire, bad faith, or perhaps even vio-lence. An authentic love cannot be the fulfillment or satisfaction of an inten-tion (in either the usual or the phenomenological sense of direction toward an object). Just as Sartre has demonstrated that my subjectivity can never be present in its (own) subjectivity, so too the Other cannot be present to me in its alterity. It is significant that immediately after his analysis of the non-positionality of subjectivity, Sartre notes that the error of the moralists who reduce all love to self-love is to have confused the priority of the pre/reflective consciousnesses. To use Sartre's example: "I pity Peter, and I go to his assistance. For my consciousness only one thing exists at that moment: Peter-having-to-be-helped. This quality of 'having-to-be-helped' lies in Peter"[67] rather than in an I wanting-to-help. The "I," whom the moralists find lurking behind my charity, has not yet appeared in the pre-reflective consciousness. To say that all love is self-love or that all desires have as their end the satisfaction of my self can only be a corruption of the reflective consciousness.

But love is not quite like the activity of pre-reflective consciousness: "being lovable" is not exactly a quality "in" a person the way "having-to-be-helped" was found in Peter. The capacity for "being loved" is, strictly speaking, not in the Other, just as the capacity for loving is not exactly in "me," not only because my love does not exist without the Other, but the "I" who loves is not the same "I" prior to the activity of loving. The "I" who insists on the equivalence between the "I" who loves and any previous "I" has *eo ipso* failed really to love (as we say in common language, I must be "transformed" by love).

Reflection exposes the "I" as nothing other than—instead of preceding—the capacity for relation.[68] I find myself only in my encounter with the Other. But in authentic relations,

> one must give up seeing the other as a subject, and for a radical reason. The other *must* remain invisible so as to offer himself to a possible love, because if, by chance, I saw him (if an intuition adequately fulfilled the intentional objective …), he would be ipso facto already disqualified as other. As soon as Orpheus wants *to see* Eurydice, he transforms her into an object and thereby disqualifies her as beloved. He makes her disappear because he does not admit her as invisible. … The other, as other, irreducible to my intention, but origin of another intention, can never be seen, by definition.[69]

This encounter with an intention that imposes itself on me—as opposed to my capacity to define myself through what I am—renders my own intention "destitute" and the Other's "gaze brings out the features of the *I* to the point where no traces remain of it other than a simply and naked *me*. … The *me* designates the *I* uncovered, stripped bare, decentered."[70] I am exposed to the Other, but I do not thereby claim the Other's nudity (as an object) in my own gaze. I do not see the Other but encounter the alterity of the Other as one who is also exposed. Only this exposure to the Other allows for the possibility of love even as, on the other hand, "I" cannot insist on being seen by the Other as an object of her intention. I cannot "expose myself" to the Other but, in love, I am exposed to the exposure of the Other (else I merely "take" the Other's nudity for myself and my enjoyment).

## IV. THE APPEARANCE OF A WORLD

> If transcendence exists between us, if we are visible and invisible to each other, the gap is enough to sustain our attraction. Why should an object between us be necessary? To be irreducible to one another can assure the two and the between, the us and the between-us.[71]

At the limit of phenomenology, the integrity of the subject was twice interrupted: not only by the Other who captivates me but also in the internal necessity of the "I" to lose itself and to be swept outside itself. It is only the chance encounter of love that creates the possibility for the derelict "I" to avoid succumbing to the temptations of languishing in its own existence and its own "desire to be." Because there is no guarantee that love shall ever exist, we are often seduced by counterfeits of love that merely reaffirm the solitude and solipsism of the ego in the face of the Other.

On the other hand, love names the possibility of tarrying at the limit between self and Other without collapsing either one into the production of the other as a fusion or a synthesis. Love appears not as a dialectic of—but in the possibility of tarrying at the limit between—self/Other, am/not, non/being, i.e., not as a "holding together" into a whole or a One but, rather, in the duality of continuous approach and withdrawal, that is, the persistent maintenance or crossing of two. As we have seen, however, crossing is possible only when the subject is de-centered (or "converted" in Sartre's terms so that it can inhabit the ambiguity of its is/not) by the experience of (authentic) love in which my flesh is both capable of and amenable to the most "subtle" touch.

Strictly speaking, the liminal touch is not a contact between one and another but the appearance of an originary Two that is reducible neither to the fusion of individuals nor to the duality of the one/multiple.[72] The lover is not the "I" who encounters another (nor vice versa) but, rather, the (crossed) Two of love is a new, unique, and absolutely singular subject ontologically and structurally distinct from what had preceded the chance encounter. The possibilities of this amorous subject are not those that were contained "in me" and are no longer "my" possibilities nor, strictly speaking, "our" possibilities. The commonality of ends in "our" possibilities defines not love but sociality and politics as attempts to define what we collectively (multiply) affirm. The amorous encounter, then, is not the fusion but the crossing of intentions. In love I do not merely seek what you seek and neither can I demand that you abide by my prerogatives; such love is conditional on the assumption of contract and exchange (e.g., when we make "equal sacrifices"). It is precisely in this refusal to identify my intentions with those of my lover (and *vice versa*)—this non-relation or non-coincidence of intentions—that constructs the relation of the Two (i.e., the appearance of love) as an opening onto a world; conjointly, in love, we discover new possibilities for encountering a world.

The Two is not merely the transformation of a subject because the possibilities of the Two were in no way contained in the self. I did not merely contain in myself the "possibility to get married," for example, for such an abstract possibility did not and could not prepare me for this particular marriage here and now. The Two arrives *ex nihilo*, outside the intentions of myself or the Other, and for which no thought could have prepared. At no point can love intend what it will be. In love, thought is stunned by what is wholly exterior to it and yet which nevertheless demands response. As Sartre's analysis of bad faith demonstrates, without the vigilance of reflection, love is easily betrayed. Reflection too, however, is often impure and thought seems only to attempt to grasp itself by objectification. At the limit of reflection, the knowing subject surrenders to the loving subject. Perhaps it is only in the "crossing" of gazes where I see the Other as a subject and as a freedom (instead of an intentional object of desire) that I might also approach "myself" as a subject: but this "self" and this "subject" are no longer "mine" (just as when I love my life ceases to be mine and who I am—what it means to be a subject—is radically called into question in the sudden appearance of the Two). The possibility and responsibility for thinking the Two can only be found in the Two itself. Just as philosophy defines itself by interrogating what it means to think, so also the Two is defined by the marvel that love is possible and that it exists only so long as it is thought to be so. In this way, love reverses the usual order of causality: love is possible only when it exists.

In the primary sense, then, the amorous subject is the Two itself. The "I" of the oath "I love you" does not precede the amorous encounter or, in other words, saying "I love you" is literally nonsensical outside the amorous event. Just as the "I" was revealed by phenomenological reflection to be nothing other than the capacity for relation, in the amorous encounter we have more than the meeting of two "I"s or the exchange of promises ("I love you because you love me"). The "I" of the "I love you" is not reducible to any other "I" (as we say in plain language, we "are changed" by the amorous event and "every love is different"). The difference between the two positions of the amorous encounter is therefore structural and not substantive or essentialist (for example, in heteronormative assumptions of what is "male" and "female"). At the limit between self and Other, and precisely there by virtue of the crossing of intentions, something new emerges, i.e., the possibility of creating something new in the world. Love, then, does not happen to a subject but provides the site from which a (new) subject appears, brought into existence as a spontaneity.

Love insists that a new existence be affirmed. Love not only appears as exuberance but also appears in a long labor easily lost, whose fragility and contingency are easily forgotten by the strength of its insistence. We insist because we address the world, for the sake of creating a world. Only love affirms the existence of the world *simpliciter*: the world is not presented as alien or indifferent (as the object of understanding) or as an injustice to be overcome. Rather, love asserts that the world is worthy of existence and that life[73] shall continue—which, previously, had merely tended toward death—not only in procreation (as one possible effect of the amorous encounter) but also in the (re)production of the forms that make life possible: the home, the sharing of speech, sexuality (as the intertwining of flesh), and so on. Love makes possible a sort of "transcendental organization"[74] of a world unique and absolutely singular. Just as the Two of the amorous encounter is specific to each event and not a mere addition of one and another (which would define a political or economic space), the world we construct exists for the sake of nothing other than love, which would not be possible without it. Love is, strictly speaking, not "in" the world because it is the creation of something new: a transformation of what had been given and presented as a world. The task of phenomenological description therefore ends when one becomes Two: just as the "I" dissolves under reflection in the amorous encounter with the Other, love begins at Two but subsequently opens onto the infinite, faced not under the threat of anguish but, rather, faced as the promise of happiness, births, vulnerabilities, compassion, and fecundity that had been foreclosed to the one who could neither love nor be loved. The Two "is" only the life and the lives it creates and only in love is there the sole possible life worthy of pure affirmation unadulterated by vanity.

## NOTES

1. José Ortega y Gasset. *On Love: Aspects of a Single Theme*, trans. Toby Talbot (New York: Meridian Books, 1957), 23–24.

2. Plato, *Symposium*, ed. John Cooper (Indianapolis: Hackett Publishing Company: 1977), 177e. Socrates' "knowledge" of love, however, is presented and voiced, not insignificantly, through the mediation of Diotima.

3. This term should be understood in its semiotic sense: each of the authors' insights discussed below should be understood and interpreted in relation to each other. Neither of these authors makes the claim at the end of the present sentence, which emerges only from the seriation of their respective ideas.

4. Although Sartre's conception of love has been criticized as sexist or otherwise inadequate by Suzanne Lilar, *A propos de Sartre et de l'Amour* (Paris: Éditions Bernard Grasset, 1967) and Toril Moi, "Freedom and Flirtation: Bad Faith in Sartre and Beauvoir," in *Situating Sartre in Twentieth Century Thought*, eds. Jean-François Fourny and Charles D. Minahen (New York: St. Martin's Press, 1997), for example, these criticisms are based on (incomplete) readings of *Being and Nothingness* without regard to some other texts (especially the *Notebooks for an Ethics*), which will be treated below.

5. Although it is not necessarily possible to separate Marion's theological work from his philosophical, the discussion below appropriates Marion's more explicitly phenomenological treatment of love and not the more celebrated theological treatment of *God without Being*.

6. On this point specifically, the *locus classicus* of the problem of domination masquerading under the guise of love is Beauvoir's *The Second Sex* in her analysis of the opposition of woman as the Other of man. See also the psychoanalytic generalization of this insight into the construction of masculinity and femininity in Benjamin (1988). Jessica Benjamin. The Bonds of Love: *Psychonanalysis, Feminism, and the Problem of Domination*. New York: Pantheon Books, 1988.

7. Many of these deformations of love have appealed to the illusion that there exists a univocal Form of love (cf. note 8 below).

8. For reasons of space I make an important assumption, without which the proceeding analysis will seem less convincing: i.e., that a love that strives to possess the Other, that reduces or predicates loving the Other to the erotic desire for the Other's body, or that seeks a beloved to satisfy some lack in the lover (money, self-esteem, children, etc.), distorts, masculinizes, alienates, fetishizes, or otherwise does violence to the integrity of the Other in the name of a fundamentally avaricious desire that is manifestly not love at all. But, conversely, as Sartre highlights in *Being and Nothingness*, so too my desire to eliminate "myself" for the sake of the Other is equally in bad faith and denies the freedom of the Other. Neither does mutual recognition seem to escape the reciprocal and ultimately legalistic demands that seem to betray the real(ity) of love. As we shall see below, love requires not the fusion of two into one—which must either do violence to one or both—but the persistent maintenance of a Two irreducible to one.

9. Jean-Paul Sartre. *Notebooks for an Ethics*, trans. David Pellauer (Chicago: University of Chicago Press), 470. Jean-Paul Sartre, *Cahiers pour une Moralé* (Paris: Presses Universitaires de France, 1983), 486. Hereafter, NE with the English pagination followed by the French.

10. A better analogy is the use of the term "limit" in mathematics, which provides a way of speaking about the behavior of a function at a certain point (which may or may not be defined within the function). If the behavior is indeterminate, then the limit does not exist at that point. A function is "closed" if two conditions are met: (1) it is defined at its boundary and (2) the limit exists at the boundary. If either of these conditions fail, the function is "unclosed." Unfortunately, just as the spatial analogy has its limitations, so too this analogy is imperfect, for instance, insofar as there exist certain continuous but non-differentiable functions and also insofar as the concept of a limit is only useful in speaking of the behavior of a function at a particular point. The strength of the mathematical analogy, however, is that the limit of a function need not be evaluated at a point that is defined in the function.

11. Note that this claim is not quite subject to the Hegelian criticism that the possibility for thought thinking its own limit requires the infinitude of thought itself (i.e., being "beyond" those limits). In love, thought encounters its limit not in thought itself but by an exteriority that both resists comprehension and that prevents thought from retreating again into itself because it demands an attention foreign to the constituting activity of a subject.

12. Iris Murdoch, *Existentialists and Mystics: Writings on Philosophy and Literature*, ed. Peter Conradi (New York: Penguin Books, 1997), 215.

13. Jean-Paul Sartre, "Intentionality: A Fundamental Idea of Husserl's Phenomenology," in *The Phenomenology Reader*, eds. Dermont Moran and Timothy Mooney (New York: Routledge, 2002), 383; emphasis added.

14. Jean-Paul Sartre, *The Transcendence of the Ego, trans. Forrest Williams and Robert Kirkpatrick* (New York: Hill and Wang, 1989), 48–49. Hereafter TE.

15. Sartre, TE, 53.

16. Ibid., 88.

17. Ibid., 74.

18. Ibid., 53.

19. Ibid., 66.

20. Sartre, "Intentionality," 383.

21. Sartre, TE, 99.

22. Ibid., 100.

23. Ibid., 103–4.

24. Jean-Paul Sartre, *Being and Nothingness*, trans. Hazel Barnes (New York: Washington Square, 1957), 344, 355. Jean-Paul Sartre, *L'Être et le Néant*. (Paris: Gallimard, 1943), 296, 304. Hereafter, BN with the English pagination followed by the French.

25. Sartre, BN, 473/402.

26. Ibid., 478/407.

27. Ibid., 479/407.

28. Ibid.

29. Ibid.

30. Ibid.

31. Sartre, BN, 473/402. Sartre had already indicated that this was the point of convergence of these two aspects of ethics, however, in *The Transcendence of the Ego*. In his later works, Husserl himself would indicate the transcendence of the subject by what it is not in his account of affection in the *Analyses Concerning Passive and Active Synthesis*.

32. Sartre, NE, 493/509.

33. Ibid., 493-6/509-12 (translator's interpolation); translator's interpolation; cf. Sartre, BN, 473/402.

34. Ibid., NE, 376/389.

35. Sartre, BN, 57-8/57.

36. Sartre, NE, 417-8/433-4; cf. 451/466.

37. Ibid., 499/515.

38. Cf. ibid., 500/515.

39. Ibid., 501/516. More precisely, this finitude is found to be the body, and "to unveil the other in his being-within-the-world is to love him in his body" (ibid.). This

idea will become important below: "Freedom per se is not lovable ... Nor is pure Being any more *lovable* in its total exteriority of indifference. But the Other's body is lovable insofar as it is freedom in the dimension of Being" (Ibid., 507/523).

40. Ibid, 477/493–4.

41. Ibid.

42. John M.E. McTaggart., *The Nature of Existence* (Cambridge: Cambridge University Press, 1988), II, 473.

43. Specifically, the willing of existence instead of the willing of being (Sartre, NE 478, 482ff/494–95, 499ff).

44. Sartre, BN, 788/667.

45. Martin Heidegger, *Being and Time*, trans. Joan Stambaugh (Albany: State University of New York Press, 1996), 31; emphasis added.

46. Jean-Luc Marion, *Being Given: Toward a Phenomenology of Givenness*, trans. Jeffrey L. Kosky (Stanford: Stanford University Press, 2002), 320. Jean-Luc Marion, *Étant Donné: Essai d'une Phenomenology de la Donation*, (Paris: Presses Universitaires de France, 1997), 439. Hereafter, BG with the English pagination followed by the French.

47. Ibid., 320–1/439–40, translation modified.

48. Ibid., 322/441–2.

49. Martin Heidegger. *The Basic Problems of Phenomenology: Winter Semester 1919/1920.* Trans. Scott M. Campbell. (London: Bloomsbury Publishing, 2013), 142.

50. Jean-Luc Marion, *The Erotic Phenomenon*, trans. Stephen E. Lewis (Chicago: University of Chicago Press, 2007), 101–2. Jean-Luc Marion, *Le Phénomène Érotique: Six Méditations* (Paris: Bernard Grasset, 2003), 162. Hereafter, EP with the English pagination followed by the French.

51. Jacques Derrida, *On Touching—Jean-Luc Nancy*, trans. Christine Irizarry (Stanford: Stanford University Press, 2005), 67–68.

52. Marion, EP, 103/164. When "crossing" is introduced in *Prolegomena to Charity,* another aspect is given more prominence: "two definitively invisible gazes (intentionality and the injunction) cross one another, and thus together trace a cross that is invisible to every gaze other than theirs alone." Jean-Luc Marion, *Prolegomena to Charity*, trans. Stephen E. Lewis (New York: Fordham University Press, 2002), 87.

53. See Marion, EP, 104/165.

54. As Robert Solomon observes, love does not merely "take" time but love is an experience *of* time. See, for example, Robert C. Solomon, *About Love: Reinventing Romance for Our Times* (New York: Simon & Schuster, 1988), 264.

55. This notion and the attendant consequences of an ego insufficient in itself, taken beyond itself, etc., makes its appearance in *The Erotic Phenomenon* in §12. It is also here that Marion says "in order to love *myself* (or at least claim to do so), I must acknowledge myself as a radically finite self: since I need someone to love me from out there, I must trace a limit—my own—beyond which this 'out there' can appear in its exteriority ..." (Marion, EP, 55/92).

56. Ibid., EP, 105/167.

57. We might say that the oath is "performed" in the time of a life constructed by this common signification. We try to say, for example, in ordinary language that in love we must "negotiate." But the economic or contractual language of negotiation (or worse, "mutual sacrifice" or "making a deal") is drastically inappropriate here insofar as it fails to address the possibility of what is properly common and not merely an exchange of services that we would otherwise like to get for free. Similarly, the emptiness of mere words ("but of course I love you!") often betokens not mere misunderstanding (I am not simply wrong in thinking that you do not love me when, "in fact," you [say that you] do) but the collapse of that which is properly common. We might say that "actions speak louder than words" because the mere declaration "I love you" has no sense apart from the life in which it is lived (and not merely in a reciprocal "I love you too").

58. As Sartre says: "in seduction I do not try to reveal my subjectivity to the Other. Moreover I could do so only by *looking at* the other; but by this look I should cause the Other's subjectivity to disappear, and it is exactly this which I want to assimilate" (Sartre, BN 484/411-12); or conversely, I make myself a fascinating object for the Other (ibid.) and reduce myself to my body that is looked at by the Other.

59. Marion, EP, 38/65.

60. Ibid., 118/186.

61. Ibid,. 118/187.

62. Ibid., 120/189.

63. Ibid.

64. Cf. Ibid., 83-4/135-6.

65. Marion, BG, 323/443.

66. In a commentary on Beckett, Badiou uses the term "numericity" to indicate the irreducibility of the Two to the addition of individuals: for example, "the numericity of love (as one, two, infinity) is the place of what Beckett, quite rightly, called happiness. Happiness also singularizes the amorous procedure, there is only happiness in love; it is the reward specific to this type of truth." Alain Badiou, *Conditions*, trans. Steven Corcoran (London: Continuum, 2008), 282.

67. Sartre, TE, 56.

68. It is for this reason that reflection on the conditions for love's appearance is also *necessary*. Nothing human merely happens without the effort of thought (and, as Heidegger provocatively asserted, what is most astonishing after all this time is that we are still perhaps not—or very rarely—thinking). Reflection "prepares" us for the appearance of love through a sort of "katharsis" (Sartre, BN, 218/190) of the tendency to languish in bad faith by insisting on the simple identity and presence of the for-itself to and for itself.

69. Marion, *Prolegomena*, 80–81.

70. Ibid., 84.

71. Luce Irigaray. *To Be Two*, trans. Monique M. Rhodes and Marco F. Cocito-Monoc (New York: Routledge, 2001), 16.

72. The figure of the Two here does not necessarily refer to the counting of bodies (nothing about the succeeding analysis prohibits the possibility of polyamory as a multiple crossing, for example). As suggested below, love *begins* at Two.

73. Whereas Marion argues, in his discussion of the erotic reduction, that vanity renders the question of being destitute, it is not *being* that fails to persevere under the threat of vanity but *life* (in Michel Henry's sense of affection).

74. This term is borrowed from Badiou's *Logics of Worlds* where the transcendental is described as the operation that organizes the degree to which a being appears in a world. See Alain Badiou, *Logics of Worlds: Being and Event, 2*, trans. Alberto Toscano (London: Continuum, 2009), 99–140.

## BIBLIOGRAPHY

Badiou, Alain. *Conditions*. Translated by Steven Corcoran. London: Continuum, 2008.

———. *Logics of Worlds: Being and Event, 2*. Translated by Alberto Toscano. London: Continuum, 2009.

Benjamin, Jessica. *The Bonds of Love: Psychoanalysis, Feminism, and the Problem of Domination*. New York: Pantheon Books, 1988.

Derrida, Jacques. *On Touching—Jean-Luc Nancy*. Translated by Christine Irizarry. Stanford: Stanford University Press, 2005.

Heidegger, Martin. *The Basic Problems of Phenomenology: Winter Semester 1919/1920. Translated by Scott M. Campbell. London: Bloomsbury Publishing, 2013.*

———. *Being and Time*. Translated by Joan Stambaugh. Albany: State University of New York Press, 1996.

Irigaray, Luce. *To Be Two*. Translated by Monique M. Rhodes and Marco F. Cocito-Monoc. New York: Routledge, 2001.

Lilar, Suzanne. *A propos de Sartre et de l'Amour*. Paris: Éditions Bernard Grasset, 1967.

Marion, Jean-Luc. *Being Given: Toward a Phenomenology of Givenness*. Translated by Jeffrey L. Kosky. Stanford: Stanford University Press, 2002.

———. *The Erotic Phenomenon*. Translated by Stephen E. Lewis. Chicago: University of Chicago Press, 2007.

———. *Étant Donné: Essai d'une Phenomenology de la Donation*. Paris: Presses Universitaires de France, 1997.

———. *Le Phénomène Érotique: Six Méditations*. Paris: Bernard Grasset, 2003.

———. *Prolegomena to Charity*. Translated by Stephen E. Lewis. New York: Fordham University Press, 2002.

McTaggart, John M.E. *The Nature of Existence*. Cambridge: Cambridge University Press, 1988.

Moi, Toril. "Freedom and Flirtation: Bad Faith in Sartre and Beauvoir." In *Situating Sartre in Twentieth Century Thought*, edited by Jean-François Fourny and Charles D. Minahen, 111–28. New York: St. Martin's Press, 1997.

Murdoch, Iris. *Existentialists and Mystics: Writings on Philosophy and Literature*, edited by Peter Conradi. New York: Penguin Books, 1997.

Ortega y Gasset, José. *On Love: Aspects of a Single Theme*. Translated by Toby Talbot. New York: Meridian Books, 1957.

Plato, *Symposium*. In *Complete Works*, edited by John Cooper. Indianapolis: Hackett Publishing Company: 1997.

Sartre, Jean-Paul. *Being and Nothingness*. Translated by Hazel E. Barnes. New York: Washington Square Press, 1956.

———. *Cahiers pour une Morale*. Paris: Presses Universitaires de France, 1983.

———. *L'Être et le Néant*. Paris: Gallimard, 1943.

———. "Intentionality: A Fundamental Idea of Husserl's Phenomenology." In *The Phenomenology Reader*, edited by Dermont Moran and Timothy Mooney, 382-84. New York: Routledge, 2002.

———. *Notebooks for an Ethics*. Translated by David Pellauer. Chicago: University of Chicago Press, 1992.

———. *Transcendence of the Ego*. Translated by Forrest Williams and Robert Kirkpatrick. New York: Hill and Wang, 1989.

Solomon, Robert C. *About Love: Reinventing Romance for Our Times*. New York: Simon & Schuster, 1988.

*Chapter Five*

# Monogamism and Polyamorism

## *A Weberian Analysis*

### Erik Jansson Boström

"You're the One That I Want." With these words Danny and Sandy sing out their love for each other in the climactic conclusion of the movie *Grease*. This is just one of the famous moments of *Grease* that may be claimed as a celebration of romantic love. No matter how complicated the love story is, the narratives of popular culture often presuppose that a happy ending means getting together with the *one* that you want. It is imbued with what we might call a monogamous worldview of romantic love. There is no denying that monogamy is central to most people's understandings of sexuality, relationships, and love. Today the centrality of monogamy is being challenged by the counter-cultural polyamorous lifestyle of having several close emotional, romantic, and sexual relationships simultaneously with the consent of all partners.[1] This chapter asks: What is the worldview that underlies the polyamorous lifestyle? How does it differ from the worldview of monogamy?[2] Polyamorism is often equated with having several relationships, but it is perhaps even more important that polyamorism changes the *meaning* of relationships. That is, polyamorism clearly indicates new possibilities not only in terms of the *quantity* of relationships, but more notably, it opens up wider variety in the *qualities* that legitimate relationships may have. Before reaching these conclusions, however, let us start with some methodological reflections.

### IDEAL TYPES

In this chapter, I am describing a set of competing worldviews concerning romantic love. By "worldview," I am referring to Max Weber's idea of *Weltanschauung*, meaning an interconnected system of thoughts, ideas, ideals and values on a specific subject that is embodied and lived. This is in contrast to rigid and explicit doctrines or ideologies. Worldviews tend to be more slippery phenomena. We do not carry around a systematic whole of thematized and clear ideas, ideals, and values that we live by in a straightforward way. As they are in many ways tacit, it is hard to explain one's worldview even when it comes to specific topics. It is still more difficult to account for the common worldview of a whole culture or group, even when they share common ways of interpreting, valuing, and judging. This might be especially true of individualistic media-driven cultures in which one is confronted with a cacophony of narratives and other messages daily. Even the basics of one's identity, worldview, and lifestyle are often complex, fuzzy, and contradictory.

The British philosopher Iris Murdoch claims that "Man is a creature who makes pictures of himself, and then comes to resemble these pictures."[3] Albeit to a large extent unarticulated, I take worldviews to be such pictures. They are neither simple empirical descriptions nor purely normative claims; they are, in fact, both at the same time. We come to resemble what our worldview tells us about how we live, what we ought to do, and how we should think and feel. Moreover, since we only *resemble* the pictures, there will always be gaps and tension between them, us, and our world. The inherent complexity and ambiguity of our worldviews make them difficult to describe both precisely and richly. Thus, one must be cautious to avoid relying on oversimplifications and stereotypes. As a response to these difficulties, I will use the Weberian ideal typical approach through which we may account for the complexity of social phenomena.[4]

Max Weber introduces this method in "The 'Objectivity' of Knowledge in Social Science and Social Policy." He writes:

> Whenever the "ideas" that govern (i.e. are diffusely active in) the human beings of a certain epoch are mental constructs of a somewhat more complicated nature, we can only grasp those ideas *themselves* with conceptual precision *in the form of an ideal type,* as they are of course empirically present in the minds of a large, indeterminate and varying number of individuals, and can be found there in a multitude of variants with regard to form and content, clarity and meaning.[5]

An ideal type is a one-sided accentuation, which "brings together certain relationships and events of historical life to form an internally consistent cosmos of *imagined* interrelations."[6] Ideal types may appear to be descriptions, and especially because of the emphasis on certain features, they may even look like stereotypes. Therefore, it is important to understand that the uniqueness of this approach does not lie in the form it describes but in how to understand and use ideal types. They do not claim to describe actual phenomena; they are tools to reach an understanding of a phenomenon. More specifically, they are meant to be used as *objects of comparison* and our task "then becomes that of establishing, in each *individual case,* how close reality is to, or how distant it is from, that ideal image."[7] Weber mainly talks about the role ideal types can have in empirical, especially historical, investigations but we can likewise make use of them in personal reflections on existential questions.[8] That is how the ideal types of this chapter are to be understood. Accordingly, the aim of this chapter is not to make any empirical claims about how anyone is thinking but to present *possible* ways of thinking about love, sex, and relationships that actual practices may or may not be founded on. Ideal types provide a basis of comparison for how we think and ideas we have encountered. As long as they help us to think about and formulate our worldview to ourselves, they have fulfilled their purpose.

Weber realized that no formulation can be neutral. Ideal types are as value-laden as any description, but unlike similar accounts, they cannot be said to have empirical validity.[9] That is, since they are only intended to be objects of comparison, they are value-free in a modest sense. They do not hope to convince us of their truth. They do not strive to push one's judgment in any predetermined direction. Moreover, ideal types are equally valuable if they conflict with our views, as if they are spot-on characterizations. They invite us to acknowledge at which points we agree and disagree, and hopefully therefore, to aid the formulation of our own well-founded judgments. Of course, every ideal type highlights certain features of a phenomenon, possibly downplaying and ignoring others; it will have what Weber calls a *value relation (Wertbeziehung).* This means that it will be formulated in relation to what one finds interesting and worth knowing from their moral, cultural, and personal point of view.[10] For this reason, it is preferable to have a palette of ideal types of the same or similar phenomena. To a large extent, the attitude of the reader determines the success of the ideal typical method; they have to read an ideal type *as* an ideal type and not as an empirical description.

## IDEAL TYPES OF MONOGAMISM AND POLYAMORISM

Throughout history, "monogamy" has signified the practice of marrying only one person, in contrast to marrying several people (polygamy). Arranged marriage has been the norm and primarily a way to organize family, legacy, and property. Over the course of history, marriage has been more closely connected to these legal, political, and material aspects of life than to love, which has mostly flourished outside of marriage.[11] Within our contemporary worldview monogamous marriage still plays a central role but only recently has transformed into a "celebration of love."[12] One basic idea of contemporary monogamism is that one *ought* to have a romantic love relationship. It is widely believed that an exclusive, stable, intimate, sexual relationship based on love is an essential part of a happy and meaningful life, and that if we are without such a relationship we are incomplete as human beings.

The core idea of polyamorism is that one can love several people at a time and be in several legitimate romantic and/or sexual relationships at a time. How does this affect the concepts of love and sexuality? To begin with, it would certainly be possible to formulate an ideal type of polyamorism that keeps the idea of the uniqueness of romantic love and therefore is structurally similar to monogamism (with the obvious exception that you can love and have romantic relationships with several people). However, the kind of polyamorism I will focus on in this chapter is essentially more *fluid* than monogamism. This means that concepts such as love, sexuality, relationships, friendship, and so on are understood as fundamentally open and flexible. On the descriptive level, it stresses that it is *possible* to have several intimate relationships at the same time; and on the prescriptive level, that it is also *permissible*. In contrast to monogamism, polyamorism does not claim that (one or more) romantic love relationships are necessary for an individual to be complete or happy. Furthermore, romantic love is not considered to be inevitably unique or ideal among types of relationships. In fluid polyamorist love, romance, attraction (both sexual and nonsexual), devotion, and care are different aspects of the many possible attachments we can feel toward others. From this palette of feelings, a unique mixture arises in each relationship; and the meaning of every relationship is to explore and develop its own potential. The relationship's title is secondary, and no label should put the relationship into a prefabricated category with nonnegotiable expectations and demands.

The central assumption of monogamism is that we can only love one person at a time and have one romantic love relationship at a time. But does this mean that it is *impossible* to love and be with many people at the same time? Or that it is *forbidden*? One can believe that it is metaphysically impossible to love several people at a time, and therefore, it is *ipso facto* also impossible to have several genuine romantic relationships at a time.[13] On the other hand, one can believe that it is possible to love several people at a time but that it is morally reprehensible to have several romantic relationships simultaneously. Keeping these distinctions in mind, there are at least three different ideal types of monogamism. The most extreme form of monogamism, which I will call *true love monogamism*, is built upon the idea that there is such a thing as someone out there that is meant for me and only me: my true love, Ms. Right, Prince Charming, my soul mate, the One.

True love monogamism dictates the impossibility of having several romantic love relationships because of the nature of love itself: If I am truly in love with someone, I do not love or want to be with anyone else and I will never come to love anyone else. In this notion of love, monogamy and sexuality are so closely connected that one will not find anyone else sexually attractive.

One will not even see other people in a way that makes that feeling possible. If one happens to fall in love with someone else, this means that his or her previous "love" was a mere chimera. This ideal type comes closest to messages we can hear from time to time in popular culture. It might be an ideal we dream of and hope for, and it is generally understood to be the message we endorse and cherish when we marry "until death do us part." This phrase in its different versions is old but has survived into our age of romantic love marriages and thus has come to be a part of the idea of what it means to truly love someone.

Another ideal type of monogamy is *serial monogamy*. This is a kind of monogamy that builds upon the idea that we can love only one person at a time, but that our love can die and that it is possible to fall in love with someone new. Serial monogamism does away with the idea of "*one* true love" without necessarily leaving the idea of "true love" behind. Thus, in serial monogamism, love can be something genuine, here and now, even if it may change over time. One aspect of serial monogamy is that if one finds oneself in love with someone other than his or her partner, this means that he or she has necessarily stopped loving his or her current partner. Although it does not have to mean that they did not love them before this new love came.

Third, we can imagine a more practically motivated monogamy, which I will simply call *pragmatic monogamism*. This form of monogamy probably has more similarities with how most people actually think. Pragmatic monogamism is the idea that we can find several people sexually attractive, that we can have a crush or maybe even be in love with several people at the same time, but that it is not viable or ethical to be in several intimate relationships simultaneously. From this perspective, a monogamous relationship may still be an ideal, either because it has intrinsic value or because of a conviction that polyamory is unworkable. However, in contrast to true love monogamism, the fact that actions on such feelings are discouraged is confirmation that they are possible. Ultimately, pragmatic monogamism would thus be a kind of monogamism that could share some basic ideas about the nature of love with polyamorism but disagree on the conclusions about how to live well.

Attraction and crushes will be understood differently within the three ideal types of monogamism. There are many ways to draw the line between, on the one hand, sexual attraction and crushes, and on the other hand, being in love. Clearly, the meaning and uses of these words vary to some extent in everyday language. For the sake of making the ideal types conceptually clear, I will say that sexual attraction and crushes can strike us suddenly, as though out of nowhere. However, love needs more time to grow. In the monogamist worldview, it is more or less impossible to find out if one loves another person, in an ethical manner, if one is in a relationship with another person, except perhaps in the case of "love at first sight." This is because for love to develop, more time and intimacy are required than are possible to have without "cheating" on one's current partner. Since according to pragmatic monogamism it is possible, but forbidden, to have a crush on someone other than one's partner or to find another person sexually attractive, these feelings are often construed as shameful and blameworthy. Love for someone else may not be just a threat to one's current relationship but a death sentence.

I would wager that most people have had a crush on, or feelings of sexual attraction to, someone other than their current partner. These feelings may be so overwhelming that one can lose all thoughts of the possible consequences of their actions. Within the monogamous worldview, there is simply no room for acting on these feelings if one wants to be responsible toward one's current partner. To act ethically, one needs to break the spell, take a step back and regain his or her composure, because the fundamental principle of monogamism is that one can have only one partner. In order to regain self-possession, first one must carefully interpret what his or her feelings mean. Then they have to decide if they want to stay in the current relationship or break up and move on. There is no clear-cut distinction between the acts of interpretation and decisions, as if they were two consecutive steps. The process of realizing what one feels is complex; emotions cannot simply be registered and labeled. To understand one's feelings may be, in a sense, to simultaneously *decide* what one feels. Even if one later determines that his or her interpretation was founded on wishful thinking and self-deception rather than on honest judgment and insight, one is required to decisively affirm his or her feelings in one direction or another.

Sexual attraction and crushes are possible without really knowing the other person and therefore they are often fleeting. One can resist the allure and hope it will simply pass. One could eventually find the other person to be simply attractive or likeable and nothing more. However, one might also realize at an early stage that there is something more to these feelings. They may feel beyond control. If they endure or grow over time, one might come to believe that they carry the potential to develop into love. Within monogamism these reflections cannot be separated from considerations on what one feels for his or her current partner. That is, the central question of what one feels in this situation is whether or not he or she *really* loves his or her current partner. Ultimately the attraction to another person ends up being a question about one's feelings for his or her current partner.

In polyamorism (but also to a certain extent in pragmatic monogamism), loving someone truly does not imply that one does not want to be with anyone else, or that they do not find other people attractive. Affection for one person does not necessarily imply anything about one's feelings for anyone else. Thus, to have a crush on, or find someone other than one's partner(s) alluring, is not automatically construed as a problem. It might cause practical complications and issues of priorities, but feelings for someone else can be understood as fundamentally positive. That is, it can be good news that one's partner has a crush on someone else because each person's happiness makes the other(s) happy. Ultimately, whether one truly loves his or her partner(s) is a question that must be answered independently of what one feels for other people. Indeed, the meaning and implications of one's feelings are to be discovered and understood anew in each individual case.

Of course, there are still opportunity costs in polyamorism; we all have limited resources of time and energy. But this is a different kind of choice than one makes in monogamy. Within polyamorism, the options are not limited to either staying with one's partner, or breaking up and exploring a crush. It is a question of proportions, of agreements on the distribution of goods. If there is an agreement that one-night stands are allowed, then one can explore a sudden meeting with an interesting person without having to decide what this means for one's primary relationship(s). If the boundaries are clear and mutual from the start, then one can go with the flow within those guidelines and see where an adventure carries them. However, in the case that one starts to fall in love with someone else, issues of time and energy management will be inevitable. One might end up in a situation where similar choices must be made as in a monogamous relationship; no one can have unlimited amounts of commitment and intimacy. One relationship might have to be sacrificed in order to keep another. The difference is that, in polyamorism, this choice occurs in a particular situation and not through abiding by a predetermined code.

The principle of amorous fidelity is not always easy to keep, and it may even become undesirable to those who have agreed to it. As such, one of its common consequences is deception, and in particular, furtive cheating. Cheating can be characterized as an unethical version of polyamory as it involves the lack of consent of at least some of the affected people. The very word "cheating" suggests breaking the agreed rules of a game to get what one desires. Cheating is equally possible within polyamorous relationships but the difference is that faithfulness does not automatically mean emotional or sexual exclusivity. Rather it means keeping explicit promises and respect for mutual agreements and personally determined boundaries. In either case, one may break promises, but the rules of monogamism are often implicit, nonnegotiable principles that are more or less internalized cultural norms and ideals. In fluid polyamorism no boundaries can be taken for granted beforehand as the relationship finds its own form.

Confronted with the fact that one's partner is attracted to someone else, one might start questioning themselves: "What am I doing wrong? What is wrong with me? If I only changed something they would stop being attracted to others." These thoughts arise from two interconnected ideas from the monogamous worldview: first of all, the idea that two people *can* be enough for each other. Second, that two people *should* be enough for each other. This follows the logic of a closed economy of relationship fulfillment with only two options: *either* keep each other satisfied, be grateful for what the other gives, and be willing to make sacrifices around what a partner cannot provide, *or* end the relationship. However, polyamorism follows a different logic: that any one person is not required, or typically even able, to fulfil another person's needs for intimate companionship. Instead partnerships can be built around existing commonalities while complementary relationships can satisfy unmet needs and desires. This means that rather than taking an all-or-nothing approach to relationship fulfilment, individual limitations need not entail that one's partner(s) make related sacrifices.

In monogamism, firm boundaries also surround the categories of friends, family, colleagues, acquaintances and so forth. These groups come with certain conceptions of what is appropriate and possible to do together and feel for people in each of these categories. Nevertheless, the brightest line is between romantic love and other kinds of relationships. Romantic love is more strictly regulated and circumvented by ideals and norms of *true love* whereas the possibility of variation is more readily acknowledged within relationships with friends, parents, siblings, and children. Since there is no strict concept of true love of one's father or sister, for example, these relationships can be defined more individually. For instance, take the love of a younger brother. It could consist in being his best friend, but it could also consist in merely watching out for and protecting him. Even a distant relationship between two grown-up brothers would not automatically be a reason for questioning their love for each other. In this case there is openness about how the relationship can appear and still involve genuine love. However, a monogamous love relationship must still meet certain expectations to avoid scrutiny. Partners must live together, have sex, and ideally, raise children together. It can be hard to convince one's partner (and maybe even oneself) that one *really* loves them if one does not want to have one of these elements of the supposedly ideal romantic relationship.

In monogamism, there are not only strict categories for relationships but there are also set goals and a fixed logic of relationship development. The monogamist ideal is not just about achieving the emotional state of romantic love; it is a *life course* with predetermined components—a series of steps in relationship development taken at a steady pace toward greater intimacy and commitment. The first step is singlehood. Being single within monogamism is a state of *not yet,* as finding someone with whom to share one's life is one of the ultimate aims. A single person can date several people, having one-night stands and "friends with benefits," as these relationships and the emotions involved are *not yet* true love, *not yet* serious, or mere preludes to the quest for a loving, monogamous relationship. A single person who is attracted to someone is imagined to be (potentially, fingers crossed) at the beginning of this predefined path. If one does not want to progress through each step, then one's love will likely be questioned or labelled problematic. One's commitment may be doubted if one does not want to move in together, get married, buy a house, and have children on the proper timeline. There is the impression that if one is *really* in love, then they will want a lifestyle in which love and sex are inseparable, and in which faithfulness is defined by sexual and emotional exclusivity. Without meeting these conditions, then the relationship "fails," and one can, at best, start over.

In fluid polyamorism there is no watershed between romantic love and other relationships. Sexuality and love are seen as separate elements to combine in variable ways. Polyamorous relationships also do not have fixed stages of development. No predefined expectations or demands follow by necessity from the discovery of a certain feeling for someone. Instead one remains open to one's development of feelings, as they dwell upon their meaning and how to act on them. This means that generally, there are not any predefined fixed limits between the categories of "partner(s)" and "friends." There is no presumed causality between people's feelings for each other and their current or future relationship status or its course of development. For many polyamorists, there is also no hierarchy of types of relationships. Friendship may even be considered more fundamental than romance, because it provides a structure upon which other elements are combined into unique individual relationships. Friendship can be just as complex and intimate as romantic love, and demand similar considerations. Family formation can happen either with partners or between friends; this includes having children and living together. The desire to become a parent within polyamorism can be separated from these notions of the ideal outcome of romantic love. There is no preconception about what a "real" family should look like; instead, we have to find our own ways of having and raising children together according to what suits our lives and personalities best.

Another key difference between polyamorism and monogamism is their perspectives on jealousy. Jealousy can certainly be experienced in any relationship. However, the meaning of these feelings and their perceived appropriateness may differ. The monogamist worldview holds that possessiveness may be appropriate between romantic partners, but inappropriate between friends or family. While one may feel equal love for a variety of people—one's parents, siblings, children, and/or friends—romantic love is an exclusive connection between two people. It is thought to be either inherently or practically impossible to have multiple, equally important, equally viable romantic loves at one time. In monogamism, jealousy is legitimated by a belief in one's *exclusive rights* to one's partner. For example, no one else has the right to have sex with one's partner and one's partner has no right to flirt with others. Moreover, if one were not jealous in such circumstances, one's love might be questioned. In contrast, sibling rivalry over parents' attention or jealousy when a friend feels ignored is measured differently. There may be a certain legitimacy to these feelings when one is being neglected, but one does not have the same right to exclusivity in these relationships. If one feels jealous of a friend spending time with others, even when the jealous one does not have time for that friend, then the proper solution to this problem is not for one's friend to stop having other friends. The person who is unwilling to share is perceived as the problem. In the monogamous worldview, friends do not have exclusive rights over one another, just as in the polyamorist worldview, no one has exclusive rights over any other person.

In both monogamism and polyamorism, there will be considerations regarding how much time and attention to give one person over another. But in monogamism, the lines are clearer in many cases. For example, one's partner is generally given priority over a friend. Family relations will typically come before friendship, but there can be more controversy between family members, such as one's spouse, parents, siblings, and children. Sometimes, other family members may even take priority over one's spouse. Exclusivity is not the rule with family, but jealousy can still become a matter of one's priorities in relation to time management, attention, expenses and so on. In the fluid polyamorist worldview, these difficult decisions must also be made in one's romantic life. One has to learn how to share one's partner or lovers, just as one must share his or her family and friends. A feeling of neglect can still lead to jealousy, but rights of exclusivity are not thereby validated. Just as parents can love multiple children with equal ardour, so can romantic partners. Within a family one can find solutions to feelings of jealousy, for example, by communicating reassurance and devotion, or renegotiating arrangements for distributing time and attention. In polyamorism the idea is that if siblings and friends can learn this, so can partners.

## CONCLUSION

From these above analyses, we can see that within monogamy, there are set norms and ideals that are more or less nonnegotiable. In addition, no partner has to take responsibility for justifying these norms since they are understood as inherent parts of what it means to be in love and in a romantic relationship. These features can be considered to be both strengths and weaknesses of monogamy. Clearly, many people value the apparent simplicity, security, and stability of monogamy. For others, however, there are unappealing trade-offs including less freedom to explore, express, and act on one's feelings. For some people, monogamy would require that they keep certain aspects of their emotional life hidden from their partner, leading to secretiveness. While some people may think of such sacrifices as a positive marker of devotion, for others they are some of the restraints that polyamorism turns against. From a polyamorous perspective, nonnegotiable, implicit norms can be at odds with what it means to be a fully flourishing human being because they deny and/or suppress important aspects of love and sexuality. It is viewed as positive and vital to discuss and negotiate all aspects of one's relationship and feelings rather than conform to an established form of the relationship. These conversations are believed to deepen intimacy within the relationship.

As pointed out in the beginning, Stephanie Coontz argues that there was a revolution in marriage practices in the twentieth century when political and material reasons for marriage were replaced by romantic love. Both monogamism and polyamorism can be based in contemporary concerns with the satisfaction of personal desires, dreams, and affections, as well as the hope for self-actualization. The difference is that monogamism asserts that these values are realized through finding one's true love, "the one that I want," while polyamorism perceives romantic and sexual exclusivity as a hindrance to their realization. At this point, one might feel inclined to ask: Which worldview is a more accurate depiction of human nature? Which one is more correct? Faced with this temptation, it is important to contemplate Murdoch's remark. If she is right that human beings are creatures that come to resemble the pictures they paint, then this question cannot be completely decided by empirical or metaphysical investigations.[14] Imperatives will already be intertwined with our accounts of reality.

Ultimately, Weber provides the method of creating ideal types as useful points of comparison among worldviews. They can aid us in seeing our descriptive or normative claims with more clarity, and therefore help us to know whether or not we are creating pictures that we consciously agree to resemble. In this instance, we have realized that the differences between monogamism and polyamorism are not merely a matter of quantity. Rather they reveal a twofold concern with quality: What does a quality relationship, in the sense of excellence, look like? And what qualities, or attributes, should a romantic relationship have? Weber provides the tool for realizing exactly how intertwined these questions can be. It will be up to the reader to determine how closely these ideal types approximate their experience, to consider their relevance in articulating their own worldviews and judgments, and perhaps to add to the palette of ideal types related to these phenomena.

*Erik Jansson Boström*

## NOTES

1. For two good introductions, see Dossie Easton and Janet W. Hardy, *The Ethical Slut: A Practical Guide to Polyamory, Open Relationships & Other Adventures* (Berkeley: Celestial Arts, 2009), and Elizabeth F. Emens, "Monogamy's Law: Compulsory Monogamy and Polyamorous Existence," *New York University Review of Law & Social Change* 29 (2004).

2. It is important to distinguish between contemporary western polyamorous lifestyles and established polygamy marriage practices throughout the world and history. Since the term "polygamy" is already strongly connected as an opposite to the more traditional and narrower usage of "monogamy" as referring to marriage practices, the term "polyamory" was coined and spread as the opposite of "monogamy" in a broader sense, even though it is not the opposite on a strictly semantic level. According to Easton and Hardy (*The Ethical Slut*, 8), it was coined by Morning Glory Ravenheart Zell. Morning Glory Ravenheart Zell, "A Bouquet of Lovers," Green Egg #89, Beltane 1990. Published online, 2010: http://www.patheos.com/Resources/Additional-Resources/Bouquet-of-Lovers. In addition, singlehood could be argued to be yet another lifestyle that purports to be an alternative to monogamy today. Consequently, one could discuss its possible underlying worldview; unfortunately this lies outside the limits of this chapter.

3. Iris Murdoch, "Metaphysics and Ethics," in *Existentialists and Mystics: Writings on Philosophy and Literature,* ed. Peter Conradi (London: Penguin Books, 1999), 75. See also Iris Murdoch, "The Idea of Perfection," ibid.

4. For a more detailed account of my interpretation of Weber's idea of the ideal type, see my dissertation (forthcoming).

5. Max Weber, "The 'Objectivity' of Knowledge in Social Science and Social Policy," in *Max Weber: Collected Methodological Writings*, eds. Hans Henrik Bruun and Sam Whimster (London: Routledge, 2012), 128.

6. Ibid., 124.

7. Ibid., 125. See also Max Weber, "The Meaning of 'Value Freedom' in the Sociological and Economic Sciences," 304–334, in *Max Weber: Collected Methodological Writings*, eds. Hans Henrik Bruun and Sam Whimster (London: Routledge, 2012), 331.

8. Such an ideal typical analysis of monogamism and polyamorism as historical ideas would be possible but too vast of a project for one chapter. The ideal types formulated in this chapter could be seen as preliminary drafts of such ideal types, but the main aim here is to aid existential reflections. The analysis below can be understood as an attempt to test the value of Weber´s ideal typical approach for philosophical reflections in practice.

9. To be sure, one of Weber's main questions in "The 'Objectivity' of Knowledge in Social Science and Social Policy" is what role ideal types are supposed to play in order for empirical scientific accounts to be valid. However, that is an entirely different question and lies outside the scope of this chapter.

10. For an overview on this topic, see Hans Henrik Bruun, *Science, Values and Politics in Max Weber's Methodology* (Aldershot: Ashgate, 2007), especially 27, but also 20–32, 109–64.

11. See Stephanie Coontz, *Marriage, a History: How Love Conquered Marriage* (New York: Penguin Books, 2006), for example, 5–10 and chapter 1 (15–23).

12. Ibid.

13. For a more elaborate discussion on this point, see Carrie Ichikawa Jenkins, "Modal Monogamy," *Ergo* 2, no.8 (2015): 175–94.

14. See Emens, "Monogamy's Law," 294–7 for a good overview of biological accounts of monogamy and polyamory.

# BIBLIOGRAPHY

Bruun, Hans Henrik. *Science, Values and Politics in Max Weber's Methodology*, new expanded edition. Aldershot: Ashgate, 2007.

Coontz, Stephanie. *Marriage, a History: How Love Conquered Marriage.* New York: Penguin Books, 2006.

Easton, Dossie, and Janet W. Hardy. *The Ethical Slut: A Practical Guide to Polyamory, Open Relationships & Other Adventures*, 2nd edition. Berkeley: Celestial Arts, 2009.

Emens, Elizabeth F. "Monogamy's Law: Compulsory Monogamy and Polyamorous Existence." *New York University Review of Law & Social Change* 29 (2004): 277–375.

*Grease*. Directed by Randal Kleiser. Los Angeles: Paramount Pictures, 1979.

Jenkins, Carrie Ichikawa. "Modal Monogamy." *Ergo* 2, no.8 (2015): 175–94.

Morning Glory Ravenheart Zell. "A Bouquet of Lovers," in *Green Egg*, #89, Beltane, 1990. Published online (2010). Available at http://www.patheos.com/Resources/Additional-Resources/Bouquet-of-Lovers. Accessed 15th November 2013.

Murdoch, Iris. "The Idea of Perfection," in *Existentialists and Mystics: Writings on Philosophy and Literature*, edited by Peter Conradi, 299—336. London: Penguin Books, 1999.

———. "Metaphysics and Ethics," in *Existentialists and Mystics: Writings on Philosophy and Literature*, edited by Peter Conradi, 59–75. London: Penguin Books, 1999.

Weber, Max. "The Meaning of 'Value Freedom' in the Sociological and Economic Sciences," in *Max Weber: Collected Methodological Writings*, edited by Hans Henrik Bruun and Sam Whimster, 304–34. London: Routledge, 2012.

———. "The 'Objectivity' of Knowledge in Social Science and Social Policy," in *Max Weber: Collected Methodological Writings*, edited by Hans Henrik Bruun and Sam Whimster, 100–138. London: Routledge, 2012.

*Part III*

# SEX, LOVE, AND AGENCY

## Chapter Six

# Friendless Women and the Myth of Male Nonage

## *Why We Need a Better Science of Love and Sex*

### Elena Clare Cuffari

The opening sentences of Kant's "What Is Enlightenment?" declare:[1]

> Enlightenment is man's emergence from his self-imposed nonage. Nonage is the inability to use one's own understanding without another's guidance. This nonage is self-imposed if its cause lies not in lack of understanding but in indecision and lack of courage to use one's own mind without another's guidance. *Dare to know!* (*Sapere aude.*) 'Have the courage to use your own understanding,' is therefore the motto of the enlightenment.[2]

The myth of male nonage, as I name the problem I find in the scientific investigations of and pop science discourse around monogamy, tells that men cannot be faithful without guidance. If they get adequate oxytocin (OXT) doses, or if they are sufficiently coerced by social norms to at least keep their public acts together, they will behave monogamously. Left to their own devices— watch out! Though to be honest, we do not really know what person-level male agency looks like. Recent years have witnessed a growing trope in television ads of the "dumb white guy."[3] This Everyman can't be trusted to manage money, feed himself, clothe his child properly, or hang out with his friends without doing something bone-headed and dangerous. Certainly he cannot interact intelligently—on equal footing—with an attractive woman. So we—as scientists, as marketers, and as women—make sure men are not expected to do any existential heavy-lifting, so to speak. This is how the myth of male nonage works for creatures like us, whose own being is an issue, who can be too afraid to know, and whose knowledge is ultimately always self-referential: The nonage is at once imposed by bad science and self-imposed by adopting the self-understanding offered in this science-inspired *endoxa*.

As the first two sections of this chapter argue, scientific and popular discourse about male fidelity in heterosexual monogamous relationships deprives men of agency, reducing their decisions either to sub-personal biological processes or to supra-personal norms and the universal rationality of cost-benefit analysis. By perpetuating the myth of male nonage, this discourse maintains an asymmetrical relation between women and their partners and undermines friendship among heterosexual women. Opposing this myth, in the next three sections I call for an ethical science of *commitment*. I sketch the conditions of this science using philosophical analysis and enactive cognitive science, according to which agency, interaction dynamics, and mortality are indispensable ingredients in human valuing, decision-making, and behavior.

The overarching claim I make takes the form of a constructive proof: we can treat monogamous commitment as a practice chosen and realized at the level of the person, and we can do so scientifically. The point of my philosophical intervention in the scientific discourse surrounding male monogamous behavior is not to argue that monogamy itself is a good thing—this is another healthy debate, as it should be, since it is a question of community value.[4] Rather, my goal is to build a conceptual bridge over which it would be possible to bring scientific investigation into line with real-life experience and values, and furthermore, to do so in a way that generally seeks to bring new and potentially transformative knowledge, rather than dig deeper the ditches in which current norms may be mired.

## NOSE-SPRAYS, NORMS, AND NON-AGENTS: ETHICAL FAILINGS OF THE CURRENT SCIENCE OF MONOGAMY

### The Data: What We Are Given

Monogamy, and particularly male fidelity, is a perennial topic of interest inside and outside the academy. I discuss here two recent scientific approaches to the sexual behavior of men vis-à-vis monogamous commitments that have garnered particular media attention: (1) the effects of the hormone oxytocin and (2) the rationalizations of college-age men who cheat. At first blush, these new inquiries and findings in neuroscience and sociology appear as provocative advancements. Yet the presuppositions and values in the background of the research are standard-issue. This is seen clearly in the media uptake of these results, and in the case of the hormone study, also seen in scientists' descriptions of their own work.

In November of 2012, the media got hot and bothered about the effects of the hormone and neuromodulator oxytocin, administered via nose-spray, on adult men in monogamous relationships.[5] The headlines herald a miracle drug that will "keep" "attached men" "monogamous" and "away from hot women"—and voluntarily![6] This news was explicitly addressed—one might even say marketed—to women, and not only by reporters. In the neuroscientists' own words: "It is clear that for these potentially fidelity-enhancing effects of OXT to be revealed, female partners would need to evoke its endogenous release immediately before contexts in which men might encounter other women."[7]

That the researchers operated with evident expectations about gender roles in human romantic relationships is thus clear in the published study: women are afraid of how the men with whom they are in relationships will behave with other women. Reading the study itself also makes clear the rather unexciting context of the much hyped findings. The only "hot"' woman the men interacted with was one of the scientists (who, to be fair, was indeed "rated as being attractive" in a follow-up questionnaire). The interaction consisted in stop-distance tests of comfortable proximity. A more accurate, though considerably less steamy, sound bite about the investigation might be, "When asked to walk toward a rated-as-attractive-when-asked female scientist, men in a relationship given oxytocin stopped ten centimeters further away than did oxytocin-dosed men not in relationships."

The actual events of the study do not stop media coverage from indulging in a slippery-slope landslide from steps taken in a lab to speculations of how men will behave "in the wild" of everyday social encounters with dreaded "other women." Yet such extension to real-life situations is not justified, as is well known to experimenters in neuropsychology and other fields as the problem of ecological validity.[8] As philosopher Gary Gutting recently argues in *The New York Times*, priming effects achieved in an experimental psychology lab are not transferrable or replicable to real-world settings and interactions:

> There is no automatic transfer of a laboratory result to the real-world events we want to control. In the natural sciences we can typically control and probe inert bodies any way we like to yield precise quantitative measures of effects. But the complexity of humans, the interdependence of key variables, and ethical limitations on constraining human subjects make such control far less likely in the human sciences.[9]

The outcome of the OXT study (which notably does not involve inert bodies) should be recognized for what it is: an isolated effect achieved in a controlled experimental environment. The fanfare surrounding this outcome must also be recognized for what it is: fodder for the myth of male non-agents and the suspicions of the women who love them. Feminist philosophers of science have well documented the reductionism that plagues brain research in the context of discussions of gender and sex.[10] Wariness is equally warranted regarding reductionism in the study of social relationships, particularly those invested and infused with the values that go into monogamous commitment.

Offering a social science perspective, UK sociologist Eric Anderson's 2012 book *The Monogamy Gap: Men, Love, and the Reality of Cheating*, based on interviews with male college students about their own cheating behavior in heterosexual monogamous relationships, met a far chillier media welcome than the OXT nose-spray findings.[11] Anderson critiques the hegemony of *monogamism* and attempts to articulate a broader and potentially more compassionate notion of commitment, albeit based on a problematic model of utilitarian calculation. According to Anderson, "Data suggest that participants who cheat do so not because of lost love, but instead cheating represents an attempt to rectify conflicting desires for monogamy and recreational sex."[12] In response, the media collectively wrote the research off as "a Cheater's Charter," an apology for male misbehavior. In a review, Anderson is described as arguing that "Men should have their cake and eat it too. [Anderson] knows this works for almost all libidinous young men, especially for gays. He has no idea whether this could work for everyone, for married people, for women with lively young children who are too tired for sex even with their spouse."[13]

Seriously alarmed by the frank anecdotes of actual men, public uptake of Anderson's research clings to hostile stereotypes and decries typical male lack of self-control.[14] Apparently, no one wants to take on the sociologist's actual argument that cheating is a rational process of cost-benefit analysis and norm-compliance that conflicted young men find themselves following.[15] What makes this research so alarming and so prone to red-herring readings? There is an obvious answer—the resulting prescription isn't hormone-dosing, but instead, painful confrontation with the conflicting desires people must negotiate in their limited lifetimes. A person may desire both the joys of support and companionship that emerge in a long-term romantic relationship and the differently positive experiences of one-night stands. Western (particularly the United States) society generally views these pursuits as mutually exclusive. There is no over-the-counter remedy here. Anderson notes that hegemonic monogamism is not ideal for the men who nonetheless find a way to (nominally) practice it, and he offers a subtle yet ambitious plea for regime change such that monogamy is no longer the only option with social benefits.[16]

But even for the brave souls willing to stare into the blazing light of reality—that is, a heap of evidence that monogamy in name means nonmonogamy in practice[17]—a dark shadow lurks in Anderson's analyses. He suggests that there is *logic* at work here, that cheating *makes sense* to men, and that at least in this epistemologically normative way, there is some *rightness* to it. This enrages critics, but they mistake Anderson to be saying that cheating is morally right, and therefore miss his own preference, which would be a different system entirely. Nonetheless, there is cause to tread carefully with this kind of supposedly nonnormative description. In this case, unlike in the sub-personal account, the man has reason on his side—so much so that he acts in ways that, according to Anderson, cause him cognitive dissonance. On this account of male rationality, the woman who worries about her partner's fidel-ity shouldn't bother with his hormone levels or even his particular behavior, but rather must reckon with a whole clever culture of men who know how to get what they want without telling.

## Love, Sex, and Science Fiction

The fear-mongering and fear-motivated media responses to research on monogamy remind us, importantly, that there is something basically right in being afraid of zombies, aliens, and robots. There is a reason that so many horror movie plots involve kids and machines running amok—there is just no reasoning with them, no hope of human connection with a possessed vehicle. But like a Stephen King hive-mind, we are writing this drama ourselves. Contrary to the myth of male nonage, a boyfriend is a person, too.

Imagine: a human man watches the news, reads magazines, and web articles, and possibly reads peer-reviewed research journals.[18] What does he see there? That his decisions are dictated by genes. That monogamy is hard because he has urges to have recreational sex with different people. That since being in a relationship maximizes social benefits, his best bet may be to handle his biological business quietly. What *doesn't* he see? That desire is complex. That all day long he makes difficult decisions between incommen-surable options, choices with uncomfortable remainders. That he is human, with great emotions and great powers, and that ultimately he is responsible in the fullest existential sense of the term *He*—not his hormones and not his boys—is the only one who will live his life and die his death.

The science we have now also perpetuates a culture in which heterosexual women are isolated in suspicion and insecurity. The terror that looms in the words "contexts in which the men might encounter other women" is palpable and likely not placed accidentally. If, in my felt sense of the relationship, the only thing standing between my husband and the sex organs of another woman is my diligent attention and sly hormonal manipulation, I cannot be his friend. At best I am his babysitter, if not his parole officer, zookeeper, or mad scientist progenitor. This is the burden the myth of male nonage places on women: they must be the constant caretakers and vigil keepers. Such a deep asymmetry built into the structure of a relationship cannot but be a prob-lem for both parties. For women, it means being profoundly alone, because they are the half of the relationship that is expected to be a fully, actualized adult person, managing her own agency and yet also tempted into bad faith by the perpetual management of another.[19]

Support from outside the monogamy-hopeful dyad is in short supply as well, since most of a woman's male "friends" are just biding their time until they are granted access to her sex organs.[20] Hence, for women, friendship with straight men is out. So, too, is the sisterhood of traveling pants or any other kind, because clearly *she* can't be counted on to have my back, especially if she's ovulating.[21] As bell hooks, Christine Overall, and other feminists have observed, sexism and the zero-sum game for male attention—life under the patriarchy—systematically undermines solidarity and friendship among women.[22] Here the universal (male) logic of cost-benefit analysis, which maintains that what she does not know will not hurt her, has it quite wrong. Not knowing drives a person mad; the paranoia infects sisters, friends, and colleagues. As Annette Baier cannily observes, "the special vulnerability which trust involves is vulnerability to not-yet-noticed harm, or to disguised ill will."[23] If Anderson is right about the strength of the taboo against cheating, expecting deception from one's partner becomes a rational option. No one is trustworthy and no one is safe.

Women can thank science under the patriarchy not only for the paranoia, isolation, and wildly unbalanced burden of responsibility, but also for actively writing our experiences out of the story. Women also cheat, or want to cheat.[24] Women, like all living humans, struggle with the weight of their own commitments. This unevenness in the discourse only cements further the myth of *male* nonage, reifying heteronormative gender roles: women (only women) are jealous and controlling, yet unproblematically desire monogamy across the board; men (only men) are unable to will or practice fidelity on their own virtue.

## TELLING A DIFFERENT STORY: THE SCIENCE OF COMMITMENT

### Defining Commitment

Having identified a mutually reinforcing evil in the discourse—friendless women and non-agentive men—I offer now a preliminary philosophical breakdown of terms guided by the goal of identifying what will count as appropriate (nonreductive) scientific inquiry into a complex human practice.[25] The object of these studies is the condition(s) that will guarantee (or fail to guarantee) monogamous action by men. For the sake of setting up terms, notice that for an action to count as monogamous, it must be carried out by a person in a committed relationship of sexual exclusivity. So while singular actions (such as approaching or maintaining distance from a woman) are the target of the hormone studies, the larger value in question is inherently long-term monogamous commitment.

It is important to note that monogamy itself is a value (a valued practice), one that not everybody holds or must hold. Furthermore, the value of commitment is available for realizing in nonmonogamous relationships, even if such arrangements are less visible in or supported by mainstream culture. One can be romantically committed to multiple people, or committed to maintaining and steadily improving disparate ongoing sexual relationships. Commitment is not the privileged or unique possession of monogamous dyads (whether heterosexual or homosexual). So an exclusive practice of a certain kind of commitment—sexual fidelity—is the defining feature of a monogamous pairing.

Nonetheless, before turning to how monogamous commitment can be defined in terms of constituent values, I want to consider commitment itself and more broadly. Commitment is an indispensable ingredient in the practice of living one's own life and realizing the values of one's choice, and it is a systematically overlooked element in scientific explanations of people's behavior in such arrangements. Then I will turn briefly to the more particular strain of monogamous commitment, constituted by sexual fidelity.

Given the dynamic and open nature of human existence, given the reality of choice and creation in all of our activities (whether we see it this way or not), all value- and virtue-realizing requires commitment. By commitment I mean the dedication of one's efforts toward a certain practice or manifestation of a certain way of life over and against other options or competing forces. Note that we are already accustomed to using this word "commitment" in the context of romantic-sexual relationships (including forms of deprivation like "commitment-phobic"). This is no coincidence. Contemporary western culture, particularly in the United States, values romantic relationships, these lifelong pursuits, perhaps above all others.[26] But we also routinely call on the value of commitment when we are talking about anything from a diet to a political ideal. Commitment is at-issue whenever something matters to us, and whenever that thing that matters requires a sustaining effort over time. Thus, a philosophical analysis of commitment is incomplete unless we address its inherent temporal aspects.

The temporality of commitment involves at least two timescales: (1) in-the-moment decisions, and (2) a global, autobiographical sense of one's life narrative.[27] As will be evident in what follows, research on decision-making in moral psychology and cognitive science tends to deal with timescale (1), while the notion of monogamy requires timescale (2). Yet the timescales are and should be studied as interrelated: choices to uphold that to which one is committed are made in the moment, but may be motivated by a 'larger' experiential sense of life narrative. Even if this sense of autobiography is not always consciously present in decision-making, decisions made necessarily go into the composing of this story—the commitment is sustained, or weakened, or left entirely.

A basic condition of commitment as the act of values-realizing across timescales is *mortality*. Human existence is temporal, not eternal. Persons "know their own mortality and are therefore open to aspirations and frustrations."[28] What we value has to do directly with our bodily situation and the corresponding reality that this situation is impermanent and finite. "Facing our finitude, we find that we care, not only whether we exist but how we exist."[29] Hence, the question of who one spends one's mortal days with, and who one has sex with during that time, is a significant question for us, one that we respond to in complex and ongoing acts of decision-making.

Once one considers commitment as a choice of being-with made in mortal life, one finds a social dimension within the particular commitment involved in monogamy. This commitment is one of reciprocally binding sexual fidelity.[30] I treat commitment as a complex temporal act, and I will soon discuss some ways that cognitive science treatments of action and interaction might handle this. But, as will become clear in those complex analyses of how people choose and uphold commitments, a wider context of value is an indispensable ingredient (the necessary friction) of such situational responding. The values in play in monogamous commitment as the practice of sexual fidelity are trust and loyalty. Monogamous commitment is commitment to enacting these values in relation to a particular other. As relational, these values have inherent temporal aspects as well. The basic structure of monogamous commitment is: if I commit to spending (some or all of) my mortal days sleeping with you and only you, I want you to do the same for me.

Loyalty can explain why one may, in looking back over a failed monogamous relationship, feel varying degrees of outrage and frustration in the final knowledge that one's partner did not uphold the expected reciprocal exclusivity. Loyalty is measured in perseverance and stick-to-it-ive-ness; it is costly in time investment and also in its privileging of one group, cause, person, identity, and so on, over above other competing claims for one's allegiance and energy.[31] To be loyal is to hang around when the going gets tough. By definition, almost, it is not a good time. Hence, to have been loyal to someone who has not been loyal in return does not engender good feelings.

We glimpse some of the temporal significance of commitment in reflections on loyalty. But I do not think the structure of this virtue or value fully captures what is at stake in monogamous commitment, that is, the threat not only of time lost or misspent but this compounded with threat of betrayal and heartbreak. Here we must speak of trust. At once pointing out the inherently social nature of trust and getting to the beating pulse of its presence in our lives, Baier writes, "without trust, what matters to me would be unsafe."[32] By her definition, trust is an attitude toward someone regarding their actions vis-à-vis something valuable to the one who trusts. The valuable something that defines monogamous relationships is sexual exclusivity. But in less analytical parlance, what people talk about entrusting in such contexts is their "heart." I think it is reasonable to give this a wide interpretation of emotional well-being in a context of emotional dependency. As Overall has effectively argued, one's self-identity is at stake in one's sexually being with another.[33] This observation accords well with Baier's observation that "the things we typically do value include such things as we cannot single-handedly either create or sustain" including "our own life, health, reputation."[34]

In addition to that which one entrusts, a trust relationship requires a trustworthy trustee. Baier develops a valuable critique of traditional moral philosophy's contractual model of trust between two relatively distant, independent, and equally powerful agents. Yet recall the discourse in which I am attempting to intervene: a discourse that assumes that men do not *choose* monogamous commitment and that attributes any long-term practice of commitment to a trick, leading by the nose, or dispassionate social coercion. As non-agent men are not trustworthy, at least not in the precarious moments when other women are present and/or their primary watchers—ahem, girlfriends or wives—are absent.

Note the radical extent of the damage done by this logic: if a man does not choose monogamy but is "kept" in it by these sub- or supra-personal forces, he also wins no credit for a history of trustworthiness. Given the high existential and emotional stakes of monogamous commitment, a woman who find herself in a relationship that is defined by sexual exclusivity, but that takes place in a scientific-discursive horizon that renders men non-agentive and untrustworthy, finds herself in a true double-bind, to which manipulation and paranoia are expected coping strategies. This situation reaches its extreme in a world where even a "good" man is perpetually susceptible to being turned: women who have no evidence of untrustworthiness are in the very same boat as the ones who do.

While arguably each of these may be treated as virtues, values, acts or practice, for present purposes, I take commitment to be a practice and trust to be a relational attitude inspired by commitment and in turn fostering the continuance of commitment. Loyalty I take as a character trait or virtue that can be attributed to people who commit successfully; it is also a value "in" commitment. In order to commit one's self to the trust of another in a monogamous bond, and in order to be a loyal partner in any meaningful sense, one must be an agent.

## Choosing Commitment

How do people realize (or fail to realize) the social values of trust, loyalty, and fidelity in the practice of monogamous commitment (if not by nasally dosing hormones, that is)? Let us consider, albeit in a preliminary fashion, humans' complex, dynamic cognitive processes of reasoning, deliberating, valuing, and choosing.

In investigating commitment as a temporally complex choice, we are invited to dialogue with cognitive science, despite its being traditionally detached from social concerns. Recent and socially attuned enactive cognitive science demonstrates that in-the-moment decision-making is no simple matter; it cannot be reduced to a single variable, nor can it be outsourced to disembodied reason.

Current efforts to naturalize moral psychology offer various dual-process hypotheses of decision-making in which "judging a situation and deciding on a course of action is not a simple cost-benefit analysis but a context-dependent mixture of rational and affective processes."[35] Approaches such as Damasio's *somatic marker hypothesis* (SMH) make plain the insufficiency of both the sub-personal and supra-personal explanations of monogamous (or nonmonogamous) behavior that we find in the research discussed above.[36] According to the SMH, body states and the bioregulatory processes that measure and react to body states can set off marker signals, which in turn condition and inform the body's response to a stimuli in the environment. Both conscious and non- or less-conscious responses involve these "markers" in the body, which Damasio defines as special sorts of feelings and emotions "that have been connected, by learning, to predicted future outcomes of certain scenarios."[37] Throughout multiple works, Damasio argues against any strict separation between affect and reason in human cognition, giving a distinctive account of emotion as a biocognitive recursive process of the body monitoring itself (in part through neural maps) from moment to moment.[38] The particular upshot of the SMH is that our choosing processes are vitally motivated, bodily informed, and preconsciously selective.[39] Moreover, Damasio shows that it is possible (and indeed necessary, on this view) to explain deliberative and evaluative processes by positing an integrated brain-body-environment system.

From a Damasioan perspective, the sub-personal focus on hormones driving OXT research misses—really quite wondrously skips over—how a chemical reaction interacts with the emotionally aware environment of a body that knows itself to be "going steady" with Rebecca. On Damasio's account, a person's autobiographical sense of self, memory, sensory-motor system, somatic markers, and other physiological and neurological structures all work in concert whenever one evaluates, responds, and acts in the world. While the details of this orchestration are beyond the scope of the present endeavor, in essence, Damasio offers a neuroscientist's version of the temporal richness of each here-and-now moment, thick with ineffable influences of the past and reaching into a value-laden future. The story to be told about how we evaluate and react emotionally in full-blown adult-human-scale *social* situations *is* complex—this is the point—but the groundwork has been laid down by psychologists and neuroscientists like Damasio who take an embodied and environment-interactive approach.[40]

A recent study refines the somatic marker hypothesis by using tools from mathematics and complex systems acting in time to investigate the claim that "Our decisions are rarely isolated events, and their interaction is rarely additive."[41] Rather, any instant of deciding what to do next emerges (and is probably being *a posteriori* identified) out of a back-and-forth jumble as actions and local conditions play off each other unpredictably and at different rates of change. Thus, to get closer to what actually happens in human choosing, researchers analyze *decision chains*, rather than isolated moments. By modeling nonlinear scenarios in which environmental feedback plays a repeat and leading role in decision-making, Bedia and Di Paolo find that even recently acquired or poorly attuned somatic markers (i.e., body-regulatory patterns that do not yet link the significance of a bodily emotion gained in a previous experience to what needs to be resolved in a current situation) help a system to learn via unnecessarily extreme reactions (reactions that are reckless or cautious, relative to the stimulus). In addition to identifying this exploratory tendency of somatic markers (SMs), they also find that "for many environments, as an evolutionary strategy involving developmental plasticity, SMs may out-compete the evolution of sophisticated deliberative capacities."[42] Therefore, the best "balance" of rational and affective processes in decision-making is then not what dual-processing theories suggest, as it is weighted more heavily toward the influence of new body markers that might be figuratively described as fledgling hypotheses with an itchy trigger finger. Over the unfolding course of reflexive acting in the world, chaos supports an ordered system, and a hectic mix of recklessness and over-caution yields a desired outcome.[43] This research furthermore indicates that even if all the sub-personal factors could be perfectly isolated, identified, quantified, proportionally weighted, and so on to predict a single decision, this result is not expandable to account for the complex relations of a decision chain. Thus, the kind of analysis offered by Bedia and Di Paolo outlines more appropriate conditions for the kind of decision-making that I have been talking about—that which enacts a life or a period of monogamous commitment.

This careful research into the complex web of sub-personal and environmental factors in agency has a significant upshot: Supra-individual explanations of action that rest on abstract social forces and norm-conformance assume a cleanly calculating rationality that does not exist. The ideal of rational decision-making has been disproven for economic decision-making, as Daniel Kahneman showed in his Noble Prize–winning research in psychology.[44] Given Kahneman's recent work on a broader range of irrational biases, and the complexity of real-time choosing just discussed, Anderson's claim that college men cheat to rationally resolve a conflict between somatic and emotional desires leads in two wrong directions.[45] First, it assumes a division between emotions, calculations, and bodily wants that is abstract to the point of being untenable. Second, and more importantly, it incorrectly assumes that there is a reason to expect or predict that someone like Tom, who holds conflicting beliefs, will cheat rather than not cheat as a calculable outcome of this dissonance: "Tom navigates two contrasting and heavily naturalized beliefs (i) that the desire for monogamy results from true love and; (ii) that men naturally desire recreational sex even when in love."[46] Tom may indeed also be in a double-bind (I find this aspect of Anderson's work quite compelling and deserving of further consideration), but one could argue this makes his cheating behavior the result of desperation, not "sensible" problem-solving.

The point I take Damasio, Bedia and Di Paolo, and Kahneman to collectively make is that human choice is neither an exercise of "pure"—objective, detached, spotless—rationality, nor a blind hijacking by sub-personal forces. To be clear, processes of somatic regulation are real and play a substantial role in evaluating, choosing, and acting; the same goes for sociocultural norms. Pure rationality is a myth, and holding on to it precludes triangulating the person-level of decision-making in this account. The person "level" is the feeling, interpreting, acting, responding entity, the one who enacts regulatory processes (both physical and social) in local, actual, and shifting ways, within the broader context of a dynamically unfolding life story.

My goal in discussing cognitive studies in decision-making is to address commitment as an agential, existential, dynamic choice that people make again and again in life. In however many moments of stopping at one drink, matching or not matching the tone of a text, promising, promise-breaking, or doing things that strengthen the bond between two people (romantic, sexual, friendship), people choose commitment (or choose against it), both in that act-moment, and over time and developing response patterns. The present purpose is not to spell out fully and in every instance how this works but only to offer a sample of ways—*scientific* ways—of thinking about realizing a value of commitment without resorting to nose-spray hysteria or detached utility maximization.

Two aspects of choosing commitment have only been alluded to in the foregoing discussion of the moral embodied psychology of decision-making: self-identity and social interaction. While affect- and chaos-inclusive models of decision-making progress ever closer to approximating lived experience, there remains a need to account for the narrative timescale, the fact that people commit to things *across* multiple instances of choosing.[47] This is precisely what committing consists in. What does it mean to be a person who understands himself as committed to a life of sexual fidelity with one other person—and who so understands himself day after day, anniversary after anniversary?

I want to pause and let that question hang in the air for a moment. This is at once a philosophical question that should guide whatever empirical or theoretical responses I might offer, and a personal question ultimately answered in particular lives and particular relationships. I will begin to sketch a part of the answer using enactive theory.

According to enactive biocognitive philosophy, identity, agency, and self-hood are direct products of a precarious organism's self-sustaining activity in the world. Such embodied activity is itself intelligent: "Living is itself a cognitive process—a process whereby a living being creates and maintains its own domain of meaningfulness, in generating and maintaining its own self-identity as embodied organism."[48] Multiple levels of autonomous and self-sustaining processes interlock and overlap as our organism interfaces, or couples to, its environment.[49] Human environments are social and cultural; this means that our whole bodily intelligence is social and cultural, all the way down to those pesky self-aggrandizing genes.[50] It also means that neither our decisions nor the self-narratives we compose in deciding can be "localized" in our brains, in a disembodied space of reasons, or in isolation from our friends, partners, or families. For the enactivist, a man is not the sole author of his intentions, actions, and behaviors. Rather, he is coauthor, along with his environment and the people who constitute the networks of interaction in which he participates.[51] This complexity does not eliminate agency; it *is* agency—in flesh and blood, rather than abstract axioms.

## Living Commitment: Restoring and Redistributing Agency in Monogamous Relationships

Overcoming the myth of male nonage requires restoring and balancing agency in a monogamous romantic relationship. In a rigid and asymmetrical dynamic, neither the friendless woman nor her non-agentive charge is well poised to regulate their ongoing interaction. The kind of nuanced social agency required by commitment is threatened or missing in the current scientific explanations of male behavior. In the cognitive science of decision-making sketched above, choice depends on a person's embodied emotional history and present momentary existence. But just as choices are not made in a physical vacuum, the choices involved in a monogamously committed life are not made in a social vacuum. Human agency emerges from affordances in interaction and not simply from an individual will to change (*pace* bell hooks).[52]

The existentialists tell us that we are what we do—*existence precedes essence*. Enactive cognitive science's treatment of social cognition takes this further, by showing that we do not act or exist alone—*co-existence precedes self-existence*. (This is also a basic claim in the social psychology found in Mead, Dewey, and Vygotsky.) Interactional encounters have affective and normative colorings, which shape the unfolding or coenacting of the encounter.[53] When the people involved have a history of interacting with each other, the way this all goes down is strongly governed by patterns that span the participants, patterns that reinforce themselves. The same old argument about keeping the blinds closed or whether the fan should be on at night; the same old way that we do or certainly do *not* comment on the attractiveness of strangers walking by in the park. The myth of male nonage comes alive in the asymmetrical dynamics of actual relationships. This is the fault of neither party, also of both, and finally of our scientific discourse. The behavior of one person in a relationship is partially creditable to the other but, more importantly, also to the dynamic that relates them to each other.

The *participatory sense-making* approach in enactive cognitive science builds on findings about how multi-agent systems, be they aggregations of single-cell organisms or garden-variety humans in inter-individual action, generate a self-regulating dynamic, which looks after its own needs and wants.[54] Cycles of interaction regulate themselves, and in turn inform the adaptivity of the individuals interacting.

Participatory sense-making is observable on a human scale both in smooth collaborative synergies and in everyday awkwardness. To give an example of the latter, I am a foreigner to my current country of work, and I initially had trouble adjusting to the local custom of the double-cheek-kiss greeting. Last year, this resulted in a near-death experience. On my way out of our building one evening, I ran into a colleague on the stairs who stopped me to meet another academic in the department, a young British man. Our building happens to be new and of modern design: a low side-table and two red swivel chairs mark the light-wood-paneled landing as a mid-staircase "hang-out." Ben reached out over these jaunty furnishings to shake my hand—or so I must have expected—and proceeded to draw me in for the dreaded double-kiss-greeting. Out of stubborn habit, or fear of the shin-height table between us, I resisted this lean-in, pulling away even as I hung onto his hand to avoid toppling backward down the remaining half of the staircase. Yet Ben's strength (or determined politeness) won out, even as horrified awareness dawned in his blue eyes and he exclaimed in my ear "Oh, you're American!"

By this point, to be sure, neither of us had any desire to complete the routine—just as neither of us had any desire to embarrass the other. But the dynamics of our bodies and cultures in interaction had taken over, and complete it we did, to mutual annoyance. As this experience shows, a person's actions are influenced by interaction processes that no "one" has control over.

It may seem paradoxical or even alarming to introduce a distributed notion of action and choice into an analysis of commitment. What about betrayal—isn't this a real, and bad, thing that one person does to another? Is this a suggestion that no one is ever the master of her own actions? On the account I am building here, the answer to both of these would most likely be yes and no. While I resist the reductive determinism of the sub- and supra-personal explanations of significant human action and choice as over-simplistic, category mistakes, or just plain incorrect, I am not denying situational and social determinism that, in very complex ways, coauthor the life a person makes for himself, including its constituent values and attendant fumbles.

The inquiry into commitment that I am advocating thus distributes agency without necessarily removing responsibility. What then comes to light as a pressing question is how commitments are maintained when members of a couple are not together in the moment and are tasked with keeping the faith of their shared commitment in new or different interaction environments.

I find one recent perspective in new interaction sciences helpful in sorting out the shared labor of commitment, that of *social* and *dialogical systems.* According to eco-linguist Sune Steffensen, a social system is "a whole in which participants are socially coordinated," and they emerge out of and are frequently coincidental with dialogical systems that are wholes "in which participants perform social coordination."[55] An example of a social system as a trans-situational and personally defined community is one's immediate family; and an example of a dialogical system is that same family sitting, eating, and talking together at the dinner table. Even when they are not together, the members of the family "carry the values and habits of the family's social system with them and they all bring these values along in their various settings. These values are upheld by the nonlocal, trans-situational and dialogical dynamics" that inform human interaction.[56] A reciprocal relationship exists between the two systems: the social system expands before and after the dialogical system on a longer timescale that stabilizes patterns emergent in dialogical interaction, but each instance of the dialogical system "pivots on interactivity that draws on non-local dynamics"—that is, the values the family has come to share.[57]

One point to take from this is that whether or not they are present, others are included in our reasoning, choosing, and values-realizing. Others are included in moments when they are copresent, but also when they are absent, if we are related in a social system based in a history of real-life interactions. So to return once again to the limits of the rationale behind the OXT nose-spray, the girlfriend does not need to administer hormones to make sure she is "a part of" her man's style of interacting with other people. This notion of social system could furthermore explain the unshakeable haunting specter of the girlfriend that torments the guilty subjects of Anderson's research.

Of course, these interactionist accounts of social coordination do not foretell just what actions will result in just what scenarios. People are not robots. Likely enough there is real possibility of one's significant other interacting meaningfully with other sexual beings. If there was not a reasonable expectation of various types of encounters emerging between people at any moment, monogamy and fidelity would not be the hot topics that they are. Valuing something makes one vulnerable, and valuing another person makes one vulnerable to her choices. The observation that these choices emerge in complex dynamics may indeed increase that vulnerability—or it just may reduce it.

This brings me to the second point I want to make on the basis of these proposals about social coordination and co-situated deciding and acting: iInteraction histories have persistent (yet perpetually transformable and susceptible) power.[58] What dynamics are being sustained and strengthened in a couple's or a family's ongoing interactions? This is where the popular science media (just like other forms of media) show up in intimate life—as trans-situational values or routines that can influence how people relate to each other. To borrow from and build on the ecological perspective, one's wider sociocultural milieu contributes some patterns, expectations, models; the established dynamics of interacting systems may afford the ongoing influence and intersection of these contributions, and some systems will do this more than others. The model of the male non-agent recurs in T.V. ads and OXT research (not to mention the Judd Apatow canon). Embodied in the dynamics of a real-life heterosexual couple, male nonage structurally sustains his partner's overbearing and suspicious tendencies—and vice versa. (More generally, both nonage and overbearing dominance are bad faith practices, existentially speaking, and reciprocally reinforcing in interaction dynamics.)

The paradoxical task is spelling out personal experiences of continuity and agency for socially created body-selves. Beauvoir would call this task *assuming ambiguity*. Being coauthor is still being an author. As embodied cognitive science and existential phenomenology both show, a person's present situation is quite rich. Through the cooperation of environment and others, one re-creates in each moment one's felt sense of identity and value, though indeed such consistency is a complex achievement and is not guaranteed. This begins to explain how commitment is practiced and hence how people may expect each other to practice it even when someone is on a business trip. The fragility of realizing values in different circumstances and over the continuously (though not infinitely) unfolding span of one's life also clarifies what happens when commitments break down and change. To put the point a bit less gently, the logical structure of monogamy is in tension with the dynamic, contingent, and impermanent nature of life and human sense-making. This tension is what calls for commitment as the dedication of one's efforts toward a certain practice or manifestation of a certain way of life over and against other options or competing forces. Commitment does not eradicate the tension; it is one way of assuming it.

Ultimately, if we enlarge our perspective on what counts as making a decision, and what counts as identity, the picture becomes more complicated, but less terrifying. We get back to a human scale, where our paths are our own messy, meandering creations "laid down in walking"[59]—a little less zombie apocalypse and a little more down-to-earth muddling. From this vantage point, heterosexual women may be able to approach their male partners as humans, and eventually as friends.

## NOTES

1. The author would like to thank Heather Lakey, Elizabeth Caldwell, George Fourlas, and Ezequiel Di Paolo for helpful comments and suggestions on initial drafts, and also Caroline R. Lundquist for great editorial guidance and patience at the end of the process. This work was supported in part by the Marie-Curie Initial Training Network, "TESIS: Towards an Embodied Science of InterSubjectivity" (FP7-PEOPLE-2010-ITN, 264828).

2. Immanuel Kant, "What Is Enlightenment?," trans. Mary C. Smith, http://www.columbia.edu/acis/ets/CCREAD/etscc/kant.html.

3. "In TV Ads, Dumb Has Become the New Clever," *Chicago Tribune*, accessed April 29, 2013, http://articles.chicagotribune.com/2011-03-08/news/ct-talk-esposito-ads-0308-20110308_1_commercials-hummus-ad; *Men Are Stupid (A Media Study)*, 2012, https://www.youtube.com/watch?v=1ILVL_MLwqI&feature=youtube_gdata_player.

4. See for example Dan Savage's lecture in November 2013: *Festival of Dangerous Ideas 2013: Dan Savage - Savage Advice*, 2013, https://www.youtube.com/watch?v=C-laWOpXxC8&feature=youtube_gdata_player, as well as the discussion surrounding Bergner's *What Women Want*: Elaine Blair, "'What Do Women Want?' by Daniel Bergner," *The New York Times*, June 13, 2013, sec. Books / Sunday Book Review. http://www.nytimes.com/2013/06/16/books/review/what-do-women-want-by-daniel-bergner.html.

5. Oxytocin and its nose-spray administration continues to receive research and media attention, both about pair bonding in romantic relationships and more general pro-sociability effects in patient–doctor relationships and in cases of autism. See for example "Intranasal Application of Oxytocin Appears to Enhance Placebo Response," *ScienceDaily*, accessed November 11, 2013, http://www.sciencedaily.com/releases/2013/10/131022170630.htm; Caitlin Shure, "Nasal Sprays Offer Therapy with a Sniff: Scientific American," accessed November 11, 2013, http://www.scientificamerican.com/article.cfm?id=nasal-sprays-offer-therapy-with-a-sniff.

6. Lindsay Abrams, "Study: Oxytocin ('the Love Hormone') Makes Men in Relationships Want to Stay Away From Other Women," *The Atlantic*, November 16, 2012, http://www.theatlantic.com/health/archive/2012/11/study-oxytocin-the-love-hormone-makes-men-in-relationships-want-to-stay-away-from-other-women/265314/. "Oxytocin Hormone Helps with Monogamy, Study Says," *GlobalPost*, accessed March 22, 2013, http://www.globalpost.com/dispatch/news/science/121114/oxytocin-hormone-helps-monogamy-study-says. "Oxytocin Keeps Attached Men Away from Hot Women," *NBC News*, accessed March 22, 2013, http://vitals.nbcnews.com/_news/2012/11/13/15144027-oxytocin-keeps-attached-men-away-from-hot-women. "Study: Hormone Oxytocin May Keep Men Monogamous," *CBS News*, accessed March 22, 2013, http://www.cbsnews.com/8301-204_162-57549944/hormone-oxytocin-may-keep-men-monogamous-study-suggests/.

7. Dirk Scheele et al., "Oxytocin Modulates Social Distance Between Males and Females," *The Journal of Neuroscience* 32, no. 46 (2012): 160.

8. Marilyn B. Brewer, "Research Design and Issues of Validity," in *Handbook of Research Methods in Social and Personality Psychology*, eds. Harry Reis and Charles Judd (Cambridge: Cambridge University Press, 2000); J. Michael Williams, "Everyday Cognition and the Ecological Validity of Intellectual and Neuropsychological Tests," in *Cognitive Approaches to Neuropsychology*, eds. J. Michael Williams and Charles J. Long, (Plenum: New York, 1988), 123–41.

9. Gary Gutting, "Psyching Us Out: The Promises of 'Priming,'" *Opinionator*, accessed November 11, 2013, http://opinionator.blogs.nytimes.com/2013/10/31/psyching-us-out/.

10. See for example Lesley Rogers, *Sexing the Brain* (New York: Columbia University Press, 2001); Cordelia Fine, *Delusions of Gender: How Our Minds, Society, and Neurosexism Create Difference* (New York: W.W. Norton, 2010).

11. Eric Anderson, *The Monogamy Gap: Men, Love, and the Reality of Cheating* (Oxford: Oxford University Press, 2012).

12. Eric Anderson, "'At Least with Cheating There is an Attempt at Monogamy': Cheating and Monogamism among Undergraduate Heterosexual Men," *Journal of Social and Personal Relationships* 27, no. 7 (2010): 851–72.

13. Catherine Hakim, "The Monogamy Gap: Men, Love and the Reality of Cheating by Eric Anderson—Review," *The Guardian*, March 1, 2012, sec. Books, http://www.guardian.co.uk/books/2012/mar/01/monogamy-gap-eric-anderson-review.

14. Vicki Larson, "Why Men Need To Cheat," *Huffington Post*, August 30, 2012, http://www.huffingtonpost.com/vicki-larson/why-men-need-to-cheat_b_1170015.html.

15. Anderson, "At Least with Cheating."

16. Interesting to note by contrast the reception of Dan Savage's talk at the Festival of Dangerous Ideas in the fall of 2013.

17. Anderson, "At Least with Cheating"; Christine Overall, "Monogamy, Nonmonogamy, and Identity," *Hypatia* 13, no. 4 (1998): 1–17; Victoria Robinson, "My Baby Just Cares for Me: Feminism, Heterosexuality and Non-Monogamy," *Journal of Gender Studies* 6, no. 2 (1997): 143–57.

18. While research is ongoing, particularly regarding the mechanisms of influence, several reviews of empirical work suggest overall correlations between entertainment media consumption and the development of sexual attitudes. See L. Monique Ward, "Understanding the Role of Entertainment Media in the Sexual Socialization of American Youth: A Review of Empirical Research," *Developmental Review* 23, no. 3 (September 2003): 347–88; S. Liliana Escobar-Chaves et al., "Impact of the Media on Adolescent Sexual Attitudes and Behaviors," *Pediatrics* (2005): 116–303.

19. Simone de Beauvoir, *The Second Sex* (New York: Knopf, 1953).

20. "Men and Women Can't Be 'Just Friends': Scientific American," accessed March 11, 2013, http://www.scientificamerican.com/article.cfm?id=men-and-women-cant-be-just-friends. See also James Conlon's "Why Lovers Can't Be Friends," in *Sex, Love, and Friendship: Studies of the Society for the Philosophy of Sex and Love: 1993-2003*, ed. Adrianne Leigh McEvoy (Rodopi, 2011), 1–8, and Johann A. Klaassen's rebuttal article, "Friends and Lovers," *Journal of Social Philosophy* 35, no. 3 (2004): 413–19.

21. "Booty Call: How to Spot a Fertile Woman," *LiveScience.com*, accessed March 22, 2013. http://www.livescience.com/10828-booty-call-spot-fertile-woman.html.

22. bell hooks, "Sisterhood: Political Solidarity between Women," *Feminist Review* no. 23 (1986): 125–38; Overall, "Monogamy, Nonmonogamy, and Identity."

23. Annette Baier, "Trust and Antitrust," *Ethics*, 96, no. 2 (1986): 239.

24. Recent review research is found for example in Daniel Bergner's *What Do Women Want? Adventures in the Science of Female Desire* (Ecco, 2013).

25. I want to note first that seeking to ameliorate this situation is not tantamount to advocating for monogamous relationships in general. Nor is it tantamount to giving advice to men or to women as such. Rather, these terms are set in consideration of how people strive to realize and practice a certain set of values in their lives.

26. bell hooks, *All about Love: New Visions* (New York: William Morrow, 2000); Wendy Langford, *Revolutions of the Heart: Gender, Power and the Delusions of Love* (London: Routledge, 2002).

27. Compare with the two senses of commitment discussed by psychologists here: Dominik Schoebi, Benjamin R. Karney, and Thomas N. Bradbury, "Stability and Change in the First 10 Years of Marriage: Does Commitment Confer Benefits Beyond the Effects of Satisfaction?," *Journal of Personality and Social Psychology* 102, no. 4 (2012): 729–42.

28. Ezequiel Di Paolo, "The Phenomenon of Life, by Hans Jonas," *Journal of the British Society for Phenomenology* 36, no. 3 (2005): 340–42.

29. Hans Jonas, *The Phenomenon of Life: Toward a Philosophical Biology* (New York: Harper & Row, 1966), 234.

30. As the foregoing shows, attempting to avoid the "loadedness" of terms like "fidelity" and "commitment" (as Overall's "Monogamy, Nonmonogamy, and Identity" does) is precisely what gets us into the bad science in the first place. Instead we need to consider logically and phenomenologically what these terms entail, namely, values and value-practices with certain conditions.

31. John Kleinig, "Loyalty," *The Stanford Encyclopedia of Philosophy* (Fall 2013 Edition), ed. Edward N. Zalta, http://plato.stanford.edu/archives/fall2013/entries/loyalty/.

32. Annette Baier, "Trust and Antitrust," *Ethics* 96, no. 2 (1986): 231.

33. Overall, "Monogamy, Nonmonogamy, and Identity." She says this is especially true for women.

34. Baier, "Trust and Antitrust," 236.

35. Ezequiel Di Paolo, "Tarkovsky's *Stalker* and the Paradoxes of Non-Linear Decision Making," *Ezequiel Di Paolo Blog*, October 9, 2012, http://ezequiel-dipaolo.wordpress.com/2012/10/09/tarkovskys-stalker-and-the-paradoxes-of-non-linear-decision-making/. Accessed April 13, 2013. For a critical evaluation of dual-process models of moral reasoning, see Mark Johnson, *Morality for Humans* (Chicago: University of Chicago Press, 2013).

36. Antonio R. Damasio, *Descartes' Error: Emotion, Reason, and the Human Brain*, (New York: Putnam, 1994); Antonio R. Damasio, "The Somatic Marker Hypothesis and the Possible Functions of the Prefrontal Cortex [and Discussion]," *Philosophical Transactions of the Royal Society of London. Series B: Biological Sciences* 351, no. 1346 (1996): 1413–20.

37. Damasio, *Descartes' Error*, 174.

38. See e.g. Antonio R. Damasio, *The Feeling of What Happens: Body and Emotion in the Making of Consciousness* (New York: Harcourt Brace, 1999).

39. Damasio, *Descartes' Error*, 173.

40. Damasio, *The Feeling of What Happens*; Don Tucker, *Mind from Body: Experience from Neural Structure* (Oxford: Oxford University Press, 2007).

41. Di Paolo, "Tarkovsky's Stalker." Manuel G. Bedia and Ezequiel Di Paolo, "Unreliable Gut Feelings Can Lead to Correct Decisions: The Somatic Marker Hypothesis in Non-Linear Decision Chains," *Frontiers in Psychology* 3 (2012).

42. Bedia and Di Paolo, *Unreliable Gut Feelings*, 12.

43. Damasio, "Somatic Marker Hypothesis"; Bedia and Di Paolo, "Unreliable Gut Feelings."

44. Daniel Kahneman and Amos Tversky, "Prospect Theory: An Analysis of Decision under Risk," *Econometrica* 47, no. 2 (1979): 263–91.

45. Daniel Kahneman, *Thinking, Fast and Slow* (New York: Farrar, Straus and Giroux, 2011).

46. Anderson, "At Least with Cheating," 859.

47. John Dewey, *Human Nature and Conduct: An Introduction to Social Psychology* (Amherst: Prometheus Books, 2002).

48. Steve Torrance, "In Search of the Enactive: Introduction to Special Issue on Enactive Experience," *Phenomenology and the Cognitive Sciences* 4, no. 4 (2005): 359.

49. Ezequiel Di Paolo, Marieke Rohde, and Hanne De Jaegher, "Horizons for the Enactive Mind: Values, Social Interaction, and Play," in *Enaction: Toward a New Paradigm for Cognitive Science*, eds. John Stewart, Olivier Gapenne, and Ezequiel A. Di Paolo, 33-88 (Cambridge: MIT Press, 2010).

50. Lesley J. Rogers, *Sexing the Brain*.

51. Hanne De Jaegher and Ezequiel Di Paolo, "Participatory Sense-Making," *Phenomenology and the Cognitive Sciences 6, no. 4 (2007)*: 485–507; Thomas Fuchs and Hanne De Jaegher, "Enactive Intersubjectivity: Participatory Sense-making and Mutual Incorporation," *Phenomenology and the Cognitive Sciences* 8, no. 4 (2009): 465–86.

52. bell hooks, *The Will to Change: Men, Masculinity, and Love* (New York: Atria Books, 2004).

53. Giovanna Colombetti and Steve Torrance, "Emotion and Ethics: An Inter-(en) active Approach," *Phenomenology and the Cognitive Sciences* 8, no. 4 (2009): 505–26.

54. De Jaegher, and Di Paolo, "Participatory Sense-Making."

55. Sune Vork Steffensen, "Care and Conversing in Dialogical Systems," *LSC Language Sciences* 34, no. 5 (2012): 519–20.

56. Steffensen, "Caring and Conversing," 519.

57. Steffensen, "Caring and Conversing," 520.

58. I take this term from De Jaegher and Di Paolo: see 2007, 2008, and 2012.

59. William Irwin Thompson, Lindisfarne Association, and Lindisfarne Fellows Conference, "Gaia, a Way of Knowing: Political Implications of the New Biology" (Lindisfarne Press, 1987); Francisco J. Varela, Evan Thompson, and Eleanor Rosch, *The Embodied Mind: Cognitive Science and Human Experience* (Cambridge: MIT Press, 1991).

## BIBLIOGRAPHY

Abrams, Lindsay. "Study: Oxytocin ('the Love Hormone') Makes Men in Relationships Want to Stay Away From Other Women." *The Atlantic*, November 16, 2012. http://www.theatlantic.com/health/archive/2012/11/study-oxytocin-the-love-hormone-makes-men-in-relationships-want-to-stay-away-from-other-women/265314/.

Anderson, Eric. " 'At Least with Cheating There Is an Attempt at Monogamy': Cheating and Monogamism among Undergraduate Heterosexual Men." *Journal of Social and Personal Relationships* 27, no. 7 (2010): 851–72.

———. *The Monogamy Gap: Men, Love, and the Reality of Cheating*. Oxford: Oxford University Press, 2012.

Baier, Annette. "Trust and Antitrust." *Ethics*, 96, no. 2 (1986): 231–60.

de Beauvoir, Simone. *The Second Sex*. Translated and edited by H.M. Parshley. New York: Knopf, 1953.

Bergner, Daniel. *What Do Women Want?: Adventures in the Science of Female Desire*. Ecco, 2013.

Blair, Elaine. " 'What Do Women Want?' by Daniel Bergner." *The New York Times*, June 13, 2013, sec. Books / Sunday Book Review. http://www.nytimes.com/2013/06/16/books/review/what-do-women-want-by-daniel-bergner.html.

"Booty Call: How to Spot a Fertile Woman." *LiveScience.com*. Accessed March 22, 2013. http://www.livescience.com/10828-booty-call-spot-fertile-woman.html.

Brewer, Marilyn B. "Research Design and Issues of Validity." In *Handbook of Research Methods in Social and Personality Psychology*, edited by Harry T. Reis and Charles M. Judd, 3-16. Cambridge: Cambridge University Press, 2000.

Colombetti, Giovanna, andSteve Torrance. "Emotion and Ethics: An Inter-(en) active Approach." *Phenomenology and the Cognitive Sciences* 8, no. 4 (2009): 505–26.

Conlon, James. "Why Lovers Can't Be Friends." In *Sex, Love, and Friendship: Studies of the Society for the Philosophy of Sex and Love: 1993-2003*, edited by Adrianne Leigh McEvoy, 1–8. Rodopi, 2011.

Damasio, Antonio R. *Descartes' Error: Emotion, Reason, and the Human Brain.* New York: Putnam, 1994.

———. *The Feeling of What Happens: Body and Emotion in the Making of Consciousness.* New York: Harcourt Brace, 1999.

———. "The Somatic Marker Hypothesis and the Possible Functions of the Prefrontal Cortex [and Discussion]." *Philosophical Transactions of the Royal Society of London. Series B: Biological Sciences* 351, no. 1346 (1996): 1413–20.

De Jaegher, Hanne, and Ezequiel Di Paolo. "Participatory Sense-Making." *Phenomenology and the Cognitive Sciences* (2007): 485–507.

Di Paolo, Ezequiel. "Tarkovsky's Stalker and the Paradoxes of Non-Linear Decision Making," *Ezequiel Di Paolo Blog,* October 9, 2012, http://ezequieldipaolo.word-press.com/2012/10/09/tarkovskys-stalker-and-the-paradoxes-of-non-linear-decision-making/.

Di Paolo, Ezequiel, Marieke Rohde, and Hanne De Jaegher. "Horizons for the Enactive Mind: Values, Social Interaction, and Play." In *Enaction: Toward a New Paradigm for Cognitive Science,* edited by John Stewart, Olivier Gapenne, and Ezequiel Di Paolo, 33–88. Cambridge: MIT Press, 2010.

Dewey, John. *Human Nature and Conduct: An Introduction to Social Psychology.* Amherst: Prometheus Books, 2002.

Escobar-Chaves, S. Liliana, Susan R. Tortolero, Christine M. Markham, Barbara J. Low, Patricia Eitel, and Patricia Thickstun. "Impact of the Media on Adolescent Sexual Attitudes and Behaviors." *Pediatrics* 2005: 116–303.

Fine, Cordelia. *Delusions of Gender: How Our Minds, Society, and Neurosexism Create Difference.* New York: W.W. Norton, 2010.

Fuchs, Thomas, and Hanne de Jaegher. "Enactive Intersubjectivity: Participatory Sense-making and Mutual Incorporation." *Phenomenology and the Cognitive Sciences* 8, no. 4 (2009): 465–86.

Gutting, Gary. "Psyching Us Out: The Promises of 'Priming.'" *Opinionator.* Accessed November 11, 2013. http://opinionator.blogs.nytimes.com/2013/10/31/psyching-us-out/.

hooks, bell. *All about Love: New Visions.* New York: William Morrow, 2000.

———. "Sisterhood: Political Solidarity between Women." *Feminist Review* no. 23 (1986): 125–38.

———. *The Will to Change: Men, Masculinity, and Love.* New York: Atria Books, 2004.

"In TV Ads, Dumb Has Become the New Clever." *Chicago Tribune.* Accessed April 29, 2013. http://articles.chicagotribune.com/2011-03-08/news/ct-talk-esposito-ads-0308-20110308_1_commercials-hummus-ad.

"Intranasal Application of Oxytocin Appears to Enhance Placebo Response." *ScienceDaily*. Accessed November 11, 2013. http://www.sciencedaily.com/releases/2013/10/131022170630.htm.

Johnson, Mark. *Morality for Humans*. Chicago: University of Chicago Press, 2013.

Jonas, Hans. *The Phenomenon of Life: Toward a Philosophical Biology*. New York: Harper & Row, 1966.

Kahneman, Daniel. *Thinking, Fast and Slow*. New York: Farrar, Straus and Giroux, 2011.

Kahneman, Daniel, and Amos Tversky. "Prospect Theory: An Analysis of Decision under Risk." *Econometrica* 47, no. 2 (1979): 263–91.

Kant, Immanuel. "What Is Enlightenment?," translated by Mary C. Smith. http://www.columbia.edu/acis/ets/CCREAD/etscc/kant.html

Klaassen, Johann A. "Friends and Lovers." *Journal of Social Philosophy* 35, no. 3 (2004): 413–19.

Kleinig, John. "Loyalty," *The Stanford Encyclopedia of Philosophy* (Fall 2013 Edition), edited by Edward N. Zalta. http://plato.stanford.edu/archives/fall2013/entries/loyalty/.

Langford, Wendy. *Revolutions of the Heart: Gender, Power and the Delusions of Love*. London: Routledge, 2002.

"Men and Women Can't Be 'Just Friends.'" *Scientific American*. Accessed March 11, 2013. http://www.scientificamerican.com/article.cfm?id=men-and-women-cant-be-just-friends.

*Men Are Stupid (A Media Study)*, 2012. https://www.youtube.com/watch?v=1ILVL_MLwqI&feature=youtube_gdata_player.

Overall, Christine. "Monogamy, Nonmonogamy, and Identity." *Hypatia* 13, no. 4 (1998): 1–17.

"Oxytocin Hormone Helps with Monogamy, Study Says." *GlobalPost*. Accessed March 22, 2013. http://www.globalpost.com/dispatch/news/science/121114/oxytocin-hormone-helps-monogamy-study-says.

"Oxytocin Keeps Attached Men Away from Hot Women." *NBC News*. Accessed March 22, 2013. http://vitals.nbcnews.com/_news/2012/11/13/15144027-oxytocin-keeps-attached-men-away-from-hot-women.

Robinson, Victoria. "My Baby Just Cares for Me: Feminism, Heterosexuality and Non-Monogamy." *Journal of Gender Studies* 6, no. 2 (1997): 143–57.

Rogers, Lesley J. *Sexing the Brain*. London: Weidenfeld & Nicolson, 1999.

Savage, Dan. *Festival of Dangerous Ideas 2013: Dan Savage - Savage Advice*, 2013. https://www.youtube.com/watch?v=C-laWOpXxC8&feature=youtube_gdata_player.

Scheele, Dirk, Nadine Striepens, Onur Güntürkun, Sandra Deutschländer, Wolfgang Maier, Keith M. Kendrick, and René Hurlemann. "Oxytocin Modulates Social Distance Between Males and Females." *Journal of Neuroscience* 32, no. 46 (2012): 16074–79.

Schoebi, Dominik, Benjamin R. Karney, and Thomas N. Bradbury. "Stability and Change in the First 10 Years of Marriage: Does Commitment Confer Benefits Beyond the Effects of Satisfaction?" *Journal of Personality and Social Psychology* 102, no. 4 (2012): 729–42.

Shure, Caitlin. "Nasal Sprays Offer Therapy with a Sniff: Scientific American." Accessed November 11, 2013. http://www.scientificamerican.com/article.cfm?id=nasal-sprays-offer-therapy-with-a-sniff.

Steffensen, Sune Vork. "Care and Conversing in Dialogical Systems." *LSC Language Sciences* 34, no. 5 (2012): 513–31.

"Study: Hormone Oxytocin May Keep Men Monogamous." *CBS News*. Accessed March 22, 2013. http://www.cbsnews.com/8301-204_162-57549944/hormone-oxytocin-may-keep-men-monogamous-study-suggests/.

Thompson, William Irwin, Lindisfarne Association, and Lindisfarne Fellows Conference. "Gaia, a Way of Knowing: Political Implications of the New Biology." Lindisfarne Press; Distributed by Inner Traditions International, 1987.

Torrance, Steve. "In Search of the Enactive: Introduction to Special Issue on Enactive Experience." *Phenomenology and the Cognitive Sciences* 4, no. 4 (2005): 357–68.

Tucker, Don. *Mind from Body: Experience from Neural Structure*. Oxford: Oxford University Press, 2007.

Varela, Francisco J., Evan Thompson, and Eleanor Rosch. *The Embodied Mind: Cognitive Science and Human Experience*. Cambridge: MIT Press, 1991.

Ward, L. Monique. "Understanding the Role of Entertainment Media in the Sexual Socialization of American Youth: A Review of Empirical Research." *Developmental Review* 23, no. 3 (2003): 347–88.

Williams, J. Michael. "Everyday Cognition and the Ecological Validity of Intellectual and Neuropsychological Tests." In *Cognitive Approaches to Neuropsychology*, edited by J. Michael Williams and Charles J. Long, 123–41. New York: Plenum, 1988.

## Chapter Seven

# The Revolutionary Politics of Love

## *Pussy Riot and Punk Rock as Feminist Practice*

### Fulden Ibrahimhakkioglu

I did not believe that a Cause which stood for a beautiful ideal, for anarchism, for release and freedom from convention and prejudice, should
demand the denial of life and joy. I insisted that our Cause could not expect
me to become a nun and that the movement would not be turned into a
cloister. If it meant that, I did not want it. "I want freedom, the right to
self-expression, everybody's right to beautiful, radiant things." Anarchism
meant that to me, and I would live it in spite of the whole world—prisons,
persecution, everything. Yes, even in spite of the condemnation of my own
closest comrades I would live my beautiful ideal.

—Emma Goldman, *Living My Life*

Pussy Riot is a Russian feminist punk rock collective that has been staging
unauthorized public performances since August 2011. The members wear
balaclavas in bright colors as a playful, punk take on "militant attire" and in
order to ensure anonymity. Their guerilla gigs are recorded, edited, and posted
online as music videos. Their songs are brash, heavy, lo-fi anarcha-punk
songs with angry, expressive singing and a feminist/queer lyrical orientation
that is highly critical of heteronormative patriarchy, the Putin government and
its gradual merging with the Russian Orthodox Church.

Three of the members, 22-year-old Nadezhda Tolokonnikova (a philosophy student), 23-year-old Maria Alyokhina (a student of journalism
and creative writing), and 29-year old Yekaterina Samutsevich (a computer
programmer), were arrested on March 2012, following their impromptu performance at Christ the Savior Cathedral. "Virgin Mary, Mother of God," they
sang, "Banish Putin, we pray thee!"[1] Held in custody until the trial, the three
members were found guilty of "hooliganism motivated by religious hatred"
on August 17, 2012, and sentenced to two years in prison because of what

they called a "punk prayer."[2] In October 2012, Samutsevich was released on probation, following an appeal, and the other two women were separated and sent to prison camps.[3]

By and large framed in terms of a free speech issue by the western media, the Russian media and the court treated the incident as an attack on religion, an act of religious *hatred*. Of course, compared to actual, historical acts of religious hatred (such as the church burnings in Norway in the early 1990s by satanic black metal musicians), Pussy Riot's peaceful protest seems rather harmless. They stated numerous times that their performance was not aimed against religion per se, but against the politically manipulative use of religion in Russia today. The results of the psychological evaluations conducted during their time in prison indicated no signs of hatred or animosity. Far from being a post-adolescent prank on Christianity (as the Russian media made it seem to be for the most part, despite the fact that post-adolescent pranks are not often punished with imprisonment), there is a self-conscious feminist reworking of religion in their punk prayer whereby Virgin Mary is called to "be a feminist" and drive Putin away, so that practice of religion can take place freely without the repressive politics of the Putin government. Mobilizing art as a site of feminist resistance, Pussy Riot's subversive politics is not driven by hatred, but a desire for freedom. This desire is to be understood in relation to "the erotic," described by Audre Lorde as a "source of power and information within our lives."[4] Lorde aligns the erotic with artistic creativity, aesthetic enjoyment, and our inherent capacity for feelings of joy and empowerment that has been corrupted by interlocking systems of oppression. Tapping into the power of the erotic brings about "the energy to pursue genuine change within our world."[5] Pussy Riot's project for social transformation entails precisely this mobilization of the erotic, and their punk rock aesthetics ("angry yet joyful") serves as a tool for this purpose.

By analyzing the affective structures of feminist activism at the conjunction of politics and aesthetics through the example of Pussy Riot, my goal is to problematize some of the common (mis)representations and (mis)interpretations of feminist fury. Feminist fury has been associated with hatred, irrationality, and incivility as a way to silence us and delegitimize our claims. The same rhetoric is being utilized to cover the recent events with Pussy Riot, as a way to dismiss and trivialize their art and politics. As Pussy Riot offers a case where rebellious punk rock could potentially become a vehicle for social change, we confront the role of anger in feminist politics whereby the aforementioned associations and their silencing effect can be undone. Further, anger is instrumental to the positive projects of antioppressive struggles, and cannot by itself sustain a movement or bear productive results. Although essential to feminist struggles, we must reinterpret our anger in its tie to the erotic. Through a reading of the letters, testimonies, and song lyrics by Pussy Riot and some feminist writings on anger, I will suggest that the driving force of our impassioned politics is the erotic, or love, to which anger is instrumental.

This project is informed and motivated by growing scholarship on the politics of emotions/emotions of politics, also known as affect theory. Although I generally keep my analysis restricted to Pussy Riot and feminist activism, when drawing parallels with other kinds of antioppressive struggles, it is important to note that these "structures of feeling," to borrow from Raymond Williams, operate in a context-dependent manner, insofar as they are lived, interpreted, and felt differently within different social and historical contexts.[6] My goal is not to decontextualize anger and love but to highlight their important role in many forms of activism. Audre Lorde's insightful account of the erotic, for example, carves a space where we can ponder how the erotic can tie many different kinds of struggles together. Today, we see many sorts of struggles all over the world taking place in a revolutionary spirit, through which people with very different, sometimes conflicting, concerns come together and organize around quite general, if not largely undefined, terms such as freedom or justice. How are we to understand these heterogeneous social movements? Are they inherently incapable of restructuring mainstream politics because of how dispersed and at times contradictory these concerns are? These are some of the questions about the larger context within which Pussy Riot's activism takes place.

Moreover, the tendency within political theory has been to analyze these struggles in terms of rational actors who make rational decisions and implement particular political agendas, which does not quite capture the ethos of these struggles. Yet far from denying the rationality of the actors, affect theory attempts to highlight the central role of emotions in political struggles. This does not suggest a disconnection between reason and emotion. On the contrary, the insistence on the rational actor theory suggests this divide, insofar as it conceptualizes reason *without* emotion. As Deb Gould writes: "A focus on emotion and feeling, then, need not, and *should* not, negate the rationality of protesters or the political nature of social movements and other forms of activism."[7] Such focus instead provides a more holistic account. The central role of emotions must not be overlooked *especially* in the case of Pussy Riot, a performance art collective. At this particular conjunction of aesthetics and politics, emotions become even more important to analyze. For here, the political functions not only on the register of reason but also on the register of sensibility.

Lastly, when I talk about anger or the erotic, I do not simply refer to subjective feelings or psychological states. Insofar as anger and love comprise a structure of feeling, they create and contribute to a general political atmosphere, which different political actors may very well experience or interpret differently. Yet it is not the subjective experience that is central to my analysis, but the *mood* that gets constructed, which in turn influences those actors who are involved. For this reason, what is important is anger not only as felt by the political actors, but also as represented, understood, and imbued with signification within the larger context.

## FEMINIST LOVE AND SERIOUS ACTIVISM

On March 3, 2013, Tolokonnikova's daughter turned five and celebrated her birthday without her mother for the second time. According to *The Times*, she sent her daughter Gera a letter which "presents a rare glimpse of Tolokonnikova's softer side."[8] Ben Hoyle, the author of the article, notes: "When they stood trial last year she and her co-accused, Maria Alyokhina and Yekaterina Samutsevich, never courted sympathy and radiated a composed sense of commitment to their cause."[9] The insinuation here is that one cannot be a radical, angry, hard-ass feminist (or perhaps any kind of political activist for that matter) and a loving person at the same time, or if one is (for instance, if she is a *mother*, like Tolokonnikova), one's "softer side" could only be caught in the form of "a rare glimpse." Of course, this is a rather strange characterization given that the HBO documentary *Pussy Riot: A Punk Prayer* depicts Tolokonnikova and Alyokhina laughing as they wait before the trial, misreading "cannabis" for "Canada" on a journalist's shirt, and joking that the press will misconstrue their cheerfulness for not taking the trial seriously. Alyokhina then says: "Let's make serious faces."

The call to make serious faces, of course, is a call to play the part. The part must have been well played, given what the article says. The framing of the article is reflective of the public imaginary where the seriousness of one's commitment to a cause demands the exclusion of sympathy, humor, or as Hoyle puts it, "softness." Love is nothing but a sign of weakness, an obstacle for "real" activism, a threat to the demanded seriousness. The birthday letter, in this sense, is strange, unexpected, and out of place. Hoyle expects his readers to be surprised that one of these angry women is also a loving mother. How can one be a loving mother and a serious political activist at the same time? This very sentiment is expressed—in the form of shaming—in one of the questions asked to Tolokonnikova in an interview. "You have a four-year-old daughter, and you must have known going into your performance in the church that arrest was a real possibility. Wasn't that irresponsible toward your child?" asks a reporter for SPIEGEL, a German online news magazine. In her response, Tolokonnikova implies that this is in fact the responsible thing to do, for she is "fighting for [her] daughter to be able to grow up in a free country."[10]

This question, as well as Hoyle's framing, is rooted in the two hundred year western history of sexual division of labor under industrial capitalism, women's confinement to the domestic realm, and the male domination of the public realm to which political activism supposedly belongs. But aside from this history, though perhaps not altogether separate from it, there is another presupposition at work. Activism is associated with seriousness, commitment, and anger, which are supposed to be the antithesis of cheerfulness, sympathy, and love. The suggestion here is that the former requires the lack of emotional bonds and any deep sense of connection with others (in short, a lack of vulnerability and care). We must ask why this is so. For it is troubling to think that the political actors are not motivated by these positive feelings, and only negative ones. It not only pathologizes activism but also suggests that any social and political change would be brought about by those who deprived themselves of love, care, and vulnerability.

Yet there is, of course, much more to activism than is suggested by this false binary. As Todd May suggests, "t.here can be no such thing as a sad revolutionary. To seek to change the world is to offer a new form of life-celebration."[11] The necessity for the activist to choose both sides at once, to change the world and to celebrate life, maps onto the two primary affects that move politics: anger and love. Even though world-changing anger is most often the focal point of the conversation when it comes to social movements (in the way in which riots or uprisings are represented in the media, for instance), it is in fact only half of the story. I intend to tell the other half here that most often gets pushed aside as accidental or inessential or not "serious" enough. The fact of the matter is that love is, and must be, central to political activism,[12] and anger only instrumental to love. Love and anger are not only intimately tied in this respect, but they also *together* keep political struggles going. Deb Gould, for example, talks about the sexually charged, joyful atmosphere of ACT UP meetings in conjunction with the confrontational methods employed in ACT UP protests. ACT UP led to the establishment of supportive communities in the midst of AIDS crisis in the 1990s. It is not anger *without* love, or love *without* anger, but precisely their very coincidence that provides impetus for many antioppressive struggles.

## THE POLITICS OF THE EROTIC AND PUSSY RIOT'S PROJECT OF BRINGING JOY

But what does love have to do with politics? In his letter to Carlos Quijano, the founder of the influential Uruguayan newspaper *Marcha*, Che Guevara writes: "At the risk of seeming ridiculous, let me say that the true revolutionary is guided by great feelings of love."[13] He continues: "It is impossible to think of a genuine revolutionary lacking this quality. Perhaps it is one of the great dramas of the leader that he or she must combine a passionate spirit with a cold intelligence and make painful decisions without flinching."[14] Love, which Che calls the "moving force" for the revolutionary, is irreducible to "small doses of daily affection," and it must be made "one and indivisible."[15] Love must be "idealized" into "love of the people, of the most sacred causes," "love of living humanity," and "transformed into actual deeds, into acts that serve as examples."[16] Love, then, is not only an interpersonal affair for Che, but a *political practice* that is essential for social transformation. It is entailed by any project of disalienation, defined as "the full realization as a human creature."[17] One's strangeness to herself, her labor can only be undone through political practices of love. In this process, Che writes, "[a] person begins to become free from thinking of the annoying fact that one needs to work to satisfy one's animal needs. Individuals start to see themselves reflected in their work and to understand their full stature as human beings ... Work ... becomes an expression of oneself."[18] The "necessities" of life, thereby, are no longer lived as an obstacle. Eradicating the effects of the capitalist logic of need, desire, and lack brings about the human capacity for enjoyment. The question for the revolutionary becomes: instead of suffering through life, why not celebrate it? Celebration here is a form of resistance; it is to create new possibilities for life, for human flourishing, against and in the face of suffering and decadence. The process of disalienation, then, is a process of rejuvenation: it is a rediscovering of joy, health, and energy, a reclaiming of our innermost drives, our will to life. It engenders a Nietzschean philosophy of joy and life affirmation through political praxis. This names an erotic politics that is not only concerned with survival, but with joy, enjoyment, pleasure, and fulfillment.

The erotic, Lorde explains, does not only pertain to sexuality,[19] but is "a resource within each of us" that is applicable to all spheres of life when activated. Lorde writes "When released from its intense and constrained pellet, [the erotic] flows through and colors my life with a kind of energy that heightens and sensitizes and strengthens all my experience."[20] It is that empowering, rejuvenating energy that has been dulled by systems of oppression, which must be recovered for any project of resistance. A significant part of being oppressed, for Lorde, is the suppression of this capacity for feeling, and especially joy. This could take many forms. As in the example of alienation, I may be incapacitated to enjoy myself, my labor or my life in a menial job. I may be pathologized in my enjoyment of certain bodies under heteronormativity. I may be left with despair, in paralyzing boredom and depression, if all that the world is willing to give me is cruelty and bitterness. Yet a part of many anti-oppressive political struggles is this reclaiming of our capacity for joy, collectively and individually, through a joyful coming together, and thus a recovery and mobilization of the erotic. This is the very project undertaken by Pussy Riot.

Tolokonnikova states in her court defense:

> I am a member of Pussy Riot. I was there when the group developed its idea of performance. The girls said that if we put on dark balaclavas people would think we are bad people. But we're good, friendly people. *We bring joy to the world.* We wear bright neon masks, or as the prosecution calls them, acidic colors. *We are jokers, jesters, holy fools* and bear no ill will towards anyone.[21]

How is that the case for a serious activist who never courts sympathy and radiates "a composed sense of commitment to [her] cause"?[22] Far from suggesting that we should not take Pussy Riot seriously, Tolokonnikova reworks our sedimented notion of militancy, particularly through the example of the kind of balaclavas they wear. Dark facemasks read too criminal, too "terrorist"-like. Yet Pussy Riot's goal is not to bring terror. It is not to offend or harm, but to bring *joy*. Yet she suggests that *this* is what people are offended by, what they cannot stand. But why?

Lorde talks about the disruptive potential the erotic entails for political change. She writes: "In order to perpetuate itself, every oppression must corrupt or distort those various sources of power within the culture of the oppressed that can provide energy for change."[23] The suppression of the erotic (which she defines as "a source of power and information,"[24] "an assertion of the lifeforce of women,"[25] "the nurturer or nursemaid of all our deepest knowledge,"[26] "open and fearless undermining of my capacity for joy,"[27] sharing of that joy[28]) has resulted in the oppression of women. "[O]nce we begin to feel deeply all the aspects of our lives," Lorde writes, "we begin to demand from ourselves and from our life-pursuits that they feel in accordance with that joy which we know ourselves to be capable of."[29] The power of the erotic, then, comes not only from an inner feeling of empowerment that brings about fulfillment and life-affirmation. It also comes from the energy the erotic yields "to pursue genuine change within our world, rather than merely settling for a shift of characters in the same weary drama."[30] "For as we begin to recognize our deepest feelings," Lorde writes, "we begin to give up, of necessity, being satisfied with suffering and self-negation, and with the numbness which so often seems like their only alternative in our society."[31] And this refusal to settle is not only a state-of-mind, nor is it divorced from material reality. It gets translated into political action that can potentially rearrange and reconfigure the structural conditions. Rejecting the dichotomy between spiritual and the political, Lorde then places the erotic at the center of political struggles as their moving force: "the bridge which connects [the spiritual and the political] is formed by the erotic—the sensual—those physical, emotional, and psychic expressions of what is deepest and strongest and richest within each of us, being shared: the passions of love, in its deepest meanings."[32]

*The passions of love*. In its deepest meanings. The erotic, as Lorde reminds us, comes from the Greek *eros*, sensual, passionate love, or as she puts it, "personification of love in all its aspects—born of Chaos, and personifying creative power and harmony."[33] Love is the very source of that intense joy that comes with the pursuit and realization of erotic possibilities. This joy, then, is not that of the isolated individual, but comes precisely from relations: how we relate to others, ourselves, our work and life. The politics of the erotic involves the implementation of this intense feeling into political practice, the pursuit of social change as guided by the erotic. This is performed by Pussy Riot in their aesthetic/political project.[34] At the heart of their subversive project lies a will to life, love, and joy.

In her letter to Slavoj Žižek, Tolokonnikova characterizes Pussy Riot in the following way:

> Borrowing Nietzsche's definition, we are the children of Dionysus, sailing in a barrel and not recognising any authority ... We are a part of this force that has no final answers or absolute truths, for our mission is to question. There are architects of apollonian statics and there are (punk) singers of dynamics and transformation.[35]

The Dionysian names the artistic impulse of intoxication, ecstasy, sensuality, excess, and self-dissolution in Nietzsche's *The Birth of Tragedy*. The Dionysian is driven by passions, like the erotic. It is in tension with the critical distance required by the Apollonian, and for Nietzsche, Greek tragedy comes out of this very tension. Tolokonnikova here highlights the disruptive forms the Dionysian impulse can take (as opposed to the order-seeking Apollonian), and the transformative possibilities this yields. Yet besides the destructive potential he embodies, Dionysus is also the god of wine—a festive, celebratory god; a god who embodies some erotic possibilities, by means of passion, by means of enjoyment.

The transformation of the political in Tolokonnikova's account depends on the interplay of Dionysian artists and what she calls the "architects of apollonian statics." This attests to the cyclical movement from construction to destruction, and then to reconstruction. She locates Pussy Riot in the spirit of Dionysus, as joyous disrupters, both world-changing and life-celebrating, radiating passion and erotic energy. *Jokers, jesters, holy fools*, but dangerous, precisely because of the excessive, disruptive force that comes from Dionysus, an erotic god.

## ANGER AND LOVE

What happens, then, to anger, if love is at the center of activism? Anger inarguably holds an important place for political movements, for it is most often the fuel of those movements. Deb Gould, for instance, explains the process of turning *grief* of losing loved ones to AIDS into *anger* against the government in the context of ACT UP. This anger, she suggests, is what mobilized the masses and kept them going. Even though anger is probably the most visible and relatable emotion when it comes to political activism, it by itself may not be adequate to sustain movements in the absence of a positive project. Gould talks about the emergence of new communities of support and care that resulted from the coexistence of anger and joy in ACT UP's protests. She notes that it was not only anger, but the joy of being together, side by side, that led to a strong, flourishing movement. Anger's critical role in the movement was supplemented by an atmosphere of love, joy, and belonging, attesting to the instrumental value of anger for social movements. In such movements, anger is intimately tied to the erotic. The disruptive project must then rest on some kind of a positive project of reconstruction. Gould names this "collective world-making."[36] She reports that ACT UP New York member Maxine Wolfe "pointed to the 'combination of serious politics and joyful living' as one of ACT UP's greatest qualities."[37] This gives us hope in that an international imagined community of angry/joyful women has been formed by Pussy Rioters, yet time will show, of course, how far this will go.

In this section, I discuss anger and its relation to love, as embodied by Pussy Riot specifically, but also in the context of feminist politics at large. Anger often comes up in Pussy Riot's testimonies, interviews, letters, and song lyrics in relation to their politics. It has a strategic function for their activism. In a letter that Tolokonnikova wrote for her supporters while she was being held in custody before the trial, she writes: "It is not the fact that I am in prison that makes me angry. I hold no grudge. I feel no personal anger. But I do feel political anger."[38] This "political anger" that is felt by Pussy Rioters has been transferred to and mobilized groups and individuals on an international scale whereby it "brought together forces so multi-directional,"[39] connecting the personal to the political, her letter tells us. "Whatever the verdict for Pussy Riot, we and you have already won," she continues, "Because we have learned to be angry and speak politically."[40]

Here, it is the sharing of anger that mobilizes people. Social movements organize around this sharing of anger. Anger has the effect of bridging the personal and the political, for there is something personal at stake as expressed in my anger, my passionate involvement. Anger here is a driving force of impassioned politics; it is an affect that reaches out to bring about change.

The mobilizing effect of anger is also expressed in the Pussy Riot song "Putin Got Scared," as they sing: "Live on Red Square/Show the freedom of civil anger."[41] It is not only that a politics fueled with anger brings about the freedom called for, whatever that may be. But there is an even more intimate link between freedom and anger suggested here. To show the freedom of civil anger means that anger *is* already a practice of freedom. In other words, as people give themselves to rage, they are engaging in a liberatory practice. This is so because anger rests on a shift in perspective, a certain realization or coming to an understanding. Just as the feminist consciousness-raising groups in the 1970s renamed the widespread depression women were feeling as "anger" that lead to a shift in the experience of that emotion, Pussy Riot here calls people to recognize their anger *as anger* and embrace it as a liberatory practice. And if they are not angry, they *must* be, because something is seriously wrong here. In a sense, anger is a claim for justice.

As the primary affective mode of punk rock as feminist practice, anger is both disruptive and creative. It disrupts the sedimented modes of being, seeing, thinking, feeling, and gives way to new ones. It is in this sense that anger by itself is a liberatory practice, for it brings one's desires into question. And it is precisely here that anger is linked to the erotic, insofar as "[i]n touch with the erotic, I become less willing to accept powerlessness, or those other supplied states of being which are not native to me, such as resignation, despair, self-effacement, depression, self-denial."[42] Thus, anger expresses the refusal to settle for anything less than the standard set by the erotic, a standard that often comes with a fantasy embodied by the erotic. Here I use "fantasy" not simply in opposition to the real, but as an *excess* of the real, which is in line with Butler's description of fantasy as that which "allows us to imagine ourselves and others otherwise; it establishes the possible in excess of the real; it points elsewhere, and when it is embodied, it brings the elsewhere home."[43] The erotic and its fantasy are the means of access to that beyond. What Tolokonnikova names "political" anger, then, is a claim for justice, in the very excess, to lay a claim to that beyond. In this sense, anger can hardly be reduced to senseless, blind rage in the way that it operates in such social movements: it is not altogether disconnected from reason.

This linking between anger and the erotic, a linking that relays a sense of affective rationality within political agency, again shows the instrumental value of anger for social movements, but it also highlights anger's link to a positive project, however undefined or vague that may sometimes be. Yet if we look at how Pussy Riot's anger has been interpreted, we see that it is misread as hatred by the court (as they were found guilty of "hooliganism motivated by religious hatred"). This willful misreading is not uncommon: the depiction of the angry feminist as a man-hater is all too familiar. Far from being a harmless caricature, this stereotype has not only been sedimented in the public imaginary now, but it also obscures the central position love holds for feminist movements, as discussed in the previous section. As Tolokonnikova puts it in SPIEGEL interview, "I love Russia, but I hate Putin." And that hatred of Putin's despotism only follows from that love, from the erotic at the heart of feminist politics.

The misconstrual of Pussy Riot's anger as hate indicates a larger problem. Just as Audre Lorde's anger as a black woman was unpalatable to white feminists when she wrote about her anger in the 1980s, the trope of the furious woman to this day stands as feminism's Other. Hence, it is not surprising to read hateful, misogynistic comments about Pussy Riot's performance such as the following: "This video is intolerable. If I wanted to hear angry Russian women yelling all the time, I would have ordered a bride from a catalog and made her life miserable for several decades."[44] It is precisely anger that makes feminism and punk rock so unpalatable, yet this obscures the fact that the anger of both is reactive, or better, responsive. Virginia Woolf explains this process in terms of a transmission of affect.

In *A Room of One's Own*, in order to address the question of women and fiction, Woolf reads some works written on women by men. As she reads a book that makes the case for the inferiority of women, she catches herself getting angry, and begins wondering why. She imagines the author as an angry man, and suggests that she "had been angry because he was angry."[45] The anger of the author is transmitted to the reader. "If he had written dispassionately about women," Woolf explains, "had used indisputable proofs to establish his argument and had shown no trace of wishing that the result should be one thing rather than another, one would not have been angry either. One would have accepted the fact, as one accepts the fact that a pea is green or a canary yellow."[46] Yet it is precisely because the text was laden with anger, with hateful, misogynistic rage, that Woolf finds herself feeling the anger of the author. Woolf's anger, consequently, is reactive, not original, but in general, feminist anger is a responsive. It is amazing how often this simple fact gets overlooked.

Similarly, Lorde explains her own anger as an internalization of "Hatred, that societal deathwish directed against us from the moment we were born Black and female in America."[47] One finds oneself to be cruel, hateful, as "[e]choes of [this Hatred] returns as cruelty and anger in our dealings with each other. For each of us bears the face that hatred seeks, and we have each learned to be at home with cruelty because we have survived so much of it within our own lives."[48] It is racist, heteropatriarchal hatred that engenders the furious feminist, anti-racist subject insofar as she comes to feminism and anti-racism in responding to the hatred of racism and sexism. Thus, when Tolokonnikova speaks of "learning to be angry," this is what she refers to. "Anger seems to be a reaction to being thwarted, frustrated or harmed,"

Marilyn Frye writes. "The frustrating situations which generate anger, as opposed to those which merely make you displeased or depressed, are those in which you see yourself not simply as obstructed or hindered, but as wronged. You become angry when you see the obstruction or hindrance as *unjust* or *unfair*."[49] One arrives at anger by way of confronting an injustice, as a means of survival in the face of a deep-seated hatred, but that confrontation only comes *after* one learns to see this injustice as an injustice. In each of these feminist accounts of anger, anger is entailed by responsiveness and care, but also (by virtue of anger's tie to the erotic) love.

Love is the driving force even in Valerie Solanas's *SCUM Manifesto*, a paragon of feminist fury, a piece many consider to be a man-hating rant at best and a feminist program devised by a deranged, homicidal woman at worst. Perhaps I am being cynical here by referring to Solana's, as she sees the solution for women's liberation in the total elimination of men. Yet strangely enough, this text that celebrates violence, despises proper etiquette, and lays out a feminist agenda of killing men is ultimately *not* driven by hatred. Solana's makes it clear in the climactic statement of the text that the real project here is *love*: "In actual fact, the female function is to explore, discover, invent, solve problems, crack jokes, make music—*all with love*. In other words, create a magic world."[50]

Many say that *SCUM Manifesto* was not meant to be taken seriously, although Solana's did put some of her ideas into practice when she shot Andy Warhol. This uncertainty regarding whether or not she was serious captures precisely the performative ambiguity of the text. And of course, strictly speaking, we cannot take seriously this ironic piece of writing laden with exaggerations and sensationalizing statements. Yet it is striking that feminist anger here in its ultimate extremity still aligns itself with love. It is the inherent incapability of love, for Solana's, that makes the male subhuman, thus dispensable: "The male is completely egocentric, trapped inside himself, incapable of empathizing or identifying with others, of love, friendship, affection or tenderness. He is a completely isolated unit, incapable of rapport with anyone."[51] The essential problem with the male that Solana's locates in the caricature of the masculine she presents is the inability to love. What is at stake here, then, in the end is love.

A performance artist herself, this manifesto written by Solana's represents feminist anger at its extremity, yet is still ultimately driven by love. The ethos of the manifesto lives on in some of the contemporary acts of feminist punk,[52] one of which is Pussy Riot. The main project for both Solana's and Pussy Riot is to "create a magic world," and feminist fury emerges as a political practice of love in the service of that creation. The term "grrrl love" coined by the riot grrrl movement that began in the late 1980s and early 1990s in the Pacific Northwest (and with which Pussy Riot is self-affiliated)[53] captures nicely the association.

There is a practice of love, philogyny, but it comes with a growl. One needs the growl insofar as anger and love coexist in feminist politics.

As Frye puts it, "The maintenance of phallocratic reality requires that the attention of women be focused on men and men's projects—the play; and that attention not be focused on women—the stagehands. Woman-loving, as a spontaneous and habitual orientation of attention is then, both directly and indirectly, inimical to the maintenance of that reality."[54] The anti-phallocratic practices of grrrl love within the riot grrrl movement included lesbianism, encouraging women to form bands, teaching each other to play instruments, having support groups where women can voice and discuss their problems, and playing shows where the stage would be surrounded by women. One flyer passed to the audience before a Bikini Kill show in England that invites women to stand by the stage explains this philogynic practice of reorienting attention: "I really wanna look at female faces while I perform. I want HER to know that she is included in this show, that what we are doing is for her to CRITISIZE/LAUGH AT/BE INSPIRED BY/HATE/WHATEVER... Because this is our fucking show; the GIRLS, the QUEERS, the WIMPS, the OUTCASTS..."[55] These practices have created a new community of young women who became politically engaged through the feminist practices of love. They were furious, but hate was not the primary affect that guided that fury. The real disruptive potential of fury lies in love.

Although Pussy Riot undertakes punk rock as feminist practice in different ways than the riot grrrls of the nineties,[56] the politics of anger and love function in punk rock as feminist practice in an analogous fashion. The rebellion, the anger … The thrill of saying "no" and the joy of saying "yes" … The erotic possibilities… Ideas seem to travel across borders through affects.

## CONCLUSION

Punk rock today as a feminist practice mobilizes performance art for political purposes. In so doing, it not only grants visibility to feminist issues, but also gives way to the emergence of certain structures of feeling that *move* politics, to borrow from Deb Gould. Pussy Riot's unauthorized performances offer an important example of this practice today, in terms of their use of joyful anger and the mobilization of the erotic. Pussy Riot opens up a space for people "to learn to be angry and speak politically." This process of coming to anger is a central political concern, as it not only paves the way for change, but is also a practice of freedom in its own right. Pussy Riot's politics reveal something important about feminist fury: that it is not driven by hatred, but primarily love and desire for freedom. In this sense, within feminist movements and many other anti-oppressive struggles, anger is deeply rooted in the erotic. Even though the erotic often gets overshadowed by displays of anger, it is nonetheless central to feminist activism and to Pussy Riot's performance art. For all these reasons, Pussy Riot's feminism and its transformative force ought not be underestimated.


## POSTSCRIPT

Since I wrote this piece in March 2013, Alyokhina and Tolokonnikova have been released from prison on December 23, 2013, under an amnesty law. They have since made a stage appearance in Amnesty International's Bringing Human Rights Home concert in Brooklyn, NY where they were introduced by Madonna, and made a cameo appearance in the television series *House of Cards* in 2015, whose end credits featured a song they wrote in English entitled "Don't Cry Genocide" (a song which Tolokonnikova stated is devoted to "the militarization of society and to American drones in particular"[57]). They also toured the United States giving talks on their experience as activists, performers, and former prisoners. These talks were entitled "A Conversation with Pussy Riot" and the tickets were sold for rather steep prices. In response other anonymous members of Pussy Riot published an open letter on February 2014 stating that Alyokhina and Tolokonnikova were no longer a part of the collective, as they have betrayed some of the collective's ideals and principles. The collective stated: "We belong to leftist anti-capitalist ideology—we charge no fees for viewing our art-work, all our videos are distributed freely on the web, the spectators to our performances are always spontaneous passersby, and we never sell tickets to our 'shows.'"[58]

While it may be important to use some media outlets to bring attention to important issues, it would not be a stretch to suggest that Alyokhina and Tolokonnikova have been cashing in on the attention they have received since their prison release, whereas the collective itself has been more or less left behind. While the name Pussy Riot has by now become identical with Alyokhina and Tolokonnikova, it is my hope that this piece about Pussy Riot is not read as focusing merely on these two individuals but rather as pertaining to the larger collective that Pussy Riot originally named, especially in its link to feminist punk rock activism at large. I wrote this piece as a fellow feminist, philosopher, activist, and punk musician/performer, and I intended it to be an analysis of the political relevance of the affects of anger and love to feminist activism, particularly as can be observed in contemporary punk rock formations. Despite the recent developments I note above, I believe that the argument put forth by the piece still stands. Anger is instrumental to a revolutionary politics of love as expressed and practiced in feminist punk rock, notwithstanding the susceptibility of political art to being coopted by the global capitalist machinery.

# NOTES

1. Pussy Riot, "Punk Prayer," translated by Carol Rumens, *The Guardian*, August 20, 2012. http://www.guardian.co.uk/books/2012/aug/20/pussy-riot-punk-prayer-lyrics accessed: March 20, 2013).

2. BBC News, "Pussy Riot Members Jailed for Two Years for Hooliganism." See reference: August 17, 2012. http://www.bbc.co.uk/news/world-europe-19297373. (accessed: March 20, 2013).

3. James Brooke, "Russia Frees One Punk Rocker, Keeps Two in Jail." see bibliography: Voice of America News, October 10, 2012. http://www.voanews.com/content/russian-courtreleases-pussy-riot-member/1523761.html. (accessed: March 20, 2013).

4. Audre Lorde, "Uses of the Erotic: The Erotic as Power," in *Sister Outsider* (Berkeley: The Crossing Press, 2007), 53.

5. Ibid, 59.

6. Raymond Williams, "Structures of Feeling," in *Marxism and Literature* (Oxford: Oxford University Press, 1977), 128–35.

7. Deb Gould, *Moving Politics: Emotion and ACT UP's Fight against AIDS*, (Chicago: University of Chicago Press, 2009), 17.

8. Ben Hoyle, "Agony of Nadezhda Tolokonnikova's Birthday Letter to Her Daughter," *The Times*, March 5, 2013. http://www.thetimes.co.uk/tto/news/world/europe/article3705450.ece. Accessed: March 20, 2013.

9. Ibid.

10. Nadezhda Tolokonnikova, interview by SPIEGEL, September 3, 2012. http://www.spiegel.de/international/world/spiegel-interview-with-pussy-riot-activist-nadezhda-tolokonnikova-a-853546.html. Accessed: March 20, 2013.

11. Todd May, "To Change the World, To Celebrate Life," *Philosophy & Social Criticism*, 31, nos. 5/6 (2005): 529.

12. I must note that the account I give here of political activism is mainly limited to left-wing struggles.

13. Che Guevara, "Socialism and Man in Cuba," in *Che Guevara Reader: Writings on Politics and Revolution* (Colombia: Ocean Press, 2012), 225.

14. Ibid., 225–26.

15. Ibid., 226.

16. Ibid., 226.

17. Ibid., 220.

18. Ibid.

19. Though she notes that it has been reduced to sexuality in our culture, reduced to what she calls the pornographic, which she explains in terms of "sensation without feeling."

20. Lorde, "Uses of the Erotic," 57.

21. *Pussy Riot: A Punk Prayer,* dir. Mike Lerner and Maxim Pozdorovkin (HBO Documentary Films, 2013), emphasis added.

22. Hoyle, "Agony of Nadezhda Tolokonnikova's Birthday Letter to Her Daughter."

23. Lorde, "Uses of the Erotic," 57.

24. Ibid.
25. Ibid., 55.
26. Ibid., 56.
27. Ibid.
28. The erotic is not about individualistic pleasures, desires or enjoyment. It is, for Lorde, fundamentally about relations with others, about sharing.
29. Ibid., 57.
30. Ibid., 59.
31. Ibid., 58.
32. Ibid., 56.
33. Ibid., 55.
34. It must be noted, of course, that Lorde delivered this paper on 1978. She is concerned with a specific historical and cultural context. Yet insofar as the erotic is linked to art (and, for Lorde, especially to poetry), one can see it operating in many other contexts. In her writing, although she is mindful of the influence of culture and history, the erotic reads more as a human capacity for creative possibilities and resistance than a context-dependent idea. Typically, Lorde writes from experience is Lorde's habit from writing from experience, putting her heart and soul the paper, rather than providing an aloof, disinterested analysis that lacks flesh and blood.
35. Nadezhda Tolokonnikova, "Nadezhda Tolokonnikova of Pussy Riot's Prison Letters to Slavoj Žižek," *The Guardian*, November 15, 2013. http://www.theguardian.com/music/2013/nov/15/pussy-riot-nadezhda-tolokonnikova-slavoj-zizek. Accessed: November 18, 2013.
36. Gould, *Moving Politics*, 158.
37. Ibid., 183.
38. Nadezhda Tolokonnikova, "Letter from Pre-Trial Detention Facility No. 6," trans. by Katya Kumkova, *Chtodelat News*, August 16, 2012 (published the next day). http://chtodelat.wordpress.com/2012/08/17/nadezhda-tolokonnikova-letter-from-jail/. Accessed: March 20, 2013.
39. Ibid.
40. Miriam Elder, "Pussy Riot Member Condemns Putin's Russia ahead of Verdict," *The Guardian*, August 16, 2012. http://www.guardian.co.uk/music/2012/aug/16/pussy-riot-putin-russia-court-verdict. Accessed: March 20, 2013
41. Pussy Riot, "Putin Got Scared," *The St. Petersburg Times*, trans. Sergey Chernov, February 1, 2012. http://sptimes.ru/index.php?action_id=2&story_id=35092. Accessed: March 20, 2013
42. Lorde, "Uses of the Erotic," 58.
43. Judith Butler, *Undoing Gender* (New York: Routledge, 2004), 29.
44. Carles, "Pussy Riot Desperately Tries to Keep Their Dead Meme Alive with Dumb Westerners," *Hipster Runoff*, September 20, 2012. http://www.hipsterrunoff.com/altreport/2012/09/pussy-riot-desperately-tries-keep-their-dead-meme-alive-dumb-westerners.html. Accessed: March 20, 2013.
45. Virginia Woolf, *A Room of One's Own* (Fort Washington: Harvest Books, 2005), 34.
46. Ibid.

47. Lorde, *Sister Outsider*, 146.

48. Ibid.

49. Marilyn Frye, *The Politics of Reality: Essays in Feminist Theory* (Trumansburg: The Crossing Press, 1983), 85.

50. Valerie Solana's, *SCUM Manifesto* (London: The Matriarchy Study Group, 1983), 13.

51. Ibid., 1-2.

52. Swedish anarcha-feminist punk band Solana's Cunts, for example.

53. See footnote 55.

54. Frye, *The Politics of Reality*, 172.

55. Julia Downes, "The Expansion of Punk Rock: Riot Grrrl Challenges to Gender Power Relations in British Indie Subcultures," *Women's Studies* 41–42 (2012): 226.

56. In an interview they gave to Chernov, Sergey, they talk about the differences and similarities in the following way: "What we have in common is impudence, politically loaded lyrics, the importance of feminist discourse, non-standard female image. The difference is that Bikini Kill performed at specific music venues, while we hold unsanctioned concerts. On the whole, Riot Grrrl was closely linked to Western cultural institutions, whose equivalents don't exist in Russia." Chernov, Sergey. "Female Fury," *The St. Petersburg Times*, Issue 1693, February 1, 2012, http://sptimes.ru/index.php?action_id=2&story_id=35092. Accessed: March 20, 2013.

57. Jason Guerrasio, "Pussy Riot Makes a Bold Cameo in 'House of Cards' Season 3," *Business Insider*, March 3 2015. http://www.businessinsider.com/house-of-cards-pussy-riot-2015-3. Accessed: May 29, 2016.

58. Jenn Pelly, "Nadia Tolokonnikova and Masha Alyokhina No Longer Members of Pussy Riot," *Pitchfork*, February 6, 2014. http://pitchfork.com/news/53860-nadia-tolokonnikova-and-masha-alyokhina-no-longer-members-of-pussy-riot/. Accessed: May 29, 2016.

## BIBLIOGRAPHY

Alyokhina, Maria, Nadezhda Tolokonnikova, and Yekaterina Samutsevich. "Closing Statements." *N+1 Magazine*, Translated by Maria Corrigan & Elena Glazov-Corrigan. August 13, 2012. http://nplusonemag.com/pussy-riot-closing-statements. Accessed: March 20, 2013.

Brooke, James. "Russia Frees One Punk Rocker, Keeps Two in Jail." *Voice of America News*, October 10, 2012. http://www.voanews.com/content/russian-court-releases-pussy-riot-member/1523761.html. Accessed: March 20, 2013.

Butler, Judith. *Undoing Gender*. New York: Routledge, 2004.

Carles, "Pussy Riot Desperately Tries to Keep Their Dead Meme Alive with Dumb Westerners." *Hipster Runoff*, September 20, 2012. http://www.hipsterrunoff.com/altreport/2012/09/pussy-riot-desperately-tries-keep-their-dead-meme-alive-dumb-westerners.html. Accessed: March 20, 2013.

Chehonadskih, Maria. "What Is Pussy Riot's 'Idea'?" *Radical Philosophy* 176, (Nov./ Dec. 2012). http://www.radicalphilosophy.com/commentary/what-is-pussy-riots-idea. Accessed: March 20, 2013.

Chernov, Sergey. "Female Fury." *The St. Petersburg Times*, Issue 1693, February 1, 2012. http://sptimes.ru/index.php?action_id=2&story_id=35092. Accessed: March 20, 2013.

Downes, Julia. "The Expansion of Punk Rock: Riot Grrrl Challenges to Gender Power Relations in British Indie Subcultures." *Women's Studies* 41–42, 2012.

Elder, Miriam. "Pussy Riot Member Condemns Putin's Russia ahead of Verdict." *The Guardian*, August 16, 2012. http://www.guardian.co.uk/music/2012/aug/16/pussy-riot-putin-russia-court-verdict. Accessed: March 20, 2013.

Frye, Marilyn. *The Politics of Reality: Essays in Feminist Theory*. Trumansburg: The Crossing Press, 1983.

Goldman, Emma. *Living My Life*. CreateSpace Independent Publishing Platform, 2011.

Gould, Deb. *Moving Politics: Emotion and ACT UP's Fight against AIDS*. Chicago: University of Chicago Press, 2009.

Guerrasio, Jason. "Pussy Riot Makes a Bold Cameo in 'House of Cards' Season 3," *Business Insider*. March 3, 2015. http://www.businessinsider.com/house-of-cards-pussy-riot-2015-3. Accessed: May 29, 2016.

Guevara, Che. "Socialism and Man in Cuba." In *Che Guevara Reader: Writings on Politics and Revolution*. Colombia: Ocean Press, 2012.

Hoyle, Ben. "Agony of Nadezhda Tolokonnikova's Birthday Letter to Her Daughter." *The Times*, March 5, 2013. http://www.thetimes.co.uk/tto/news/world/europe/article3705450.ece. Accessed: March 20, 2013.

Lorde, Audre. In *Sister Outsider*. Berkeley: The Crossing Press, 2007.

———. "Uses of the Erotic: Erotic as Power." In *Sister Outsider*. Berkeley: The Crossing Press, 2007.

Malpas, Anna. "Pussy Riot Women Disown Husband as Group's Spokesman." The Daily Star Lebanon, October 12, 2012. http://www.dailystar.com.lb/News/International/2012/Oct-12/191169-pussy-riot-women-disown-husband-as-groups-spokesman.ashx#axzz2JPtMhSNn. Accessed: March 20, 2013.

May, Todd. "To Change the World, To Celebrate Life." *Philosophy & Social Criticism*, 31, nos. 5–6 (2005): 517–31.

Pelly, Jenn. "Nadia Tolokonnikova and Masha Alyokhina No Longer Members of Pussy Riot." *Pitchfork*, February 6, 2014. http://pitchfork.com/news/53860-nadia-tolokonnikova-and-masha-alyokhina-no-longer-members-of-pussy-riot/. Accessed: May 29, 2016.

Pussy Riot. "Punk Prayer." Translated by Carol Rumens. *The Guardian*, August 20, 2012. http://www.guardian.co.uk/books/2012/aug/20/pussy-riot-punk-prayer-lyrics. Accessed: March 20, 2013.

———. "Putin Got Scared." Translated by Sergey Chernov. *The St. Petersburg Times*, February 1, 2012. http://sptimes.ru/index.php?action_id=2&story_id=35092. Accessed: March 20, 2013.

*Pussy Riot: A Punk Prayer.* Directed by Mike Lerner and Maxim Pozdorovkin. HBO Documentary Films, 2013. Film.

"Pussy Riot Members Jailed for Two Years for Hooliganism." *BBC News*, August 17, 2012. http://www.bbc.co.uk/news/world-europe-19297373. Accessed: March 20, 2013.

Solana's, Valerie. *SCUM Manifesto*. London: The Matriarchy Study Group, 1983.

Tolokonnikova, Nadezhda. Interview by *SPIEGEL*. September 3, 2012. http://www.spiegel.de/international/world/spiegel-interview-with-pussy-riot-activist-nadezhda-tolokonnikova-a-853546.html. Accessed: March 20, 2013.

———. "Letter from Pre-Trial Detention Facility No. 6." Translated by Katya Kumkova. *Chtodelat News*, August 16, 2012 (published the next day). http://chtodelat.wordpress.com/2012/08/17/nadezhda-tolokonnikova-letter-from-jail/. Accessed: March 20, 2013.

———. "Nadezhda Tolokonnikova of Pussy Riot's Prison Letters to Slavoj Žižek." *The Guardian*, November 15, 2013. http://www.theguardian.com/music/2013/nov/15/pussy-riot-nadezhda-tolokonnikova-slavoj-zizek. Accessed: November 18, 2013.

Williams, Raymond. "Structures of Feeling." In *Marxism and Literature*, 128–35. Oxford: Oxford University Press, 1977, 128–35.

Woolf, Virginia. *A Room of One's Own*. Fort Washington: Harvest Books, 2005.

*Chapter Eight*

# Paradox in Practice

## *What We Can Learn about Love from Relationships between Parents and Young Adult Children*

### Christine Overall

Your children are not your children …

They come through you but not from you,

And though they are with you yet they belong not to you.

—Kahlil Gibran, "On Children"

Contemporary western culture depicts love primarily in terms of romantic and sexual feelings.[1] We are also encouraged to think of the standard case of love as being between approximate equals. Admittedly, the predominant cultural meme of love recognizes certain kinds of differences. For example, it romanticizes the "wrong side of the tracks" relationship between those who are not socioeconomic equals, or between individuals from different racial, ethnic, or religious backgrounds. But love between romantic partners remains the paradigm case, which means not only that it is a particular kind of love involving romance and sexual intimacy, but also that it (1) standardly involves two people who are at comparable life stages, who (2) form a relationship after they leave childhood, and who (3) change and grow (if they do) in parallel and reasonably symmetrical ways.

There isn't much pop music that extolls the love between family members—especially the love between parents and children. Even when western culture permits attention to the love of parents for children, the dominant focus is on young children, often under ten, or at least not yet out of their teens. It is more unusual to consider what it means for a parent to love her adult child, that is, her child who is past the age of adolescence. Such love is exactly the topic of this chapter. My main focus is upon parental relationships with young adult children, that is, those in their twenties and thirties. Part of my motive is simply to acknowledge and explore a kind of love that gets little recognition in western culture—a love in which the two persons are at very different stages of life, and whose development vis-à-vis each other is inevitably different. This kind of love, I argue, has survived and thrived throughout a vast amount of change—change that is asymmetrical in a particular kind of way: The child has become an adult during the relationship, but in social terms, the parent is always already an adult during the relationship.

In addition, I believe there is something more general to be learned about love from examining these kinds of relationships. There is, first, the ontological aspect: It is important to consider who and what the persons are who are in the love relationship. And second, there is the epistemological aspect: It is important to consider what the persons in the love relationship can and cannot know about each other. The relationship between parents and their adult children exemplifies the ways in which both the ontology and the epistemology of the love relationship change over time, even while the love is sustained. Consistency of status, equality, or roughly comparable places in life is not at all necessary to ensure the continuity of love. Loving one's adult children, I want to say, means continuing to love during change both in who the persons are and in what can be known about them.

The philosophical literature about parents[2] and children focuses primarily on the *ethical* obligations generated by the bond between them, particularly the obligations of parents to small children. There is also a well-developed record of philosophical debate about the content of and moral basis for the obligations of adult children to their parents, especially aging parents.[3] There is relatively little philosophical discussion of the obligations of parents to young adult children.[4] Such obligations may change and evolve as the children and parents get older, and as their relationship takes new forms, which may depend on the participants' needs and dependence. These obligations could include, for example, parental obligations with respect to communication, contact, and psychological support, as well as financial assistance, living accommodation, and other material needs of young adult children. Moral questions also arise about appropriate parental responses to adult children's choices about relationships, education, employment, housing, religion, alcohol and drug use, sexuality, marital status, procreation and parenting, politics, moral values, and lifestyle, especially those with which the parents do not agree.

The goal of this chapter is not, however, to legislate with respect to these obligations. Instead, I shall discuss some of the more fundamental challenges of a loving parent/young adult child relationship.[5] These include recognizing both continuity and change in one's offspring, reordering one's perspective on one's child to encompass both his past and his present, and adjusting to the changing needs and perspectives of a maturing, autonomous human being who was once dependent, a being who both is and is not a child. These challenges, I suggest, are grounded both in the relationship's underlying ontological structure—that is, who and what parents and adult children are, vis-à-vis each other—and in its epistemological structure—that is, what they do and can know about each other.

Interestingly, there has been relatively little empirical investigation into the effects on midlife parents of parenting young adult children, at least by comparison with empirical studies of other stages of the parent/child relationship—for example, the significance of early parenting on young children, the effects of parents on young adult children, and the significance of the relationship between middle-aged children and aged parents.[6] Carol D. Ryff and Marsha Mailick Seltzer point out:

> The general paucity of knowledge about the middle years of the parental experience occurs, ironically, during a most interesting time in the parental experience: when parents watch their children grow from adolescence to adulthood and begin to see how their strengths and weaknesses are played out in life choices. It is also the time when parents begin to establish adult-to-adult relations with them.[7]

In this discussion, a different picture would probably emerge if it were written from the point of view of an adult child, but I shall not attempt to convey that perspective. This chapter is inspired primarily by my relationship with my son.[8] I am grateful for what I have learned from him. However, since one's background as an adult child of one's own parents may affect one's relationship with one's adult children,[9] my thinking has, not surprisingly, been shaped by my experiences as the adult child of my mother.

In writing about the parent/young adult child relationship, I am assuming that the child grew up in close contact with the parent, that both parent and adult child are (have become) autonomous and competent beings, that the relationship between them is sustained and supportive, and that neither one suffers from serious mental or psychological disabilities. I also acknowledge that the claims about the parent/adult child relationship made in this chapter may be culturally specific and limited by my middle class, white, heterosexual identity.[10] Indeed, the situation may appear to be so qualified as to be ungeneralizable. But the basic components—who we are in a loving relationship, and what we can know about the person whom we love and who loves us, especially over the course of profound change in one or both—are, I claim, foundational to understanding love. In analyzing the love of a parent for an adult child, I am not trying to legislate the axiology of the relationship, but rather to delineate its ontological and epistemological bones.

## ONTOLOGY

In this section, I discuss what I call the "ontology" of the parent/young adult child relationship, by which I simply mean the ways in which who and what the parent and the young adult child are affect the nature of their love.

As Norvin Richards puts it, "The fact is that your adult son or daughter is not your child in the sense of still being under your care."[11] Parents have to recognize that choices about what their child does now belong to the child, and that the child is now responsible for the kind of person he is.[12] But the ways in which one's son or daughter is or is not still one's child are more complicated than that.

Meg Wolitzer writes:

> Being an adult child was an awkward, inevitable position. You went about your business in the world: tooling around, giving orders, being taken seriously, but there were still these two people lurking somewhere who in a split second could reduce you to *nothing*. In their presence, you were a big-headed baby again, crawling instead of walking.[13]

The quotation reflects the fact that the phrase "adult child" is an apparently self-contradictory one, indicating something important about the ambiguous nature of the relationship between parent and adult child. The ambiguity of the phrase "adult child" is evident in its contemporary, new age application, which is used to refer to those adults who have survived various forms of trauma or abuse in childhood. Consider the term "adult child of alcoholics":

> The label 'adult child' acknowledges a reality: as adults, we are also the children of our past. We can remember our childhood as it was, not the way we wished it could have been or the way we were told it was. And we can think about ourselves as adults, affected in a multitude of ways by our childhood experience. ... [This is a] meaning of 'adult child' that establishes a dual identity and looks at individuals as adults chronologically and functionally, and, at the same time, as 'adult children' with a past that influences the present.[14]

Think also of more general references to the "child" within each of us adults, who supposedly still exists and may have unmet wants and unexpressed desires. According to Harold H. Bloomfield, "Within each of us, no matter how adult we may think or act, is an inner child who still carries unresolved hurts, needs and demands."[15,16]

These new age terms, metaphysically coherent or not, reflect the onto-logical ambiguity of the concept of the adult child. Contemporary parents are encouraged to wonder about the child who supposedly persists within their adult offspring. Thus, as I contemplate the history of my connection with my son, I may wonder where I might have failed him, and what disappoint-ments or needs he may secretly harbor. Are there any ways in which I should be reaching out to the "child" who may still live on in him, rather than only treating him as an adult? (The fact that he has not raised these issues himself does not necessarily obviate their existence.) The uses of these terms stress the ways in which adults are marked, shaped, and even injured by childhood experiences, especially those with their parents. In this sense, then, the "adult child" exists as a potential reproach (and less frequently, perhaps, a credit) to his parents.

The term also has a metaphysical implication—that there is a surviving person within us who is an earlier, less socialized, and more vulnerable ver-sion of the person we are now. This surviving person retains crucial aspects of childhood and may have strong influences on the choices we make in the present. Of course, this Russian-doll metaphor is not literally accurate: There is not a small person existing inside each adult child who is striving to be revealed. Yet the ambiguity of the parent/adult child relationship is a function of the long-lasting process of individuation and self-definition that begins when the child is very young. During the first eighteen years or so of the relationship, the child is a developing and dependent being, at first helpless, then relatively weak and vulnerable, always learning and growing physically, mentally, and psychologically, and proceeding along a gradient from non-competence to the gradual acquisition of more or less complete autonomy over his or her life.

The parent must come to recognize that her child has a life separate from her; that (in the case of the biological mother) from the moment he exited her body, he ceased to be a part of her; and that he develops a life plan and moral trajectory that are independent of her. Francine Toder says, "You must believe, and be willing to accept, that you and your child have separate destinies."[17] But how separate, and when should separation occur? Kathy Weingarten argues that there is a cultural imperative to support separation of the child from the mother, to such an extent that "a mother's involvement is easily defined as intrusion, care as invasion of privacy, and responsibility as overprotection."[18] She believes that mothers who attempt to maintain close-ness with children nearing adulthood are stigmatized as "bad."[19]

No person is static; everyone is a work in progress, but perhaps most of all a growing child. As the child grows up, the parent is constantly off balance, trying to understand, relate to, keep up with, and love the changing individ-ual. Parents must learn to move "from hierarchical relationships toward those which are more egalitarian."[20]

The constant changes within the child render inevitable changes within his parent. For, as Mary L. Shanley writes: "When someone is considered in the role of parent, he or she cannot be viewed apart from the child that makes him or her a parent; an 'autonomous' (in the sense of unfettered or atomistic) individual is precisely what a parent is *not*."[21] This description applies even when the "child" in question is past adolescence. A parent is permanently reconstituted as a person who is *in relation with* someone who once was crucially dependent upon her. Parent/child relationships are most assuredly not like the "voluntary contractual relationships that dominate market-oriented societies like ours."[22] Even once the child is grown and the concentrated work of parenting is finished, even once the original conditions of dependence, need, and vulnerability that defined the original parent/child relationship have been transcended, still the parent remains a parent and the adult child, a child. My identity as a mother continues to be (re)generated in and through my relationship with my adult child.

Hence, my relationship to my adult son is affected by the fact that I have to (re)constitute myself as a new being. Similarly, when her daughter departed for college, Mary Rose O'Reilley wrote, "It's foolish to fuss over a giddy girl packing for college. But perhaps I am also in mourning for my own life. She will not be here, and therefore I will not be here, either. Without her, who will I be? Who will I care for? And where is the 'we of me'?"[23] Like O'Reilley, I am learning to detach myself from a major component of my customary self-definition. It is a truism that it can be hard for mid-life women to give up their reproductive role, to stop full-time mothering. As an academic for the last three decades, I was never a full-time parent according to the outmoded fifties model of in-home, always-present mothering. Yet in another way I was, for even while at work, I did not stop being the mother of my children—worrying about them, thinking about them, and always on call if they had any problems. So, if a child persists in my son, so also a mother persists within me. Yet as this phase of my life draws to a close, I am dealing with the emergence of a new self of my own. Just as for my son this stage is a crucial one in defining his sense of selfhood and his possibilities, this stage is a crucial one for me, his parent, as I redefine my sense of myself at midlife, both consolidating the gains and contemplating the losses attached to this time of life.

The parent appears to create and shape who and what the child is, and it may therefore seem as if the child does not and cannot reciprocate, for obviously the parent became an adult long before and independently of the child. Joseph Kupfer, for example, says that in the early years not only does the parent run the child's life; the parent also, more radically, shapes the child's nature according to the parent's own goals. "While the parent may be changed dramatically *as a result* of rearing the child, the parent is not shaped *by* the child."[24] Hence the parent is more responsible for the child's identity than the child is for the parent's identity. Moreover, once the child reaches adulthood, "Because it includes the history of the unequal relationship with the parent, the adult child's self-concept limits the degree to which she can function autonomously with the parents." Kupfer thinks that even a grown child who may be more autonomous in general than his parents nonetheless in interaction with them is *less* autonomous than his parents. "Adult children can't quite 'be themselves,' at least not all of the selves they've become apart from their parents."[25]

Although Kupfer highlights some important ontological asymmetries in the parent/adult child relationship, I believe he greatly exaggerates their implications. While it is true that the parent contributes to shaping the child during times when the child is young, vulnerable, and close to helpless, and hence makes special contributions to the child's identity, the child is not a formless lump of clay bearing only the imprint of the sculptor. As Amy Mullin notes, "We often do not recognize ways in which children, especially babies and very young children, shape reciprocal interactions with parents. ... We often fail to notice that children pay close attention to their caregivers and respond to cues they receive from them."[26] As developing persons with abilities, weaknesses, goals, and experiences of their own, children also influence their parents through the communication of their opinions, demands, and proclivities. By the very nature of the fact that the parent/child relationship *is* a relationship, in which two people, however different their ages, interact with each other, the effects on the participants are mutual and reciprocal, despite the inequality of power in the early years. Melissa Burchard writes of her adopted, formerly abused children:

> To change the self in any small way is often experienced as an enormous effort. To ... learn to trust the world and the (kind of) persons (adults, even parents) who have betrayed and violated; this is probably a lifelong project, and one of the things that has been most difficult for us, as parents of deeply wounded children, is that not just the kids, but we will be doing this work in one way or another for the rest of our lives. As the project of self-construction is an ongoing, lifelong project in general, we understand that we will be supporting our children in this work for as long as we can.[27]

Nor does it follow that adult children cannot "be themselves" with their parents or that their self-concept limits their autonomy vis-à-vis the parents. It is of course true that the adult child's sense of privacy, independence, and personal dignity will likely lead him to keep confidential certain aspects of his life, and to cease to be the confiding and open little person that he was when he was, let's say, four years old. The development of control over the expression of feelings, discretion about whom to trust, and caution about what information to share are hallmarks of the concept of mature adulthood in North America. In almost every relationship, including close and long-standing friendships, individuals may still not reveal everything about themselves, and may preserve some parts of their thoughts or feelings that are "off limits." However, this tendency to maintain some personal privacy even in a close relationship is not incompatible with being fully oneself, or all of one's selves, within that relationship. It is partly *because* one can feel confident that the other person will not pry into what one does not want to show, or press for details when one does not wish to provide them, that one can be oneself without fear of excessive vulnerability.[28] Paradoxically, it is through the mutual limitation, in a love relationship, of totally unrestrained self-expression that self-expression in that relationship is facilitated. One's autonomy and self-possession in interactions are enhanced through the assurance that other persons will exert morally appropriate restraints on the expression of their autonomy.

Ideally, I would say, adult children are more likely to "be themselves" and to be fully realized selves with their parents than with many other people, at least in a good relationship, which is what Kupfer hypothesizes. Their parents witnessed the adult child's history and development, they love and respect him, and they consequently are able to be open to and accepting of the adult child in ways that other people can be neither obliged nor expected to express. Moreover, Kupfer overestimates the degree to which parents may engage in what he calls "the strong sense of 'exercising autonomy'" with respect to shaping their child's very nature. First, parents are unlikely to want to produce children that are mere replicas of themselves. Most parents hope that their children will live lives expressive of their own individuality, and many parents also hope that in growing up, their children will avoid their own weaknesses and errors. Second, children are far more resilient, more deeply themselves almost from conception, let alone birth, than he is willing to recognize. If it were possible to shape children as profoundly as he thinks, then parents would be able to determine their children's sexual and romantic leanings; children would follow the interests and career trajectories that their parents present to and map out for them; and law-abiding parents would never spawn law-breakers. But given the amount of deviation from most parents' projects that children present, I think we can safely assume that although parental influence is by no means negligible, it also not as powerful as Kupfer pretends.

In addition, although obviously the child cannot shape his parent's childhood, Kupfer is just mistaken when he says that the parent is not shaped by the child.[29] Admittedly, the child cannot control the parent; the child cannot deeply remold the parent's nature by reference to the child's own goals. Still, the child contributes to the parent's identity. He does so first and most simply by virtue of making the parent a parent. But the child also manipulates the parent's identity and sense of herself in more complex ways. For example, the child may "call forth" from the parent feelings and behaviors, such as nurturing, supporting, counseling, and disciplining, that the parent would not otherwise evince or even recognize in herself.[30] Moreover, the child may generate the opportunity for the parent to experience and enjoy activities and fields of endeavor, like sports, games, crafts, hobbies, arts, or sciences, that the parent would not have otherwise encountered or chosen. The child also provides the opportunity and even the necessity to meet other people, such as other parents, neighbors, teachers, coaches, and health care workers, whom the parent would not otherwise have gotten to know.

In addition, living with one's children provides the parent with a second-hand glimpse at the systemic oppression of children, and a lived demonstration of the need for children's liberation. By this I do not simply mean that the parent receives an introduction to children's vulnerabilities and need for care, or even that the parent acquires a measure of empathy for the ways in which other children may suffer. I mean that rearing a child introduces one to the political status of children: that although we live in a pronatalist culture, it remains in many ways anti-child, treating children as if they were a different kind of being from adults, rather than persons who are still in the process of maturing. Parents learn to see, and care about, the cultural ignorance or underestimation of children's capacities for self-determination; the built environment that is often not set up to meet children's needs (so that children are, effectively, temporarily disabled by their smallness in the face of a world built for those who are over five feet tall); condescension toward children; the use of children in many parts of the world as mere laborers or as soldiers; and even the abuse of children, whether physical, sexual, or psychological.

Finally, raising a child challenges a thoughtful parent to keep up with the child's intellectual, psychological, and moral growth, to rethink a lot of shibboleths about human beings and human development, and to be humble and open to the insights that the child can offer. Caroline Whitbeck suggests that "the idea of learning with and from a 'weaker being,' such as a child, [is hard to accept because it] goes too much against the culture's preoccupation with hierarchy and domination."[31] Perhaps our sense of the "weakness" of the child is exacerbated in cases where children have or will have disabilities. But this preoccupation with inequality and vulnerability makes it difficult for us to recognize that, intentionally or not, the child helps to shape the parent's identity.[32] Despite the ontological asymmetry of the parent/adult child relationship, each person contributes to the constitution of the other's individuality.

Although the adult child is obviously no longer a child in the sense of "young human being below the age of puberty," he is still a child in the other sense of "offspring" of his parents. As a mother, then, I know that my son is both an adult, in that he has grown physically and psychologically to maturity, and also still a child, my child. Kupfer writes, "While children should

outlive their childhoods, they remain their parents' children."[33] The challenge
of love between a parent and her adult child is in part to recognize and to deal
with the apparent paradoxes that the adult child embodies, not necessarily to
himself (although he might), but rather to his parent.


## EPISTEMOLOGY

In this section, I discuss what I call the "epistemology" of the loving parent/
young adult child relationship, by which I simply mean the nature of and
constraints on what the participants can and do know about each other.

The adult child's status as child in the sense of offspring may make it difficult for the parent to recognize that he is no longer a child in the sense of
young human being. In my relationship with my son, I find I have to understand and respond to a kind of epistemological bewilderment: What happened
to the little boy who used to follow me around? The child who is still so vivid
in my memories has disappeared; in his place is an adult. Where did that child
go? Is it possible to see the little boy as being both distinct from and yet continuous with the young man?

Kupfer argues that there is a fundamental inequality between parents and
their adult children because of the fact that, while the parent has an "intimate knowledge of the young child's development, including knowledge
of the child before she knows herself," the child can never be a comparable
authority on or have comparable access to his or her parent's personal identity.[34] Moreover, "[p]recisely because parents know their children so well
qua children they may be kept from truly seeing and appreciating who the
child is as an adult, the image of the young child coloring the parent's later
perceptions."[35],[36] Laurence Thomas worries that parents retain, even after the
children reach adulthood, a "presumption" that they can determine the good
for their children, and make "authoritative assessments" of their children's
behavior. As a result, says Thomas, parents and adult children can rarely form
a "bond of trust" with each other, for such a bond requires that each person
be able to examine her life "without there being any sense, on the part of
either party, that the hearer is entitled to make authoritative assessments of the
speaker's life and is entitled to the speaker's deference with respect to those
assessments."[37] Like Kupfer, then, he thinks that there is an epistemological inequality between parents and adult children that creates emotional and
moral boundaries between them.

It is always a challenge to develop an ongoing and realistic understanding
of a developing, growing, and changing being. As Mullin explains, "parents
have a great influence on the directions in which a child develops his or her
skills and to what the child aspires. This requires the love between children

and parents to be very accommodating of change, and it explains why parents are often willing to accommodate changes they have helped to bring about."[38] That challenge does not disappear once the child reaches young adulthood. As Toder remarks, "We, as parents, continue to grow and change throughout our lives; we don't stop at adulthood. To complicate matters, our adult-children continue to grow and change during *their* adult lives. At any moment in time, when we wish to communicate with them, we are all in a unique, dynamic state that differs from another point in time."[39] The parent/adult child relationship is complicated by the fact that in epistemic terms, the two persons are differently situated. Kupfer is correct to acknowledge an epistemological asymmetry in their relationship. Two friends or relatives of approximately the same age can hope to remember the same events for which they were both present, however differently they may remember them, but not so in my relationship to my adult child, whose perspective on the early events of his life—at which we were both present—is necessarily intrinsically different from mine. Our relationship now is complicated by the different memories we have. I remember him as a fetus, as a two-month-old, as a toddler, as a kindergartner. Not only does he not have comparable memories of me as a little one, he does not even remember me as I was when he was very little.

But I think Kupfer overestimates the epistemological asymmetry in the relationship. He claims that the parent is "an expert on the formation of his adult child's temperament and tastes, aspirations and humiliations."[40] Yet this expertise is, surely, limited, and begins to decline in accuracy and depth as soon as the child begins social relationships of his own. Children have thoughts and feelings that are hidden from their parents. Parents sometimes learn only in retrospect of a child's struggle with a bully in grade three, or special friendship in grade six, or crush on a teacher in grade nine. Indeed, as the child gets older he becomes more able and more willing to conceal his private life from his parents. So, *contra* Thomas, I believe that a parent who retains a belief in her power to make "authoritative assessments" of her grown child lacks an appropriate degree of what I would call epistemic realism, and to that extent is failing to gain a genuine understanding of the adult child.

A parent who accepts that she is gradually losing whatever "expertise" she may briefly have possessed with respect to her offspring, and that her child has both a life and a mind of his own, has the opportunity to appreciate her adult child for who he really is. According to Kupfer, neither parent nor child "can really 'discover' an independently existing other" within their relationship, for the parent's image of the child *qua* child inhibits the vision of the adult child as he truly is.[41] And it is true that the parent's consciousness of the child's development and of her own relationship with the child is likely to linger within her perception of that child. Kupfer is correct in pointing to an ambiguity in the parent's vision: The parent both knows her adult child and does not know him. The parent was once the most important person in his life and is now relegated, comparatively, to bit-part status. But although it poses an epistemological challenge, I don't think this perspective makes it impossible to see the child for what he is: just more difficult, and more of a challenge. In my own experience, it has been interesting to notice how often my son has surprised me. Just when I think I know who he is, he reveals other aspects of himself that I had not previously suspected or observed. Being an epistemic realist with respect to one's adult child requires that one be open and receptive to these surprises.

Kupfer argues that the very relationship with the parent compromises the adult child's behavior. He says that the adult child's autonomy is inevitably limited in relation to his or her parents because of the child's "enduring habits and attitudes" toward parents, such as "respect and loyalty, as well as habits of deference and accommodation engendered in youth [which] persist into adulthood. As a result, the adult child is less likely than her parent to press disagreement or criticism in their interaction; she is less likely to assert herself."[42]

Respect and loyalty are indeed highly desirable virtues, but they are necessary to any loving relationship, and I do not see that they necessarily inhibit disagreement and criticism. Indeed, one might be moved to disagree with someone precisely because one respects and is loyal to her; that is, one might feel a responsibility to be open about one's opinions and to suggest, gently but clearly, where one thinks the other is going wrong. Deference and accommodation, on the other hand, may be appropriate at times, but if they are the defining characteristics of the adult child's interactions with his parent then I would argue that the parent who has raised a child who is in this uncomfortable situation has not done a good job of parenting. This parent has failed to nurture the conditions by which the child gradually achieves cognitive and axiological independence. Such a parent would be preventing her child from being fully authentic; she would be requiring him to disown part of himself.[43,44]

On the contrary, if parents have raised a genuinely autonomous child, one who is capable of independent thought and assessment, he will be only too able to see the parent for what she is, and is unlikely to defer to or accommodate the parent unless it makes sense on other grounds to do so. As Jeffrey Blustein points out, people gain self-knowledge and self-confidence through continued contact with their parents: "Continued access to my family of origin enables me to experience my life as evolving over time; confronted with many vivid reminders of my earlier self, my personality can attain a coherence that it might not otherwise have."[45] I believe that these characteristics enable the adult child to be open and expressive with his parents. "[C]hildren who are confident of their parents' continued love feel that their relationship is resilient enough to withstand open criticism of parents' actions or beliefs, and this can strengthen the bond between them."[46] Children who have been offered and have seen modeled processes of critical thinking, lively discussion, and thoughtful disagreement are unlikely to repress these capacities in themselves, just because they are with their parents. Indeed, precisely because parents have indicated, throughout the child's life, that these critical and evaluative capacities are valuable and worthy of exercise, the adult child is even more likely to exercise them with the parent, who both approves of lively discussion and is likely to constitute, even when the child is past childhood, a safe haven for trying out new and audacious ideas.

Kupfer also claims that the adult child can never have the "special access" to the adult's personal identity that he believes the parent has to the child's.[47] But I would say that next to the parent's spouse or partner, if any, it is often the child who knows the parent best, especially as their relationship develops and gets older. The parent/adult child relationship is asymmetrical, but not as unequal as Kupfer would have us believe, for children of all ages are observant and alert, and are likely to come to a special and indeed unique knowledge and understanding of their parents. Epistemic realism requires that the parent recognize that her child has been observing her throughout his life. The child has lived with the parent in the privacy of their home; has seen the parent in vulnerable, unguarded moments; and has been subjected to the parent's feelings and thoughts that might have been filtered or repressed if nonrelatives were around. The child has witnessed the parent in the formation and development of a significant part of her selfhood—her identity as parent. The child has observed and interacted with the parent during the parent's journey from relative youth to midlife, as well as during her struggles with work, whether inside or outside the home, and relationships, whether inside or outside the immediate family. The parent and the adult child have a great deal of shared history, even if they may not share all their values. Although the parent and the adult child are asymmetrically situated with respect to their knowledge of each other, each has a special, unique, and epistemically privileged perspective on the other's history and identity.

It is not uncommon to claim that certain loving relationships are a form of friendship. For example, some couples speak of having married their "best friend," and some adult daughters may describe their mother as their "best friend."[48] Certainly friendships and parent/adult child relationships share some commonalities: mutual support and assistance, reciprocity, enjoyment in spending time and activities together, sharing of personal information, and pleasure in each other's joys and accomplishments.

Still, the shared history of the parent and adult child, and what I have argued is the epistemically privileged perspective that parents and adult

children have on each other, do not, in my view, mean that they are or
become friends. The fact that the parent helped to generate the child (literally, in the case of biological parents, and socially, in the case of all parents)
and watched him grow up makes her relationship to him intrinsically different from friendship. The differences arise, I think, from the epistemological
and ontological differences between a parent/adult child relationship and a
friendship. In a friendship, two people gradually get to know each other and
to enjoy spending time together. They more or less set out from the same
starting point. Friendship, like romantic love, is usually between equals.
That is not to say that there cannot be friendships between people of different ages, but a defining characteristic of the parent/adult child relationship is
that in the beginning it necessarily involves a significant difference in power
and dependence, a difference that is only gradually evened out. Friendship
does not typically originate between persons with large differences in power,
vulnerability, need, and dependence. More importantly, friendships can and
do end—for example, if the friends move far away, finish school, or change
jobs; or if the friends gradually "drift apart" through changing interests or
goals, or simply because other friends come to take priority. Their situation
is different from that of the parent and her adult child. There is a lifelong
commitment that is at least implicit in the relationship of parent and adult
child. Whatever may happen, I am still my son's mother. Even if he were to
move to the other side of the world, change his life drastically, or take up
with persons or activities utterly foreign to me, I would still be related to
him and in relation with him. Other relationships will not take priority over
my relationship with him; as my son he is unique, in a way that makes our
love unique.

## CONCLUSION

The ontological and epistemological ambiguities of a loving parent/adult
child relationship can make it difficult for the parent to know how to act
with her adult child. Human maturation does not always consist of discrete
stages, and human development is a continuous process. There are no solid
lines between dependence and autonomy, immaturity and maturity, noncom-
petence and self-sufficiency. There is no visible line at which a child becomes
an adult, and no point at which a parent ceases to be a parent. Instead, as
Richards describes it, "insofar as a child is less competent at something than
an adult, that is often due to differences between a child's level of experience and that of an adult. These differences do not vanish instantly when the
child becomes an adult, but they do fade away in time. At some point, it is no
longer true that the parent has had more experience in some matter or that the

child has had insufficient experience, but only that the experiences each has had have been different ones."[49]

It can therefore be a challenge for the parent to acknowledge the increasing independence, autonomy, and self-reliance of the young adult child, while also remembering the unique history and cherishing the connections that the parent/child relationship creates. The ambiguity of loving relationships between parents and their young adult children is situated not only in the fact that the young person is both adult and child, but also in the fact that the parent is and must be a parent to both of them, while at the same time creating a new way of living the parenthood role.

Yet it is in these ambiguities that the best prospects for the future development of their love lie. Letty Cottin Pogrebin, the mother of three young adult children, captures these prospects when she writes, "[T]he more independent they [her children] become, the more adult their concerns. The more adult their concerns, the more I have in common with them. The more we have in common, the closer our relationship. Ergo, separation yields closeness."[50] But Weingarten cautions that parents should not confuse separation with what she calls *differentiation*. What she seems to mean is that adult children can—and should—differentiate themselves from their parents, but such a differentiation need not compromise intimacy—defined as "mutual meaning making"—between them.[51] The sustenance of a relationship does not require a "clean break" between parent and child, because each remains vital to the other through sharing of concerns and reciprocity of attention.[52] While the parent/child relationship is asymmetrical with respect to its history of power, authority, and responsibility, it is always in important ways interactive and mutually influential. Ideally, in her relationship with her young adult children, the parent gradually divests herself of power and authority, moving toward a more egalitarian relationship and redefining the nature of her responsibility to and connection with the adult child. The parent's recognition of the child's independence and the acknowledgment of his autonomy are necessary conditions for the sustenance of communicative love and mutual respect between parent and young adult child.

As the child reaches young adulthood, his parent needs to acknowledge that the child both is and is not her child, and that she both knows and does not know her child. The recognition of this paradox in practice is the basis of a loving relationship between parent and young adult child. But I also suggest that explicitly recognizing the changing ontological and epistemological frameworks of relationships may enrich our understanding of all forms of love, not only those between parent and adult child. What that relationship vividly demonstrates is that consistency of status, equality, and roughly comparable places in life are not at all necessary to ensure the continuity and intensity of love.

## NOTES

1. Thank you to Yolanda Estes for her insightful comments on an early version of this chapter. And I am deeply grateful to Caroline R. Lundquist for helping me to reshape the chapter to focus more clearly on love.

2. Jeffrey Blustein reminds us that a better term than "parents" would be "child-rearers," since not all (biological) parents raise their children, since social practices may allot childrearing to non-parents, and since what is of ethical interest is the relationship between children and those who raise them, whoever they may be (Jeffrey Blustein, "On the Duties of Parents and Children," *Southern Journal of Philosophy* 15 (1977): 427–41). However, in this chapter, I am exclusively interested in the relationship between adult children and those who are defined as their parents (provided the parents rear their children), including guardians and adoptive parents, whether or not they are biologically related. While the experiences of birthmothers who relinquish their children are of interest for their own sake, and some such women have a relationship with their offspring even when the offspring are not in their lives at all (e.g., Dorothy Rogers, "Birthmothers and Maternal Identity: The Terms of Relinquishment," in *Coming to Life: Philosophies of Pregnancy, Childbirth and Mothering*, eds. Sarah LaChance Adams and Caroline R. Lundquist (New York: Fordham University Press, 2013), 120–37), I shall focus on parents who have fairly continuous interactions with their children, over the course of their children's lives, even if the children do not always live with the parents. This focus could, then, include stepparents (see, e.g., Beckey Sukovaty, "On Stepmothers as Hybrid Beings and World Travelers: Toward a New Model for Care-Full Ethics," in *Philosophical Inquiries into Pregnancy, Childbirth, and Mothering: Maternal Subjects*, eds. Sheila Lintott and Maureen Sander-Staudt (New York: Routledge, 2012), 151–61).

3. For example, Jeffrey Blustein, "On the Duties of Parents and Children," *Southern Journal of Philosophy* 15 (1977): 427–41; Jeffrey Blustein, *Parents and Children: The Ethics of the Family* (New York: Oxford, 1982); Nicholas Dixon, "The Friendship Model of Filial Obligations," *Journal of Applied Philosophy* 12, no. 1 (1995): 77–87; Jane English, "What Do Grown Children Owe Their Parents?" in *Having Children: Philosophical and Legal Reflections on Parenthood*, eds. Onora O'Neill and William Ruddick (New York: Oxford, 1979), 351–56; Joseph Kupfer, "Can Parents and Children Be Friends?" *American Philosophical Quarterly* 27, no. 1 (1990): 15–26; Christina Hoff Sommers, "Filial Morality," in *Women and Moral Theory*, eds. Eva Feder Kittay and Diana T. Meyers (Totowa: Rowman & Littlefield, 1987), 69–84.

4. One insightful exception is Norvin Richards, whose book, *The Ethics of Parenthood* (Oxford: Oxford University Press, 2010), contains a chapter entitled "Having Grown Children." Toder's research indicates that what people at this stage in their life are concerned with in relationship to their parents is "independence, separateness, and control. What this group want[s] most from their parents [is] acknowledgment of their adult status and sharing of their experiences without criticism, judgment, or advice. If these young adults' tenuous footing [is] noticed, they want[] their parents to remain silent until specifically asked for help" (Francine Toder,

*Your Kids Are Grown: Moving on with and without Them* [New York: Insight Books, 1994], 15).

5. I shall use both empirical literature on parent/adult child relationships, and philosophical writings on friendships between parents and children. For the former, see, for example, John R. Logan and Glenna D. Spitze, *Family Ties: Enduring Relations between Parents and Their Grown Children* (Philadelphia: Temple University Press, 1996); Constance L. Shehan, and Jeffrey W. Dwyer, "Parent-Child Exchanges in the Middle Years: Attachment and Autonomy in the Transition to Adulthood," in *Aging Parents and Adult Children*, ed. Jay A. Mancini (Lexington: Lexington Books, 1989), 99–116; Joan E. Norris and Joseph A. Tindale, *Among Generations: The Cycle of Adult Relationships* (New York: W.H. Freeman, 1994). For the latter, see, for example, Nicholas Dixon, "The Friendship Model,"; Kupfer, "Can Parents and Children Be Friends?"; Laurence Thomas, "Friendship," *Synthese* 72 (1987): 217–36.

6. Carol D. Ryff, and Marsha Mailick Seltzer, eds., *The Parental Experience in Midlife* (Chicago: University of Chicago Press, 1996).

7. Ibid., 8.

8. I won't be able to examine in detail either the possible differences between how mothers and fathers relate to their adult children (see, for example, Caroline Whitbeck, "A Different Reality: Feminist Ontology," in *Beyond Domination: New Perspectives on Women and Philosophy*, ed. Carol C. Gould [Totowa: Rowman & Allanheld, 1983], 64–88), or the gender differences between men and women as young adults in relationship with their parents (see, for example, Shehan and Dwyer, "Parent-Child Exchanges," 100; Cate Dooley and Nikki Fedele, "Raising Relational Boys," in *Mother Outlaws: Theories and Practices of Empowered Mothering*, ed. Andrea O'Reilly [Toronto: Women's Press, 2004], 357–85); Alison M. Thomas , "Swimming against the Tide: Feminists' Accounts of Mothering Sons," in *Mother Outlaws: Theories and Practices of Empowered Mothering*, edited by Andrea O'Reilly, 341–56. For one view of the difference that sexual identity makes to parenting, see Laura Benkov, "Yes, I Am a Swan: Reflections on Families Headed by Lesbians and Gay Men," in *Against the Odds: Diverse Voices of Contemporary Mothers*, eds. Cynthia García Coll, Janet L. Surrey, and Kathy Weingarten (New York: Guilford Press, 1998), 113–33.

9. See Harold H. Bloomfield, *Making Peace with Your Parents* (New York: Random House, 1983); Letty Cottin Pogrebin, *Getting Over Getting Older: An Intimate Journey* (New York: Berkley Books, 1996); Shauna L. Smith, *Making Peace with Your Adult Children* (New York: Plenum Press, 1991).

10. Throughout this chapter, I shall refer to the adult child using masculine pronouns, mostly in order to differentiate him from the parent, for whom I use feminine pronouns. I am adopting these terms for clarity and convenience only, and I do not assume that only women are parents, or that only men are adult children!

11. Richards, *The Ethics of Parenthood*, 225.

12. Ibid., 226.

13. Wolitzer quoted in Rosalie Maggio, *The New Beacon Book of Quotations by Women* (Boston: Beacon Press, 1996), 504–5.

14. Stephanie Brown, *Safe Passage: Recovery for Adult Children of Alcoholics* (New York: Wiley, 1992), 11–12.

15. Bloomfield, *Making Peace with Your Parents*, 98.

16. Shauna L. Smith writes, "My own picture of the child within is one that conceptualizes the child as the core of a person—the natural self that is born basically innocent and unarmed. ... Defenses begin to grow and barriers are set up to shield the child from hurt. The layers are like onion skins which grow around the child and gradually hide her, often even from herself" (Smith, *Making Peace with Your Adult Children*, 95).

17. Toder, *Your Kids are Grown*, 92.

18. Weingarten, "Sidelined no More," 21.

19. But the degree to which separation is *socially* required may be a function of gender. Alison M. Thomas writes of the fears some mothers have of " 'losing' their sons to patriarchy [because of] the demands and expectations to be 'masculine'" ("Swimming against the Tide: Feminists' Accounts of Mothering Sons," in *Mother Outlaws: Theories and Practices of Empowered Mothering*, ed. Andrea O'Reilly (Toronto: Women's Press, 2004), 348). Cate Dooley and Nikki Fedele cite the old saying, "A daughter is a daughter for the rest of your life; a son is a son 'til he takes a wife," and speak of "numerous negative images in the media of close mother–son relationships [and] exaggerated stereotypes that mockingly refer to adult men who are close to their mothers as 'mama's boys'" (Dooley and Fedele, "Raising Relational Boys," 382).

20. Norris and Tindale, *Among Generations*, 49.

21. Mary L. Shanley, "Fathers' Rights, Mothers' Wrongs? Reflections on Unwed Fathers' Rights and Sex Equality," in *Having and Raising Children: Unconventional Families, Hard Choices, and the Social Good*, eds. Uma Narayan and Julia J. Bartkowiak (University Park: Pennsylvania State University Press, 1999), 56, her emphasis.

22. Laura M. Purdy, "Boundaries of Authority: Should Children Be Able to Divorce Their Parents?" in *Having and Raising Children: Unconventional Families, Hard Choices, and the Social Good*, eds. Uma Narayan and Julia J. Bartkowiak (University Park: Pennsylvania State University Press, 1999), 159.

23. Mary Rose O'Reilley, *The Barn at the End of the World: The Apprenticeship of a Quaker, Buddhist Shepherd* (Minneapolis: Milkweed Editions, 2000), 72.

24. Kupfer, "Can Parents and Children be Friends?," 16, his emphasis.

25. Ibid., 17.

26. Amy Mullin, "Parents and Children: An Alternative to Selfless and Unconditional Loven" *Hypatia* 21, no. 1 (2006): 184.

27. Melissa Burchard, an Adoptive Mother to Do? When Your Child's Desires Are a Problem," in *Coming to Life: Philosophies of Pregnancy, Childbirth and Mothering*, eds. by Sarah hance Adams and Caroline R. Lundquist (New York: Fordham University Press, 2013), 151.

28. Kupfer claims that behaviors such as "complaining to his grown child about the other parent; telling sexual stories or jokes; or, an unmarried parent going with the adult child to socialize with others in sexually oriented ways" are out of place in the parent/adult child relationship. He says their *verboten* status is a function of the "authority" of the parent and reflects the "inequality in autonomy" between the two (Kupfer, "Can Parents and Children be Friends?," 18). However, the fact that these behaviors may sometimes (but not always, surely) be inappropriate has more to do

with factors such as loyalty to the other parent or respect for one's child's sexual privacy, than with inequality in autonomy.

29. This claim is related to the equally mistaken idea that young children do not give to their parents, but merely take. For example, Blustein claims that in the early childrearing years, "parents do most of the giving and children most of the taking" (Blustein, "On the Duties of Parents and Children," 194). It is true that the responsibility is entirely one way, with parents responsible for their children and not vice versa, and it is also true that parents provide material things for children that their offspring cannot possibly reciprocate at that time. But any parent who has received a freshly picked dandelion, a sticky kiss, or a song from a small child knows how much children give to their parents.

30. Whitbeck, "A Different Reality," 83, note 3.

31. Caroline Whitbeck, "The Maternal Instinct," in *Mothering: Essays in Feminist Theory*, ed. Joyce Trebilcot (Totowa: Rowman & Allanheld, 1983), 193.

32. Melissa Burchard points out the power of young people, even those who have been abused: "Children who have suffered abuse in their families ... may have responded by forming an intense desire to be in control. This may take the forms of "bossing" others, including adults, anticipating directives and acting before receiving instructions or permission, or undermining the authority of adults through manipulation, misdirection, or even flat-out refusal" (Burchard, "What's an Adoptive Mother to Do," 153).

33. Kupfer, "Can Parents and Children be Friends?" 18.

34. Ibid., 17.

35. Ibid., 18.

36. Likewise, however, it might be thought that because children know their parents well *qua* parents, they could be prevented from fully recognizing and appreciating the parents for who they are.

37. Laurence Thomas, "Friendship," *Synthese* 72 (1987): 222.

38. Mullin, "Parents and Children," 189.

39. Toder, *Your Kids are Grown*, 45, her emphasis.

40. Kupfer, "Can Parents and Children be Friends?" 18.

41. Ibid., 20, 18.

42. Ibid., 17.

43. Dixon, "The Friendship Model," 80.

44. Kupfer suggests that if one parent criticizes the other parent to his or her adult child, this behavior is wrong, in part because it subtly tells the child that "she is the parents' moral equal, someone fit to judge the criticized parent" (Kupfer, "Can Parents and Children be Friends?" 19). But any parent who can*not* recognize her adult child as a moral equal is making a moral and intellectual error, lacks epistemic realism, and has not successfully made the transition to being the parent of an adult child. Instead, I would say, the error is of another kind, perhaps the lack of respect for privacy.

45. Blustein, "On the Duties of Parents and Children," 250.

46. Ibid., 192.

47. Kupfer, "Can Parents and Children Be Friends?" 17.

48. But this claim may be gendered in the parent/child context: I suspect that it would be more unusual for a son to describe his mother—or even his father—as his best friend.
49. Richards, *The Ethics of Parenthood*, 227.
50. Letty Cottin Pogrebin, *Getting Over Getting Older: An Intimate Journey* (New York: Berkley Books, 1996), 237.
51. Weingarten, "Sidelined no More," 27.
52. Ibid., 23–25.

# BIBLIOGRAPHY

Benkov, Laura. "Yes, I Am a Swan: Reflections on Families Headed by Lesbians and Gay Men." In *Against the Odds: Diverse Voices of Contemporary Mothers*, edited by Cynthia García Coll, Janet L. Surrey, and Kathy Weingarten, 113–33. New York: Guilford Press, 1998.
Bloomfield, Harold H. *Making Peace with Your Parents*. New York: Random House, 1983.
Blustein, Jeffrey. "On the Duties of Parents and Children." *Southern Journal of Philosophy* 15 (1977): 427–41.
———. *Parents and Children: The Ethics of the Family*. New York: Oxford, 1982.
Brown, Stephanie. *Safe Passage: Recovery for Adult Children of Alcoholics*. New York: Wiley, 1992.
Burchard, Melissa. "What's an Adoptive Mother to Do? When Your Child's Desires Are a Problem." In *Coming to Life: Philosophies of Pregnancy, Childbirth and Mothering*, edited by Sarah LaChance Adams and Caroline R. Lundquist, 138–68. New York: Fordham University Press, 2013.
Dixon, Nicholas. "The Friendship Model of Filial Obligations." *Journal of Applied Philosophy* 12, no. 1 (1995): 77–87.
Dooley, Cate, and Nikki Fedele. "Raising Relational Boys." In *Mother Outlaws: Theories and Practices of Empowered Mothering*, edited by Andrea O'Reilly, 357–85. Toronto: Women's Press, 2004.
English, Jane. "What Do Grown Children Owe Their Parents?" In *Having Children: Philosophical and Legal Reflections on Parenthood*, edited by Onora O'Neill and William Ruddick, 351–56. New York: Oxford, 1979.
Kupfer, Joseph. "Can Parents and Children Be Friends?" *American Philosophical Quarterly* 27, no. 1 (1990): 15–26.
Logan, John R., and Glenna D. Spitze. *Family Ties: Enduring Relations between Parents and Their Grown Children*. Philadelphia: Temple University Press, 1996.
Maggio, Rosalie. *The New Beacon Book of Quotations by Women*. Boston: Beacon Press, 1996.
Mullin, Amy. "Parents and Children: An Alternative to Selfless and Unconditional Love." *Hypatia* 21, no. 1 (2006): 181–200.
Norris, Joan E., and Joseph A. Tindale. *Among Generations: The Cycle of Adult Relationships*. New York: W.H. Freeman, 1994.

O'Reilley, Mary Rose. *The Barn at the End of the World: The Apprenticeship of a Quaker, Buddhist Shepherd*. Minneapolis: Milkweed Editions, 2000.

Pogrebin, Letty Cottin. *Getting Over Getting Older: An Intimate Journey*. New York: Berkley Books, 1996.

Purdy, Laura M. "Boundaries of Authority: Should Children Be Able to Divorce Their Parents?" In *Having and Raising Children: Unconventional Families, Hard Choices, and the Social Good*, edited by Uma Narayan and Julia J. Bartkowiak, 153–62. University Park: Pennsylvania State University Press, 1999.

Richards, Norvin. *The Ethics of Parenthood*. Oxford University Press, 2010.

Rogers, Dorothy. "Birthmothers and Maternal Identity: The Terms of Relinquishment." In *Coming to Life: Philosophies of Pregnancy, Childbirth and Mothering*, edited by Sarah LaChance Adams and Caroline R. Lundquist, 120–37. New York: Fordham University Press, 2013.

Ryff, Carol D., and Marsha Mailick Seltzer, editors, *The Parental Experience in Midlife*. Chicago: University of Chicago Press, 1996.

———. "The Uncharted Years of Midlife Parenting." In *The Parental Experience in Midlife*, edited by Carol D. Ryff and Marsha Mailick Seltzer, 3–9. Chicago: University of Chicago Press, 1996.

Shanley, Mary L. "Fathers' Rights, Mothers' Wrongs? Reflections on Unwed Fathers' Rights and Sex Equality." In *Having and Raising Children: Unconventional Families, Hard Choices, and the Social Good*, edited by Uma Narayan and Julia J. Bartkowiak, 39–63. University Park: Pennsylvania State University Press, 1999.

Shehan, Constance L., and Jeffrey W. Dwyer. "Parent-Child Exchanges in the Middle Years: Attachment and Autonomy in the Transition to Adulthood." In *Aging Parents and Adult Children*, edited by Jay A. Mancini, 99–116. Lexington: Lexington Books, 1989.

Smith, Shauna L. *Making Peace with Your Adult Children*. New York: Plenum Press, 1991.

Sommers, Christina Hoff. "Filial Morality." In *Women and Moral Theory*, edited by Eva Feder Kittay and Diana T. Meyers, 69–84. Totowa: Rowman & Littlefield, 1987.

Sukovaty, Beckey. "On Stepmothers as Hybrid Beings and World Travelers: Toward a New Model for Care-Full Ethics." In *Philosophical Inquiries into Pregnancy, Childbirth, and Mothering: Maternal Subjects*, edited by Sheila Lintott and Maureen Sander-Staudt, 151–61. New York: Routledge, 2012.

Thomas, Alison M. "Swimming against the Tide: Feminists' Accounts of Mothering Sons." In *Mother Outlaws: Theories and Practices of Empowered Mothering*, edited by Andrea O'Reilly, 341–56. Toronto: Women's Press, 2004.

Thomas, Laurence. "Friendship." *Synthese* 72 (1987): 217–36.

Toder, Francine A. *Your Kids Are Grown: Moving on With and Without Them*. New York: Insight Books, 1994.

Weingarten, Kathy. "Sidelined No More: Promoting Mothers of Adolescents as a Resource for their Growth and Development." In *Against the Odds: Diverse Voices of Contemporary Mothers*, edited by Cynthia García Coll, Janet L. Surrey, and Kathy Weingarten, 15–36. New York: Guilford Press, 1998.

Whitbeck, Caroline. "A Different Reality: Feminist Ontology." In *Beyond Domination: New Perspectives on Women and Philosophy*, edited by Carol C. Gould, 64–88. Totowa: Rowman & Allanheld, 1983.

———. "Afterword to 'The Maternal Instinct.'" In *Mothering: Essays in Feminist Theory*, edited by Joyce Trebilcot, 192–98. Totowa: Rowman & Allanheld, 1983.

———. "The Maternal Instinct." In *Mothering: Essays in Feminist Theory*, edited by Joyce Trebilcot, 185–92. Totowa: Rowman & Allanheld, 1983.

*Part IV*

# EMBODIMENT AND CULTURE

## Chapter Nine

# Orchid Love

## Phoebe Hart

Both bodies in a single body mix,

A single body with a double sex.

—Ovid, *Metamorphoses*

Allow me to introduce myself. My name is Phoebe. I am a filmmaker, journal writer, academic, and a mother to our adopted daughter, Rachel. I am recently separated from my husband of more than a decade, feeling the distinct and terrifying possibilities not unlike that of a young adult about to leave the family home and embark on a new life. Additionally, I am a 46XY chromosomal woman: I am intersex.

Provocation #1: *What is this strange feeling in my chest? Is it worry for my child's future and my own? I wonder if I'll experience true love and passion ever again. I have fears as to the kind of example my ex is setting, or the aspersions he may care to cast in my direction ... I must keep a cool head. I must lead by example. He can't expect me to emote for him anymore. Not anymore.*

"Intersex" occurs in individuals where the reproductive organs are at variance with the genetic sex. Historically, a person with an intersex variation may have been known as a hermaphrodite.[1] Nowadays, many intersex peer-support groups and health care specialists also term an "intersex" variation as a Disorder of Sex Development or DSD.[2] It is my preference to use the term "intersex," yet at the same time allowing myself full permission to use whichever turn of phrase I feel is most appropriate and poetic at any given point.

Androgen Insensitivity Syndrome (AIS) is the congenital intersex variation I have, which can occur spontaneously at conception, or is passed down the generations via the matriarchal line. People with AIS have 46XY

169

chromosomes (i.e., the typical male pattern) but develop atypical reproductive organs as a result of their bodies being insensitive to androgens (male hormones, which include testosterone). The insensitivity to androgen can vary from "complete" insensitivity (CAIS) to "partial" insensitivity (PAIS). Consequently, physical appearance at birth can vary across the spectrum of female to male, and people with AIS can identify as being male, female, or intersex.[3] However, most individuals with CAIS, myself included, identify as women. In all cases, the gonads are actually undescended or only partially descended testes.[4]

By virtue of our common intersex variation, AIS, we enjoy distinctive physical features unlike many other adult human beings. We lack axillary and pubic hair; we have a feminine appearance, and a clear complexion (due to the ineffectiveness of testosterone on the AIS body, variations such as acne, which is caused by testosterone, are not a problem). As a result, in the eyes of some unwitting onlookers, we are often uncommonly beautiful and desirable.

Depending on which variations are described as intersex or a disorder of sexual development, the incidence of intersex globally is a matter of much conjecture and controversy; some scientists have suggested a frequency as high as between 1 or 2 in every 200 individuals.[5] Normally, people with intersex are sterile and suffer nonconsensual medical treatment and surgery as infants and children.[6] For myself, this intrusive pathologization included a round of surgery to remove my undescended testes, vaginal dilation and a lifetime of hormonal replacement therapy. As a result, shame, secrecy, and stigma have surrounded my life.

In 2010, in the spirit of Socrates's adage of the unexamined life not being worth living, I produced the feature documentary film Orchids: My Intersex Adventure— an autobiographical account of my life as a person with intersex. 25 Similarly, the title of this chapter is *Orchid Love*, as these ornamental flowers of the genus *Orchideae* are an especially potent symbol for people with intersex variations, particular for those with AIS. The etymology of the word "orchid" derives from Latin *orchis* and from Greek *orkhis*, which mean "testicle." Certainly, the protuberances within the orchid's flowering structure are reminiscent of the male gonads. Many people with AIS undergo an *orchidectomy* or the removal of internal testes to reduce the risk of cancer at some point in their lives, and, as such, often refer to themselves as orchids in their own life writing.[7] Therefore, I have appropriated these flowers as a resonant symbol throughout.

Provocation #2: *I went out on a date last night—lovely guy and we had fun—but at the end of the evening, only a vague "so we'll go out again sometime, huh?" What's up with that? And does that mean I need to do the inviting? I guess I am kind of gutless with this kind of thing.*

Arguably feminist phenomenology provides the best framework for philosophical investigation of the subjective gendered lived experience of intersex.[8] Intersex, by its very fluidity, problematizes standard, deterministic definitions of sex and gender, as often posited in the "nature versus nurture" polemic. Clearly, the ambiguously gendering of intersex bodies, such as my own, "seems to be extremely disconcerting or unsettling."[9] In 1990, Judith Butler's tome *Gender Trouble* posited that gender, like other aspects of identity, is a performance reinforced by repetition.[10] Butler acknowledges that hetero-normative imperatives of sex, desire, and gender are maintained by the psychological placement of self against "'incoherent' or 'discontinuous' gendered beings who appear to be persons but who fail to conform to the gendered norms of cultural intelligibility by which persons are defined."[11]

Here, Butler makes specific reference to intersex, citing the journal of nineteenth-century hermaphrodite Herculine Barbin, and its introduction by Michel Foucault:[12] "Herculine deploys and redistributes the terms of a binary system, but ... the very redistribution disrupts and proliferates those terms outside the binary itself."[13]

Like *Orchids*, Barbin's writings detail "the lived, first-person account of her ambiguous embodiment."[14] Perhaps, these accounts affected and mediated by historical context cannot be read as absolute "truth," but phenomenologies of gendered difference are useful in feminist investigations, where, as Foucault elucidates, "cultural practices intertwine with private sensations, pleasures, and pains."[15] Feminist phenomenology also provides a framework for understanding "ambiguous embodiment" in first-person filmmaking.

Agnès Varda's semi-autobiographical documentary *The Gleaners and I* (2000) is an example of embodied filmmaking. *The Gleaners and I* is a lyrical and visually arresting film about people who choose to pick over society's waste to find food, shelter, clothing, inspiration, or even fun. Varda, who, as a filmmaker, is a gleaner of sorts, draws extensively on the visual power of the reflection, as she passes a comment on her own aging body by juxtaposing self-portraits against a discarded clock with no hands (in effect, halting time), and using a mirror to study her maturing face. Rutherford notes that "all spectatorship is potentially affective" and describes the affective experience contained within this inspiring documentary:

> Ethics, the legal code, self-scrutiny and parody all jostle for position with the sweet taste of a ripened fig, the beauty of afternoon light in an apple orchard and the experience of old age ... [In *The Gleaners and* I] there is no implicit hierarchy here between image and word, no phobia of the image or its potential indeterminacy—the full capacity of the sound and image is put into play, and with it the affective experience of the spectator.[16]

Inspired by Varda, *Orchids: My Intersex Adventure* ruptures through the artistic manipulation of sound and image. Montages of bright, day-lit sequences of my journeying through picturesque Australian landscapes create affect, as

do scenes of my sister Bonnie, who also has AIS, and I *gleaning* eccentric
rural "op shops" (known as "thrift stores" elsewhere) in order to find treas-
ured objects. Photographs and personal objects from the characters' lives
are shot and edited to arrest the attention of the viewer, and the rich sexual
shapes and textures of the film's symbol—the orchids—are intended to be
beautiful and fascinating. However, the lens also attempts to make whole
the corporeal experience of being intersex and/or differently gendered. One
sequence shows me filming the landscape of scars on my body in close up,
a testament to the medical erasure of surgical intervention I have endured.
Another sequence poses Bonnie comparing dilators (prescribed by our doctors and used to stretch our vaginal canals to an acceptable length) to broom
sticks. Many of these scenes are filmed in intimate, enclosed spaces.

Kate Ince discerns in the film, "a performance of feminist phenomenology
deriving from her woman-subject's desire, experience, and vision."[17] Here,
Ince draws upon Young's seminal work on feminine embodied experience,
*Throwing like a Girl*, stating that Varda's work "privilege[s] female subjectivity and embodiment at the expense of representing as a cultural construct, either in the narratives or the material structure of her film-texts."[18]
Similarly, *Orchids: My Intersex Adventure* seeks to privilege intersex subjectivity, to tell our stories and, via affective sound and imagery, demonstrate
our bodily experiences, our thoughts and feelings, and our outlooks, loves,
and longings.

Interviewed some years after the publication of *Gender Trouble*, Butler
reiterated the value of creating works and acts "that challenge our practices of
reading, that make us uncertain about how to read, or make us think that we
have to renegotiate the way in which we read public signs."[19] Her sentiments
offer encouragement to myself as the author, bolstering the deconstructive
aims of my project, which were set upon the demystification and destabiliza-
tion of assumed knowledge.

Further, in *Bodies That Matter*, Butler elaborates upon the precursors of
the subversive act. She recognizes that individuals identify a "normative
phantasm of 'sex'" by rejecting the abject body, a "threatening specter" that
inhabits "those 'unlivable' and 'uninhabitable' zones of social life."[20] Clearly,
Butler was influenced by Julia Kristeva's view of abjection, a psychological
process that occurs during the creation of one's ego and "borders between self
and other."[21] Here, the initial step in a life-long process of abjection occurs
at an early stage of childhood, when a child first rejects what is dangerous to
him or her, such as sour milk:

> Loathing an item of food, a piece of filth, waste, or dung. The spasms and vomit-
> ing that protect me. The repugnance, the retching that thrusts me to the side and
> turns me away from defilement, sewage, and muck. The shame of compromise,

of being in the middle of treachery. The fascinated start that leads me toward and separates me from them ... But since the food is not an "other" for "me," who am only in their desire, I expel *myself*, I spit *myself* out, I abject myself within the same motion through which "I" claim to establish *myself*.[22]

Butler asserts that the identification of a hetero-normative sense of self occurs by rejecting the "abject" body that falls outside the limited classifications of "male" and "female" in the mind of the subject. For most individuals, the hermaphroditic body philosophically dwells in this abject realm.

Here, it is relevant to mention the work of Erving Goffman, a Canadian sociologist and writer, whose 1963 work *Stigma: Notes on the Management of Spoiled Identity* led to a greater transparency of the operations of social stigma in classifying and managing categories of persons "of a less desirable kind."[23] Goffman explores the relationship between attribute and stereotype that divides the "handicapped," or those with a flaw or weakness of some description, from the "normals," or those who have no discreditable attributes. Invariably, such a socially enforced divide leads the discredited or discreditable individuals to come to view him or herself as inferior, ashamed, and unaccepted.[24]

Provocation #3: *So, I hooked up with my date from last week. I just find him very sweet if somewhat mysterious. I felt very relaxed, but then a whole bunch of doubts started to creep in. I haven't told him about the AIS yet but we shared a really nice intimate time with one another, which is rare and to be cherished. I like him.*

As the speaker in Orchids: My Intersex Adventure, by using my voiceover narration and interviews, I gradually selected to reveal information about my variation and myself in order to effect a transformative interaction with the varied audience.[26] Many of these revelations emerged organically during the production process. Initially, I may not have wished them to be known, but as my trust of the camera grew, and my confidence in the power of the project became enhanced, I realized the inherent potential of such revelations. I also convinced my younger sister Bonnie of this potential, and together we attempted to create a series of self-directed and heart-felt "reveals" for *Orchids*. In *Orchids*, revelations such as trying to unsuccessfully insert a tampon, being prescribed dilators by our doctors to lengthen our vaginal canals, our subsequent relationships with our bodies that led us both to have eating disorders, my first sexual experiences—all these elements were conscious decisions to share something intensely private about our lives. Moreover, *Orchids* is an exploration of issues around love: be it familial, spousal, or communal.

However, part of these "reveals" relies on the invitation to the audience, the watcher, to join us on our journey. This is effectively an attempt to create a contract with the audience in order to establish a supportive relationship that cherishes openness. A sense of trust is invaluable to my own ontological security, but also opens a space for a "pure relationship" between me and the viewer(s) based upon mutual disclosure.[27] Perhaps this shall be realized by audience discussion after screenings of the film ("Q&A"), personal correspondence, and weblogs via the Internet presence the production proposes to develop. In the introduction to the film, I attempt to establish that multi-layered contract, by stating who I am, my insider credentials, the purpose for making this film and what I hope to achieve by doing so. Although a member of an audience is still able to reject or regulate his or her individual engagement, I feel that I have unmistakably offered an invitation for others to "come along for the intersex ride."

Another way that the empowered reveal was realized in the film relates to my decision to film myself (or to have my sister Bonnie film me) as I "outed" myself to random strangers. There was not much of a system to it; I just selected people whom I thought might be open to what I had to say. The first time I did this in the film was at an "op shop" in rural New South Wales. Fifi, the kindly Frenchwoman behind the counter, was curious about what we were doing, and her friendly disposition inspired me to ask if she minded if we filmed her while I told her about the project. Although this woman has little investment in our story or mission, such interaction, now captured on videotape and edited into the film, serves as a point where normative audiences might grasp that such an exchange could be a privilege and an opportunity. This creates an open space, and a place for active engagement that may help give mainstream viewers access to the intersex gaze.

Laura Mulvey, influenced by the work of French theorist Jacques Lacan, investigated the psyche of the cinema spectator, and described the pleasures of the scopophilic, voyeuristic [male] gaze.[28] Separated within a dark auditorium and dazzled by a brilliant, flickering screen, "a hermetically sealed world which unwinds magically, indifferent to the presence of the audience," the spectator is induced into an "illusion of voyeuristic separation."[29] In this state, men are the agents of a gaze upon "the [erotic] spectacle of the female body,"[30] and a "shifting tension" develops between the gaze of the male star and the gaze of men within the audience.[31] Paradoxically, Mulvey argues that the female form, while fascinating, is also threatening. The female's power is her psychic ability to castrate and diminish the male viewer's authoritative gaze, and hence [male] filmmakers counteract by sadistically disciplining or fetishizing the female character on the silver screen, as evident in the films of von Sternberg and Hitchcock.[32]

However, Mulvey's account of the "active male agent" and "passive female object" has been criticized for ignoring the possible viewing positions of those individuals "whose class, racial, national, and sexual orientation generally went unnamed."³³ Researchers have recently turned to the task of examining the mechanics of gay and lesbian cinema spectatorship, and these investigators have frequently found Mulvey's psychoanalytic work to be lacking.³⁴ For example, Straayer states that, according to feminist understandings of cinema spectatorship, a hypothetical lesbian heroine can only be viewed as "male" even though "maleness is potentially irrelevant to lesbianism."³⁵ Others (including herself) have also challenged Mulvey's early work by suggesting that the spectator is rarely passive, engaging with the cinematic experience on manifold levels.³⁶

More questions have arisen within film studies, challenging how self-identified homosexual viewers engaged with same-sex characters on screen, discussing the possibility of women and men as *both* agents and objects of desire. Richard Dyer, for instance, locates a complex system of identification in gay male viewers of Judy Garland films.³⁷ Debates over the "nonequivalence" of sexual objectification and narcissistic identification with an object (a legacy again of Lacan) become primary.³⁸ In her analysis of mainstream cinema from a lesbian spectator perspective, Jackie Stacey notes that "the rigid distinction between *either* desire *or* identification, so characteristic of psychoanalytic film theory, fails to address the construction of desires which involve a specific interplay of both processes."³⁹ Stacey suggests that, rather than the either/or choice of desiring a character or simply identifying with a character, it may be that the two are "meshed."⁴⁰

In my film, I feel I can only come back to how I speak and see, and then present what is heard and seen. I have adopted a psychological approach of assertive engagement in order to create an access point for the multifarious viewer. A part of this approach is the empowered reveal, which represents an invitation to access the intersex gaze. The framing of my ex-husband James is another example of a particular reveal, and the invitation to *see what I see*, although I have agonized whether some aspects of his inclusion could be read as mere titillation or voyeurism. Legally, current Queensland law sanctions our union as man and wife, yet our relationship could be seen as contentious. When James states on camera that he worried that he might be gay at the time when he and I first made love, *Orchids* attempts to create a space and reach a concern that may be felt by any male, heterosexual viewer. By making such an open declaration, James identifies a homophobic "knee jerk" reaction many men may have to the prospect of being with a woman who is, possibly, male. As such, I decided that it was important to include James' interview, as it not only serves to reach a new audience, but also forcefully addresses the multifarious nature of desire, and the complexity of human love relationships. This interview with James actually gives a crucial point of access to the intersex gaze, and the possibility of acceptance of non-heteronormatively gendered and sexualized identities for those people who could or would be *Orchids'* most antagonistic or reluctant audience members.

Theoretician Bill Nichols has identified not so much an erotic object of desire in documentary films but an *epistephilia*, or "pleasure of knowing."[41] However, Renov rebuts Nichols' assertion that the spectator could only desire knowledge, and argues instead that there are other "less rational" motivations to watch.[42] Referring to documentary filmmaking in the 1920s, Renov locates sites where "the journey to discursive sobriety at the level of documentary is temporarily set adrift by fantasy ... Documentary spectatorship is shown to be the site of multiple, even conflictual, desires that traverse the presumed barriers between conscious and unconscious processes."[43] Therefore, spectator identification can only ever be understood as "shifting, oscillating, inconsistent, and fluid."[44]

Provocation #4: *Wow! What a rollercoaster of emotions!! At first excited to be catching up with A (even if his text messages seemed to me to be somewhat off-handed) then really disappointed when he postponed. I really imagined the worst! Is this rejection? I must be too raw to get into any kind of relationship still; I need to do a lot more work on myself before I have the confidence to let it be. Then he texted this afternoon and was utterly charming ... Maybe I'm expecting too much?*

In the nineteenth century, when gonads were considered the true marker of sex, a woman with testes desiring a man would have been seen as unnatural. In fact, to medical practitioners of the time, it would have made more sense for such a woman to desire other women.[45] Not all of these medical understandings and fears have dissipated completely. Whenever I reveal my body or my story to a lover, I worry that he might think himself gay for being with a woman with male chromosomes. Open revelation forcefully addresses the multifarious nature of desire, and the complexity of human relationships. The possibility that someone may not accept my non-heteronormatively gendered body is cause for deep personal anxiety. Undoubtedly, my fears extend from a deep sense of shame, guarded secrecy, and the interventions I endured as a teenager. After my surgery, I wanted to disappear. Bodies with intersex are routinely "stripped of their ability to pleasure and be pleasured" by medicalization and social erasure. My decision to now live as a sexual, loving human being ruptures the rule of "asexual preinscription."[46]

Evidently, western cultures place a high value on possessing a "normal" body, and then urge us toward flawlessness. We strive for the perfect body, which has become persistently visible in our media-saturated environment, inversely leading to the invisibility and erasure of the nonnormative body in society.[47] Thus, medicine and the deity function of doctors are invoked to fix the disabled in both mind and body, as "restoring normal function and appearance are the purposes of rehabilitation."[48]

Our bodies cause ruptures also. Beauty equates to normalcy in our world at this moment; women who are considered beautiful are often the ones who have altered their bodies in extreme ways in order to conform.[49] People with intersex variations also undergo cosmetic procedures (sometimes without their permission) to obtain the prize of normalcy. As a teenager, I was like-wise driven to do anything at all that would make me more like a "normal" girl. But my body continued and continues to fall through the cracks. The scars on my body still show the wounds—the sites of entry and alteration. My [male] chromosomes still speak the truth. I am abject, yet there is beauty in my body, as there is beauty in the bodies of all the participants in *Orchids*. In many ways, my body fulfills the beauty standard, but is contradictory. I have excellent flawless skin, I am tall, and I am feminine; yet I am chromosomally male, and, pre-surgery, I had testes. I use my nearly normal body as some-thing I enjoy, rather than an obstacle to overcome. My body is able to create art and experience emotions such as love, and it has the ability to give and receive sexual pleasure.

Provocation #5: *For the last few days, I've been working myself into an absolute tizz. In my mind, A has rejected me because on our last date, I revealed I have AIS and he now knows I'm part male (although, really, I feel like a woman!). I thought I delivered the information so awkwardly and I was blaming myself for not having any of my former chutzpah about it. But actu-ally I can now see he is struggling with his own (fragile?) sense of masculin-ity. He's quite preoccupied with "getting ripped" and bring up his perceived differences between men and women quite a lot. But I think I was originally attracted to him because he has such a gentle feminine side!*

Evidently, my ambiguously gendered experience is complicated, queering normative expectations of love. I would like to celebrate the subjective, lived difference of the "abject" body, my body—to "reclaim [my] own impassioned, desirable, and desirous [body]."[50] Indeed, my body (and my narrative) has the power to disrupt, or, as espoused by transgendered advocate Constantine Giannaris, to create *genderfuck* and enact "play and performance which desta-bilize subject positions."[51] Gender variant visual artist and filmmaker Del La Grace Volcano likens our embodied experience to that of a chimera:

> I want to be seen for what I am: a chimera, a hybrid, a herm. After seven years of living as a herm I have to question if it is even possible for others to see beyond the binary and validate those of us who choose to live outside its confines, as well as those who have never been given the chance to.[52]

Like Volcano, I am difficult to grasp; I am neither completely male nor wholly female. My likes and dislikes, dreams and goals, needs and desires change over time. My body ages, and the people who populated my life at one point move on or evolve in their own life journeys. I cannot be arrested or fully explained by the moving image (nor anyone else for that matter). I can only measure the success of this auto/biography, which ultimately I must, by increments of political, cultural, social, and personal transformation. Like others, I seek intimacy—both physical and emotional—but love is illusive, and how do I (or should I even) confess my difference to my lovers? Often my indistinct body gives silent clues to those who are observant, but, most times, for another to comprehend, my words must fill the spaces. My filmmaking provides a discourse of difference and desire, but "the phenomenological method only begins with first-person descriptions of experience."[53] My embodied experience continues beyond the narrative confines of the documentary production, now as a single mother back on the dating scene.

In many ways, my film work and my life highlights how intersex love works on many varied, ambiguous layers. These ambivalences, while at times the source of great personal anxiety, nonetheless, continue to form a sexual provocation. As I embrace my new lovers, many of whom steadfastly declare their tenuous heteronormativity and have little understanding or knowledge of gender difference, both the reality of postdivorce dating and my fantasy life come crashing together. Can I truly find perfect love and sex with another when my body lies so far out from the range of "normal" variation? Will I be accepted and loved for who and what I am? Indeed, there is an emotional risk and vulnerability when entering into any *affair de coeur* to which no one is immune, whether one is intersex or not:

> Melancholy is amorous passion's sombre lining. A sorrowful pleasure, this lugubrious intoxication constitutes the banal background from which our ideals or euphoria break away as much as that fleeting lucidity which breaks the trance entwining two people together. Conscious that we are destined to lose our loves, we are perhaps even more grieved to notice in our lover the shadow of a loved object, already lost.[54]

I think the answer may come not from without, but within. In the meantime, I resolve to battle on as I seek human contact, affection, deep understanding and love in a quest that is not easy. As feminist-poet Adrienne Rich notes, "[a]n honorable human relationship—that is, one in which two people have the right to use the word 'love'—is a process, delicate, violent, often terrifying to both persons involved, a process of refining the truths they can tell each other. ... It is important to do this because in doing so we do justice to our own complexity."

Provocation #6: *So it's over. I feel like the anxiety has lifted. I feel heartbroken. But there are no regrets. I'm grateful to have loved (and lost) and I'm glad to know it was not so much about the AIS. I have a kernel of hope within me still ... I'll find someone else right soon.*

I presented *Orchids: My Intersex Adventure* as an exploration of my memory, history and love, and, concurrently, an examination and a celebration of the encircling institutions of family, community, and society. During the creative practice process, I struggled with the politics and aesthetics of attempting to engage such a broad audience. In my mind's eye, I imagined who might be watching the final film at its initial screening. In part, the film is my message to my mother, and my family, who brought me into the world and shaped my understanding of it. Significantly, I am also speaking to others with an intersex variation, saying *this is how I see it*, and asking *do you see it this way too?* It is an intimate message, a shared agreement of intersubjectivity, which, in many ways, is latent in the text, perhaps unwritten, made manifest by those who understand its language. It is a language written on the intersex body; a phenomenological language of cuts, lies, sensations, feelings, and fears. It is a way of looking, a way of *speaking, seeing,* and *knowing* what is unspoken and unseen or unknown by others.

While creatively addressing and embodying these issues, I believe my embodied experience of love, whether mediated or lived, has the power to destigmatize a sector of society that is *biologically* different by recognizing "the flexibility of the biological [human] organism and the complexity of the interaction between genes and experience during development."[55] In effect, my body and my memoir is a form of emancipation through artistic reinvention, which aims to split the bio-determinism nexus, that is, the use of genetic difference as an instrument of control, for example, "to justify the oppression of races, classes, and minority groups."[56] Moreover, beyond demonstrating the flexibility of the human organism, I continue to explore the kinship bonds between people with intersex, and to challenge society's "will-to-normalize the non-standard body."[57]

## NOTES

1. Alice Domurat Dreger, "Hermaphrodites in Love: The Truth of Gonads," in *Science and Homosexualities*, ed. Vernon A. Rosario (New York: Routledge, 1997), 47.

2. Sherri Groveman Morris, "DSD but Intersex Too: Shifting Paradigms without Abandoning Roots." (2006) Accessed 29 March, 2007. http://www.isna.org/node/1067; Ieuan A. Hughes, Peter A. Lee, Christopher P. Houk and S. Faisal Ahmed, "Consensus Statement on Management of Intersex Disorders," *Journal of Pediatric Urology* 2 (2006): e 488. http://pediatrics.aappublications.org/cgi/reprint/118/2/e488.

3. Other intersex variations include Congenital Adrenal Hyperplasia (CAH: virilized individuals with 46XX chromosomes), Gonadal Dysgenesis (an abnormal development of the gonads, which could be caused by a number of intersex variations,

including Turner, Swyer, and Perrault Syndromes), and Klinefelter's Syndrome (chromosomal aneuploidy resulting in the duplication of sex chromosomes, e.g., 47-XXY, 48-XXXY, 49-XXXXY, 48-XXYY, etc.).

4. Milton Diamond, "Androgen Insensitivity Syndrome and Klinefelter's Syndrome: Sex and Gender Considerations," *Child and Adolescent Psychiatric Clinics of North America* 13, no.3 (2004): 623–25.

5. Leonard Sax, "How Common Is Intersex? A Response to Anne Fausto-Sterling," *The Journal of Sex Research* 39 (3) (2002): 174; Anne Fausto-Sterling. "The Five Sexes: Why Male and Female are Not Enough." The Sciences March/April (1993): 20.

6. Tony Briffa, Accessed April 14. Last modified April 04, 2005. http://home.vicnet.net.au/~aissg/.

7. Ibid.

8. Linda Fisher, "Gendering Embodied Memory," in *Time in Feminist Phenomenology*, eds. Christina Schues, Dorothea E. Olkowski and Helen A. Fielding (Bloomington: Indiana University Press, 2011), 91.

9. Ibid., 95.

10. Judith Butler, *Gender Trouble: Feminism and the Subversion of Identity* (New York: Routledge, 1990).

11. Ibid., 17.

12. Herculine Barbin and Michel Foucault, *Herculine Barbin: Being the Recently Discovered Memoirs of a Nineteenth-Century Hermaphrodite,* trans. Richard McDougall (New York: Pantheon, 1980).

13. Butler, *Gender Trouble*, 23.

14. Johanna Oksala, "Sexual Experience: Foucault, Phenomenology, and Feminist Theory," *Hypatia* 26, no.1 (2011): 217.

15. Cited in Oksala, "Sexual Experience," 218.

16. Anne Rutherford, "The Poetics of a Potato: Documentary That Gets Under the Skin," *Metro Magazine* 137 (2003): 129.

17. Jill Franz, Marissa Lindquist and Grace Bitner, "Educating for Change: A Case for Pedagogy of Desire in Design Education" (essay presented at the DesignEd Asia Conference 2011, Hong Kong Convention & Exhibition Centre, Hong Kong), 613.

18. Ibid.

19. Cited in Judith Butler, "Gender as Performance," in *A Critical Sense: Interviews with Intellectuals*, ed. Peter Osborne (New York: Routledge, 1996).

20. Judith Butler, *Bodies That Matter: On The Discursive Limits of "Sex"* (New York: Routledge, 1993), 3.

21. Cited in Noelle McAfee, *Julia Kristeva*, ed. Robert Eaglestone, *Routledge Critical Thinkers* (New York: Routledge, 2004), 45.

22. Julia Kristeva, *Powers of Horror: An Essay on Abjection* (New York: Columbia University Press, 1982), 2–3.

23. Erving Goffman, "Selections from *Stigma*," in *The Disability Studies Reader*, ed. Lennard J. Davis (New York: Routledge, 2006), 131.

24. Ibid., 133.

25. Phoebe Hart, *Orchids: My Intersex Adventure.* Phoebe Hart. Performed Brisbane, Australia: Hartflicker, 2010.

26. By 'transformative' I mean a radical and spontaneous change in the minds and lives of those watching, hopefully for the better, around the issue of intersex.

27. Anthony Giddens, *Modernity and Self-Identity: Self and Society in the Late Modern Age* (Cambridge: Polity Press, 1991), 6.

28. Laura Mulvey, "Visual Pleasure and Narrative Cinema," in *The Audience Studies Reader*, eds. Will Brooker and Deborah Jermyn (New York: Routledge, 2003 [1975]), 135.

29. Ibid., 135.

30. Richard Allen, "Psychoanalytic Film Theory," in *A Companion to Film Theory*, eds. Toby Miller and Robert Stam (Oxford: Blackwell, 2004), 137.

31. Mulvey, *Visual Pleasure*, 137.

32. Ibid., 140–41.

33. Julia Erhart, "Laura Mulvey Meets Catherine Tramell Meets the She-Man: Counter-History, Reclamation, and Incongruity in Lesbian, Gay, and Queer Film and Media Criticism," in *A Companion to Film Theory*, eds. Toby Miller and Robert Stam (Oxford: Blackwell Publishing, 2004) 171.

34. Ibid., 171–72.

35. Chris Straayer, *Deviant Eyes, Deviant Bodies: Sexual Re-Orientation in Film and Video*, ed. John Belton, *Film and Culture* (New York: Colombia University Press, 1996), 11.

36. Jacqueline Rose, "Paranoia and the Film System," in *Feminism and Film Theory*, ed. Jacqueline Rose (New York: Routledge, 1988); Constance Penley, *Future of an Illusion: Film, Feminism, and Psychoanalysis, Media and Society* (Minneapolis: University of Minnesota Press, 1989).

37. Richard Dyer, "Judy Garland and Gay Men," in *Queer Cinema: The Film Reader*, eds. Harry Benshoff and Sean Griffin (New York: Routledge, 2004).

38. Erhart, "Laura Mulvey Meets Catherine Tramell," 172.

39. Cited in Caroline Evans and Lorraine Gammon, "Reviewing Queer Viewing," in *Queer Cinema: The Film Reader*, eds. Harry Benshoff and Sean Griffin (New York: Routledge, 2004), 212.

40. Ibid.

41. Bill Nichols, *Introduction to Documentary* (Bloomington: Indiana University Press, 2001).

42. Michael Renov, *The Subject of Documentary*, eds. Michael Renov, Faye Ginsberg and Jane Gaines. Vol. 16, *Visible Evidence* (Minnesota: University of Minnesota Press, 2004), 93.

43. Ibid., 102–3.

44. Evans and Gammon, *Reviewing Queer Viewing*, 217.

45. Dreger, "Hermaphrodites in Love," 49–50.

46. Sumi Colligan, "Why the Intersexed Shouldn't be Fixed: Insights from Queer Theory and Disability Studies," in *Gendering Disability*, eds. Bonnie G. Smith and Beth Hutchinson (New Brunswick: Rutgers University Press, 2004), 50.

47. Sharon Dale Stone, "The Myth of Bodily Perfection," *Disability and Society* 10 (4) (1995): 413.

48. Philip Hancock, Bill Huges, Elizabeth Jagger, Kevin Paterson, Rachel Russell, Emmanuelle Tulle-Winton and Melissa Tyler, *The Body, Culture and Society: An Introduction* (Philadelphia: Open University Press, 2000), 33.

49. Rosemarie Garland Thomson, "Integrating Disability, Transforming Feminist Theory," in *The Disability Studies Reader*, ed. Lennard J. Davis (New York: Routledge, 2006), 263.

50. Colligan, "Why the Intersexed Shouldn't Be Fixed," 50.

51. Cited in Evans and Gammon, "Reviewing Queer Viewing," 219.

52. Del LaGrace Volcano and Indra Windh, "GenderFusion," in *Queer Theory*, eds. Iain Morland and Annabelle Willox (New York: Palgrave MacMillan, 2005), 134.

53. Oksala, "Sexual Experience," 220.

54. Julia Kristeva, "On the Melancholic Imaginary," *New Formations* 3 (1987): 5.

55. Gisela T. Kaplan and Lesley J. Rogers, *Gene Worship: Moving Beyond the Nature/Nurture Debate Over Genes, Brain, and Gender* (New York: Other Press, 2003), 4.

56. Cited in Kaplan and Rogers, *Gene Worship*, 31.

57. Rosemarie Garland Thomson, "Integrating Disability," in *Gendering Disability*, ed. Bonnie G. Smith and Beth Hutchinson (New Brunswick: Rutgers University Press, 2005), 264.

## BIBLIOGRAPHY

Allen, Richard. "Psychoanalytic Film Theory." In *A Companion to Film Theory*, edited by Toby Miller and Robert Stam, 123–45. Oxford: Blackwell, 2004.

Barbin, Herculine, and Michel Foucault. *Herculine Barbin: Being the Recently Discovered Memoirs of a Nineteenth-Century Hermaphrodite*. Translated by Richard McDougall. New York: Pantheon, 1980.

Briffa, Tony. Accessed April 14. Last modified April 04, 2005. http://home.vicnet.net.au/~aissg/.

Butler, Judith. *Bodies That Matter: On The Discursive Limits of "Sex."* New York: Routledge, 1993.

———. "Gender as Performance." In *A Critical Sense: Interviews with Intellectuals*, edited by Peter Osborne, 109–26. New York: Routledge, 1996.

———. *Gender Trouble: Feminism and the Subversion of Identity*. New York: Routledge, 1990.

Colligan, Sumi. "Why the Intersexed Shouldn't Be Fixed: Insights from Queer Theory and Disability Studies." In *Gendering Disability*, edited by Bonnie G. Smith and Beth Hutchinson, 45–60. New Brunswick: Rutgers University Press, 2004.

Diamond, Milton. "Androgen Insensitivity Syndrome and Klinefelter's Syndrome: Sex and Gender Considerations." *Child and Adolescent Psychiatric Clinics of North America* 13, no.3 (2004): 623–40.

Dreger, Alice Domurat. "Hermaphrodites in Love: The Truth of Gonads." In *Science and Homosexualities,* edited by Vernon A. Rosario, 46–66. New York: Routledge, 1997.

Dyer, Richard. "Judy Garland and Gay Men." In *Queer Cinema: The Film Reader,* edited by Harry Benshoff and Sean Griffin, 153–166. New York: Routledge, 2004.

Erhart, Julia. "Laura Mulvey Meets Catherine Tramell Meets the She-Man: Counter-History, Reclamation, and Incongruity in Lesbian, Gay, and Queer Film and Media Criticism." In *A Companion to Film Theory,* edited by Toby Miller and Robert Stam, 165–181. Oxford: Blackwell Publishing, 2004.

Evans, Caroline, and Lorraine Gammon. "Reviewing Queer Viewing." In *Queer Cinema: The Film Reader,* edited by Harry Benshoff and Sean Griffin, 209–24. New York: Routledge, 2004.

Fausto-Sterling, Anne. "The Five Sexes: Why Male and Female are Not Enough." *The Sciences* March/April (1993): 20–25.

Fisher, Linda. "Gendering Embodied Memory." In *Time in Feminist Phenomenology,* edited by Christina Schues, Dorothea E. Olkowski, and Helen A. Fielding, 91–110. Bloomington: Indiana University Press, 2011.

Franz, Jill, Marissa Lindquist, and Grace Bitner. "Educating for Change: A Case for Pedagogy of Desire in Design Education." Essay presented at the DesignEd Asia Conference, Hong Kong Convention & Exhibition Centre, Hong Kong, 2011.

Garland Thomson, Rosemarie. "Integrating Disability." In *Gendering Disability,* edited by Bonnie G. Smith and Beth Hutchinson, 73–103. New Brunswick: Rutgers University Press, 2005.

———. "Integrating Disability, Transforming Feminist Theory." In *The Disability Studies Reader,* edited by Lennard J. Davis, 257–74. New York: Routledge, 2006.

Giddens, Anthony. *Modernity and Self-Identity: Self and Society in the Late Modern Age.* Cambridge: Polity Press, 1991.

Goffman, Erving. "Selections from Stigma." In *The Disability Studies Reader,* edited by Lennard J. Davis, 131–40. New York: Routledge, 2006.

Groveman Morris, Sherri. "DSD but Intersex Too: Shifting Paradigms without Abandoning Roots." (2006) Accessed 29 March, 2007. http://www.isna.org/node/1067.

Hancock, Philip, Bill Huges, Elizabeth Jagger, Kevin Paterson, Rachel Russell, Emmanuelle Tulle-Winton, and Melissa Tyler. *The Body, Culture and Society: An Introduction.* Philadelphia: Open University Press, 2000.

Hart, Phoebe. *Orchids: My Intersex Adventure.* Phoebe Hart. Performed Brisbane, Australia: Hartflicker, 2010.

Hughes, Ieuan A., Peter A. Lee, Christopher P. Houk, and S. Faisal Ahmed. "Consensus Statement on Management of Intersex Disorders " *Journal of Pediatric Urology* 2 (2006): 148–62. http://pediatrics.aappublications.org/cgi/reprint/118/2/e488.

Kaplan, Gisela T., and Lesley J. Rogers. *Gene Worship: Moving Beyond the Nature/ Nurture Debate Over Genes, Brain, and Gender.* New York: Other Press, 2003.

Kristeva, Julia. "On the Melancholic Imaginary." *New Formations* 3 (1987): 5–18.

———. *Powers of Horror: An Essay on Abjection.* New York: Columbia University Press, 1982.

McAfee, Noelle. *Julia Kristeva,* edited by Robert Eaglestone, *Routledge Critical Thinkers.* New York: Routledge, 2004.

Mulvey, Laura. "Visual Pleasure and Narrative Cinema." In *The Audience Studies Reader*, edited by Will Brooker and Deborah Jermyn, 133–142. New York: Routledge, 2003 [1975].

Nichols, Bill. *Introduction to Documentary*. Bloomington: Indiana University Press, 2001.

Oksala, Johanna. "Sexual Experience: Foucault, Phenomenology, and Feminist Theory." *Hypatia* 26, no.1 (2011): 207–23.

Ovid. "*Metamorphoses*: Book IV." In *Poetica Erotica: A Collection of Rare and Curious Amatory Verse*, edited by T. R. Smith. New York: Crown Publishers, 1921.

Penley, Constance. *Future of an Illusion: Film, Feminism, and Psychoanalysis, Media and Society* Minneapolis: University of Minnesota Press, 1989.

Renov, Michael. *The Subject of Documentary*, edited by Michael Renov, Faye Ginsberg and Jane Gaines. 16 vols. Vol. 16, *Visible Evidence*. Minnesota: University of Minnesota Press, 2004.

Rich, Adrienne. *On Lies, Secrets, and Silence: Selected Prose 1966–1978*. New York: W.W. Norton & Company, 1979.

Rose, Jacqueline. "Paranoia and the Film System." In *Feminism and Film Theory*, edited by Jacqueline Rose, 141–58. New York: Routledge, 1988.

Rutherford, Anne. "The Poetics of a Potato: Documentary That Gets Under the Skin." *Metro Magazine* 137 (2003): 126–31.

Sax, Leonard. "How Common Is Intersex? A Response to Anne Fausto-Sterling." *The Journal of Sex Research* 39, no.3 (2002): 174–78.

Stone, Sharon Dale. "The Myth of Bodily Perfection." *Disability and Society* 10 (4) (1995): 413–24.

Straayer, Chris. *Deviant Eyes, Deviant Bodies: Sexual Re-Orientation in Film and Video*, edited by John Belton, *Film and Culture*. New York: Colombia University Press, 1996.

Varda, Agnès. *The Gleaners and I*. Canal + and La Procirep Cine-Tamaris with the Participation of Centre National du Cinema. Performed France: Zeitgeist Video. Theatrical Release, 2000.

Volcano, Del LaGrace and Indra Windh. "GenderFusion." In *Queer Theory*, edited by Iain Morland and Annabelle Willox, 130–41. New York: Palgrave MacMillan, 2005.

*Chapter Ten*

# Failed Medicalization and the Cultural Iconography of Feminine Sexuality

## Rebecca Kukla

In this chapter, I look at the medical history of "female sexual disorders" as an example of a narrative of *failed medicalization*. Deep-rooted ideological pressures prevent a medicalization of female sexuality analogous to the very successful medicalization of male sexuality that occurred in the 1990s, I claim. In the post-Foucaultian era, narratives of medicalization are common ways of revealing the contingent social history of what appears to be a natural phenomenon or a given condition. It is easy to find histories of the medicalization of erectile dysfunction (ED), alcoholism, fetal alcohol syndrome, disorders of sexual development, and so forth. But we rarely examine cases where medicalization fails, even though these are at least as revealing of the social production of medical and bodily facts and knowledge.

Since the FDA approval of Viagra in 1998, men's sexuality (at least in developed capitalist nations) has been massively medicalized through the lens of "ED." The creation and expansion of ED, and the role that the pharmaceutical industry and direct-to-consumer advertising played in that process, is widely acknowledged as a textbook example of how disease-generation is driven by economic forces and social meanings.[1]

Viagra was originally under development as a drug for pulmonary hypertension, and its impact on men's ability to obtain and maintain an erection was discovered serendipitously. Pfizer quickly recognized a marketing opportunity, at first framing ED as a secondary effect of other morbidities, but rapidly recasting it as a self-standing disease. Early marketing targeted at elderly men quickly expanded to include reasonably young and otherwise able men; meanwhile, early spokesmen of the "elderly statesman" variety such as Bob Dole were replaced with younger, more romantic figures such as Cuba Gooding, Jr. Initially targeting men who had a total or near-total inability to get and stay erect, Pfizer worked to expand its market by casting *any* failure to get and stay erect when desired as a *medical symptom* as opposed to a normal, perhaps situational, fluctuation in libido or biochemistry. Thus, ED became a disease that almost any man could worry about having. With the success of Viagra, other pharmaceutical companies jumped into the fray, with copycat drugs such as Cialis and shady alternatives such as Enzyte flooding the market.[2]

The effect of this market broadening was not merely the sale of more ED drugs; it brought about a far-reaching medicalization of male sexuality. Almost any man, during the normal course of his sex life, could now experience "symptoms" widely understood as appropriately brought under medical surveillance and management. Accordingly, maintaining a "normal" sex life came to require pharmaceutical support for a huge swath of otherwise healthy men. Arguably, our very conception of male sexuality itself was reconstituted, or at least sharpened and streamlined. With the advent of ED, genital performance serves as the official measure of sexual normalcy and function for men.[3]

Given the commercial success of ED, it is no surprise that in the early 2000s, there was a flurry of concerted attempts to medicalize female sexual dysfunction—or "FSD"—in some analogous way. So began a race to find the "female Viagra." In particular, the Boston University Department of Urology, heavily backed by pharmaceutical money, quickly positioned itself as the leading center for the biomedical study of FSD.

But whereas there has been little disagreement over where to look for male sexual dysfunction—that is, look directly at the penis and its mechanical ability to get and stay hard on cue—the medical community and pharmaceutical industry found it a far from straightforward task to locate and define FSD. The first burst of post-Viagra research on female sexuality took the form of a rush to develop indices, measures, and diagnostic criteria for female sexual function and dysfunction. The early 2000s saw the development of the Female Sexual Function Index, the Female Sexual Distress Scale, and several other quasi- or pseudo-quantitative measures of FSD. In turn, and in sharp contrast to the male case, this work did not lead to a single, narrow definition of FSD, but on the contrary to a sudden proliferation of official diagnoses for women, including but not restricted to:

- Sexual interest/desire disorder
- Subjective sexual arousal disorder
- Genital sexual arousal disorder
- Orgasmic disorder
- Sexual aversion disorder
- Dysparenuia (pain from penetration)
- Vaginismus (pelvic contractions inhibiting penetration)

Almost as quickly as it began, scholars and activists began publishing critiques of the nascent medicalization of female sexuality. These critiques took familiar forms, arguing that women's sex lives—much like childbirth, young boys' inability to sit still, and other everyday phenomena deeply embedded within social and material life—were being coopted and overhauled for profit by the medical and pharmaceutical industries. Correspondingly, our conception of sexual normalcy was being narrowed, normal human variation was being pathologized, socially rooted problems and discomforts were being reduced to biochemical mechanical breakdowns, standard heteronormative conceptions of sexual life and identity were being reinscribed and given scientific imprimatur, and bodily self-knowledge was being undermined by an expert-based epistemology.

Among the most visible of these critics was (and is) Leonore Tiefer, who has organized a major campaign against the medicalization of FSD, virtually headquartered at www.newviewcampaign.org. Tiefer has helped organize successful lobbies against the approval of several proposed FSD drugs, and she has been a major voice making vivid the dangers of medicalization. Meanwhile, Ray Moynihan, in a much-cited 2003 article in the *British Medical Journal*, insisted that "the corporate sponsored creation of a disease is not a new phenomenon, but the making of FSD is the freshest, clearest example we have."[4]

Let me be perfectly clear that I agree with Moynihan, Tiefer, and others that there are significant social and medical risks involved in the medicalization of female sexuality and the development of FSD as a disease, especially as spearheaded by the pharmaceutical industry. These critics' concerns are real and pressing. However, the situation is more complex than Moynihan makes it sound. We continue to see a lot of highly motivated *attempts* at the medicalization of FSD, and there are real reasons to worry about these attempts and about the consequences we would face were they successful. But so far, FSD is a partial, messy, failed exercise in medicalization, not a "clear" one.

Indeed, what interests me most for the purpose of this chapter is the extent to which the attempts to medicalize female sexuality over the last ten to fifteen years have *failed* in multiple ways. In stark contrast to the case of male sexuality, and despite many research dollars being poured into the process, we still have no clear medical conception of FSD. FSD has not been branded or reduced to a simple narrative. The one medication that has been approved for treating FSD—Addyi (flibanserin)—made it through the FDA approval process in late 2015 amidst huge scientific and ethical controversy and much ongoing expert disagreement over its efficacy and safety. It comes with a box warning and special constraints on its prescription due to its severe potential side effects. Unlike Viagra, it must be taken regularly for a long term, and in its most successful testing it raised the number of "satisfying

sexual events" for women by 0.5 per month over placebo, after 6–12 months
of use. Perhaps most relevantly, the mechanism by which it works is completely unknown.[5] Women do not know when to go to their doctor to get help
with their sex lives, nor do doctors have reliable treatments or diagnoses at
the ready. Medical surveillance and management of women's sex lives is
not the norm.

FSD has not yielded a standard, unidirectional, medicalization narrative,
such as we saw with ED, ADHD, alcoholism, and other famous cases of
medicalization. Instead, it has been a tension-ridden process during which,
I argue, the pressures to medicalize have mixed uneasily with ideological and
conceptual pressures to preserve female sexuality as a phenomenon immune
from scientific and biomedical assimilation.

In the rest of this chapter, I demonstrate that the reasons for this failure
are philosophically interesting. An important upshot of this chapter will be
that what we *don't* successfully medicalize can be as interesting and telling
as what we do.[6] We are by now familiar with a multitude of post-Foucaultian
stories about how micro-forces and vectors of power collude to medicalize a
condition. Just as interesting, but much less discussed, are narratives of how
such micro-forces and vectors can collude to undermine or block medicalization, even when there are profit motives driving it forward.

## WHAT IS MEDICALIZATION AND
## WHEN IS IT APPROPRIATE?

What is at stake when we claim that a condition or set of experiences has
been, or is being, medicalized? There is no one agreed-upon definition of
medicalization.[7] Roughly, it is the process of bringing some dimension or
mode of human experience or bodily functioning under medical surveillance
and control. I think it is helpful to understand medicalization as involving (at
least) four dimensions. Although these four dimensions are causally intertwined, in any given case medicalization may be partial, and a condition may
be medicalized in some of these ways and not others.

1. *Institutional*: This is the most obvious. When a condition becomes medicalized, it is brought under the epistemic and practical authority of the
   institutions of medicine. Health professionals become the arbiters of
   diagnostic standards and individual diagnoses, and likewise, the expert
   determiners of normalcy and pathology. Medical surveillance, control, and
   management become appropriate. In recent decades, we have seen this sort
   of institutional medicalization of female infertility and transgender identity, for instance.

2. *Epistemological:* Medicalization is not just bound up with *who* has expert knowledge, namely, health professionals, but also with *how* a condition is detected and diagnosed. Medicalized conditions are diagnosed through the examination of single bodies, isolated in clinics, using the tools and skills of medicine (visual and tactile examination, blood tests, scanning technology, questionnaires, etc.). For example, ADHD is not diagnosed by watching a child act and interact in his daily social environment and material space, which might give quite different kinds of information, but through clinical examination that he does on his own.

3. *Metaphysical:* Correspondingly, medicalized disorders and pathologies are the right sorts of entities to be revealed by these epistemic methods; they are dysfunctions of particular body parts or systems, inherent in individual bodies (as opposed to, for instance, relational or social properties). They are also the right sorts of entities to be managed by medical institutions; they are amenable to treatment or mitigation through targeted bodily interventions such as drugs or surgery.

4. *Ethical:* Medicalization often counteracts moralization. It involves a "move from badness to sickness," as Peter Conrad put it.[8] Conditions taken as indicating poor character, weakness of the will, laziness, sinfulness, and the like can at least partially shed these moral meanings through medicalization; consider the medicalization of alcoholism, obesity, and chronic fatigue syndrome, for instance. Meanwhile, medicalization invests parts of the body with direct normative (albeit amoral) meaning; they become pathological or dysfunctional, in need of fixing rather than accommodation if possible.

Medicalization per se is neither "good" nor "bad." Whether it does more overall good or harm depends on many factors. Some of these include how effective our medical tools are at relieving the relevant sorts of human suffering and discomfort, the social context in which medicalization occurs, the extent to which the process generates and constitutes human suffering and discomfort rather than responding to it, the particular power interests invested in medicalization, and the intensity of the ideology of moralization and blame that preceded medicalization.

In most cases, successful medicalization comes along a complex combination of good and bad effects. As for good effects, most obviously, many treatments alleviate suffering and reduce risk. Furthermore, many people, as they are transformed into "patients," in addition to benefiting from the alleviation of harmful symptoms, find social legitimization for their suffering and limitations. Medicalization can also aid in creating and giving access to communities based around shared experiences, and it can encourage the devotion of social resources to a problem. The move from a rhetorical and ethical logic of blame and character flaws to that of pathology and dysfunction is almost always a moral and political improvement.

On the negative side, medicalization typically goes along with a narrowing down of our sense of the normal and a limitation of diversity, together with a pathologization of human variation. Because of its epistemological and metaphysical commitments, medicalization tends to mask social and relational determinants of embodied experience, including those shaped by systematic oppression and injustice. In ossifying a narrow sense of the normal, that sense tends to be one that reentrenches widespread social norms, including sexist, heterocentric, and classist ones. Because of the social authority afforded to medical professionals and institutions, medicalization can also block the critical interrogation of the norms it entrenches or reentrenches. Furthermore, medicalization enhances the power over bodies and lives held by social institutions whose interests may not align with patients' own interests, such as pharmaceutical and insurance companies. And often it gives problematic "gatekeeping" powers to medical professionals, who get to control who has access to diagnoses and interventions—and often, by extension, to entire identities.

In critiquing the medicalization of FSD specifically, Moynihan accuses those searching for FSD drugs of "turning healthy people into patients."[9] Thea Cacchioni and Leonore Tiefer worry about "the genitalization of sexuality (and its inadvertent androcentrism)"[10] that is threatened by the medicalization of FSD. Janine Farrell and Cacchioni also point out the deep heteronormativity of the FSD literature, which focuses almost exclusively on women's physical and psychological ability to engage in "proper" penis-in-vagina-culminating-in-orgasm sex.[11] Tiefer's New View Campaign produced a fact sheet on one proposed FSD drug, arguing that the developing company's rhetorical focus on the "right to choose" the medication "misdirects outrage over gender injustice toward consumer product choices… Drugs and drug companies cannot provide the groundwork for social change that improves women's lives, and they confuse the public by conflating consumer choice with social and personal empowerment."[12] She points out that emphasizing the autonomy that comes with making the drug available cannot be divorced from a context in which women are pressured to be available to men for genital intercourse.[13] A recent documentary on the medicalization of FSD points out that a huge number of women have such poor sex education that they don't even know how to identify their clitoris or that clitoral stimulation is the most common route to orgasm for women, making a pharmaceutical "solution" a distraction from more important social barriers to women's sexual fulfillment.[14]

Conversely, effective medicalization might well enhance women's sexual pleasure and self-esteem, legitimize various kinds of suffering currently treated as too private and shameful to be shared or even articulated, and help undo social myths of sexual appetite and pleasure as fundamentally masculine.

I (incompletely) summarize these benefits and risks here to drive home the point that I am neither vilifying nor lobbying for the medicalization of female sexuality. Medicalization is a rich and complicated social process, rife with messy normative consequences of many kinds. How helpful or damaging the medicalization of female sexuality would be depends on the details, including how FSD ends up getting operationalized and what ideological assumptions are built into that operationalization. Failed medicalization—my interest here—is a much less studied but equally rich phenomenon.

## BIG PHARMA AND THE HARD PHALLUS

It is unsurprising that male sexual dysfunction was so easily operationalizable and so ripe for medicalization, given how we already imagined men's sexuality. It is easy to locate male sexual success or failure—it resides in the penis. "Proper," functional men get and keep erections when they want to. This reductive image of male sexuality is pervasive and long standing. We portray ED as having social and relational *effects*, such as shame, breakdowns of relationships, and emasculation. But we assume the *causes* of male sexual dysfunction to be physiological, and we assume its *expression* to be mechanical. It is easy for us to accept that we can fix such physiological and mechanical breakdowns through pharmaceutical interventions and medical management, thereby effectively restoring social and relational normalcy.

This is a classic version of the medicalization narrative, and interestingly, it is arguably one that has more often been applied to women. Historically, shady diagnoses such as hysteria and overextended legitimate diagnoses such as depression have been used to reduce women's social and relationship breakdowns to individualized physiological breakdowns, accompanied by the promise that medical intervention will heal social relationships. Direct-to-consumer drug advertisements aimed at women often portray a progression from social and relational breakdown, to a pharmaceutical fix, to social healing. Woven into the narrative is the idea that the woman has a moral responsibility to fix herself, out of fairness to her partner and children (see figure 10.1). Similar marketing techniques have been used for depression, hormone replacement therapy for menopause, and reproductive technologies for infertility, for instance.

Advertisements for ED drugs often use this characteristically feminized narrative strategy on a distinctively male condition. ED advertisements typically focus first and foremost on the impact of the condition

**Figure 10.1**

on relationships, billing a physiological intervention as able to heal social breakdowns. One 2007 ad, entitled "good morning," features a string of happy, fulfilled, peppy middle-aged women clearly having a wonderful morning, delightedly heading out to work and the like, followed by an image of Viagra.[15] In order for these narratives of social breach and pharmaceutical repair to stick, we must find it plausible that the etiology of the social breakdown is some sort of locatable, determinate bodily dysfunction plausibly targeted by a unified physiological intervention. ED has proven highly amenable to this strategy.

## FEMALE SEXUAL DYSFUNCTION: THE STATE OF THE SCIENCE

Since the spectacular success of Viagra and the medicalization of ED, concerted efforts have been underway to operationalize "FSD" and find marketable pharmaceutical "solutions" for it. Such efforts are media darlings, and when new drugs show up on the horizon there are multiple headlines about the quest for the "little pink pill" that can be the female counterpart to Viagra.[16] Despite the economic and cultural hunger for such a thing, there have been surprisingly few actual clinical trials of drugs for FSD. Hardly any dedicated FSD drugs have been developed or proposed. An exception was Flibanserin, which was designed by a relatively obscure pharmaceutical company, Boehringer Ingelheim. The drug was designed to boost female sexual desire by working at the neural level; unlike Viagra, its function is psychotropic. Originally, the FDA rejected this drug by unanimous vote as well, although a new company, Sprout Pharmaceuticals, rekindled research on Flibanserin (now known as Addyi) as of 2013, and as we saw at the start it was approved with strict constraints in 2015, amidst controversy. Its efficacy is modest at best, its mechanism is unknown, and using it is both burdensome and risky for patients. By any measure it does not count as anything like the "magic bullet" that Viagra and similar ED drugs appear to be. We still don't have a clear taxonomy or etiology of FSD, and indeed much research effort is still being directed at the classification of forms of FSD, and the development and validation of diagnostic tools.

Many of the clinical trials on proposed FSD fixes have been designed to test whether some already available medication such as Viagra, testosterone supplements, or hormone replacement therapy can additionally alleviate some version of FSD. As it turns out, Viagra moderately helps women already on SSRIs to achieve orgasm, but it does not help the general population of women, nor does it help with desire or arousal. Testosterone seems to boost libido in postmenopausal women, but again, not in the general population, and it comes along with serious side effects and nontrivial risks. A low-dose testosterone patch, "Intrinsa," was developed by Procter and Gamble, but unanimously turned down for approval by the FDA (although it has been approved in the EU). A decade ago, a company named Vivus developed a drug called Alista, designed to increase blood flow to the genitalia, but the company failed to produce statistically significant evidence that the drug helped with any sexuality-related issues; in a white paper from 2005, Vivus admits that while "progress is being made" on FSD treatments, so far, no pharmaceutical solutions have panned out. A new drug, Lybrido, currently in the testing stage, basically combines two previously unsuccessful approaches: it increases genital blood flow, like Viagra and Alista, and also operates on the balance of serotonin and dopamine, much like Flibanserin. Other than this, there have not really been any traditional medical interventions proposed for FSD.

## THE FAILURE OF THE ATTEMPT TO
## MEDICALIZE FEMALE SEXUALITY

I interpret the attempt to medicalize female sexuality and FSD as a failure, rather than just as a nascent, incomplete program. Unlike in the cases of ED, ADHD, depression, and so forth, the standard medicalization narrative—in which we identify and sharpen a physiological dysfunction that stands as proxy for a complex social dysfunction, and then bring it under medical surveillance and management, offering medical interventions as social fixes—has failed to get off the ground.

One reason for the tepid response to the vigorous call for medicalization seems to be that—unlike in the male case—there is still nothing resembling agreement as to what physiological dysfunction such a drug ought to address. We already saw that FSD is actually a cover term for a wide range of "diagnoses," and one striking feature of this list is that the purported dysfunctions it covers are Borgesian in their lack of fit with one another; they do not even concern the same body parts or systems. They range from physical pain, to muscular response, to lack of "normal" propositional attitudes such as desire for intercourse, to emotions such as fear, to general existential malaise.

Once one puts all these possible "dysfunctions" together, it appears that between 40% and 63% of all women "suffer from" at least some form of sexual disorder.[17] At these rates of "dysfunction," the case for the existence of a meaningfully unified disorder becomes seriously attenuated. It is, of course, possible for a single disorder to afflict a huge percentage of a population—even a majority. It is also sometimes useful to lump together diverse sets of symptoms and dysfunctions under a single disease label. However, given that FSD is not a unified syndrome with a single set of symptoms, and given that no one makes any pretense to believing in a shared physiological pathway behind the various versions of FSD, it seems like the only grounds we might have for lumping these things together and medicalizing them would be if we could identify a statistically abnormal group of women in need of some sort of common response. But in fact if the rate of the "disorder" is hovering around 50%, then there is no sense in which the women who fall under its label are statistically abnormal at all. This means there is as yet no plausible case for a unified medical condition here, even if we accept all the normal presuppositions and motivations behind pushes to medicalize.

Furthermore, with remarkable consistency, attempts to understand FSD in medical terms end up *deferring* attention to other, more traditional, already medicalized conditions. In the scientific literature, women's sexual dysfunction is typically seen as caused by—or at least studied through the lens of—depression, menopause, infertility, postpartum depression, past sexual abuse, or (perhaps most interestingly) their male partner's own sexual dysfunction. For instance, Fugl-Meyer and Fugl-Meyer[18] blame women's low sexual desire and satisfaction primarily on men's sexual dysfunction. Clinical studies of proposed FSD treatments are most often performed on populations that already have one of these other diagnoses—perimenopausal women, depressed women, and the like.[19]

This is in sharp contrast to male sexual dysfunction, which, as we saw, is framed as the *cause of* social and relationship breakdown and other socially damaging states like depression, rather than as an *outgrowth* of them. If FSD is indeed a side effect of some other condition or range of conditions—and particularly if it's an effect of a social dysfunction—then it would make sense that it would not lend itself to direct pharmaceutical address; instead, the underlying condition should be the primary target of treatment. Male sexual dysfunction, we saw, showed up first as a secondary effect of this kind but quickly took on life as a self-standing and independently treatable disorder. But FSD has remained primarily framed as such an effect, and has not been operationalized in a way that gives it the unity it needs to start searching for a convincing pharmaceutical fix.

Given the strong financial incentives behind medicalizing FSD, why has the medical community, including the pharmaceutical community, had such a comparatively hard time settling on a plausible meaning for the term or even a relevant system of the body? And why has it seemingly proved difficult to turn the medical gaze *directly* upon FSD at all? Why is it so routinely interpreted and identified in the context of other medical and social dysfunctions that show up as more fundamental? My hypothesis is that there are deeply rooted ideological pressures that prevent the medicalization of female sexuality and explain these odd evasions and incoherences. However intense the pressure toward medicalization is, there are countervailing pressures built into our cultural imaginary.

## IMAGINING FEMALE SEXUALITY AND
## THE MYTH OF FEMININE MYSTERY

It is built into the logic of medicalization that the medical gaze seeks clear, self-contained bodily parts and systems that can be identified as physiologically dysfunctional in a clinic. Yet the scientific literature—along with vast swaths of our fiction, pop psychology, television, movies, advertisements and more—typically takes as its starting point that female sexuality is inherently and essentially complex, mysterious, elusive, shifting, disorderly, unpredictable, and fragile. This image surely predates but is elegantly encapsulated by Freud's famous insistence that "The sexual life of adult women is a "dark continent" for psychology," and that women's sexual desire is "veiled in an impenetrable obscurity."[20] But this picture is antithetical to the isolating, unifying, and simplifying project of medicalization.

There are at least four separable features of how we imagine feminine sexuality that help it resist medicalization. According to our cultural imaginary, feminine sexuality is (1) inherently mysterious and unpredictable, (2) not locatable in any particular part of the body, (3) in the first instance, used *strategically* as a tool of social negotiation, rather than being first and foremost a source of pleasure valuable in its own right, and (4) fragile and highly context-dependent. I will discuss these in turn. In each case, my goal is not to come down on whether these *really are or aren't* distinctive features of feminine sexuality (which would be hard to even frame as a well-formed empirical question, given the mutual interdependence of cultural ideology and individual bodily experience).[21] Rather, my point is that these *starting assumptions* about feminine sexuality make the project of medicalization show up as incoherent or nearly hopeless from the beginning.

First, the idea that feminine sexuality is epistemically impenetrable—that no one (implying no man) could puzzle out what women "really want"—is clearly a source of endless jokes and narrative plots, and not just of Freudian melodramatic racialized imagery. In a recent *Psychology Today* article on feminine sexuality, Noam Shpancer begins, "What do women want? Sigmund Freud famously asked the question, but he didn't have an answer. Even today, the question of what motivates female sexual desire continues to resound. Definitive answers have proven elusive. What men want we understand quite well. In general, their sexual desire is orderly, consistent, and narrowly directed"[22] What counts as "orderly" or "disorderly" is interestingly relative to expectations about what sorts of regularities one will find. It is an aesthetic measure of a sort. The idea that women's sexuality is "disorderly," and hence incomprehensible, runs deep in our imagination, and also reflects androcentric principles built into our scientific and lay methods of explanation. In contrast, Shpancer claims, "Viagra's success demonstrates the simplicity of the male mechanism." Here, the connection between the purported messy incomprehensibility of feminine sexuality and the difficulty in medicalizing it is explicit.

Second, while medicalization involves *locating and isolating* a dysfunctional body part or system, we imagine feminine sexuality as inherently unlocatable—as shifting across the body. This unlocatability contributes to the epistemic impenetrability I just described. This is crystalized in the work of Luce Irigaray, for instance, who claims that "Whence the mystery that woman represents in a culture claiming to count everything, to number everything by units, to inventory everything as individualities ... She resists all adequate definition ... And her sexual organ, which is not *one* organ, is counted as *none* ... But *woman has sex organs more or less everywhere.*"[23] The direction of women's desire is purportedly shifting and unstable as well. Shpancer writes, "The female body, studies show, likes everything."[24]

Third, we have a millennia-old tradition of portraying women as using their sexuality strategically, as a tool of social negotiation, rather than as seeking out sexual stimulation and pleasure for its own sake. We imagine feminine sexuality as a powerful tool used to arrange social space through manipulating male behavior. Lysistrata persuades Greek women to withhold sex in order to control their military actions. Rousseau's tutor of Emile gives Sophie detailed lessons explaining how she should grant and withhold sex and erotic affection in order to mold Emile into a virtuous husband and citizen. Countless contemporary sitcoms, magazine articles, and the like continue the trope. But if a woman's sexuality is instrumental in this way, and keyed to *social* needs and narratives, then there is no reason to think that a *physiological* intervention will "fix" her or make her more "orderly" in her sexual responses.

Fourth, even when women are not using their sexuality strategically, their sexual desire and sexual pleasure are framed as highly—indeed overwhelmingly—dependent upon emotional and social context. Whereas men, we think, desire sex as a kind of physical need, women desire sex when they are feeling emotionally intimate, or as situated within a monogamous relationship, or whatever it may be.[25] For women, the story goes like this: Sexual pleasure is not a self-standing need or an end in itself, but something that is woven into social narratives. Women want sex and can take pleasure in it when they feel secure and emotionally connected, pretty much regardless of the stimulus, whereas men want sex whenever they are presented with appropriate stimuli, as long as everything is mechanically in order.[26] With this context-dependence goes a fundamental fragility: Women's sexual interest and pleasure can supposedly vanish at a moment's notice, capriciously, based on subtle social and emotional shifts, and this adds to their basic "disorderliness."

As with the sex-as-strategy point above, this social and emotional conceptuality and fragility make it much harder to operationalize female sexuality in a way that lends it to predictable physiological intervention. In a medical journal article that seeks to define FSD and explore its relationship with menopause, Joan Pitkin calls women's sexuality "complex ... vague and intimate." Like many others, she bemoans the difficulty in separating "true" sexual dysfunction from "natural" female responsiveness to context.[27] An ABC news item on the development of Flibanserin quotes a drug company representative as saying: "Viagra is a blood-flow issue, a mechanical issue ... Scientists have known for years [sic] that a woman's most significant sexual organ is actually her brain, which is what makes female desire disorders so hard to treat."[28] Critics of medicalization like Tiefer share this starting point, asserting that female sexual problems are "different" from men's as they more often stem from social, relational, and emotional issues.[29]

When we put all of this together, we get a picture of a phenomenon that is antithetical to the logic of medicalization—inherently impenetrable and complex, too unstable to be predictable, relationally rather than individualistically determined, and essentially located within social rather than clinical or physiological narratives. Deep-seated ideological tropes push back against our conceiving of female sexuality as epistemically accessible to science or to the clinical gaze, or as manageable and predictable by other people (especially men), or indeed as *bodily* at all.[30]

## FEMALE SEXUALITY IN THE SCIENTIFIC IMAGINATION

It is routine for scientific and popular articles on FSD to begin with a discussion of the relative complexity, obscurity, instrumentality, and context-sensitivity of female sexuality, along with warnings that this makes medical solutions difficult from the get-go. Indeed, we see this picture concretely visualized in many scientific articles on FSD that bemoan the complexity of their own research subject. For instance, in figure 10.2, we see what I like to think of as the flower of FSD.

This diagram illustrates both sides of the tension around the medicalization of FSD. On the one hand, its point is the complex set of overlapping shapes; there is no determinate answer to *how many* phenomena there are here. On the other, the diagram also focuses our attention at the intersection in the center. So the image both resists and affirms the presence of a unified

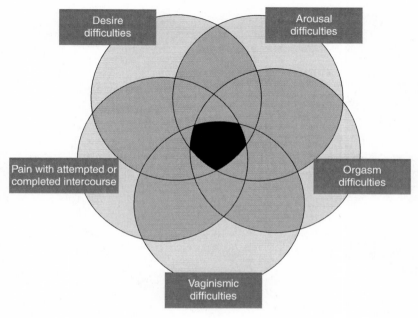

**Figure 10.2**

phenomenon of the sort medicine seeks for purposes of medicalization. At the same time, the diagram is fascinatingly *meaningless*. What exactly are the overlapping flower petals supposed to represent, besides vaguely invoking a flowery vagina? Wouldn't a list of possible barriers to sexual pleasure convey the same information? What exactly is the significance of the solid, colored area in the middle? The force of the diagram seems to be less epistemic than imagistic.

One popular trope in discussions of FSD is the idea that there is no linear causality when it comes to female sexuality. Unlike (purported) male sexual response, female sexual response is tangled in a set of causal feedback loops that make it difficult to isolate and affect through targeted intervention, as in the swirly diagram of figure 10.3.

More generally, diagrams "making sense" of female sexuality are often pointlessly elaborate, seemingly designed more to prove the impenetrability of the phenomenon than to clarify it, as in figure 10.4.

This chart's arrows seem to be nearly randomly distributed. It is fairly safe to bet that an equivalent chart for male sexual response would present a single, phallic arrow.

There is virtually no talk in the literature on male sexual dysfunction about willingness to have sex, aversion to sex, the communicative force

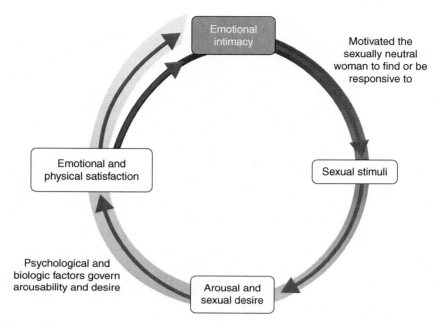

**Figure 10.3**

of sex, incentives to have sex, the "nonsexual" rewards of sex, or sexual satisfaction that doesn't necessarily involve orgasm (in contrast to figure 10.4). Men can experience all of these things, obviously, and conversely it is not clear that all these things need to be on the table every time a woman has sex. Thus, our cultural imagery overinflates the complexity of female sexuality and reductively simplifies the complexity of male sexuality—to the detriment of both, one suspects. This cultural imagery infiltrates and pervades both the scientific efforts at medicalization and the scholarly critiques of those efforts.

To see how differently we frame male and female sexuality, and the differences this leads to in conceptualizing what *dysfunction* involves, it is helpful to compare the webmd.com entries on "Sexual problems in women" and "Sexual problems in men" (figure 10.5):

The rhetorical differences between these two entries are telling. The language in the male case is clearly much more medicalized. Meanwhile, there is an immediate emphasis on complexity and on relationality in the female case; sexual pleasure itself shows up as secondary to a need for "closeness and intimacy." Similarly interesting is the emphasis on the women's page on

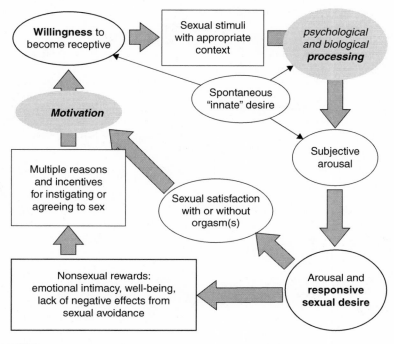

**Figure 10.4**

*self*-diagnosis and self-reflection, compared to the emphasis on the men's page on *expert* medical examination and diagnosis. This is predictable, given my analysis: women's sexuality is impenetrable to the clinical gaze, whereas men's sexuality has been medically coopted and brought under expert management and epistemic control.

While this last split may seem (and in some ways is) empowering to women, it's worth remembering again that many women have such poor and repressive sexual education that they don't know how to find their own clitoris, nor do they know basic facts about female sexuality, such as the rarity of vaginal orgasm.[31] So their ability to "recognize a sexual problem" in themselves may be quite limited. At the same time, our hyper-medicalized approach to men's sexuality makes invisible all of the complexity of men's lives that may shape their sexual happiness and the range of things they find pleasurable and uncomfortable, as well as reinforcing heteronormativity and a narrow conception of "successful" sexual performance and experience.

**SEXUAL PROBLEMS IN WOMEN: TOPIC OVERVIEW**

**What are some causes of sexual problems in women?** Female sexuality is complex. At its core is a need for closeness and intimacy. Women also have physical needs. When there is a problem in either the emotional or physical part of your life, you can have sexual problems.

**How are sexual problems in women diagnosed?** Women often recognize a sxual problem when they notice a change in desire or sexual satisfaction. When this happens, it helps to look at what is and isn't working in the body and in life. For example ... Do you have a caring, respectful connection with a partner? Do you and your partner have the time and privacy to relax together?...

**SEXUAL PROBLEMS IN MEN: TOPIC OVERVIEW**

**What causes male sexual problems?** Sexual dysfunction can be a result of a physical or a psychological problem. Many physical and/or medical conditions can cause problems with sexual function. These conditions include diabetes, heart and vascular (blood vessel) disease, neurological disorders ...

**How are male sexual problems diagnosed?** The doctor likely will begin with a thorough history of symptoms and a physical exam. He or she may order other tests to rule out any medical problems that may be contributing to the dysfunction...

**Figure 10.5**

## CONCLUSION

In the end, we are left with very different images of sexually dysfunctional males and females, and these differences show up vividly in marketing imagery. The paradigmatic image of a man with ED is of a lively, robust middle-aged man with a highly localized problem in his penis—a mechanical problem isolated from the rest of his identity and appropriately diagnosed by doctors and pharmaceutically managed. Meanwhile, our image of a woman with sexual dysfunction is of a sickly, depressed woman trapped in an unfulfilling relationship, perhaps troubled by other failures of femininity such as infertility or menopause—one whose problems are not visible to the scientific eye and are not orderly or stable enough to pin down (figures 10.6 and 10.7).

As we saw at the start, medicalization is generally a mixed blessing. Pharmaceutical and other medical interventions regularly provide genuine relief and improved daily lives, and having such interventions available to alleviate suffering is a good thing. Meanwhile, medicalizing a condition demystifies, legitimizes, and demoralizes it, in ways that can be productive and enfranchising. On the flip side, the logic of medicalization tends to be reductive and is typically driven at least in part by market considerations. It occludes social determinants of experience and problematic power relations

**Figure 10.6**

and systems that impede flourishing. It cedes expertise and control to a narrow group of professionals. As Lenore Tiefer puts it on the New View Campaign webpage, in the logic of medicalization, "factors that are far more often sources of women's sexual complaints—relational and cultural conflicts, for example, or sexual ignorance or fear—are downplayed and dismissed."[32]

*Rebecca Kukla*

**Some of the common causes of sexual dysfunction are:**

- unskilled or uncaring partner
- communication problems
- anxiety, depression or fear
- a gynecologic disease
- deep-seated psychological problems
- prior history of sexual abuse

**Figure 10.7**

All in, then, women should neither envy/covet the medicalization of men's sexuality nor should they celebrate the lack of medicalization of their own; the real story is more complex and lies in the details. While it is gratifying to watch the pharmaceutical industry flounder in its attempts to corporatize female sexuality despite serious profit motivations, it is also frustrating that this failure is apparently underwritten by a reactionary understanding of the supposedly mysterious, fragile, and merely instrumental character of feminine sexuality, and the disempowering image of the sexually "dysfunctional" woman. What is most interesting to me is how background ideological forces and images help shape the narrative of medicalization and its failure, while in turn this narrative shapes cultural ideologies. The medicalization of male sexuality arguably helped shape how men experience and understand sexual success and failure; correspondingly, the *failed* medicalization of FSD and the cultural discourse surrounding it can both constitute and reinforce women's experience and interpretation of their own sexuality.

# NOTES

1. Joel Lexchin, "Bigger and Better: How Pfizer Redefined Erectile Dysfunction," *PloS Medicine*, 3:4 (2006): e132.

2. Ibid; Richard Carpiano, "Passive Medicalization: The Case of Viagra and Erectile Dysfunction," *Sociological Spectrum* 21, no.3 (2001): 441–50.

3. This is problematically distorting: good sex—pleasurable erotic play between people—is cast as pathological if it does not involve an extended erection for any man involved. Conversely, bad sex—unpleasurable, perfunctory, uncomfortable, or upsetting sex—is cast as healthy as long as any man involved can keep his erections as needed. I will come back to the distortions involved in the medicalization of sexuality later.

4. Ray Moynihan, "The Making of a Disease: Female Sexual Dysfunction," *British Medical Journal* 326 (2003): 45–47.

5. http://www.fda.gov/NewsEvents/Newsroom/PressAnnouncements/ucm458734.htm, accessed 3/20/2016.

6. Male fertility is a nice, analogous example of non-medicalization, which would be worth exploring in depth.

7. Classic sources discussing the nature of medicalization include Peter Conrad, "Medicalization and Social Control," *Annual Review of Sociology* 18 (1992): 209–32; Peter Conrad, *The Medicalization of Society: On the Transformation of Human Conditions into Treatable Disorders* (Baltimore: Johns Hopkins University Press, 2007); Michel Foucault, *The Birth of the Clinic: An Archaeology of Medical Perception* (New York: Vintage Press, 1994); Michel Foucault, "The Birth of Social Medicine," in *The Essential Works of Michel Foucault*, Volume 3, ed. James Faubion (New York: The New Press, 2000); Ray Moynihan, "The Making of a Disease"; Ray Moynihan, *Selling Sickness: How the World's Biggest Pharmaceutical Companies are Turning Us All into Patients* (New York: Nation Books, 2005); Thomas Szasz, *The Medicalization of Everyday Life* (Syracuse: Syracuse University Press, 2007).

8. Conrad, "Medicalization and Social Control."

9. Moynihan, "The Making of a Disease."

10. Thea Cacchioni and Leonore Tiefer, "Why Medicalization? Introduction to the Special Issue on the Medicalization of Sex," *Journal of Sex Research* 49, no.4 (2012), 307–10.

11. Janine Farrell and Thea Cacchioni, "The Medicalization of Sexual Pain," *Journal of Sex Research* 49, no.4 (2012), 328–36.

12. New View Campaign, "Fact Sheet on Flibanserin: Gender and Choice," http://www.newviewcampaign.org/media/pdfs/FlibanserinFactsheet_choice.pdf. 2010.

13. Ibid.

14. *Orgasm, Inc.: The Strange Science of Female Pleasure* (2009), directed and produced by Liz Canner.

15. https://www.youtube.com/watch?v=rE0up432ohY.

16. To cite just a few examples, see Jill Rollet, "The Quest for a Little Pink Pill: Female Sexual Dysfunction Finally Attracting Attention," *Advance Healthcare Network* 13, no. 4 (2005), 51; Samantha Smithstein, "Women, Sexuality, and 'The

Little Pink Pill,'" *Psychology Today Blog* (2010); ABC News, "Fight Over 'Little Pink Pill' Raises Sexism Questions" (2014); Mona Iskander, "The Little Pink Pill," PBS (2010).

17. The most common rate cited is 43%—a figure that originates in Edward Lauman, Anthony Paik, and Raymond Rosen, "Sexual Dysfunction in the United States: Prevalence and Predictors," *JAMA* 281 (1999): 537–44. The 63% figure shows up in Sammy Elsamra, et al., "Female Sexual Dysfunction in Urology Patients," *BJU International* 106, no.4 (2010): 524–6. There, the number applies only to urology patients, as the title implies. However, this 63% figure has been taken up by other sources, including in *Orgasm, Inc.* (2009).

18. K. Sjögren Fugl-Meyer and Axel R. Fugl-Meyer, "Sexual Disabilities are not Singularities," *International Journal of Impotence Research* 14 (2002): 487–93.

19. Interestingly—and I am not sure how to interpret this—the conditions that FSD most often gets hooked onto are themselves examples of relatively recent intense medicalization. Menopause, infertility, and postpartum depression are excellent examples.

20. Sigmund Freud, *The Question of Lay Analysis*, (New York: Norton, 1990).

21. That is, one's experience of one's own sexuality is surely highly subject to "looping effects" in Ian Hacking's sense. See for instance Ian Hacking "Making Up People," in *The Science Studies Reader*, ed. by Mario Biagioli (New York: Routledge, 1999) 161–171.

22. Noam Shpancer, "What Do Women Really Want?" *Psychology Today Blog* (2013).

23. Luce Irigaray, *This Sex which Is Not One*, trans. Catherine Porter (Ithaca: Cornell University Press, 1985).

24. Shpancer, "What do Women Really Want?"

25. In fact, there's some evidence that the opposite is true and that women lose their sexual interest in monogamous relationships faster than do men, and are more aroused by novelty and stranger sex than are men; but such is not the hegemonic cultural narrative. See for instance Daniel Bergner, "Unexcited? There May Be a Pill for That," *New York Times* (2013).

26. Once again, my goal here is to make explicit a set of cultural images and assumptions and not to assess their truth value, but I can't help but point out how dubious, scant, and ideologically suspect the science is behind these claims.

27. Joan Pitkin, "Sexuality and the Menopause," *Best Practice and Research in Clinical Obstetrics and Gynaecology* 23, no.1 (2009): 33–52.

28. "Fight Over 'Little Pink Pill' Raises Sexism Questions."

29. www.newviewcampaign.org

30. Katherine Angel, "The History of 'Female Sexual Dysfunction' as a Mental Disorder in the 20th Century," *Current Opinions in Psychiatry* 23, no.6 (2010): 536–41.

31. *Orgasm, Inc.* (2009).

32. www.newviewcampaign.org, "Fact Sheet on Flibanserin."

# BIBLIOGRAPHY

Angel, Katherine. "The History of 'Female Sexual Dysfunction' as a Mental Disorder in the 20th Century." *Current Opinions in Psychiatry* 23, no. 6 (2010): 536–41.

Bergner, Daniel. "Unexcited? There May Be a Pill for That." *New York Times,* May 22, 2013.

Cacchioni, Thea, and Leonore Tiefer. "Why Medicalization? Introduction to the Special Issue on the Medicalization of Sex." *Journal of Sex Research* 49, no. 4 (2012): 307–10.

Canner, Liz. *Orgasm, Inc.: The Strange Science of Female Pleasure.* Directed and produced by Liz Canner (2009). Film.

Carpiano, Richard. "Passive Medicalization: The Case of Viagra and Erectile Dysfunction." *Sociological Spectrum* 21, no. 3 (2001): 441–50.

Conrad, Peter. "Medicalization and Social Control." *Annual Review of Sociology* 18 (1992): 209–32.

———. *The Medicalization of Society: On the Transformation of Human Conditions into Treatable Disorders.* Baltimore: Johns Hopkins University Press, 2007.

Elsamra, Sammy, Michael Nazmy, David Shin, Harry Fisch, Ihor Sawczuk, and Debra Fromer. "Female Sexual Dysfunction in Urology Patients." *BJU International* 106, no. 4 (2010): 524–26.

Farrell, Janine, and Thea Cacchioni. "The Medicalization of Sexual Pain." *Journal of Sex Research* 49, no. 4 (2012): 328–36.

"Fight Over 'Little Pink Pill' Raises Sexism Questions." *ABC News,* May 21, 2014.

Foucault, Michel. *The Birth of the Clinic: An Archaeology of Medical Perception.* New York: Vintage Press, 1994.

———. "The Birth of Social Medicine." In *The Essential Works of Michel Foucault,* Volume 3, edited by James Faubion, 134–156. New York: The New Press, 2000.

Freud, Sigmund. *The Question of Lay Analysis.* New York: Norton, 1990.

Fugl-Meyer, K. Sjögren, and Axel R. Fugl-Meyer. "Sexual Disabilities Are Not Singularities." *International Journal of Impotence Research* 14 (2002): 487–93.

Hacking, Ian. "Making Up People." In *The Science Studies Reader*, edited by Mario Biagioli, 161–171. New York: Routledge, 1999.

Irigaray, Luce. *This Sex which Is Not One*, translated by Catherine Porter. Ithaca: Cornell University Press, 1985.

Lauman, Edward,\ Anthony Paik, and Raymond Rosen. "Sexual Dysfunction in the United States: Prevalence and Predictors." *JAMA* 281 (1999): 537–44.

Lexchin, Joel. "Bigger and Better: How Pfizer Redefined Erectile Dysfunction." *PLoS Medicine,* 3, no. 4 (2006): e132.

Moynihan, Ray. "The Making of a Disease: Female Sexual Dysfunction." *British Medical Journal* 326 (2003): 45–47.

———. *Selling Sickness: How the World's Biggest Pharmaceutical Companies are Turning Us All into Patients.* New York: Nation Books, 2005.

New View Campaign. "Fact Sheet on Flibanserin: Gender and Choice." 2010. http://www.newviewcampaign.org/media/pdfs/FlibanserinFactsheet_choice.pdf

Pitkin, Joan. "Sexuality and the Menopause." *Best Practice and Research in Clinical Obstetrics and Gynaecology* 23, no.1 (2009): 33–52.

Rollet, Jill. "The Quest for a Little Pink Pill: Female Sexual Dysfunction Finally Attracting Attention." *Advance Healthcare Network* 13, no. 4 (2005): 51.

Shpancer, Noam. "What Do Women Really Want?" *Psychology Today Blog*, August 22, 2013.

Smithstein, Samantha. "Women, Sexuality, and 'The Little Pink Pill.'" *Psychology Today Blog*, June 29, 2010.

Szasz, Thomas. *The Medicalization of Everyday Life*. Syracuse: Syracuse University Press, 2007.

"The Little Pink Pill," PBS.org, posted July 2, 2010.

*Chapter Eleven*

# Being Through Love

## *The Collaborative Construction of a Sexual Body*

### Amy E. Taylor

In the *Phenomenology of Perception,* Maurice Merleau-Ponty suggests that if we "try to see how a thing or being begins to exist for us through desire or love ... we shall thereby come to understand better how things and beings can exist in general."[1] This chapter explains how a sexual body comes to be in the world. It describes the body as involved in a continual process that involves self-narration while it is, at the same time, held in place by the world of people and things. It is an ongoing creation between subject and object, between one's experience and the world in which this experience takes place. Others take up the body as an object, and one's lived experience as a body that exists on a continuum between activity and passivity is significant in sexuality as well as in developing and maintaining an identity.

This chapter takes the form of a response to Merleau-Ponty's reflections on "the relation between sexuality and existence."[2] It critiques Merleau-Ponty's specific notion of sexuality (as heteronormative, sexist, and able-ist) while preserving the spirit in which Merleau-Ponty takes up his elaboration of "the body in its sexual being." It also attends to the role and identity of the other in relation to whom sexuality emerges; specifically, this chapter presents the female subject missing from Merleau-Ponty's description, as well as describing aspects of sexual experience that are implicit in Merleau-Ponty's account but not elaborated. Sexuality reveals itself as an imaginative and cocreated invention, which has implications for the intersubjective nature of embodiment generally.

# INTRODUCTION

*Despite my reservations, I eventually agreed to experiment with a strap-on dildo. My expectations, though, were muted. At most, I thought I might be able to please my partner. But I honestly did not envision recreating a fully satisfying sexual experience.*

—Warkentin, K., Gray, R., & Wassersug, R., 2006, 391

The above quotation comes from a person who, in the remaining portions of this chapter, shall be referred to as "Michael." Michael was in his late fifties when he became fully physiologically impotent following hormone-based prostate cancer treatments, including a complete prostatectomy and Androgen Deprivation Treatment (ADT). After receiving these treatments, Michael felt depressed and lifeless, flawed, and believed he no longer had the capacity to achieve sexual satisfaction. Michael describes encountering traditional treatments for physiological impotence (surgically inserting an inflatable device into his penis, injecting drugs into his penis, or using a vacuum pump device), which either do not work for him or that he finds too painful and unappealing to try. Michael feels desperate and depressed, believing his sexual life has ended. He describes himself as "sexually inca-pacitated" and his penis as a "functional failure."[3] After spending more than a year in this condition, Michael follows the advice of his close lesbian friend and tries intercourse using a strap-on dildo. To his great surprise, sexual satisfaction became possible again. This included orgasm, satisfying sexual pleasure without orgasm, multiple orgasms, and other nuances of experiencing himself as sexual, sexed, and gendered, which he describes in his first-person narrative in the case study by K. Warkentin, R. Gray, and R. Wassersug.[4]

Michael also "discussed extensively" with his female partner (to whom I give the name "Susan") the possibility of using a dildo for penetrative sex. Susan is "supportive of the exploration" and they have sex with Michael wearing the strap-on dildo.[5] Michael is amazed and delighted by the "natu-ralness" of the act, stating, "It caught me by total surprise how natural intercourse felt with this strap-on device."[6] Michael and Susan continue to engage in dildo sex with increasingly positive results. "[S]exual satisfaction has become easier, because both of us have come to accept the dildo as part of our sex play."[7]

Michael describes trying various sexual positions with the dildo and reports that he and Susan "have both been able to have orgasms many times using the dildo."[8] He adds that there are some things he is able to do with the dildo that were not possible when he was able to have erections. For instance, he says "with the dildo, I am able to continue pelvic thrusts long and hard enough that [my partner] now regularly achieves an orgasm in the missionary position."[9] Michael also says, "I discovered that I ... could enjoy sex without orgasms," and "I can ... have multiple orgasms!"[10] He describes the sexual experimentation that he and Susan engage in, and says that eventually, he is even able to attain pleasure from receiving oral sex while he is wearing the dildo.

Through this process, Michael changes the way he thinks of himself, moving from "functional failure" to "joyfully empowered." He says that sex becomes more playful than it was prior to using the strap-on dildo, and states that he can enjoy "the 'play' part of sex"[11] and that he thinks of the dildo as " 'a toy.'"[12] Michael's partner adds to this atmosphere of erotic playfulness. Michael describes one morning when he walked into the bathroom to discover "the dildo sitting upright on the counter-top wearing one of my favorite neckties,"[13] interpreting this as a signal of Susan's "personification and personalization" of the dildo, and her pleasure and acceptance in the dildo as a part of Michael. Michael comes to experience a "transference from 'object' to 'organ'"[14] with respect to the dildo, which also transforms from "a piece of purple plastic" at the beginning of his narrative to "the dildo," which finally becomes "our dildo," meaning his and Susan's, by the end of his narrative.

Michael's case presents a phenomenon that is at once believable and astonishing, shedding light on a real but unarticulated (or under-articulated) phenomenon, adding to multiple conversations about the self and the body. It raises questions about the relationship of the body to external material objects; these include: How is it possible for a person to achieve orgasm by means of an external object? How does this object become a part of the felt and sensed body such that Michael can experience pleasure with it? What does the phenomenon of the body extending itself with an external object reveal about human corporeality generally? The case also has relevance for questions about the relationship of the body to a person's sense of identity, particularly in terms of the person's sex or gender. What does it mean about the body that it can acquire a new sexual organ, or an organ with significance for sexual identity? What might it reveal about the relationship between gender or sexual identity and what the body feels like? What is the relation of the dildo to the penis, and more generally, what is the relation of a bodily modification or addition to a person's body and that person's identity? Finally, this phenomenon is relevant for understanding sexuality, or the sexual body (or as a translation of the fourth chapter of Merleau-Ponty's *Phenomenology of Perception* phrases this, "the body in its sexual being"). What does Michael's change in terms of sexual functioning and experience during the process of dildo incorporation imply about sexuality generally? How does the sexual body adapt to change, and how is it possible for it to change? How does Michael's case challenge common constructions of sexuality?

It seems that there is a great deal to learn from this phenomenon. Here, I will focus on (1) the question of how it is possible for the strap-on dildo to go from, in Michael's words, "object to organ" such that he is able to experience it as part of his body, and (2) how conceptualizing identity as embodied and coming to be in relationships, or thinking of the self as emerging at the point of interface with another, can help to elucidate this phenomenon. This chapter builds upon Merleau-Ponty's elaboration to address how Michael's post-prostate cancer sexual body emerges at the level of bodily sensation, as well as how the emergence of this sexual body constitutes a change in Michael's identity. Broadly, I argue that the body and mind are not distinct and the self is bodily-based in such a way that it emerges through interactions between bodies, so in interaction with Susan, Michael enters a playful constitutive space in which he develops a new sense of his own body.

## MERLEAU-PONTY AND THE SEXUAL BODY

In *Phenomenology of Perception,* as a part of his project to "elucidate the primary function where we bring into existence ... space, the object or instrument, and describe the body as a place where this appropriation occurs," Merleau-Ponty describes "how a thing or being begins to exist for us through desire or love."[15] To understand the body's hold on the world, Merleau-Ponty examines a particular kind of hold; that is, he examines the kind of hold on the world present in sexuality. He states, "sexuality, without being the object of any intended act of consciousness, can underlie and guide specified forms of my experience."[16]

Sexuality as a kind of force that "underlies and guides" existence contrasts with ways of understanding sexuality that present it as a superficial or contingent aspect of human existence. Merleau-Ponty presents sexuality as "interfused with existence ... so that it is impossible to determine, in a given decision or action, the proportion of sexual to other motivations, impossible to label a decision or act 'sexual' or 'non-sexual.'"[17] Sexuality is a *modality* of existence, as opposed to a set of drives or reflexive, physiological responses.[18] This also means that certain kinds of injuries will have an effect on sexual life that one would not expect if sexuality were a mere response to a physical stimulus, or a reflex, as Merleau-Ponty discusses in the case of Schneider. Rather, sexuality is "co-extensive with life," and "It is at all times present there like an atmosphere."[19]

In Merleau-Ponty's view, sexuality is a part of expression in the world, not a symbolic representation or cognitive function. It "condenses [a person's] basic mode of relating to the world," meaning particularly the world of others and how one relates to them.[20] It is not "self-enclosed" but "referential" and is "intentional in the sense that it modalizes a relationship between an embodied subject and a concrete situation."[21] In other words, like other aspects of embodiment, sexuality takes place in the world and places one in relation to the world. Sexuality is a way in which one is called into the world and shaped by the world.

The importance sexuality occupies in human life emerges from "a more general drama which arises from the metaphysical structure of my body, which is both an object for others and a subject for myself."[22] Merleau-Ponty writes that "sexual experience ... [is] an opportunity ... of acquainting oneself with the human lot in its most general aspects of autonomy and dependence" and "begins with the opening out upon 'another.'"[23] It is the mode in which one is caught up in the world of others, thus a foundational aspect of human existence. Rather than representations or reflexes, it is a foundational part of how a person lives from moment to moment, with and as shaped by others. It follows that transformations to the embodied self create transformations in sexuality, and the following shall explore how Michael and others (including Merleau-Ponty's Schneider and persons whose bodies are often miscategorized by others) are transformed sexually with a change in embodiment.

## Schneider

Merleau-Ponty approaches the question of how the sexual body orients to the world through the existential analysis of a case study of Schneider. Schneider is impotent.[24] He is a 24-year-old man with brain injuries resulting from being hit by "mine splinters." These injuries result in "psychical blindness," and Schneider seems blind to a variety of images.[25] As Merleau-Ponty writes, "It was through his sight that the mind in him was impaired."[26] The observable result of Schneider's injury is an inability to perceive holistically. Sensory data flows to him without meaning and objects become unrecognizable disparate bits. He suffers various "intellectual, perceptual and motor disturbances"[27] including "sexual inertia" and a generalized lack of initiative.[28] Schneider says with reference to his actions, "I am scarcely aware of any voluntary initiative ... It all happens independently of me."[29] Schneider is describing how the "intentional arc," which "projects round about us our past, our future, our human setting, our physical, ideological, and moral situation, or rather which results in our being situated in all these respects" has, in him, "[gone] limp."[30]

Because sexuality is continuous with existence, Schneider's sexual problems are a component of his overall symptomatology. His problem manifests itself in his sexual life in Schneider's seeming loss of all capacity for sexual satisfaction. In fact, "the very word satisfaction has no longer any meaning for him."[31] The world of women's bodies does not call to him: "A woman's body has no particular essence ... physically they are all the same."[32] Schneider "no longer asks, of his environment, this mute and permanent question which constitutes normal sexuality."[33] This question presumably has to do with whether the object he has settled his eyes upon is a sexually attractive object, or perhaps a sexually available one. He does not see "the visible body ... subtended by a sexual schema ... emphasizing the erogenous areas, outlining a sexual physiognomy."[34] The sensory data he perceives, particularly the visual data, does not coalesce into a whole or an essence. As a consequence, Schneider "no longer seeks sexual intercourse of his own accord"[35] and he has no interest in looking at pornography or attractive bodies or sexual conversation. It seems that "what has disappeared from the patient is his power of projecting before himself a sexual world."[36]

Sullivan elaborates that normally, human beings have a "centrifugal" capacity for projection or to produce a "backdrop of a meaningful world against and in which I live."[37] Schneider's existence is centripetal and "operates against a given background."[38] That is to say, rather than providing his own meanings, he accepts given meanings. Sullivan describes Schneider as "constrained" and states that "the meaning of his world is that which presses in against him."[39] Similarly, once Schneider's sexual partners are no longer pressing against him and producing sensation for Schneider, deciding for themselves that the sexual act is over, Schneider does not pursue his own orgasm.[40] Schneider's sexual activity is not teleological—he neither appears to be concerned with orgasm (the apparent meaning of "satisfaction" in Merleau-Ponty's discussion) nor is he an aggressor sexually. His centripetal existence appears via Merleau-Ponty's descriptions as a particular passivity. "Close physical contact causes only a 'vague feeling,' the knowledge of 'an indeterminate something' which is never enough to 'spark off' sexual behavior and create a situation which requires a definite mode of resolution."[41] Because Schneider does not "require" a "definite resolution" to a sexual situation, he "accepts and thus is restricted by the meaning his partner has given to [the erotic situation]."[42]

To summarize, Schneider's abnormal sexuality is characterized by several failures. First, Schneider fails to view women's visible bodies in a sexual way generally. He also fails to enjoy pornography or to be attracted primarily to the visual body. Instead, "it is, he says, preeminently character which makes a woman attractive."[43] He does not actively pursue sex and behaves passively in his role as a sexual partner, becoming aroused only in response to a partner's initiation of sexual activity or primarily responding to his partner's desire during sex rather than pursuing a desire of his own (although he will make "active movements ... a few seconds before the orgasm."[44] Finally, Schneider fails to approach sex as a teleological act with the specific purpose of reaching climax. Based on Merleau-Ponty's way of describing sexuality, Schneider seems to have become nonsexual, as the world has lost its "sexual context."[45]

## Normative Sexuality

Looking more closely at Schneider, however, it seems that Schneider's sexuality has not vanished nor has he become asexual, but instead that his sexuality or the sexual dimension of his existence has *changed*. It is, perhaps, unrecognizable as sexuality in light of the normative sexuality implicitly posited by Merleau-Ponty. Specifically, it seems that Merleau-Ponty's definition of normal sexuality refers to a style of sexuality that generalizes its objects, is based on visual data, and is aimed toward orgasm, as well as being a sexuality that belongs to a strictly heterosexual male.

Butler critiques this sense of "normal sexuality" set up in contrast to Schneider. She notes that Schneider's deference in sex (described by Merleau-Ponty in the statement, "if orgasm occurs first in the partner and she moves away, the half fulfilled desire vanishes") "signifies masculine 'incapacity', as if the normal male would seek satisfaction regardless of the desires of his female partner."[46] Indeed, this seems to be what Merleau-Ponty means that Schneider lacks when he describes Schneider as "impotent."[47]

Butler also points out that Schneider's lack of visual interest in bodies is presented as evidence of his sexual abnormality (i.e., his claim that women's bodies look the same to him and that personality interests him instead, and his lack of interest in pornography). "Central to Merleau-Ponty's assessment of Schneider's sexuality as abnormal is the presumption that the decontextualized female body, the body alluded to in conversation, the anonymous body which passes by on the street, exudes a natural attraction."[48] It also seems that this anonymous body is what one may be drawn to in a given partner, in contrast to Schneider's concern with the particularities of his sexual partners. The normal male subject's "sexuality is strangely non-corporeal" by contrast (particularly strange in the context of the significance Merleau-Ponty places on touch and bodily sensation, as opposed to visual input), and Merleau-Ponty emphasizes the "visible body... subtended by a sexual schema."[49]

Butler also notes that Merleau-Ponty's description does not appear to consider the experience of Schneider's sexual partner—"the erotic experience belongs exclusively to the perceiving subject."[50] However, it seems that the most remarkable way in which Schneider's sexuality diverges from the norm Merleau-Ponty establishes, or the most remarkable way that Schneider's sexuality changes following the changes in his physical body, is that his sexuality has become *relational* in a way that it was not before. It is not a production of the perceiving subject, but takes place *between* partners. Schneider's sexuality takes place less "within" Schneider, and more between himself and his partner—his sexuality is even more "in the world" (as in, it is less Schneider's and more an event between Schneider and another) than it was before his accident. The female subject who is mostly absent as an actor from Merleau-Ponty's account ("female bodies... have an essence which is itself physical [and] designates the female body as an object rather than a subject of perception" and "she is never seeing, always seen" seems to play a significant, if not an orchestrating, role in Schneider's sexuality.[51]

Furthermore, Schneider acknowledges this. He admits that he is drawn to women's characters rather than their bodies, emphasizing the significance of who his partner *is* for his sexual response. He also reports that his partners take the lead sexually, and that he responds to their desires. Rather than taking this as evidence that Schneider is sexually repressed or otherwise damaged as a sexual body, one may instead conclude that "Schneider is more true to Merleau-Ponty's phenomenological account of bodily existence than Merleau-Ponty himself" because for Schneider, his partner's body is "expressive of the life of consciousness."[52] Schneider's sexual partner's body is subtended not by a mere physical essence but bound up in her character, part of a subject whose sexuality, body, consciousness, and existence are inseparable. This relational aspect of Schneider's sexuality, oddly missing from Merleau-Ponty's presentation of normal sexuality, finds a parallel in Michael's experience, detailed later on in this chapter.

## Normative Bodies

In Merleau-Ponty's description, a particular kind of sexuality is established as normal, thereby excluding or pathologizing a number of other possible sexualities. In order to piece together this norm and gather "a concrete description of lived experience, it seems crucial to ask whose sexuality and whose bodies are being described."[53] Before offering an alternative description of the lived experience of sexuality, we must ask, whose body is the ideal body, or, whose body provides the basis for normative sexuality? In describing the significance of the sensory body in human experience, Merleau-Ponty writes, "[If] we conceive man in terms of his experience ... his distinctive way of patterning the world, and if we reintegrate the 'organs' into the functional totality in which they play their part, a handless or sexless man is inconceivable as one without the power of thought."[54] Merleau-Ponty is here making the point that a human being (or "man") is not composed of distinct parts that can be separated out, because the body makes up a whole. Cognitive abilities are neither separable from nor more important than physical sensation, and cannot be pulled from a body as though cognition were the essence of what it means to be human while the body was merely casing for thought. This idea contrasts with the notion that cognition is a more significant component of human experience than any other human component. This includes body parts; hands or genitals are no more characteristic of what it means to be human than cognition. Therefore, a person missing any of "his" component parts is no longer a "functional totality," for all of these parts contribute to "his distinctive way of patterning the world."[55]

The problem, however, is that Merleau-Ponty implies a *particular* whole. While Merleau-Ponty may not privilege cognition over body parts, he does seem to privilege some bodies, body parts, or ways of living one's body over others. Sara Heinämaa, by way of Simone de Beauvoir, notes that the examples "hands" and "genitals" are misleading comparisons, as "genitals" is an ambiguous term: "All normal human bodies have hands but not a similar or analogous 'sexual apparatus.'"[56] To posit a single norm is to overlook the presence of two possible norms of the human body—female and male bodies—and the female body becomes a deviation from the male norm.[57] Bodies that fit neither of these norms, such as intersexed bodies, are of course also excluded from the implied norm of embodiment.

Furthermore, the norm appears to be not only a male body but a specific kind of male embodiment, which is "healthy, implicitly athletic," "externally focused," and "transparent" ("transparent" referring to the body as a means of action rather than an object of attention).[58] Beyond setting up a normative sexuality by way of contrast with Schneider, "Merleau-Ponty sets up a dialectic between what could be called a *normative body experience* and the pathological experience that is only indirectly noted in his famous Schneider."[59] The normative body "contrasts with the debilities of Schneider—but also by extension with virtually any other form of unhealthy, or even less than well-conditioned sense of body."[60] Disabled bodies are also excluded from this norm, for Merleau-Ponty posits that we all tend toward a particular body, that there is in each of us "an I committed to a certain physical and inter-human world, who continues to tend towards his world despite handicaps and amputations and who, to this extent, does not recognize them *de jure*."[61] The ways in which one diverges from this normal body are presented here as absences or failures for which one strives to make up. In sum, the "normal" body seems to exclude *most* bodies.

Merleau-Ponty overlooks the particularities of bodies, implying an ideal body or way of being embodied, such that most bodies (in particular, female bodies, bodies that are not male or female or that are both, and disabled bodies of any variety) are only recognizable as deficient, not as alternative embodiments. The bodies that neither fit the ideal nor attempt to approximate a "normal" human body are absent from Merleau-Ponty's discussion. There is still room, however, to understand forms of embodiment that are not specifically described by Merleau-Ponty (and also still by means of Merleau-Ponty's approach to embodiment and sexuality, as will become apparent later on in this chapter). In describing these embodiments, "if we refuse to establish a singular sexual norm, those who were once 'outsiders' will no longer be considered illegitimate or unnatural. In accepting other sexual orientations as normal occurrences in the world, we also allow for a greater number of accounts of embodiment."[62] It is precisely by reorienting himself, with help, as a new body *de jure*—not a pathological body, nor a deficient male, nor necessarily male at all—that Michael becomes able to develop an alternative sexual embodiment and experience sexual satisfaction anew.[63]

## Alternative Sexualities

By understanding Schneider's case as a snapshot of a particular kind of sexuality, rather than framing Schneider as a sexual failure or deficient body, we may understand more about sexuality generally (rather than normative sexuality alone). Just as Schneider is presented as a pathological alternative to a normal body, Michael initially presents himself in his narrative as a deficient or damaged body. Indeed, Michael has been castrated, deprived of androgens (male hormones) and is unable to develop an erection. Prior to using the strap-on dildo, Michael feels as though all that is left for him is to "give up on life."[64] Michael is separated from a component of human experience, feeling his existence is unbearably limited. He regards his penis, and by extension, himself, as a "functional failure."[65]

However, during the process of dildo incorporation, Michael's sexuality not only reappears but also expands. His orgasms are more expansive ("radiating across my pelvis").[66] Michael acquires more pleasure from sex, describing sex as more purely "playful." Sex no longer has a goal or particular structure, and does not aim simply for climax. Instead, Michael can enjoy sex without orgasm, have multiple orgasms, and can continue sex after his orgasm if his partner desires.[67] "Castration" (the effect of hormonal prostate cancer treatment and prostate removal) does not mean that Michael's sexuality has been cut off. Michael had imagined that his world would close once he lost his functioning penis, and that he would no longer have a connection to the world via sexuality. Instead, his world opens broadly. This is similar to the experience of "Dr. A" who identifies as a "eunuch" after undergoing androgen deprivation therapy for prostate cancer. Dr. A no longer experiences himself or his sexuality in the same way but does not cease to be a sexual body. Instead, he becomes "more open to sexual exploration, as he is no longer driven in a narrow, testosterone-determined, direction to achieve orgasm through coitus."[68]

In contrast to the way Merleau-Ponty presents the case of Schneider, Michael's loss of functioning ultimately becomes a gain in terms of his ability for "projecting before himself a sexual world."[69] Michael's horizons expand beyond where they were prior to dildo incorporation. This transformation takes place gradually, from object to instrument to organ to libido-invested image that is both a part of Michael's body and a part of the world, the mere sight of which is erotically arousing.

The following section will elaborate the way in which Michael's sexuality is expanded following what initially appears to be a loss, and offers a description of the role of his partner the voice left out of Merleau-Ponty's account of sexuality, in mediating this transformation. The next section is also intended to contrast and supplement Merleau-Ponty's description of the sexual body via his discussion of Schneider's sexuality.

## THE EVENT OF SEXUALITY

Sexuality takes place in the world of others, shaped and cocreated by those around us. We are "given over from the start ... it would seem that our being beside ourselves, outside ourselves, is there as a function of sexuality itself ... not the key or bedrock of our existence, but ... as coextensive with existence."[70] If sexuality is a phenomenon that takes place in the liminal space between self and other (or indeed, something that emerges in the context of, or because of, the significance of this liminal space in human life), how is it that the sexual body comes to be in this space? What is the other's role in shaping one's sexuality and sexual body?

Michael and Schneider's sexual transformations both illuminate sexuality as a phenomenon that takes place *in the world of others*. That is, sexuality is not located in an individual (neither Michael nor Schneider), but emerges with others. Based on descriptions from Schneider's case, Schneider's sexuality appears to emerge between Schneider and his partner(s). Referring to Merleau-Ponty's statement about Schneider that, "If orgasm occurs first in the partner and she moves away, the half-fulfilled desire vanishes," Sullivan makes the significant point that "Schneider accepts and is thus restricted by the meaning that his partner has given to [the erotic situation]."[71,73] Schneider's inability to "project" means that one could characterize Schneider as passive: "The ultimate meaning and result of this situation are things that are given to Schneider by his world" because he does not instead "take up the situation and follow it through to its fulfillment (i.e., his own orgasm)."[72] This also seems to mean that Schneider's sexuality has become more dependent upon his partner's desires. Michael's experience parallels Schneider's here, but he does not regard his passivity or sexual dependence upon his partner as pathological.

The following section elaborates the way in which sexuality emerges between Michael and his sexual partner (whom we are calling "Susan"), including Susan's role in helping Michael accept the dildo as a part of his sexual body. It fills in the missing female subject from Merleau-Ponty's account, as well as the missing description of sexual passivity or shared sexual experience that is implicitly present in Merleau-Ponty's account of Schneider. Sexuality may be regarded as an "event," neither caused nor owned by a single agent. This elaboration follows the spirit of Merleau-Ponty's phenomenology without following the letter; that is, the following is an attempt to present sexuality as "the opening out upon 'another'"[74] and the expression of the life of consciousness through the body, but without the biases, described above, that appear in some parts of Merleau-Ponty's account of sexuality.

## Sex as Imaginative Play

Michael's narrative presents two people as essential to his ability to achieve sexual satisfaction using the dildo: his lesbian friend, who helps Michael open himself to the possibility that dildo sex could be sexually satisfying, and his sexual partner, Susan, with whom Michael fulfills this possibility.

Michael's friend sets the stage for the dildo as a tool for play. Michael states that "she insisted I consider [the dildo] a 'toy.'"[75] Michael and Susan also treat the dildo as a toy by approaching dildo sex as playful. In Michael's narrative, Susan comes across as supportive, thoughtful (in terms of planning ahead and surprising Michael in ways that ease his anxiety), and in possession of an affectionate sense of humor. Michael approaches dildo sex initially as an event taking place in "the theater of the absurd;" that is, he is entering a space of imaginative play and acting, in which one may try on different roles.[76] Susan is "ultimately supportive of the exploration," also treating dildo sex as an exploratory, improvisational act.[77]

Susan and Michael continue to "accept the dildo as part of our sex play."[78] It is worth noting that Michael uses the term "play" repeatedly to describe the sexual atmosphere between himself and Susan, indicating that they operate within the ambiguous space of sexuality and explore the possibilities of the sexual body. Susan and Michael together extend the boundaries of their play and the possibilities of strap-on dildo sex. For example, Susan "started playing with the dildo in a flirtatious fashion outside of the bedroom,"[79] which Michael experiences as erotic. Susan also performs oral sex on the dildo (Michael states, "My partner and I took on the challenge"), further extending the range of their shared sexual experience. I interpreted this as a signal to me that the dildo pleased her and did so because of its association with me."[81] It seems that just as Michael interprets Susan's actions here as indicative of an association she has formed between pleasure, Michael, and the dildo, he has also formed a parallel association between the dildo and pleasure he experiences with Susan. Because of her playful participation, the dildo has taken on a sexual meaning for Michael. He reflects this with the statement, "Each time [Susan and I] use [the strap-on dildo], it becomes further imbued with the knowledge of the previous sexual satisfaction it has provided."[82] Gradually the dildo becomes "a normal at the same time erotic part of *our lives*."[83] His sexuality seems not only contained in another object in the world, but in other people in the world; specifically, his sexuality is held in the two-person, imaginative sexual world constructed with his partner. The dildo, as a symbol of this sexuality, is owned neither by Michael nor by Susan. Sexuality is created in the space between partners and shared; an ongoing invention.

## "Passivity" in the Creation of Sexuality

Michael observes that when using the dildo, "I find it easiest to achieve orgasms when my partner wants me to, especially in the context of mutually satisfying dildo intercourse, but far more difficult on my own."[84] Michael's world appears to be "given" to him by Susan, and he says, "I discussed extensively with my partner whether she was willing to have sex with me wearing a strap-on dildo. She was at first hesitant but ultimately supportive of the exploration."[85] Only in the context of Susan's support and collaborative framing of dildo-use as an "exploration" was Michael willing to attempt to use a strap-on dildo. The space of exploration could only come about between them. Michael is surprised and pleased that he "carried the act through to orgasm, to the sexual satisfaction of both my partner *and* myself," emphasizing the importance of his partner in his sexual encounters.[86] Schneider's sexual receptivity and approach to sex as responsiveness to his partner's desires rather than the pursuit of his own are characterized as disconnection from his own satisfaction. Michael finds satisfaction in this very situation. He states, in contrast to Merleau-Ponty's interpretation of Schneider's lack of focus on achieving orgasm as disinterest in sex or sexual gratification:

> When I had a prostate gland, sexual arousal that did not lead to ejaculation was frustrating, and I found it incomprehensible when a woman claimed she had pleasure from sexual stimulation yet had not had an orgasm. After my prostate was removed, I discovered that I too could have incremental pleasure from sexual stimulation and enjoy sex without orgasms.[87]

Indeed, for Michael (and one may suspect for Schneider), sexual "satisfaction" is not synonymous with sexual discharge, just as Michael discovers (and as his lesbian friend knew all along) that having a functional penis is not essential for sexual enjoyment.

A non-pathologizing way to understand this phenomenon may be to view Michael as inhabiting the aspect of his body that Feenberg calls a "dependent body," or a mode of embodiment as the body is they are *given over to* the world and reacted to by the world. Feenberg writes, "We live our body not only as actors in the world but also as beings who invite action on our bodies by others."[88] *This is not to say that these bodies no longer have agency nor that they are entirely dependent or passive*, but rather to acknowledge the ways in which our bodies belong to, or are handed over to, the world. Human beings are "dependent" in the sense that we depend upon others, to varying degrees at various times, to create our experiences.

Merleau-Ponty's concept of "reversibility" helps to illustrate the way in which one may inhabit the dependent aspect of one's embodied existence, yet still remain an agent or a subject:

> When I press my two hands together, it is not a matter of two sensations felt together as one perceives two objects placed side by side, but ... of an ambiguous set-up in which both hands can alternate roles of 'touching' and being 'touched' ... In other words, in this bundle of bones and muscles which my right hand presents to my left, I can anticipate for an instant the integument or incarnation of that other right hand ... The body catches itself from the outside ... it tries to touch itself while being touched, and initiates a 'kind of reflection' which is sufficient to distinguish it from objects.[89]

One may be in the position of touched and at once be a body that is able to initiate touch. Merleau-Ponty describes this in terms of two hands touching one another, but this seems to apply to two bodies in a sexual encounter, as well. Because Michael can respond to Susan's touch and identify himself as one who is touching back, he is not a lifeless object-body. He possesses the possibility of "reversing" the situation by accepting or responding to Susan's actions, creating an ambiguity between being the one who is touched and the one who is touching. Michael's experiences of himself as a body, including as a sexual body, come from his experience of being an active body, but also from his experiences of his body being acted upon.

The body described here as a "dependent body" is a particular type of *passive body* in which "our time horizon shrinks as we no longer control or plan the next sensation, yet we remain exquisitely alert."[90] The dependent body conveys the "lived first-person experience of our own instrumentalized status."[91] Michael seems to "hand himself over" to the new experience of dildo sex, as well as handing himself over as a dildonic body to Susan, in their first sexual experience with the strap-on dildo. Michael is "caught ... by total surprise" at how "natural" sex feels when he is using the strap-on dildo.[92] It seems that Michael did not have a plan or a goal for this act. Part of Michael's surprise is a response to Susan's actions. Michael describes that during this first instance of dildo sex, Susan "reached down and held my penis in her hand ... There was little sensory difference between this act and intercourse—my penis was not in her vagina but it did not know that."[93] Michael says "I had not expected to achieve an orgasm and was astonished that it happened."[94] Susan's independent actions provide the first steps to incorporating the dildo into Michael's sexual body and into their shared sexual life.

The dependent body as an aspect of the sexual body seems to be particularly relevant for aspects of Michael's and Schneider's experience that are overlooked in Merleau-Ponty's account of normal sexuality (which seems to emphasize active pursuit of sexual climax). In sex, the body may lose its position as a spectator or object for itself, and instead become a more "immediate" form of consciousness.[95] In other words, sex is "a relation between subjectivized bodies."[96] Each subject attempts to bring about this subject-mode in the other, calling the other more into immediate experience and sensation. "Sex is the construction of the dependent body of this other."[97] Merleau-Ponty's account of normal sexuality seems to overlook the experience of having oneself called forth as a dependent body, or the experience of being the body that is touched. Again, this body retains subjectivity and is not a mere object-body. In fact, the experience of being called into the immediate moment or experiencing himself as a dependent body is the opposite of Michael's experience prior to dildo incorporation, when he felt depressed and rejected multiple interventions upon his object-body as viable solutions (i.e., "Viagra... a vacuum erection device ... a surgically implanted penile prosthesis."[98] The experience of a body in pain or disease is described by Drew Leder: "I no longer simply 'am' my body, the set of unthematized powers from which I exist. Now I 'have' a body, a perceived object in the world."[99] The body itself is a clumsy, incomplete, or pathological object viewed from without. Alternately, with the help of his partner, Michael's body goes from being a pathological object to a sexual body, and the dildo goes from being an external object to an extension of himself.

Michael, and to some extent an alternative reading of Schneider's case, give a response to the question of what it is like to be an object of action, or to have the lived experience of sexual passivity as an aspect of overall sexual being. Their responsiveness or receptiveness in sex, rather than demonstrating deficient sexuality, reveal the dependence upon the other that partially characterizes sexuality. Schneider lacks an ability to objectively assess a situation, that is, to tell the difference between a story and a riddle, to tell the difference between play-acting and reality and seems stuck in the immediate, to the point that he is unable to think into the future beyond the tasks immediately before him.[100] This seems to place Schneider in a permanent mode of dependent sexual partner, existing in the immediate moment.

Michael describes coming to feel that sexuality is restored after feeling accepted by his partner, or rather, feeling that his dildo-body has been accepted: "Sexual satisfaction has become easier, because both of us have come to accept the dildo as part of our sex play."[101] This acceptance allows his observing consciousness to recede and he simply enjoys sex in the immediate moment. He is immersed in the imaginative sexual realm and experiences the dildo as an extension of his flesh. Michael describes sex using the dildo, even the first time, as feeling "natural," meaning the dildo has already become a "transparent" part of his experience or "ready to hand."[102] Acceptance allows Michael to return to his body and return to immediate experience.

## Passing, Acceptance, and Love

Feenberg elaborates a second kind of passive body, which he calls the "extended body," characterized not by our ability to extend our body schema through the incorporation of tools, but instead by what this incorporation signifies to others. He notes that the body not only "acts through a technical mediation, but also ... signifies itself through that mediation," suggesting ways for others to respond to one's body.[103] Merleau-Ponty's famous example of the blind man whose body schema is extended by a walking stick, for instance, does not merely experience bodily extension in the realm of body activity: "The cane does more than sense the world; it also reveals the blind man as blind" meaning his body is extended "also in the passive dimension of its own objectivity."[104] This leads others to recognize and respond (helpfully, Feenberg assumes) to his blindness, and the blind man "has a non-specific awareness" of these responses and the general world they compose for him.[105] The extended body denotes the aspect of experience, which is about the "consequences for bodily objectivity and the subject's awareness of those consequences."[106]

Of course, there are a range of ways that others might respond to one's body, and the way in which a body is instrumentally extended might provide a suggestion to others but does not necessarily elicit a particular response. Butler writes, "to be a body is to be given over to others even as a body is, emphatically, 'one's own,'" and "my body is and is not mine ... my body relates me—*against my will* and from the start—to others."[107] Feenberg seems to assume that others, upon recognizing the blind man's cane as a signifier of his blindness will respond to his dependent body *helpfully*, but there are a range of responses possible once his body is handed over to the world in this way. We are left quite vulnerable to the responses of others to and upon our bodies. We are our bodies, but our bodies are not entirely our own. The way in which our bodies are given over to others also indicates the limitations of sexual autonomy and how others shape our sexuality. The extended body "signifies itself through mediation" and the subject's awareness of its "bodily objectivity" to others shape experience.[108] This includes significations of sex, gender, sexual orientation, and so on among other aspects of self-presentation.

Hale notes that "the operation" for Female to male transsexual (FTMs), often naively conceived as a phalloplasty or a "phallic cure" for the "transsexual man's ... condition" is a "distorting imposition."[109] To conceive of "the operation" in this way is to understand the FTM's "gender identification as being primarily about absence of and desire for a cock."[110] Indeed, if the aim of transition is to be one's felt sex or gender, then one aim of the operation is to change one's signifying, object body such that what it signifies to others is consistent with who one feels one is or desires to be. This is more than a visual change. If the goal of transformations on the passive body (as one aspect of embodied experience, the aspect in which one is given over to others) is to communicate one's identity to others in order that others are better able to cocreate one's world, such that one can have a different experience of his own embodiment, then top surgery (removing and reshaping breasts into a male-looking chest) would be more significant than bottom surgery (constructing a penis for an FTM): "The most heavily weighted physical characteristic in making the gender attribution "female" to adults is the presence of breasts, whereas the most heavily weighted physical characteristic in making the attribution "male" is the presence of a penis."[111] Zita explains that "passing" is not a strong enough term, given the importance of others' responses to the passive body. " 'Passing' implies pretense and lying, not a new ontological reading of the body's sex," adding that "when our 'male lesbian' fails to maintain a consistent female identity at all times, this is ... an indication of the individual's inability to control over-determined hegemonic readings from the outside world forced on the body."[112] The "new ontology" implies a stable state and something maintained "at all times," but difficult to maintain when in conflict with hegemonic ideas about how body and identity align. "The very 'I' is called into question by its relation to the one to whom I address myself."[113] Consistent reading of one's body by others as different than one desires that it be read, as in the example of the male lesbian, "definitively 'sexes' his body."[114] Thus, how others read and interpret the body impacts one's felt identity, and leads this identity to waver when one is continually misread and affects one's experience from moment to moment.

It is through Susan's mediation that Michael comes to inhabit his new dildonic sexual body, or through which the dildo comes to signify a sexual extension of Michael's body (rather than a medical device or a means for mockery, as Michael envisions the dildo prior to Susan's mediation). Susan enables particular forms of experience in him, but there is certainly not a single, given way of responding to him. Indeed, Michael seems to sense this with his reluctance to "go into a sex shop to buy a dildo," fantasizing that he, and the dildonically extended body he had just allowed himself to envision becoming, would be "identified and mocked by someone who knew me" instead of embraced and adored, as it is by his partner.[115] Beyond this, it is Susan's mediation that allows Michael to form a new sexual identity that includes the dildo. Michael "passes" as a dildonic sexual body through Susan's recognition, or in other words, Susan allows Michael's sexual body to inhabit the dildo, and his transformation begins. This feat is especially impressive given the constraining forces set against alternative modes of sexuality.

Walker & Robinson, in their study of heterosexual couples in which the male partner has undergone the same hormonal prostate cancer treatment as Michael, find that these couples continue having satisfying sex lives when they are "unwilling to accept a loss of sex," are "open-minded about specific strategies," and "placed great emphasis on increasing relational intimacy."[116] Together, the partners develop a way of understanding and responding to the androgen deprivation therapy and prostate cancer that does not render the male partner asexual or deficient. They become flexible and open to new modes of sexuality and maintain a loving, intimate relationship. In their analysis of an interview of a woman whose husband had undergone prostate removal, Rennie and Fergus comment on the way this couple shares experience: "[The love] has taken shape on its own, so that one [becomes] transformed by it."[117] In Michael's case, love is a force of literal transformation, allowing his new body to come into being. Michael's case demonstrates "how a thing or being begins to exist for us through desire or love."[118]

## IV. CONCLUSION

As Merleau-Ponty describes, sexuality is a mode of relation. Identity and sexualities exist in the world of others and objects, not simply in the individual mind or in reflexive action. This chapter has been an attempt to elaborate sexuality as a mode of relation by presenting sexuality as an "event" between people, rather than something that emerges as a purposive action from a single (male) person. This chapter has also attempted to place sexuality outside of normative ways of viewing the body and sexual behavior, instead presenting sexuality as a complex aspect of self that is bound up with identity. Recognizing the variability of bodies and refusing to establish a body norm also allows bodies to become more playful—they are not attempting to approximate "normal" bodies nor are they resigned to a partial life as partial and broken bodies, but instead offer a new narrative of the self. Michael emerges from his experience with a new body and new sexual horizon, suggesting a complex and intersubjective relationship between sexuality, embodiment, and identity that permits space for redefinition and development. As we are all sexual, social, and embodied beings, this has implications more broadly, presenting an expanded horizon and more complex version of human being.

## NOTES

1. Maurice Merleau-Ponty, *Phenomenology of Perception*, trans. Colin Smith (London: Routledge, 1962), 178.

2. Silvia Stoller, "Expressivity and Performativity: Merleau-Ponty and Butler," *Continental Philosophy Review* 43, no. 1 (2010): 104.

3. Karen M. Warkentin, Ross E. Gray and Richard J. Wassersug, "Restoration of Satisfying Sex for a Castrated Cancer Patient with Complete Impotence: A Case Study," *Journal of Sex & Marital Therapy* 32, no. 5 (2006): 391.

4. Ibid.

5. Ibid.

6. Ibid.

7. Ibid., 392.

8. Ibid.

9. Ibid.

10. Ibid., 391.

11. Ibid., 393.

12. Ibid., 391.

13. Ibid., 392.

14. Ibid., 393.

15. Merleau-Ponty, *Phenomenology of Perception*, 178.

16. Ibid., 196.

17. Ibid.

18. Elizabeth Grosz, *Volatile Bodies: Toward a Corporeal Feminism* (Bloomington: Indiana University Press, 1994).

19. Merleau-Ponty, *Phenomenology of Perception*, 196 and 195.

20. Sara Heinämaa, *Toward a Phenomenology of Sexual Difference: Husserl, Merleau-Ponty, Beauvoir* (Lanham: Rowman & Littlefield Publishers Inc., 2003), 66.

21. Judith Butler, "Sexual Ideology and Phenomenological Description: A Feminist Critique of Merleau-Ponty's Phenomenology of Perception," in *The Thinking Muse: Feminism and Modern French Philosophy*, eds. Jeffner Allen and Iris Marion Young (Bloomington: Indiana University Press, 1989), 87.

22. Merleau-Ponty, *Phenomenology of Perception*, 194.

23. Ibid.

24. Ibid., 181.

25. Adhémar Gelb and Kurt Goldstein, "Psychologische Analysen Hirnpathologischer Fälle," *Psychological Research* 6, no. 1 (1925).

26. Merleau-Ponty, *Phenomenology of Perception*, 145.

27. Ibid., 150.

28. Ibid., 179.

29. Ibid., 120.

30. Ibid., 157.

31. Ibid., 181.

32. Ibid., 180.

33. Ibid., 181.

34. Ibid., 180.

35. Ibid., 179.

36. Ibid., 181.

37. Shannon Sullivan, "Domination and Dialogue in Merleau-Ponty's Phenomenology of Perception," *Hypatia* 12, no. 1 (1997): 2.

38. Ibid.

39. Ibid.

40. Merleau-Ponty, *Phenomenology of Perception*.

41. Ibid., 180–181.

42. Sullivan, "Domination and Dialogue, 2.

43. Merleau-Ponty, *Phenomenology of Perception*, 180.

44. Ibid., 179. Although "Exactly how and why a man who has no interest in sex has an orgasm, however brief, neither Goldstein and Gelb nor Merleau-Ponty explain" (Grosz, *Volatile Bodies*, 108).

45. Merleau-Ponty, *Phenomenology of Perception*, 181.

46. Butler, "Sexual Ideology," 92.

47. Merleau-Ponty, *Phenomenology of Perception*, 181.

48. Butler, "Sexual Ideology," 92.

49. Ibid., 93.

50. Ibid., 93.

51. Ibid., 94.

52. Butler, "Sexual Ideology," 95.

53. Butler, "Sexual Ideology," 98.

54. Merleau-Ponty, *Phenomenology of Perception*, 197.

55. Ibid.

56. Heinämaa, *Toward a Phenomenology of Sexual Difference*, 87.

57. Ibid.

58. Don Ihde, *Bodies in Technology* (Minneapolis: University of Minnesota Press, 2002), 18.

59. Ibid., 17, italics mine.

60. Ibid., 18.

61. Merleau-Ponty, *Phenomenology of Perception*, 94.

62. Jillian Canode, "Thinking the Body: Sexual Difference in Philosophy an Examination of Maurice Merleau-Ponty's Account of Embodiment in Phenomenology of Perception," *McNair Scholars Journal* 6, no. 1 (2002): 34.

63. Warkentin et al., "Restoration of Satisfying Sex."

64. Ibid.

65. Ibid.

66. Ibid., 392.

67. Ibid.

68. Richard Wassersug, "Mastering Emasculation," *Journal of Clinical Oncology* 27, no. 4 (2009): 635.

69. Merleau-Ponty, *Phenomenology of Perception*, 181.

70. Judith Butler, *Undoing Gender* (London: Routledge, 2004), 33.

71. Shannon Sullivan, "Domination and Dialogue in Merleau-Ponty's Phenomenology of Perception," *Hypatia* 12, no. 1 (1997): 2.

72. Ibid.

73. Merleau-Ponty, *Phenomenology of Perception*, 179.

74. Ibid., 194.

75. Warkentin et al., "Restoration of Satisfying Sex," 391.

76. Ibid., 391.

77. Ibid.

78. Ibid., 392.

79. Ibid., 393.

80. Ibid.

81. Ibid., 392.

82. Ibid.

83. Ibid, 392, emphasis mine.

84. Ibid.

85. Ibid., 391.

86. Ibid., 392.

87. Ibid. 391.

88. Andrew Feenberg, "Active and Passive Bodies: Comments on Don Ihde's Bodies in Technology," in *Expanding Phenomenology: A Critical Companion to Ihde*, ed. Evan Selinger (Albany: State University of New York Press, 2006), 103.

89. Merleau-Ponty, *Phenomenology of Perception*, 106–107.

90. Feenberg, "Active and Passive Bodies," 103.

91. Ibid., 103.

92. Warkentin et al., "Restoration of Satisfying Sex," 391.

93. Ibid.

94. Ibid.

95. Feenberg, "Active and Passive Bodies."

96. Ibid, 103.

97. Ibid.

98. Warkentin et al., "Restoration of Satisfying Sex," 390.

99. Drew Leder, *The Absent Body*, (Chicago: University of Chicago Press, 1990), 77.

100. Merleau-Ponty, *Phenomenology of Perception*.

101. Warkentin et al., "Restoration of Satisfying Sex," 392.

102. Ibid., 391.

103. Feenberg, "Active and Passive Bodies," 105.

104. Ibid.

105. Ibid.

106. Ibid., 104.

107. Butler, *Undoing Gender*, 20-1, emphasis mine.

108. Feenberg, "Active and Passive Bodies."

109. Jacob C. Hale, "Consuming the Living, Dis(re)membering the Dead in the Butch/ FTM Borderlands," *GLQ: A Journal of Lesbian and Gay Studies* 4, no. 2 (1998): 328–9.

110. Ibid., 329.
111. Ibid., 330.
112. Jacquely N. Zita, *Body Talk: Philosophical Reflections on Sex and Gender* (New York: Columbia University Press, 1998), 106.
113. Butler, *Undoing Gender*, 19.
114. Zita, *Body Talk*, 106.
115. Warkentin et al., "Restoration of Satisfying Sex," 391.
116. Lauren M. Walker and John W. Robinson, "A Description of Heterosexual Couples' Sexual Adjustment to Androgen Deprivation Therapy for Prostate Cancer," *Psycho-Oncology* 20, no. 8 (2011): 885.
117. David L. Rennie and Karen D. Fergus, "Embodied Categorizing in the Grounded Theory Method," *Theory & Psychology* 16, no. 4 (2006): 492.
118. Merleau-Ponty, *Phenomenology of Perception*, 178.

## BIBLIOGRAPHY

Butler, Judith. *Gender Trouble: Feminism and the Subversion of Identity.* New York: Routledge, 1990.
———. "Sexual Ideology and Phenomenological Description: A Feminist Critique of Merleau-Ponty's Phenomenology of Perception." In *The Thinking Muse: Feminism and Modern French Philosophy*, edited by Jeffner Allen and Iris Marion Young, 85–100. Bloomington: Indiana University Press, 1989.
———. *Undoing Gender*. London: Routledge, 2004.
Canode, Jillian. "Thinking the Body: Sexual Difference in Philosophy an Examination of Maurice Merleau-Ponty's Account of Embodiment in Phenomenology of Perception." *McNair Scholars Journal*, 6, no. 1 (2002): 31–36.
Feenberg, Andrew. "Active and Passive Bodies: Comments on Don Ihde's Bodies in Technology." In *Expanding Phenomenology: A Critical Companion to Ihde*, edited by Evan Selinger, 189–96. Albany: State University of New York Press, 2006.
Gelb, Adhémar, and Kurt Goldstein. "Psychologische Analysen Hirnpathologischer Fälle." *Psychological Research*, 6, no. 1 (1925): 127–86.
Grosz, Elizabeth. *Volatile Bodies: Toward a Corporeal Feminism*. Bloomington: Indiana University Press, 1994.
Hale, Jacob C. "Consuming the Living, Dis(re)membering the Dead in the Butch/FTM Borderlands." *GLQ: A Journal of Lesbian and Gay Studies* 4, no.2 (1998): 311–48.
Heinämaa, Sara. *Toward a Phenomenology of Sexual Difference: Husserl, Merleau-Ponty, Beauvoir.* Lanham: Rowman & Littlefield Publishers Inc., 2003.
Ihde, Don. *Bodies in Technology*. Minneapolis: University of Minnesota Press, 2002.
Leder, Drew. *The Absent Body*. Chicago: University of Chicago Press, 1990.
Merleau-Ponty, Maurice. *Phenomenology of Perception*, translated by Colin Smith. London: Routledge, 1962.
Rennie, David L., and Karen D. Fergus. "Embodied Categorizing in the Grounded Theory Method." *Theory & Psychology* 16, no. 4 (2006): 483–503.

Stoller, Silvia. "Expressivity and Performativity: Merleau-Ponty and Butler." *Continental Philosophy Review* 43, no. 1 (2010): 97–110.

Sullivan, Shannon. "Domination and Dialogue in Merleau-Ponty's Phenomenology of Perception." *Hypatia* 12, no. 1 (1997): 1–19.

Walker, Lauren M., and John W. Robinson. "A Description of Heterosexual Couples' Sexual Adjustment to Androgen Deprivation Therapy for Prostate Cancer." *Psycho-Oncology* 20, no. 8 (2011): 880–88.

Warkentin, Karen M., Ross E. Gray, and Richard J. Wassersug. "Restoration of Satisfying Sex for a Castrated Cancer Patient with Complete Impotence: A Case Study." *Journal of Sex & Marital Therapy* 32, no. 5 (2006): 389–99.

Wassersug, Richard J. "Mastering Emasculation." *Journal of Clinical Oncology* 27, no. 4 (2009): 634–36.

Zita, Jacquelyn N. *Body Talk: Philosophical Reflections on Sex and Gender.* New York: Columbia University Press, 1998.

*Part V*

# TRUTH AND DECEPTION

## Chapter Twelve

# The Power of Seduction

## Alain Beauclair

Seduction does not primarily aim to force sexual compliance, but rather to *produce desire*. However, desire itself is shifting and opaque. There is not always a clear or lasting quality to "what I want." Furthermore, since desire is subject-producing, then to influence another's desires is to participate in their self-formation. Seductive persuasion proceeds not by rational argument but through play, poetry, and allusion. It might be more accurately associated with beguilement than *logos*. Even more concerning, seduction involves power-plays that can reinforce oppressive roles and facilitate exploitation. Thus, one might rightly worry that seduction is nothing but disguised coercion.

Plato's *Phaedrus* examines this concern in considerable depth. One of its central questions is: Can seduction be both persuasive and just? In its opening myth, Oreithuia is "taken" by Boreas, the North Wind. It is unclear whether she was abducted and raped, or seduced. Under the influence of Pharmaceia, did she have adequate judgment to consent? Or did Pharmaceia enable her to lose her inhibitions and liberate her true desires and her true character? When Phaedrus asks Socrates's if he believes the myth to be true, Socrates's redirects the conversation toward his concern with self-knowledge. Socrates's asks whether he, himself, is similar to or different from Typhon—father of the four winds and the embodiment of hubris and violence. What is his true character? Is he consumed by lust and possessed by nature? Or does he have divinely inspired temperance? The answer depends on another question: What is the relationship between seduction and truth?

According to Socrates's, the more "artful" one's seductive speech, the more it may be deceptive. That is, one is being strategic if they "begin with their conclusion," *assuming* it is true and trying to persuade another of this truth, rather than *exploring* the truth via dialogue. Strategic speech is often achieved through flattery, telling the audience what they want to hear—what they are already inclined to believe—taking advantage of their biases while nudging them toward what the orator wants them to believe. Thus, seduction has a dual nature. It can be exploitation of one's vulnerability, coopting of one's desires by another, and ultimately a self-betrayal by the one seduced. Or it can be an art of friendly dialogic inquiry, an exploration of what one truly desires, a test of the self. At its best, seduction takes the form of the latter, a practice of collaborative self-discovery and self-formation among friends.

## THE CHARACTER OF SEXUAL COMMUNICATION

While contemporary discussions surrounding sexual consent rightly focus a great deal of attention on the *conditions* of communication, we must also inquire into its *character*. For starters, sexual consent is often (though not solely) pursued through a peculiar mode of discourse known as seduction. Though a great deal of seduction involves extra-linguistic modes of communication, the aim of all forms of seduction is to persuade, forging an indelible link to the human capacity for speech. However, while other consensus-seeking modes of speech tend to have at least a loosely defined set of norms and criteria that can assist in the validation of any agreement (e.g., science appeals to the experimental method, while economic discourse relies upon a model of fairness grounded in a contractual scheme), seduction as a form of discourse is far more open and playful, and does not appear to be clearly governed by any specific set of rules or criteria. In this regard, seductive speech is often associated more with poetry and elusive allusions than to rational argument and straightforward factual claims. Not only is it difficult to determine what counts as right reasons in this sphere, given the strong connection between seduction and desire, some might say that to agree on these terms is to countermand the very dictates of rationality. In fact, given that seductive speech is often associated with flattery and beguilement if not outright trickery, one has to wonder if consent that is garnered through such discourse can ever be granted legitimacy.

To be sure, it would be wrong to separate out the conditions of inequality that inform sexual communication from a critical analysis of the nature of seduction. Very often how we speak and what we say exploit these conditions in an attempt to coerce the subordinate other into engaging in an act they would ordinarily find less than desirable. Similarly, the norms, expectations, and patterns of seduction are powerfully structured by gender constructs and other relations of power, meaning that the situation is not something that imposes itself on the act of consent from without but also organizes what is said from within.

One need look no further than how common seductive tropes function to recognize how women are often placed in a position of extreme vulnerability in relation to men. It is still common for a man to put on displays of physical strength or act aggressively in order to increase his sexual appeal, while women are still expected to be coquettish, play "hard to get," and even at times feign resistance in order to appear even more enticing. However, when these roles are examined in light of the current epidemic of sexual assault and acquaintance rape, they do not appear so innocent. Take for example the recent popularity of controversial seduction manuals such as "Above the Game: A Guide to Getting Awesome With Women,"[1] which has gained recent media attention thanks in part to its incredible and unexpected success raising money through a kickstarter program. Beyond its surprising ability to raise funds, this book has gained notoriety for its harmful approach to seduction, in effect encouraging its readers to engage in acts of sexual assault in order to win the affections of their would-be target: "Physically pick up (the woman) and sit her on your lap. Don't ask for permission. Be dominant. Force her to rebuff your advances. ... Pull out your cock and put her hand on it. Remember, she is letting you do this because you have established yourself as a leader. Don't ask for permission, grab her hand, and put it right on your dick." Passages such as these do not just reveal the moral depravity of the author; they shed light on the dangerous and oppressive function of traditional gender roles that laud male dominance while encouraging female submission. The fact that this author is unable to recognize the difference between persuading (let alone inveigling) and coercing a woman is telling, offering us a window into the predatory model that structures the game of seduction, imposing a stark power imbalance that on its most basic level grants agency to the male while denying it to the female.

In cases such as this, it would appear that the actual art of seduction is merely a product of these conditions of inequality, and that the rules of this language game are not only vulnerable to the practices of patriarchy, but are largely determined by them. The fault then lies not so much with the act of seduction itself, but more with the conditions under which it is pursued (conditions that place one of the parties on an unequal footing prior to the initiation of any seductive act). If this is the case, then what is required is that we correct these conditions of inequality, thus paving the way for a legitimate and meaningful pursuit of consent. But perhaps matters are even more complex. One must wonder whether the art of seduction is inherently power-neutral and only corrupted by the conditions under which it is pursued, or whether seduction is itself in some ways constitutive of the interactions, identities, and practices that comprise the realm of human sexuality. That is, might the very form of this discourse precipitate a relation of dominance, and thus play a determining role in the nature and character of our sexual identities and behaviors? Just as Catharine MacKinnon once noted that gender is not only socially constructed but *constructing*,[2] might we not ask the same question of the nature of seduction?

What makes this such a complex issue is that seduction is a mode of discourse predicated on the production of desire. Seduction not only aims to persuade the other to engage in sexual acts of gratification, but to persuade the other to *want* to engage in these acts. This is a crucial detail, for it excludes all methods of persuasion that rely upon explicitly coercive measures, though it might involve more covert modes of coercion. For example, we do not consider it a matter of seduction when one is persuaded to perform sexual acts under the threat of violence or because the alternative is less than desirable (such as loss of job, public humiliation, etc.). Instead, what marks out seduction is that it leads the other to perceive the *act itself* as desirable. At first it might appear that this condition would settle the problem of consent— how can we deny the validity of such an agreement if this is in fact what the consenting party wants? Unfortunately, it is the very nature of desire to be fleeting and obscure, making us vulnerable to confusion, deception, and inner conflict. It is not uncommon to believe what we want is one thing when in truth it is another, or for our desires to be in a state of disagreement, to dissipate, or to transform. This is to say nothing of the potential to be deceived by the object of our desire—is it not a fundamental part of the game of seduction to present oneself not merely in the best possible light, but often as something we are not? How then can we know if the desire that comes as a result of seduction is either genuine or valid?

As a result, in order to determine the legitimacy of seductive speech, we are led to the most basic Freudian question: 'What do I want?' As Freud convincingly demonstrated, this question stands at the center of the task for self-knowledge, for who we are is intimately bound up with what we desire. Insofar as seduction constitutes a desire-producing activity, the role of this discourse takes on a very interesting dimension in reference to the question of self-knowledge. To take it one step further, the true aim of seduction is not simply to produce desire but to *overwhelm* the other with desire, an aim which raises the stakes of Freud's inquiry, forcing us to ask to what extent the self is formed and/or victimized by seduction. Just as Freudian analysis concedes that we may be *betrayed* (in all the myriad senses of the word) by our desires at the same time we are constituted by them, we may wonder whether betrayal is not an immanent feature of seduction. Though it is difficult to determine what implications seduction may have on the nature of the self, we can begin our inquiry with the following questions: How might seduction come to organize, structure, and even form our desires, does this discourse constitute a subject-producing activity, and to what extent is it implicated in the machinations of power? All of this culminates in a serious question of propriety, not only in terms of what is appropriate, but as a question of what is truly one's own. If the art of seduction does engage in a process of what Foucault called subjectification, we must question to what extent this discourse is involved in the formation of a subordinate self. In the most basic sense, our inquiry revolves around the following question: Is to be seduced to be subjugated?

## THE EXAMINATION OF SEDUCTION IN PLATO'S *PHAEDRUS*: THE TALE OF OREITHUIA

While the issue of seduction is considered on throughout Plato's *Phaedrus*, this chapter will focus its attention on the opening few pages with the modest hope of establishing the parameters under which an inquiry into the character of seduction can be pursued. This is not to deny the importance of what is said in the later pages, or to claim that they are somehow unrelated to the question of seduction. However, insofar as this is where the stage is set and terms are established, there is no better place from which to launch an opening salvo into the topic. The unifying question that is pursued throughout is: In what way can seduction take on the character of persuasion and remain both legitimate and just?

This question is provocatively raised by the dialogue's framing myth—when Socrates's arrives with Phaedrus at the picturesque setting beyond the city walls, Phaedrus asks, "isn't it somewhere along here on the Ilissus that Boreas is said to have abducted Oreithuia?"[3] As the story goes, Boreas was smitten with Oreithuia, and initially tried to woo her through conventional means. However, having failed to seduce Oreithuia, he is said to have abducted and raped her as she danced with Pharmacia along the Ilissus. There are three odd aspects to the way the myth is characterized by both Phaedrus and Socrates's. First, the word that Phaedrus uses for "abduction"—ἁρπάσαι—can be interpreted in a number of ways. While it has both connotations that are consistent with the myth as it is traditionally received—it can be translated as to be carried off or abducted as well as to be plundered or raped—this word also has the additional meaning of being captivated or ravished. The question we are forced to ask is what, if any, is the difference?

Second, Socrates's adds the additional detail that she was kidnapped while playing with Pharmaceia. The word from which her playmate's name is derived—φαρμακός—is one familiar to readers of Plato, denoting a drug that can be used to either heal or harm, and was used in one of these two ways (depending on one's perspective) to bring Socrates's' life to an end. This connection to the *pharmakon* has a number of interesting connotations. For starters, to claim that Oreithuia was taken by Boreas while playing with

Pharmaceia might simply mean that she was "stoned," obviously jeopardizing her ability to provide meaningful consent for her tryst with the north wind. However, as far as Greek myths go, the implication is that Oreithuia was overcome by a bout of madness both commonly associated with such indulgences, and also linked to divine inspiration. Thus, we have here a connection between the *play* of Oreithuia and the divinely inspired madness of the *pharmakon*. This connection raises a number of questions given the dubious role madness often plays in Greek poetry and religion, questions that hold a place of prominence in the dialogue's three speeches on love.

One such question involves the bearing erotic madness has on sound judgment. Much in the way it is commonly believed that "high" people lack both good judgment and an appropriate level of inhibition, it is commonly assumed that madness tends to place reason and passion at odds, whereby the latter is said to overpower the former (an effect also associated with the overwhelming desire invoked by a successful act of seduction). Nevertheless, it is not entirely clear, as Socrates's will later point out, that all madness constitutes a desire that lacks *logos*, or if madness may incite us toward or lead us astray of what is best. There are a variety of forms of madness, and the nature of desire—whether it is at odds or consonant with sound judgment—is left an open question, leading us to ask, what impact does Oreithuia's play have on her ability to make good decisions, and is this the very kind of vulnerability seduction seeks to exploit and/or produce?

Next, erotic madness has the potential to dissolve those safeguards that shield the self, concealing our true aims, projects, and aspirations. As many of us are well aware, when the orderliness of the soul is overtaken by desire we are left bare, defenseless, and radically exposed. However, it is in such moments of vulnerability that we most fully confront those desires and sentiments that have remained hidden, even to ourselves. Socrates's actually invokes this sense of madness moments later when he proclaims that Phaedrus had "found the prescription (φάρμακον) to bring me out," as though Socrates's were being "drawn out of his shell" and forced to expose his desires to the clear light of day.[4] In light of this effect of madness, we might ask in what way Oreithuia's play is revelatory, eroding those inhibitions that keep the truth of the self at bay, and in what way Oreithuia's play grants us access to her true desires.

Lastly, there is an issue concerning the liberating capacity of erotic madness, its tendency to lead us beyond our ordinary limits, a question that has deep implications on our sense of responsibility and on the nature of the self. The disorderliness of madness introduces an element of uncertainty and risk into our conduct, often leading us to a point where we no longer know where we are going. Am I responsible for actions that are a result of madness, are such actions slavish (ἀνδραποδωδῶς) or voluntary, are these actions expressions of my true desires, and to what extent do these actions represent or even constitute my character?

This characteristic of madness can be clarified in terms of the driving force behind most romantic comedies, where newly inspired passion allows our hero to break their old and tired patterns and embark on some exciting new adventure. Examined in this way, one could imagine Drew Barrymore playing Oreithuia who, thanks to the madness induced by her newfound love interest sees the world anew, full of fresh and happy possibilities. However, there is a danger that emerges in conjunction with this break with the past, one which often results in the tired plot twist that has our hero make a retreat back into her old form of life (typically at the behest of an overbearing father who is unwilling to give up his patriarchal authority). All told, we must wonder whether Oreithuia's play frees her from the shackles of indurated habit, opening up novel passages and unfamiliar paths, or if it is just a fanciful and potentially dangerous manner of misinterpreting reality. These questions take on even greater significance in light of the connection between madness and seduction, raising once again the specter of the *pharmakon*'s dubious ability to either heal or corrupt—does the madness of seduction-induced desire mark out a healing or corruption of the soul?

Finally, we can turn to the third and potentially strangest feature of the myth: Phaedrus does not ask Socrates's about this story simply because they have stumbled upon its alleged locale, but because he is curious as to whether or not Socrates's believes it to be true (ἀληθές). Socrates' response to this question, like a good episode of *Arrested Development*, offers us one of the most layered moments in all of the Platonic dialogues:

If I believed it, as the wise do, I wouldn't be odd. In that case, being wise, I might say that while she was playing with Pharmaceia a puff of wind pushed her off the nearby rocks, and that when she came to her end in this manner she was said to have been carried off by Boreas ... I myself, Phaedrus, believe that such things, while amusing, are the work of a man who is exceedingly clever and industrious but not at all fortunate for no other reason than that after this he must account for the form of the Centaurs and then for that of the Chimaera ... I myself have no leisure at all for such business, and the reason for that my friend is this: I'm not yet able, in accordance with the Delphic inscription, to know myself, and it seems ridiculous to me to investigate things that don't concern me while still lacking that knowledge. So, I leave those matters alone, and being persuaded by what is traditionally maintained about them, I investigate (as I was saying just now) not those things but myself, as to whether I happen to be a beast more complex and agitated than Typhon, or a gentler and simpler animal, possessing by nature a divine and un-Typhonic lot.[5]

Many commentators rightly point out the fact that Socrates's does not dispute the truth of this tale, and actually employs another image when stating his chief concern: Socrates's sees little value in refuting popular myths when he has not yet satisfied the far more important objective to "know thyself." Thus, this comment appears to fly in the face of the popular assumption that Socrates's was highly condemnatory of myths and the myth-making poets behind them.

But we should not stand content with this single insight, and instead ask why Socrates's broaches the question of self-knowledge by reference to a specific mythical being: the titan Typhon. This figure, often depicted as split between a human body and a head made up of countless serpents, is known as the embodiment of hubris, an excessive and violent character that sought to subdue all it came into contact with. Much like the typhoon, which is his namesake, Typhon is a monstrous being that seeks to overturn all that which is unfortunate enough to fall within his wake. Trading heavily on the metaphor of wind in this passage, Socrates's alludes to the *pharmakon*-like dual nature of the elemental force of desire-induced madness.

First, Typhon is said to be the father of the four winds, and though his specific relation to Boreas is unclear, it is the excessive force of the wind that is said to have absconded with Oreithuia. Second, the word τῦφος from which the name Τυφῶν is derived stems from the related metaphor of smoke (a cognate of Typhon and itself a kind of blinding veil). This word can mean anything from delusion to affectation, from vanity to arrogance. In terms of the matrix of the self, desire, and seduction, this is a fascinating reference, and is further enriched when Socrates's asks if he is more agitated (ἐπιτεθυμμένον) than Typhon, employing a word that is drawn from the titan's name (ἐπιτύφομαι), literally translated as "to be consumed by lust." Third, the phrase used to describe Typhon's contrary: "possessed by nature (φύσει) of a divine (θείας) and un-Typhonic (ἀτύφου) lot," employs a number of derivatives of the word "blow": φύσει can come from the word φυσάω, which can mean to distend or blow up as well as to blow out; θείας can be a form of the word θειάζω, which translates as to be inspired, literally meaning to receive the breath of the gods; while ἀτύφου literally translates as to be "not puffed up" (meaning to lack vanity). This is an ironic turn of phrase, more or less asking if Socrates's is filled up by the gods in a way that prevents his head (or any other part of his anatomy) from becoming swollen. Put more clearly, Socrates's here asks whether or not temperance can be a product of divinely inspired madness.

These various references to the image of wind bear on both sides of the seducer-seduced equation, offering insight into the potential consequences of a desire-induced madness. On the one hand, we might ask if seduction is fundamentally a form of masking one's true intent, or worse, a vicious expression of a vain individual who conceals his true worth. On the other, we might wonder whether the product of seduction is delusion, or if it goes even further to constitute a violent conquest of the other. On both sides we are exposed to the influence of power as standing at the heart of Socrates's question of self-knowledge. Given that Socrates's takes on the role of both seducer and seduced in this dialogue, Socrates's quest for self-knowledge takes on an astonishing dimension, effectively asking whether he is more consumed or driven by lust than that dissembling, vain, and deluded creature Typhon, the potential father of Boreas, kidnapper/captivator of Oreithuia, or whether he is a more simple and straightforward (ἁπλούστερον) being, blessed by the gods with the virtue of sound-mindedness. Put simply, Socrates's employs the myth of Typhon in order to ask: "Who is the self that emerges from the event of seduction?"

The answer to all of these questions hinges on one specific detail—what is the relationship between seduction and truth? We must recall that the question of seduction is a question concerning a peculiar mode of discourse. It is this question—what is the relation between various forms of rhetoric and truth—that is taken up in the latter half of the dialogue where our heroes seek the right measure for evaluating the justness of seductive discourse. Furthermore, given that it is discourse in its myriad forms that tends to hold dominion over the power of persuasion, we must ask: What are the means employed to accomplish these ends? Again, what makes seduction peculiar is that it aims to persuade through the production of desire. But how is it these desires are summoned or invoked? Through lies? Through flattery? Through rational argument? Through madness? Through the playful unveiling of truth? We are thus returned to Phaedrus' most pressing question concerning the tale of Oreithuia: "Are you persuaded this myth is true?" (σὺ τοῦτο τὸ μυθολόγημα πείθῃ ἀληθὲς εἶναι;).[6]

It is a familiar move in the Platonic dialogues for Socrates's to redirect this question of truth to a question concerning his own identity. In other dialogues, Socrates's is commonly identified with a peculiar mode of discourse—a relation to the *logos* that relentlessly pursues truth through the dialogical play of question and answer. Thus, to question the nature of Socrates's is to scrutinize not only his strange manner of speaking, but to examine why this "second sailing" is taken up by Socrates's as the primary mode of unearthing truth. Furthermore, Socrates's relation to the *logos* and pursuit of truth must be understood in the context of his occupation—as a philosopher Socrates's identity is bound to a strange kind of *eros*—he is a lover of wisdom. However, the object of Socrates's desire—what it is wisdom actually entails—remains perpetually out of view. Seen in this way, it appears Socrates's quest to 'know thyself' is bound up in a complex pattern of desire, discourse, and truth. Returning to Socrates's reference to Typhon, we are called upon to discern in what way these three aspects of his identity (both separately and combined) bear the markings of this titan.

As far as desire and discourse are concerned, the metaphor appears relatively uncomplicated. Regarding the former, Socrates's is likely making reference to Typhon's hubris, and wondering whether his desires are excessive and if he suffers from a kind of unruliness that threatens to destroy him. As for the latter, Socrates's reference resonates with the various meanings of *typhos*, expressing the worry that his speech is in fact deceptive, bearing the possibility of leading his interlocutors astray. But what impact does this metaphor have on Socrates's quest for truth?

Again, Socrates's may be invoking the various meanings of *typhos*, which would have the clear implication of 'playing one false'—to speak like Typhon would be to actively withhold the truth. But the reference to truth and falsehood is perhaps even more specific—the character of truth and falsehood is qualified by the characteristics attributed to both Typhon and his opposite. Rather than simply wondering whether or not Socrates's is similar to Typhon or shares in some of his traits, Socrates's expressly asks: "Am I a being more agitated than Typhon or a simpler, more gentle creature?" Literally translated, the sentence might read: 'Am I a being more given to *typhos* than Typhon, or am I a more straightforward and direct animal'? When we read this statement in terms of Socrates' concern over his ability to speak the truth we are presented with a striking contrast. On the one hand, we have truth, said to be *direct* and *clear-cut*, utterly lacking in duplicity and obfuscation, a description that is captured by the word Socrates employs to describe the alternative to Typhon—ἁπλούστερον. These "simple" truths comprise the realm of factual propositions, such as the belief that far from being kidnapped by Boreas, Oreithuia instead got stoned on a breezy day and took a header off a cliff. On the other hand, we have false propositions, likened to that being who is more "Typhonic and complex than Typhon"—propositions that are deceptive, dissembling, and direct us away from things as they are. Thus, on the one side we have truth, which corresponds to matters of fact, while on the other side, we have falsehood, which conjures up a fictional state of affairs. In this way we are presented with a dualistic portrait of truth, one grounded in a correspondence theory that grounds the validity of all propositions in their ability to accurately depict real states of affairs. Any proposition that fails in this endeavor is thus dismissed as both deceptive and false.

If Socrates is to be measured against this correspondence notion of truth, then the question will be: Does Socrates state matters of fact, or does he fall into the opposite category of falsehood? To this question, he offers a remarkable response: He proposes that there are *other* truths worth seeking, but that these truths cannot be presented directly through propositions of fact. Such truths appear in the guise of images, myths, and allusions (such as Socrates' own reference to Typhon). They force us to look away from what is immediately present, and like Oreithuia, are playful, love to hide, and conceal just as they disclose. Clearly, Socrates is unsatisfied with the premise of Phaedrus' question that the only two options are to take the myth at face value or deny it as deceptive. Thus, his response calls into question the sufficiency of the opposition—truth as accurate proposition vs. falsehood as noncorrespondence—in which the question of Socrates' identity is to be decided—is he a being "more complex than Typhon" or a "gentler and more simple creature?" Socrates thus presents us with an image that is neither deceptive nor straightforward, but instead calls us to see this image *as* an image.

This odd response also has important repercussions on the subject matter under investigation in the dialogue—where are we to locate seductive speech in relation to this portrait of truth? Keep in mind, Socrates is identified with an *erotic* manner of speaking, and as a result we should not separate the question of seduction from Socrates' quest for self-knowledge. In light of this connection, we are left with an interesting problem regarding the nature of seductive speech: Does it involve statements of fact? Is it deceptive and false, or might it belong under Socrates' third way? Clearly, seduction does not fall into the former category—everyone knows that it is never a good idea to bore the object of seduction with an endless rendition of how you *actually* feel (as though it were just that easy to comprehend and communicate one's desires). In all seriousness, the force of seductive discourse is not premised upon statements of fact but on statements that are far more "complex and incendiary" (πολυπλοκώτερον καὶ μᾶλλον ἐπιτεθυμμένον—another potential translation of the words used by Socrates to describe the titan Typhon). Does this mean that such speech must be located on the opposite end of the spectrum, to be seen as patently false and deceptive?

In light of Socrates' reference to Typhon, we might restate our questions in the following ways: Is seduction the work of an overly puffed-up, vain, dissembling individual who seeks to mask their true character? Is the seduced the victim of trickery, deluded by the hypnotic skill of the seducer, overwhelmed by false desires and inflamed by misguided passions? Or might the persuasive force of seduction be grounded in an enigmatic truth, one that is both revelatory and transformative? Of course, none of these questions can be answered until we actually test what has been said, for, just as Socrates intimates in the *Republic* concerning the nature of myth (and much like the problem of the *pharmakon* and its consequent madness), that which has the power to corrupt also has the power to save, so long as we are persuaded in the right way.[7]

## THE JOURNEY OF PHAEDRUS

In order to test the justness of Socrates' seductive mode of speech, it is worth turning our attention to the strange dynamic that constitutes the complex interaction between Socrates, Lysias, and Phaedrus. The dialogue opens with the following lines: "My friend Phaedrus, where are you coming from and where are you going?"[8] Phaedrus has just arrived from the home of the great orator Lysias who recently offered a feast of speeches, one of which concerned the attempted seduction of a young boy by an older man. Before we get into the bearing this topic has on the drama of the dialogue, we must look more closely at Phaedrus' journey. Regarding his past travels, we are given little detail other than that he has been enchanted by the words of Lysias and has left the city in order to better comprehend what has been said. The speech in question is said to be erotic, though it remains unclear if this is merely in reference to its subject matter, or in reference to its effect.[9] However, given the praise that Phaedrus heaps upon this speech, it seems likely Phaedrus found it to be persuasive, and if nothing else he was (for lack of a better word) seduced by the prose. Lysias' speech initiates a number of actions, pursuits, and desires on the part of Phaedrus, not the least of which is the drive to share his love for this speech with others. Thus, it would appear as though the youth Phaedrus had been charmed by the older and more established Lysias, and has only recently emerged from his potent influence.

It is at the edge of the city where Phaedrus and Socrates meet. From here Socrates is led by Phaedrus beyond the city walls into the countryside, where they arrive upon an almost magical location, a place Socrates claims is unfamiliar and, because of its breathtaking scenery, renders him decidedly vulnerable.[10] Socrates is also "led on" in a more traditional sense: Beneath his cloak, Phaedrus hides in his left hand an object we can assume to be long, cylindrical, and hard. Desperate to see what is in Phaedrus' grasp, Socrates in effect asks, "is that a scroll in your pocket or are you just happy to see me?" The answer, of course, is a scroll—one containing the content of Lysias' speech, which Socrates declares to be the true object of his desire.[11] While we may find the truth a little G-rated, Socrates' reaction is the opposite: He grows inflamed and confesses his inability to resist, submitting on a number of fronts to the unsolicited demands of Phaedrus.[12]

These passages mark an ironic turn of events in relation to the traditional character of the lover-beloved dynamic. In Ancient Greek culture, it tended to be the older, wiser man who sought to seduce the more attractive but naïve youth through mesmerizing words. However, here we have Phaedrus who is attempting to spark a flame in the heart of the older Socrates, and lead him to a place where he will succumb to his advances. Role reversals like this are a common occurrence in the dialogues and often serve to reveal what is most fundamental to these relations of dominance, as when Socrates moves from the subject-position of teacher to student, and in so doing provides insight into the essence of education, or when he takes on the role of prosecutor at his own trial to shed light on the nature of good judgment. Such moments disrupt the power dynamics inherent to various modes of discourse, in effect laying bare the vulnerabilities and risks that are constitutive of those in the subordinate position. At the same time, these reversals undermine the apparent contradictory nature of the pair, showing how the true realization of each concept is dependent on performing an act often ascribed to its opposite, such as when we see how the best student is one who is capable of giving accounts while the best teacher possesses the capacity to listen. Here, the reversal is no different, dislodging many of the structures that constitute the inequalities often exploited by the seducer. For instance, the irony behind the reversal in subject-positions is not merely a matter of age or wisdom (with Phaedrus, the youth seducing the older, wiser Socrates). Instead, as Martha Nussbaum points out, it also highlights the power dynamic that Phaedrus would be implicated in as a young man about to embark on his career, pursued by a number of suitors in positions of enduring influence (an issue that takes center stage in the first speech).[13] Plato calls attention to the coercive mechanisms that could corrupt these proceedings by turning the tables on Socrates, not only by proclaiming (in a humorous manner) the defenselessness of Socrates, but also by making the object of his desire something less than carnal—speeches.

This reversal also reveals something essential about the conditions that tend to structure seductive speech by providing us with an ironic frame, one that grants us the distance necessary not only to laugh, but to have the truth stand forth free from our own immediate projects and aims. It is a classic example of what Kierkegaard referred to as Socratic irony, understood as the ability "to say something in jest that is meant in earnest,"[14] a playful manner of dislocating and unsettling concepts, pulling apart and exposing those constructs that ordinarily orient our thinking. Allowing us to hover freely above the complex power structures that inform traditional Greek courtship, Plato's ironic frame provides us with the elbow room necessary to question the nature of seduction in a more radical and originary way.

This brings us back to our earlier claim concerning the way in which seduction is not only constructed, but constructing. What this reversal does is direct our attention to the fact that the question "where are we being led?" cannot be answered without reference to the question "what is it to be led?" That is, the ends of seduction cannot be separated from the means. Even further, these reversals have the tendency to turn our concepts back in on themselves, undermining the assumed primacy of certain ideas while demonstrating a complex apparatus of constructions and causalities, something that becomes exceedingly apparent when we are confronted with the constant subject-reversals that take place between Socrates and Phaedrus—reversals that consistently force us to ask perhaps the most important question: 'Who is leading whom?'

## THE ART OF SEDUCTION

We are thus returned to the subject matter of Lysias' speech, one which concerns "an attempted seduction of a handsome boy—but not by a lover!"[15] In this speech, we are presented with an older man who is requesting to be "gratified" by an attractive youth. What is peculiar about this request is the older man does not attempt to woo the boy in the traditional manner, with lyrical phrases and flattering comments, but instead provides what appears to be a cold, calculating, logical argument. Unlike the *pharmakon*, Lysias argues that the madness of desire serves only to poison and never to heal. To follow desire free from the guidance of the *logos* is to be enslaved by the passions, it is to be *compelled* by what is merely pleasant rather than *choose* what is best. This leads us to the paradoxical (and potentially impossible) conclusion that the best lover is a non-lover, for only the non-lover is not led astray by desire, and as a result is far less likely to do injustice to the beloved—a conclusion that at its root places desire and what is best at loggerheads.

Unfortunately, as Socrates points out, Lysias' speech is anything but a model of good dialectic. His argument is somewhat scattered, and contrary to Phaedrus' words of praise, far from complete. Instead, its persuasive power is grounded more on its style and flourish than in its capacity to reveal the truth. In fact, at no point does Phaedrus ever praise Lysias' speech for its capacity to reveal truth. Instead, its success is premised upon instilling in its listener that very state of being it proclaims is so dangerous—it makes its listener mad with desire. As such, while the speech may fail as a form of dialectic (the mark of which is the failure of this account to reveal truth), insofar as it persuades its listener through the invocation of desire, it succeeds as a form of seduction. But what then is its relation to truth? Do we view it as a form of parody, withholding the truth in a comedic manner that obliges us to laugh at the ridiculous nature of its argument? Or do we take the account literally, as offering up an argument worthy of examination and critique?

Socrates examines Lysias's speech by first exploring the art (*techne*) of speaking and writing, an art described by Phaedrus as rooted in the capacity to persuade through an appeal to how things seem rather than how things are.[16] In his estimation, the skill of rhetoric is grounded not merely in one's knowledge of the subject matter under discussion but also in the ability to exploit what merely "seems so to the masses who will be passing judgment."[17] Socrates then elaborates, claiming this art involves the ability to exploit similarities, making something appear as something it is not.[18] However, Socrates points out that in order to effectively exploit similarities in the effort to produce a compelling image of truth one must have at least some knowledge of the thing to be imaged. In fact, Socrates goes so far as to claim that the stronger one's grasp of the truth, the more competent they will be in their effort to distort it. Given that *techne* concerns a productive form of knowledge, it would appear that the true measure of rhetorical mastery is captured by the orator's capacity to deceive, embodied by the power to *knowingly* make one and the same thing appear as both itself and its opposite, or more simply, to persuade us that the image of a thing is in fact its truth.[19]

When rhetoric is viewed in this way, where persuasion is isolated from truth, the art of persuasion becomes at one and the same time an art of deception. Thus, the implication is that only the *knowing* speaker who plays with similarities while taking advantage of the audience's ignorance is capable of speaking "artfully."[20] Socrates, who credits divine inspiration as the source of his speeches and consequently renounces knowledge of his chosen subject matter denies having a share in this "art."[21] In other words, Socrates' erotic speeches are not to be understood as an example of *techne*—skillfully crafted accounts that seek to persuade Phaedrus of a given conclusion. Whether or not Lysias' speech can be judged artful is another matter.

Obviously, this is a strange way to introduce an analysis of Lysias' argument, offering backhanded praise (if Lysias' speech proves to be artful, keeping to the terms set by Phaedrus it would be deemed such precisely because it is successful in its deceit) at the same time he disavows any personal skill as an orator. First, let us begin with the concept of "artlessness." According to Socrates, what makes an orator's work "artless" is a lack of knowledge of the subject matter at hand, for to lack this knowledge would be to lack the ability to recognize and thus exploit likenesses and similarities. Having established this first premise, Socrates proceeds to offer an account that at first view appears to be focused on superficial matters of style and organization. However, when carefully examined, we find that his critique is far more potent.

Socrates begins by condemning the fact that Lysias' speech "begins with what his lover should say to his darling at the conclusion."[22] Socrates is almost obsessed with the opening lines, even going so far as to have Phaedrus repeat them not once, but twice. Again, though at first it appears that Socrates' worry is merely an ornamental one (as though Lysias' speech could have been arranged better), we should recall that how one speaks is determinative in many ways of what one means. In the case of Lysias, Socrates is making a basic point, one reiterated by Phaedrus in the very next line: τελευτή, περί οὗ τόν λόγον ποιεῖται.[23] This line can be translated in many ways, such as "the end is what the speech is made about," "he does begin the speech at the end," or even "the end is that which is before the speech's production." The implication is not merely that Lysias starts his speech at the wrong place or on the wrong note but that standing at the origin (ἄρχεται) of the speech is his conclusion.[24] In other words, the conclusion is never *tested* but merely *assumed*, and the speech is constructed in order to best defend this assumption, regardless of whether or not this conclusion would prove itself true.

Oddly enough, to criticize Lysias for crafting his speech in accordance with a predetermined conclusion is to criticize the very precondition of any and all *techne*. First, we must keep in mind that *techne* refers to a special kind of practical knowledge, one that goes beyond a competence based on mere rote, repetition, or experience and instead involves a kind of expertise grounded in a firm understanding of the fundamental principles that determine the thing to be produced. In this way, the master craftsperson does not approach their work haphazardly, and any improvisation that must take place will always be informed by a generalizable knowledge of the thing to be produced. As such, all *techne* is *teleological*, in the sense that it must be *strategic*. It is the end, the *telos* (τελευτή) to be realized that must inform this knowledge, and as a result all crafts must begin with their conclusion.

Likewise, for rhetoric to be considered a genuine art, one must be in possession not only of the purpose of this art but also of an image of the thing to be produced. So what is the end of rhetoric, in the sense of both purpose and product? If, on the one hand, we agree with Phaedrus' initial claim that the art of rhetoric is the art of persuasion, the aim of these speeches is relatively straightforward—they aim to effect the soul of the audience such that what is said is taken as true. Thus, the essence of rhetoric appears to coincide with the essence of seduction, for it involves generating an attraction in the listener toward the conclusion of the speech. And, as we saw through Lysias' act of seduction, it makes no difference whether or not this attraction is grounded in truth, only that the audience believes it to be so.[25] This leads Socrates to declare that in order to effectively convince one's audience, one must possess knowledge of not only the subject matter discussed such that what they say can *appear* true, but also possess knowledge of the nature of the human soul, such that what is said will appear true *to their audience*. In effect, like Lysias, a good rhetorician must know their audience such that they are better able to tell them what they are already inclined to believe.

This calls to mind the discussion in the *Gorgias*, which equates rhetoric, understood primarily as a mode of persuasion, with flattery.[26] Typically we might assume that this would involve the sort of activities often associated with seduction—that we feed the ego of our listener such that they are more inclined to take our side. However, flattery is not simply to be understood as one of a variety of rhetorical strategies, employed merely to "soften up" our audience. Instead, flattery is understood as comprising the very essence of rhetoric (understood as the art of persuasion), where persuasion is accomplished by telling the audience exactly what they want to hear. Above and beyond complimentary phrases of admiration, this also includes telling the audience what they are already inclined to believe, reinforcing and making use of already firmly based assumptions. Understood in this way, flattery becomes a process where persuasive speech takes advantage of the audience's personal biases and prejudices, allowing belief to persist as a matter of convenience, and all the while gently nudging us toward whatever conclusion the orator would have us believe. Consequently, we are led to confuse what is best with what is pleasant (convenient and easy). When viewed in this way, we are led to another odd kind of reversal—instead of seeing seduction as a mode of rhetoric, we are also called to recognize how rhetoric constitutes a form of seduction. As flattery, rhetoric aims to gratify and please the audience, exploiting our desire to believe what is convenient and easy, and through these means the speaker produces a condition of conviction in the spectator's soul.[27] However, in order to be successful one must possess clear knowledge of their audience such that these assumptions can be exploited. And, it is for this reason that Socrates' inquiry into the art of rhetoric leads Socrates to embark on a lengthy examination of the nature of the soul.

## THE DUAL NATURE OF SEDUCTION

It seems we have now answered many of the questions that prompted our examination of Lysias' speech. First, are the desires that emerge as a product of seduction either genuine or valid? Given that the desires fashioned out of seduction are grounded upon a fundamental deception the answer would appear to be no. The strategic dimension of this art of persuasion is rooted in exploiting the indeterminacy of our desires such that we are led to confuse an image of truth with how things actually stand. The seduced is thus blinded from the true nature of their interests, and as a result of this blindness, they are compelled to gratify the interests of the seducer while neglecting their own.

This also provides an answer to our second question: Is betrayal an immanent feature of seduction? As we have seen, not only does seduction involve a betrayal of trust on the part of the seducer who seeks to exploit our ignorance and coopt our desires, it also involves a kind of self-betrayal, where we lose control of our desires such that they now stand in the way of our capacity to choose what is best. As a result, seduction would appear to corrupt, rather than heal the soul (thus answering our third question concerning the status of the madness that comes as a result of seduction). Based on Lysias' clear attempt to not only deceive Phaedrus but to exploit his love of speeches and assumptions concerning the blinding force of desire for his own personal gratification, we can now see how to be seduced is in fact to be subjugated. Given the strategic form of this rhetoric, and its base disregard for truth, it seems as though Lysias is by no means attempting to heal the soul of Phaedrus, but quite the opposite—by telling Phaedrus exactly what he wants to hear Phaedrus loses his grip on himself, and is transformed into something decidedly slavish.

However, must seduction always take the deceitful path of Lysias, a path that stands in the way of self-knowledge and self-mastery? Or is there another side to the art of seduction, one that does not exploit and coopt desires but instead allows us to confront the truth of our desires? For one, it appears that the power dynamic that emerges from Lysias' form of seduction is premised upon his understanding of rhetoric—as the art of persuasion. But what if rhetoric was understood differently: not as the strategic art of exploiting ignorance in an effort to lead us toward a mere semblance of truth, but as the *art of inquiry*? Is it not possible that Socrates not only demonstrates an alternative relationship to speech in his dialogue with Phaedrus but also an alternative form of seduction, one that does not seek to conceal the true nature of our desires, but instead takes as its chief aim the uncovering of their truth? If we consider rhetoric in the latter sense, it becomes clear that it is no longer sufficient for a rhetorician to employ the strategy of telling us what we want to hear, but instead must adopt other means of relating to our desires. Understood as an art of inquiry, rhetoric would concern the art of self-perception. Given our analysis of Lysias' speech, it would appear that his notion of seduction can play no part in this art, for Lysian seduction is the art of disguising what is false as what is true. This conclusion is based on the assumption that seduction can only appear in the form of a Lysian deception, where the lover exploits the ignorance of the beloved. Luckily, the seductive path carved out by Socrates may demonstrate there is another way.

We find support for the possibility of this dual nature when we look at the etymology of the Greek word for "seduction": πειρώμενόν.[28] This is a compound word, originating from the Greek πείρω and μένον. The former means to pierce or cleave, invoking a sense of breaking through some fixed barrier. The latter means to stand fast, to tarry, or hold firm. Taken together, the word seems to invoke an attempt to break through one's defenses. This image of combat is deeply engrained in the Western construction of sexuality, and seems to imply right from the get-go a show of power immanent to this form of discourse. As Lysias' speech intimates, yielding to the force of seduction constitutes a kind of surrender, and has a bearing on our tendency toward self-mastery or slavishness—to be seduced is not merely to be overcome by an external force, but connotes a loss of the self. Seduction thus constitutes the process by which this vulnerability is both precipitated and exploited, where the desire of the other ceases to be their own, but coopted by another. The puritan sense of corrupted virtue is invoked here, but is even more radical given the Greek meaning of αρετή—excellence—referring to any and all qualities through which a thing can realize its utmost potential. In reference to humanity, virtue denotes both intellectual qualities such as wisdom and sound judgment as well as character traits including courage and temperance, basically naming all of those modes of human excellence that direct us toward a life of flourishing. As a result, far from merely threatening one's chastity, seduction has the power to estrange us from what is truly best for our thriving.

However, there is another meaning to the Greek word for seduction, πειρώμενόν, that leads us in another direction—literally translated it means "to test the self." While this phrase echoes some of the combative language mentioned above, the notion of "test" does not lend itself so easily to the idea of conquest. Though to be tested is to be challenged, the purpose of a test is not to overcome but to reveal the self. It is through a test that we confront our limits, our weaknesses and failings, as well as come to see our resilience, our character, and strength. But what, if anything, does this have to do with seduction? Much like the *pharmakon* and erotic madness, the desire-producing activity of seduction has a dual nature. While it can deceive and dissemble, it can also uncover and disclose.

To understand how seduction can perform the latter, it is helpful to contrast Lysias' manner of speaking with that of Socrates. As we have seen, Lysias' artfulness hinges on his ability to "begin with his conclusion"—he strategically constructs his speech in a manner that exploits Phaedrus' assumptions, telling him exactly what he wants to hear in a way that leads him to a predetermined end. Far from challenging Phaedrus, Lysias instead confirms through the construction of false images what is already believed. Socrates, on the other hand, does not begin at the end. As Socrates himself states, he is not in possession of this art, and his mode of speaking is far more playful than strategic. Unlike Lysias, Socrates does not presume to know what it is Phaedrus wants, nor does he attempt to lead him toward a given conclusion. In fact, ever the philosopher, Socrates lacks knowledge of their destination, aiming only to discover what it is Phaedrus truly wants. It is in this way that Socrates begins not with a conclusion, but with a *question*: What is it that Phaedrus truly desires? Through this question Socrates takes an interest in Phaedrus' interests, an attitude surely lacking in Lysias, and yet one fundamental to any relation that seeks to be grounded in meaningful consent. At the same time, but taking an interest in Phaedrus' interests, Socrates also tests Phaedrus, forcing him to question what he wants, as well as answer for those ends he chooses to pursue.

This art of inquiry constitutes not only an inquisitive activity, but a formative one as well. To question your desires is not merely to bring them into view, but to give them shape, direction, and substance. Our desire is not simply imbued in us by nature, preformed and unalterable, but something that can be constituted, transformed, and redirected through dialogue. By challenging Phaedrus to know the truth behind his desires, Socrates engages in the desire-producing activity of seduction. However, for Socrates, this is not an activity where one comes to commandeer and deform the desires of the other, leading them on a path of confusion and deception toward a state of slavishness and subordination. The images we receive from Socrates are not intended to play us false, lead us astray, or obscure the truth. Rather, they are presented *as* images, put forth as a hypothesis to be tested. The images of Socrates harbor a deeper truth, one that can only be seen so long as we allow the image to carry us beyond what merely *seems* true and toward what actually *is*.

For Socrates, seductive speech is not an art of persuasion, but a manner of questioning fundamental to the pursuit of self-knowledge. It is a manner of fashioning one's desires, not in order to subdue the Other but by virtue of *opening oneself up to the Other.* This is the seductive character of Socratic speech: His is a playful mode of self-discovery, where one engages the other not as a subordinate, combatant, or authority, but as an ally, not only in the shared pursuit of the truth that lays behind our desire, but with the hope—indeed, the conviction—that the Good is something to be held in common, not only as lovers, but also as friends.

## NOTES

1. To the best of my knowledge, this book is self-published by the author Ken Hoisky, and available only through his website. However, critique of this book was widespread, receiving coverage from a variety of media outlets including most prominently the Huffington Post and New Yorker. For a nice overview of the controversy with a compelling feminist analysis see: Katie Baker, "Is There Such a Thing as a Feminist Pick-Up Artist?," *Jezebel:* http://jezebel.com/is-there-such-a-thing-as-a-feminist-pick-up-artist-564354894 and Katie Baker, "Redditor's PUA Kickstarter Project Recomments Sexual Assault," *Jezebel*: http://jezebel.com/redditors-pua-kickstarter-project-recommends-sexual-as-514264056.

2. See Catherine MacKinnon, *Toward a Feminist Theory of State* (Cambridge: Harvard University Press, 1989).

3. Plato, *Phaedrus*, in *Plato's Erotic Dialogues*, trans. William S. Cobb. (Albany: State University of New York Press, 1993), 229b. All future translations are from this volume unless otherwise noted.

4. Ibid., 230d.
5. Ibid., 229c–30a.
6. Ibid., 229c.
7. Plato, *The Republic*, translated by Joe Sachs (Newburyport: Focus Publishing, 2008), 621c.
8. Plato, *Phaedrus*, 227a.
9. Ibid., 227c.
10. Ibid., 230d–e.
11. Ibid., 228d–e.
12. Ibid., 230e.
13. Martha Nussbaum, *The Fragility of Goodness*, (New York: Cambridge University Press, 2001), 207–8.
14. Sören Kierkegaard, *On the Concept of Irony*, (Princeton: Princeton University Press, 1989) 248.
15. Plato, *Phaedrus*, 227c.
16. Ibid., 260a.
17. Ibid.
18. Ibid., 261e.
19. Plato, *Phaedrus*, 261d.
20. Ibid., 262b-c.
21. Ibid., 262d.
22. Ibid., 264a.
23. Ibid., 264b.
24. Ibid., 264a.
25. Ibid., 260a.
26. Plato, *Gorgias*, in *Gorgias and Rhetoric*, trans. Joe Sachs, (Newburyport: Focus Publishing, 2009), 461a–65d.
27. Ibid., 502a–c.
28. Plato, *Phaedrus*, 227c.

## BIBLIOGRAPHY

Baker, Katie. "Is There Such a Thing as a Feminist Pick-Up Artist?," *Jezebel:* http://jezebel.com/is-there-such-a-thing-as-a-feminist-pick-up-artist-564354894
———. "Redditor's PUA Kickstarter Project Recommends Sexual Assault," *Jezebel*: http://jezebel.com/redditors-pua-kickstarter-project-recommends-sexual-as-514264056
Hoisky, Ken. *Above the Game: A Guide to Getting Awesome with Women.* Self-Published.
Kierkegaard, Sören. *On the Concept of Irony*. Princeton: Princeton University Press, 1989.
MacKinnon, Catherine. *Toward a Feminist Theory of State*. Cambridge: Harvard University Press, 1989.

Nussbaum, Martha. *The Fragility of Goodness*. New York: Cambridge University Press, 2001.

Plato. *Gorgias*, in *Gorgias and Rhetoric*, translated by Joe Sachs. Newburyport: Focus Publishing, 2009.

————. *Phaedrus*, in *Plato's Erotic Dialogues*, translated by William S. Cobb. Albany: State University of New York Press, 1993.

————. *The Republic*, translated by Joe Sachs. Newburyport: Focus Publishing, 2008.

*Chapter Thirteen*

# Some Notes on Faking

## Hildur Kalman

In 2007, while planning for a feminist anthology on the subject of faked orgasms, Susanna Alakoski and Amanda Mogensen invited Swedish women, by way of newspaper advertisement, e-mail postings, and so on, to write anonymously about their orgasms, faked or real.[1] The e-mail postings also reached women in other Scandinavian countries and Finland. They received an abundance of answers from the Nordic countries, a selection of which were published. Some of the contributors chose not to be anonymous, having made their own analysis and interpretation of their experiences. Two rather unexpected things turned up. The first was that the first letter to arrive was from a man, and eventually they received more examples of male experiences of faking. The editors were also surprised by letters from lesbian women asking why they were not interested in their experiences of faking as well. At first they were hesitant to include such stories as their plan had been to give a picture of, and investigate, the heterosexual norm for sexuality from women's points of view. But eventually they decided to include the broader empirical material, which gave an even more complex and compelling picture of the norms for sexuality today. Further, they decided to invite experts and academics—such as social workers, historians, counsellors, and myself as a philosopher—to write on the book's theme.[2] In the book *Fejkad orgasm* (hereafter referred to as *FO)*, the participating women and men provide many examples of experiences of faking along with their analyses and musings on the reasons for and circumstances surrounding faking.[3] The contributors telling of their faked orgasms describe how they might move about, groan, and moan a little extra, as well as say something about how good it was. Pleasure and enjoyment are overstated in direct and indirect terms. In 2007, RFSU (the Swedish Association for Sexuality Education) together with the TV programme *Lustgården* carried out a survey among 1000 women aged

18–35, and around 25% of these women had at some point faked an orgasm. The most common explanation given for faking in this survey was that it was a way to put an end to sex.[4] Moreover, a common question posed to RFSU (the Swedish Association for Sexuality Education) deals with lack of desire. Not only are women faking and complaining of lack of desire, but men are as well. This empirical background forms a point of departure for this chapter, the aim of which is to explore the phenomenon of faked orgasms and some reasons for faking through the lenses of feminist theory and phenomenological reflection.

It seems that contemporary ideals surrounding sexuality converge with quests for not only pleasure and love but also for experiencing what is conceived of as normal and "successful" sexuality. This chapter suggests that even deception that is performed out of love risks becoming self-defeating. Not only is there a risk of deterioration of trust within that relationship but also the experience of controlling sexual encounters through faking may become habitual. That is, this strategy to gain some control of the sexual situation may ultimately, and contrary to intentions, make it difficult *not* to respond with faking in similar circumstances later on.

## IMPORTANT ENOUGH TO BE FAKED

For faking to be an option, there must first of all be an idea of orgasm—based either on earlier or vicarious experiential understanding. Russell Keat and John Urry have distinguished a sense of "understanding" they label "vicarious experiential understanding," as it is closely related to experiential understanding.[5] By this they claim that we "not only know other people's subjective states, but are somehow able to understand them in the sort of way that we would if we had previously had similar experiences ourselves."[6] Thus, as a result, we have the capacity to extend the range of our own experiences through the presentation to us of other people's experiences. This may be the case when we, for example, read novels, poetry, and drama, or for that matter see popular depictions of what supposedly is "great" sex in films and plays. Second, to be worth faking, the orgasm must be assigned some importance or value. Third, the orgasm must be conceived of being possible to mediate through pretence, that is, faked. Not even knowing it was possible to fake an orgasm, one woman writes about her first sexual intercourse: "Had I thought that a faked orgasm was expected of me, I would have cried out for the King and motherland. Thank God for ignorance."[7,8]

In *FO* many different circumstances and reasons for faking are given—but two major kinds surface: faking in the name of love by meeting the expectation and hope for a consummate erotic encounter and faking to put an end to sex. Some of the other reasons for faking that emerge include a wish for control or the desire to feel "normal." Regardless of the reason, the question remains: What is the significance of orgasm such that it is important enough to be faked?

## A SIGN OF SUCCESS

Faking orgasms may be consistent with erotic encounters more broadly speaking as they are often are marked by play—be it imitation, role-play, something like hide-and-seek or "Simon Says." Given the nature of role-play, it is hardly surprising that a faked orgasm may be unintended as well, and surface as an effect of misunderstanding, where the partner perceived expressions of pleasure as signs of orgasm. In such cases, the faker may well choose to stick to the more or less unintended faked orgasm, so as not to break the pleasurable and playful mood: "Oh, you've been longing for me, my boyfriend cooed, and naturally he enjoyed it when I (in complete honesty) more or less screamed with delight, and (completely falsely) seemed to have been quick to come. And I didn't have the heart to tell him."[9] More often, however, the importance of an orgasm does seem to go well beyond the longing or hope for playful, reciprocal pleasure. Orgasm is a sign, the meaning of which is manifest in the interpretations that it generates. Orgasm is considered an achievement; and not having one is understood as a failure. From the experiences shared in *FO*, we learn that it is a triumph to be able to "give" another person an orgasm; a partner's orgasm is sign of one's own success. For some people, it is clear that it is even more important to be able to *give* an orgasm than to *experience* one. As one 25-year-old male writes, "The times when my buddies and I have talked about faked orgasms, it's been about our own. It's as if it's a greater defeat when the girl you're having sex with fakes it than when you do it yourself."[10]

Even when a person lacks sufficient desire or arousal to orgasm, they may still wish to make their partner feel like an accomplished lover. "I faked on my wedding night. I didn't want to make the bridegroom sad" one woman writes.[11] Along the same lines, one man reports: "There were nights when I didn't make it all the way ... But still I wanted her to feel that ... No offence meant. It was simply my little gift to her. No more, no less."[12] When an orgasm is faked, the non-faking partner may feel special, having been able to "give" and share the experience of something so intimate and gratifying.

Faking can also be a convenient way to put an end to sex without insulting one's lover's abilities:

But now I do not want to take part in this any longer, there is no way out. I cannot hurt him, because he is a nice guy, and I cannot be bothered to try to teach him ... His picture of me as a sex goddess will not be the same if I tell him: No, I am not close, stop nagging, come if you want to, and then we can cuddle some afterwards. So I do what I have done so many times before, I moan as the worst porn dame, I twitch and turn and now he comes and now he is thinking that he is a sex god without comparison. I like it when you scream, he says. So do I, I reply.[13]

Giving priority to a partner's enjoyment may be connected to other pay-offs such as conforming to an ideal, to feeling "normal," or being a "real woman." One woman writes of her first fake as a teenager:

I knew exactly what was expected of me. I was a good actress already then and scratched his back with my nails. Not too hard, but a little—the way it was described in the romantic magazines. I also made a couple of discreet sounds of *mmm*, without letting it go too far ... Afterwards I felt like a real woman. It was wonderful.[14]

The longing to fit in with what is conceived of as "normal" or a "real woman" may at times result in sexual practices best described as "ambivalent," as in the case of young women engaging in vaginal intercourse despite associated pain.[15] In an interview study with young Swedish women (14–20 years) who suffered variable degrees of coital pain during sexual intercourse, the women had sex for their partner's sake, and considered their own experiences of pain insignificant compared with their partner's pleasure. These women strove for affirmation that they fit what "a sexually normal woman should be like." Moreover, they experienced themselves as "women" only if they had sexual intercourse, and not otherwise.[16] As one of them said: "Well, I wanted it to be perfect, you know ... that it should be like in the love movies, when they have sex with each other and like 'oh, God it feels good,' sort of."[17] This ideal woman and perfect girlfriend was one who would be "willing to have sexual intercourse ... perceptive of their partner's sexual needs, and ... able to satisfy them."

In some cases, faking can also be an expression of defeated resignation, apparently the only way out of an annoying encounter as in one passage from Simone de Beauvoir's novel *Les mandarins*: A woman—during intercourse with a man obsessed with synchronicity—is rather irritated, and thinks to herself that they would be no less separated even if they were to experience orgasm simultaneously. She gives in to sighing and moaning, albeit not convincingly enough, because he asks her whether she came. Giving an affirmative answer, she thinks to herself that he has been defeated as well, as he did not pursue the question.

## SOCIAL CONSTITUTION OF BODIES, SOCIAL CONDITIONING OF EXPERIENCE

On the fringe of our encounters in love and sex, as part of what socially conditions our experiences of these encounters, are cultural and social myths, "scripts" that shape our growth into adult women and men. For example, we have come to know in different ways what an orgasm should be like, and we even know what a faked orgasm should be like. There are common references within popular culture to faked female orgasm such as the film "When Harry met Sally" and episodes in the TV series "Seinfeld" and "Sex and the City." Although these examples are taken from American popular culture, the circulation and impact of American popular culture in Sweden, for example, can hardly be overestimated.[18]

In a tangible and embodied sense, every human being carries his or her own time, culture, and society with them, even when they engage in a sexual encounter. Phenomenology sheds light on the way in which the *lived body* encompasses and expresses its history and lived experience as well as its presently lived relation to the world. It helps us see how our sexualities are formed in cultural and historical contexts. In other words, our societies and cultures—our gender and sexuality, our ways of perceiving ourselves, our having confidence in ourselves, and activities such as walking, running, throwing a ball, or making love—are all embodied.[19] Some of the cultural expressions of embodiment and bodily appearances, such as a hairstyle or the skinny jeans of last year, can be more easily changed than others. But the expressions given through the ways in which we "live" our bodies are not as easily changed.

In the essay "Picture Perfect," Douglas Rushkoff gives a compelling example of both the social constitution of bodies, and the social conditioning of experience, when he relates how he—fending off bullying accusations of not being a "real boy"—started what he labels his "straight-boy self-education" like most American males: with porn.[20] After some time of pursuit, he finally laid hands on an issue of his father's *Playboy*. But as he had not as yet "associated pictures of female body parts with erotic excitement," he did not fully understand how the pictures and his excitement were to be connected: "Somewhere between breasts and lens, photos and eyes, frontal lobe and hand, the erotic circuit between Miss July and my penis was not completed."[21] Eventually, about a year later, he managed to find an image or state of mind that "had etched itself onto the printed circuit board" directing his sexual response for decades to come.[22] First, the values and ideals of society are inscribed in our bodies, through the ways in which body and sexuality are framed in general discourse, and through the ways these are represented in the media, films, myths, and in counselling. Second, the body is constituted *through lived life*. In this way, social conditions are incorporated and can be seen in embodied habits—habits such as kissing, caressing, and even in the reaching of an erection by looking at pornographic imagery, as in Rushkoff's story.

Maurice Merleau-Ponty further explains how social conditions and cultural values become sedimented, so to speak, becoming part and parcel of our experiences when he writes:

> It is no more natural, and no less conventional, to shout in anger or to kiss in love than to call a table 'a table.' Feelings and passional conduct are invented like words. Even those which, like paternity, seem to be part and parcel of the human make-up are in reality institutions. It is impossible to superimpose on man a lower layer of behaviour which one chooses to call 'natural,' followed by a manufactured cultural or spiritual world. Everything is both manufactured and natural in man, as it were, in the sense that there is not a word, not a form of behaviour which does not owe something to purely biological being—and which at the same time does not elude the simplicity of animal life, and cause forms of vital behaviour to deviate from their pre-ordained direction, through a sort of *leakage* and through a genius for ambiguity which might serve to define man.[23]

In his analysis of perception, Merleau-Ponty distinguishes between the "personal" and the "anonymous" body to focus on different aspects of experience. He suggests that our habits, our personal style, *our personal way of seeing and experiencing* are formed like a fold in fabric,[24] or like "a wave on the sea surface."[25] The surface on which the fold is formed, or the wave occurs, is the anonymous body with the ability to respond to touch, sound, light, heat, and so on. The *personal* body inherits these abilities, as it were, where *lived experience shapes our perception*. Engaging ourselves in a field of interest, for example, may tune and refine our attention in that area, whereas it may continue to be rather numb, or be numbed, in others.[26] In this way, current experience is partly constitutive of future experiences.

This is nicely illustrated in Rushkoff's essay when he points out that "[g]etting aroused by looking at body parts owned exclusively by women is a learned skill," and argues that this skill in our culture is achieved primarily for the purpose of differentiating boys and men from the feminine.[27] The image of the woman that did the trick, that gave him what he refers to as his "first culturally sanctioned hard-on," became for him an image of "the ultimate woman" because she had distinguished him as a man.[28] His grim conclusion is: "It's called classic conditioning. Jerk off looking at pictures of horses for long enough, and you'll get a hard-on looking at them, too."[29]

Differing cultural expectations on boys and girls seem to be especially explicit with reference to masturbation and one's bodily self-relation. The straight-boy expectations and self-education in masturbation related by Rushkoff, can be seen in relation to the early and quite common shaming of girls' bodies. In the 1980's, through the method of memory-work, Frigga Haug and a group of women collectively worked on and thematized their experiences of female socialization, and of sexuality as one such form of socialization.[30] The focus of their research was to unveil and distinguish how womanhood is constituted (produced and reproduced) as a distinct form of experience—shown in ways of living the body, in routines, in interplay—that is as part and parcel of the social structures and relations one is living. An important finding of theirs was how early, deeply, and to what extent, girls' bodies and body parts became the objects of shame. An early cultural conditioning of shame with a related ambivalence toward their vulvas and vaginas may be one reason for why several women in *FO* relate how they had never experienced an orgasm until a tender and interested lover (same-sex or otherwise) showed them how.

In *The Second Sex,* Simone de Beauvoir explains that social and cultural myths tell us that it is considered widely desirable for a woman to passively exist to meet the needs of others.[31] At the same time, these myths portray it as appropriate for a man to be offered this kind of self-denial by a woman. She pointed to how women in our culture become used to perceiving themselves through the eyes of others, and to responding to and taking care of the needs of others, and how there is a risk that, even in the sexual domain, a woman will see herself as, and make herself into, an object for others.[32] Consistent with the narratives presented earlier, faking an orgasm out of love might be a way for a woman to perceive herself through her lover's eyes as one who cares for others.

Where contemporary notions of love follow the gender-binary and heteronormative ideals, loving care is coded as womanly/feminine. Political scientist Anna G. Jónasdóttir has focused on what is taken for granted as normal in the Nordic countries of today—love that is freely given and freely taken. She argues that love, and the existential forces at the heart of its power, is the driving force of society. Moreover, she suggests that the typical relation between women and men *as sexes* today is one of *political* power, and that sexuality—as it is typically organized in contemporary Western societies—"affirms and fortifies essential social relations and distinctions between groups of people."[33] Problematizing the practice of love, she points to a specific kind of exploitation—the exploitation of loving capacities. She writes: "[I]f 'politics' has any particular core of significance it is about a field of power for wills and the consequences for will-power, where it is determined how we are with each other." She claims that sex/gender relations constitute a relatively independent field of power, in which there is "a complex and tangible struggle over who is master of the situation, who has the power to decide *who is/does and /gets what, when and how.*"[34] Social relations always consist of societal practices—actions that reproduce these same relations. In this context, love is to be understood as a social, socio-sexual practice, where the two main elements of love are *loving care* and *erotic ecstasy*. She claims that the ways in which heterosexual love is institutionalized in contemporary society result in these two elements being positioned as opposites. Thus, according to Jónasdóttir, when (formally free and equal) women and men meet as sexes, the societal frames that condition these meetings are not equal. Women therefore tend to practice loving care, whereas men get to live/experience ecstasy, which becomes a means toward the end of self-assurance and personal growth.

The theoretical outline suggested by Jónasdóttir already in 1991 was later given empirical support in the socio-psychological research of Carin Holmberg.[35] Holmberg interviewed young, equal (as judged by others and themselves) couples without children, and analysed how their love and care were expressed in the actions and negotiations of everyday life. It turned out that while the women in these relationships tended to show more loving care than the men did, they often simultaneously suppressed their own needs, calling that "love." Questions of sexuality were not pursued at length in Holmberg's study, not for lack of interest but because she thought this would require an in-depth study of its own.[36] Still we can see how faking orgasms in the name of love has similarities with the loving care under scrutiny in Holmberg's investigation. In women's quest to fulfil men's wish to be special, women often fake orgasms to express loving care

If faking in the name of love is taken to be a sign of loving care, *FO* shows us that there are both women and men in Sweden who are prone to engage in such practices within an intimate relationship. Thus, the gendered, and heteronormative, binary of romantic love is not strictly realized, but in the gendered practices of loving care in which both the "giving" of orgasm and the "delivery" of orgasm remain important. Both signal the success of the sexual encounter, to the effect that both parties may experience the self-assurance of being successful lovers.

## HETERONORMATIVITY IN THE CULTURAL SIGNIFICATION OF ORGASMS

The contributions to *FO* show that faking does not necessarily coincide with the female gender, as there are examples of men faking, as well as faking in same-sex relationships. Note, also, that Beauvoir's account of how women become used to responding to and taking care of the needs of others, in no way ascribes these differing roles to women and men in essential terms. Her philosophical account, including many historical examples, points to the *situation* of women and the ways in which we become women as socio-cultural beings. Naturally, the gendered roles of women and men in Beauvoir's France of 1949, where women had had the vote for only five years, cannot be simply equated with the gender roles of contemporary Sweden, which, together with the other Nordic countries, is ranked as having the greatest equality in the world according to the *World Economic Forum's* Global Gender Gap Report from 2011. But although some of the heteronormativity inherent to Western thought may have changed slightly, other problems have been more persistent.

Complaints about male theorists either having taken their own experiences as exemplary and as the norm and model for descriptions of sexuality, or for attempting to control female sexuality, are common among feminist theorists and activists. In *The Second Sex*, Beauvoir criticizes Freud among others for their mistaken views on female sexuality.[37] Partly echoing Beauvoir's critique, Anne Koedt points to how Freud greatly influenced the norms for female sexuality when he "contended that the clitoral orgasm was adolescent, and that upon puberty, when women began having intercourse with men, women should transfer the center of the orgasm to the vagina."[38]

One example of how the symbolically male has informed the norms and ideas surrounding orgasm is mediated in language. As an example, Jennifer Saul highlights the differentiation between "sex" and "foreplay." "Sex" is taken to refer to an activity in which someone (hopefully) achieves orgasm. Foreplay, on the other hand, is something else, not quite sex, but something that prepares us for the important and "real" activity. Foreplay is thus rendered a second-rate sexual activity, even though many women experience orgasm during activities referred to as foreplay.[39] Note that this should not be taken to mean that the division reflects the experiences of most women, or those of most men, nor that what is referred to as foreplay should necessarily be of special interest to women. What is conveyed through this linguistic division is not innocent, however, as it helps shape our thoughts and experiences regarding such matters.

The symbolically male also comes forth in the representation of "real sex" having occurred— that is, in the image of a male orgasm. The model that serves for this phallic and normative ideal is what is perceived of as *the* male orgasm, by which male orgasm equals ejaculation. Pelle Ullholm, engaged in education at RFSU (the Swedish Association for Sexuality Education) and specializing in masculinity and sexuality, argues that the male faker's best friend is the massive lack of knowledge about how ejaculation does not necessarily coincide with an orgasm; if the ejaculation is seen as a guarantee of orgasm, the man who fakes does not even have to fake very well—if he can hide behind an ejaculation. "Let's start at the end. Orgasm and ejaculation are for many people the same as the end of sex. That is the overarching reason for faking; you want to get the sex over with when it's not working for you. With a credible faked orgasm, there is no need for inconvenient truth."[40] A complaint among male contributors to *FO*—with reference to former partners as well as to many sexual counsellors writing in weekly magazines—is that these people seem to think that, for men, ejaculation is equivalent to orgasm. If so, there would be only two gradations: ejaculation or not equals orgasm or not—one or zero. But as one of the informants in *FO* states, "An ejaculation can be as enjoyable as blowing your nose, or like a vision of the cosmos, with all the gradations in between."[41] The women in FO express similar thoughts, orgasms for women being a vast and varied experience as well, coming as it were, in all different shapes and sizes.

Another aspect of orgasm is its being connected to a heterosexual norm, by which the notion of a "right" time and a "right" place is conveyed. Tacit assumptions of erection as well as penetration are inherent to this ideal, and connected to its role within an ideal of heterosexual marriage. This means that a man's orgasm is supposed to occur within a woman's vagina, where it plays its "natural" role in the procreation of children, at times referred to as the "reproductive model."[42]

In parallel fashion, female orgasm is expected to be complementary to male pleasure and orgasm. The expectations for women are equally heteronormative and connected to the production of children. Thus the "right" time and place for a female orgasm is to be in accordance with what is expected of the male orgasm, through which the woman might get pregnant. In short: Women are expected to have vaginal orgasms in conjunction with penetrating intercourse.

As a consequence of this norm, other sexual practices are rendered less visible, and an understanding of male pleasure is restricted in ways that may have discriminatory undertones with regard to, for example, age and homosexuality. A historical, albeit influential, example of the devaluation of ageing men's non-erectile practices is, for example, to be found in the Kinsey Reports, despite its pronounced nonnormative ambitions:

> In some of these males, ejaculation may occur without erection as a result of the utilization of special techniques in intercourse. In many older persons, erectile impotence is, fortunately, accompanied by a decline in and usually complete cessation of erotic response.[43]

Historian of ideas Åsa Andersson notes that the researchers' use of the term "fortunately" gives a hint as to why it is just as well that old men with erectile problems stop having sex—as if an ejaculation or orgasm without erection would somehow be wrong or tragic. She points to how, albeit not explicitly, a norm has been set for what heterosexual intercourse ought to be, where it seems that certain kinds of performance are more highly valued than sensations of pleasure.[44]

The norm constructs some sexual practices as more correct, which makes other practices appear deviant, lacking or less successful.[45] It is not surprising then that there are both women and men in *FO* who write about having "faked away" their orgasms, in situations when they felt the orgasms came about at an inappropriate moment, that is, prior to a penetrating sex act.[46] Several contributors in *FO* tell of feelings of inadequacy with regard to their own bodies, such as feeling ashamed or being the object of shame for not being able to have orgasms in a relationship, or for not having them in accordance with some normative principle dictating when and how they should happen. The associated unhappiness has caused some of them to fake orgasms in order to appear normal and successful.

Heteronormative depictions of orgasm are additionally problematic insofar as cultural "scripts" portray male sexuality as being conditioned in terms of violence or subordination. Catherine MacKinnon and Andrea Dworkin have argued that pornography depicts the subordination of woman as a condition for male orgasm. That is, in their view, female subordination is represented as something that kindles desire and therefore comes to condition orgasm. They argue that pornography thus fashions women's as well as men's desire to fit the roles of victim and perpetrator, respectively, and that these roles are then portrayed and experienced as being natural forms of sexual expression and of the sexes.[47]

In their investigation of Internet pornography sites, Heider and Harp note that even as new media have changed the terrain of communications, "these sites reinforce traditional constructions of men's power over women in the forms of hierarchy, objectification, submission and violence."[48] There women are portrayed as "submissive, willing participants in sexual acts" with "a seemingly unending appetite for sex," and who are being "sexually satisfied by whatever the men in the film do."[49]

It is easy to connect such cultural representations of natural roles within a heterosexual matrix: until recently, rape within marriage did not exist as a legal concept, and was not criminalized in Sweden until 1965. It was long seen neither as a societal problem nor as a concern for the public prosecutor. To put it crudely: The "right thing" had happened in the "right place." In the United States, spousal rape was not criminalized in all states until 1993, under at least one section of the sexual offenses codes. There were differences in-between states, however, with the existence of some spousal exemptions in the majority of states. To date such exemptions still remain in some. The notion of the "right things" happening in the "right places" has in later years found a deeply homophobic and violent expression in the hate crime *corrective rape*. For example, lesbian women in South Africa have come forward to tell of systematic rapes, where the perpetrators ascribe a "corrective" function to rape.[50]

## FAKING ORGASMS AND THE LOSS OF PLAYFUL LOVING

Even in the absence of violence or subordination, there are always some kinds of scripts that seemingly "have to be" followed, and persons of both sexes may feel they are expected to be interested in having or continuing to have sex at times when they actually are not. Should we be surprised, then, that there are women, as well as men, who complain of not even experiencing desire? It is also important to bear in mind that the script provided to men is as conditioned by historical and cultural context as that provided to women.

> Many men claim they find it hard to say no to sex even when they do not feel like it. It may clash with expectations. ... those of others as well as their own. It is not unusual for men to assume they are "on" all the time, despite the fact that desire varies and is connected to how you feel otherwise.[51]

Failing to achieve orgasm may signal an overall lack of desire, as well as lack of pleasure. When people contact RFSU about sexual problems (instead of, for example, concerns about pregnancy or sexually transmitted diseases), the most common question concerns lack of desire (more often posed by women), closely followed by questions about erectile problems (commonly posed by men). One might ask whether changed norms for male sexuality would make it easier for men to address the question of lack of pleasure and desire, instead of having it framed as a matter of erectile dysfunction.

The rigidity of sexual norms could be one source of inhibited desires. There is a distinct lack of spontaneity and openness in cultural expectations that can make it harder to enjoy many sexual activities as ends in themselves, such as dwelling in a sexually charged encounter—enjoying looks, touch, play and arousal. Here, some readers may remember the cuddling, kisses, and petting of their youth, along with the pleasurable discovery of bodies—their own and others'—as being an almost ecstatic state in which space and time could become blurred. To make love playfully entails preserving some uncertainty. The ambiguity lies in the absence of rules, or rules that might suddenly be changed—neither party knows where the playful attitude will take them. María Lugones describes how the *attitude* of playfulness turns an activity into play, *the attitude that carries us through the activity, a playful attitude, turns the activity into play.* Our activity has no rules, though it is certainly intentional activity and we both understand what we are doing. The playfulness that gives meaning to our activity includes uncertainty, but in this case the uncertainty is an *openness to surprise.* This is a particular metaphysical attitude that does not expect the world to be neatly packaged, ruly. Rules may fail to explain what we are doing. We are not self-important, we are not fixed in particular constructions of ourselves, which is part of saying that we are *open to self-construction.* We may not have rules, and when we do have rules, there are no rules that are to us sacred. We are not worried by competence. We are not wedded to a particular way of doing things ... We *are there creatively.*[52]

A playful attitude renders us accessible to the surprise of the body's capacity for joy and pleasure, and the associated openness to outcome will then not implicitly hinge on an orgasm. Closeness and the accompanying possibility of play belie the use of a script with a self-evident end.

Movement, touch, and gestures are filled with meaning, just as our words are, and it is through our bodies that we understand other people.[53] What becomes especially marked in an erotic encounter is that we do not only get to know the other person through our body, but we also get to know our own body through the other person's.[54] For example, in a loving caress of my hip, I do not only feel my skin being touched—I also sense and experience the swell of my hip as pleasurable through the touch of my partner. Beauvoir also affirms this in her description of a lesbian act of love; she relates how the body of a lover may be seen as a possibility to recreate oneself in reciprocity.[55] In encounters of genuine closeness accompanied by the open-ended possibility of play both our bodies may be experienced as speaking to, calling on, enticing, or making appeals to us, and we may come to know *our own body as well as the other person's* as being happy, beautiful, and wonderful.[56]

The body often eludes our deliberate attempts at control, such as when one cannot fall asleep, or when an orgasm does not come as easily as one might wish. It may surprise us as well such as when we get goose bumps from listening to a piece of music, or when a smile and a glance from one's partner literally makes one's limbs kindle with desire. But this lack of control does not render us helpless. For example, sneezing and sleeping cannot be willed, nor can sexual pleasure—but they can be "invited." Merleau-Ponty describes how we can welcome sleep by lying down or sitting comfortably, by emptying the mind and breathing slowly.[57] Along similar lines, several contributors to *FO* write about having discovered ways to *invite* sensuous and ecstatic experience for themselves, and in playful interaction with their partners. As one woman in *FO* states: "If there is something I have learned, ... it's that it's up to me, that it does require a bit of concentration and fiddling about."[58,59] Several contributors point out that an orgasm is not something you *get* (from your lover), and one woman claims: "You are not given an orgasm, you take it,"[60] where another stresses participation: "For me it has always been natural to take responsibility for my own sexuality, to participate myself in achieving an orgasm. I would never blame a partner for the failure of pleasure to come off."[61]

The playful invitation to erotic pleasure is opposed to the habitual faking of orgasms. As was stated earlier in the chapter, two reasons given for faking in *FO* were faking in the name of love and faking to put an end to sex. Although there seem to be some notable differences between these two types of faking; both kinds are *instrumental*. They are performed in order to achieve something else. The sounds and movements signalling pleasure are used as a means to an essentialized end—the orgasm. This is in contrast to when the expressions of pleasure are ends in themselves, as a source of enjoyment regardless of what follows.

In an instrumental approach, one's attention is focussed on the movements and expressions of the other person as things to be dealt with, or even manipulated, thereby simultaneously reducing the partner to a reified being rather than a playmate. Similarly, one's own body is reduced to a thing, as the focus is not on feeling and experiencing whatever happens; it becomes a tool used to manoeuvre a situation.

A loving faker may believe he or she is performing an act of love. But one may well ask to what extent faking can be an act of love, regardless of how lovingly it is performed? Love and acts of love are typically understood as being ends in themselves. If a partner erroneously perceives acts of love as fluid and reciprocal when they turn out to have been instrumental, he or she may be prone to feel manipulated and trust will be difficult to restore. Trust and its counterpoint, distrust, are self-reinforcing.[62] Several stories in *FO* support this kind of process, where the disclosure of earlier faked orgasms has had a detrimental effect on the relationship. But even if faked orgasms are not disclosed, an opportunity for genuine closeness is lost. Moreover, there is a risk that in the face of future sexual encounters, the ability/skill of switching on to faking has become the conditioned "solution."

For some the lived experience of faking, of distancing oneself, the instrumental attitude and behaviour develops into a habit. As Merleau-Ponty points out, we acquire the ability to react to certain situations using certain kinds of solutions.[63] The body is a situation, and it is the body that "'understands' when a habit is acquired."[64] In the habit, our body is our anchor between what our aim and what we do. Thus, when encountering situations similar to those in which the habit was once acquired, our body is our means of handling the situation, and practice has made perfect. One way of dealing with *certain* situations has become a habit, such that *the habit becomes the terms on which one experiences similar situations*. Several stories in *FO* support these notions, in that contributors report experiencing difficulty not responding with faking at later occasions—especially with that same partner, but in some cases also with other partners. Thus, a practice that was intended to "resolve" certain situations may eventually end up as a lasting tendency.[65]

## FAKING—THE GOOD NEWS

As has been described earlier in this chapter, women and men may choose to fake out of loving care, or to stay with an unintended fake, in order to let their partner enjoy what might be taken as a fully reciprocal consummate erotic encounter. This choice of action might at times be ascribed to the wish to let the partner experience the role of an accomplished lover. However, if not hinged on the idea of "successful" sex or accomplishment, this choice of action may also rest on the knowledge that it *matters* to one's partner's erotic and sexual enjoyment of the sexual act. Just like arousal and desire can be kindled and heightened in reciprocal response, so can the orgasm. Read in this light, we can also see how in the sexual realm the wilful or unintended fake may blend into and touch upon the reciprocal consummate erotic encounter.

## NOTES

1. Earlier versions of this chapter have been published, as Hildur Kalman, "Faking Orgasms and the Idea of Successful Sexuality," *Janus Head: Special Issue on Feminist Phenomenology* 13 (1), 97–118, and presented, as "Faking-Feat or Self-Deceit?," at the SPSL (Society for the Philosophy of Sex and Love) session at the 2015 Pacific APA in Vancouver. I thank the audience at the SPSL and the editors of this volume for helpful and creative comments and suggestions.

2. None of the contributors, academic or otherwise, or the editors are receiving any payment or royalty for their contributions to the book. In the invitation to write, it was stated that every contribution was considered a gift to the project and to humanity. All income generated by the book is given to an organization, NSKK, working at the grassroots level outside of Kolkata in India with sexual education for young people, and supplying sanitary towels to young women.

3. Susanna Alakoski and Amanda Mogensen, eds., *Fejkad orgasm* [*Faked Orgasm*] (Stockholm: Ordfront Förlag, 2008).

4. Alakoski and Mogensen, *Fejkad orgasm*, 88.

5. Russell Keat and John Urry, *Social Theory as Science*, (London: Routledge & Kegan Paul, 1975).

6. Keat and Urry, *Social Theory as Science*, 169.

7. Alakoski and Mogensen, *Fejkad orgasm*, 37.

8. This and all the following translations of citations from the anthology *Fejkad orgasm* are mine.

9. Ibid., 241.

10. Ibid., 198.

11. Ibid., 78.

12. Ibid., 200.

13. Ibid., 26.

14. Ibid., 11.

15. Eva Elmerstig, Painful Ideals: Young Swedish Women's Ideal Sexual Situations and Experiences of Pain During Vaginal Intercourse (PhD diss., Linköping: Linköpings Universitet, 2009).

16. Eva Elmerstig, Barbro Wijma and Carine Berterö, "Why do Young Women Continue to Have Sexual Intercourse Despite Pain?," *The Journal of Adolescent Health: Official Publication of The Society For Adolescent Medicine* 43(4) (2008): 360–1.

17. Elmerstig, Wijma, and Berterö, "Why Do Young Women Continue to Have Sexual Intercourse Despite Pain?" 361.

18. These examples from American popular culture are not foreign to the Swedish public—on the contrary, these series and the film have been shown and rerun on several Swedish TV channels for many years. The impact of American popular culture can hardly be overestimated, as, for example, more than 40% of what was shown on the five biggest TV channels in 2010 was produced in the United States, which is comparable to the amount produced in Sweden. If productions of British origin are added to the American productions, these make up 50% of what is offered to the Swedish televiewer. Cinema film premieres in Sweden show comparable numbers: circa 50% are of North American origin. If one focuses on what viewers between 15 and 24 watch most of the time, that is drama, series and films (57% of their TV watching time in 2010), the North American cultural dominance is even greater (all statistics from NORDICOM, *Nordic Information Centre for Media and Communication Research*: http://www.nordicom.gu.se/eng.php - retrieved 2012-04-17). The question of impact on the audience is another issue, of course, but two examples may give a hint. When teaching ethics in the Basic Training Programme for Police Officers at Umeå University, my colleague teachers who were police officers told me that nowadays, when Swedish police officers are about to make a search of a premises, they are commonly asked to present "the search warrant." This is noteworthy as according to Swedish law there is no need for a search warrant. The expectation is obviously based on what people have seen on TV—that is, American legal practice. And most Swedish lay persons know more about American procedures in the court room, from having watched a series of dramas, and so on, on the sub-ject—whereas few have seen the inside and know the practices of a Swedish court room. The next example is from the topic of weddings: It has become common when planning for a wedding that young women in Sweden ask for a ceremony in which their fathers walk them down the aisle in order to "give them away." This has evoked some debate, and many pastors refuse to abide by this wish or at least question it. The reason is that this "giving away" of the bride is perceived of as a patriarchal

tradition, foreign and opposed to the Swedish custom, which is for the two parties to walk down the aisle side by side as two equals. This gradual change in customs, where young women perceive of the "giving away" as a romantic part of a wedding, is often interpreted as an effect of the obvious fact that most people have witnessed more American weddings on TV and in films than Swedish weddings in real life or on TV. Thus, when the Swedish crown princess and the king, in their preparations for her wedding the 19th of June 2010, expressed the wish that the king walk her down the aisle, there was a heated public debate. This led to a historical compromise whereby the king walked the princess halfway down the aisle, where the bridegroom was waiting, and then the couple continued their walk according to the Swedish custom. See Maria Sundén Jelmini, "Överlämningen en kompromiss [The Delivery a Compromise]," in *Svenska Dagbladet* (Stockholm, 2010); Mattias Sandberg, " 'Ta över Victoria': När alla skandaler briserade räddade hon familjens rykte ['Take over Victoria': When All the Scandals Exploded She Saved the Family Reputation]," in *Aftonbladet* (Stockholm, 2010).

19. Iris Marion Young, *On Female Body Experience: "Throwing Like a Girl" and Other Essays* (Oxford: Oxford University Press, 2005).

20. Douglas Rushkoff, "Picture Perfect," in *What Makes a Man: 22 Writers Imagine the Future*, ed. Rebecca Walker (New York: Riverhead Books, 2004).

21. Ibid., 56.

22. Ibid., 56.

23. Maurice Merleau-Ponty, *Phenomenology of Perception* (London: Routledge, 1962, 189 [1945]).

24. Merleau-Ponty, *Phenomenology of Perception*, 215.

25. Sara Heinämaa, *Toward a Phenomenology of Sexual Difference: Husserl, Merleau-Ponty, Beauvoir* (Lanham: Rowman & Littlefield Publishers, 2003), 51 n. 35.

26. Merleau-Ponty, *Phenomenology of Perception*, 212 ff., 240.

27. Rushkoff, "Picture Perfect," 57.

28. Ibid., 56–57.

29. Ibid., 57.

30. Frigga Haug, *Female Sexualization: A Collective Work of Memory* (London: Verso, 1990).

31. Simone de Beauvoir, *The Second Sex* (New York: Alfred A. Knopf, 2010 [1949]), 273, 294–95, 311, 334–35.

32. Ibid., 273, 294–95.

33. Anna G. Jónasdóttir, *Love Power and Political Interests: Towards a Theory of Patriarchy in Contemporary Western Societies*, (PhD diss., Göteborg: University Örebro, 1991), 224–25.

34. Jónasdóttir, *Love Power and Political Interests*, 38.

35. Carin Holmberg, *Det kallas kärlek: En socialpsykologisk studie om kvinnors underordning och mäns överordning bland unga jämställda par* [*It's Called Love: A Social Psychological Study of the Woman's Subordination and the Man's Superordination Among Young, Equal Couples*] (Göteborg: Anamma Förlag, 1993).

36. Carin Holmberg, *Det kallas kärlek*, 169.

274 Hildur Kalman

37. Beauvoir, *The Second Sex*, 16–17, 418-19; Heinämaa, *Toward a Phenomenology of Sexual Difference*, 73.
38. Anne Koedt, "The Myth of the Vaginal Orgasm," in *Radical Feminism*, eds. Anne Koedt, Ellen Levine, and Anita Rapone (New York: Quadrangle, 1973), 199.
39. Jennifer Saul, "Feminist Philosophy of Language," in *The Stanford Encyclopedia of Philosophy* (Fall 2010 Edition), ed. Edward N. Zalta, http://plato.stanford.edu/archives/fall2010/entries/feminism-language/.
40. Pelle Ullholm, "Visst fejkar män [Indeed—Men are Faking]!," in *Fejkad Orgasm* [*Faked orgasm*], eds. Susanna Alakoski & Amanda Mogensen (Stockholm: Ordfront Förlag, 2008), 201.
41. Alakoski and Mogensen, *Fejkad orgasm*, 203.
42. Sandra Dahlén, "Varför fejkar så många kvinnor orgasm [Why Are So Many Women Faking Orgasms],?" in *Fejkad orgasm* [*Faked Orgasm*], eds. Susanna Alakoski & Amanda Mogensen (Stockholm: Ordfront Förlag, 2008), 164.
43. Alfred C. Kinsey, Wardell B. Pomeroy and Clyde E. Martin, *Sexual Behavior in the Human Male* (Philadelphia: Saunders, 1948), 237.
44. Åsa Andersson, "Från fula gubbar och liderliga gummor till vitala casanovor och glada änkor: Om 1900-Talets förändrade synsätt på äldres sexualitet [From Dirty Old Men and Lascivious Old Women to Vigorous Casanovas and Merry Widows: On the Changed Perspectives on the Sexuality of Elderly During the 20th Century]," *Tidskrift för Genusvetenskap* 4 (2009).
45. Ibid.; Brent Pickett "Homosexuality," in *The Stanford Encyclopedia of Philosophy (Spring 2011 Edition)*, ed. Edward N. Zalta, http://plato.stanford.edu/archives/spr2011/entries/homosexuality/; Saul, *Feminist Philosophy of Language*.
46. See, for example, Alakoski and Mogensen, *Fejkad orgasm*, 111, 207.
47. See Andrea Dworkin, *Pornography: Men Possessing Women* (London: Women's Press, 1981); Andrea Dworkin, *Letters From a War Zone: Writings 1976–1989* (New York: Dutton, 1989); Catharine MacKinnon, *Feminism Unmodified: Discourses on Life and Law*, (Cambridge: Harvard University Press, 1987); Catharine MacKinnon, *Only Words* (Cambridge: Harvard University Press, 1993).
48. Don Heider and Dustine Harp, "New Hope or Old Power: Democracy, Pornography and the Internet," *Howard Journal of Communications* 13 (4) (2002): 297.
49. Heider and Harp, "New Hope or Old Power," 294.
50. See, for example, Yolanda Mufweba, "Corrective Rape Makes You an African Woman," *IOL: News for South Africa and the World* (published 2003-11-07) http://www.int.iol.co.za/index.php?click_id=139&art_id=ct20031107212728265P430805&set_id=1 (retrieved February 11th 2008); Vasu Reddy, Cheryl-Ann Potgieter and Nonhlanhla Mkhize, "Cloud Over Rainbow Nation," *HSRC Review* vol. 5, no. 1 (March 2007). http://www.hsrc.ac.za/HSRC_Review_Article-51.phtml (retrieved February 11th 2008).
51. Ullholm, "Indeed—Men are Faking," 201.
52. María Lugones, "Playfulness, 'World'-Traveling, and Loving Perception," in *Women, Knowledge, and Reality*, eds. Ann Garry and Marilyn Pearsall (New York: Routledge, 1996), 431; italics in original.
53. Merleau-Ponty, *Phenomenology of Perception*, 185–86; cf. 92–93.

54. cf. Hildur Kalman, *The Structure of Knowing: Existential Trust as an Epistemological Category* (PhD diss., Umeå: Universitet Umeå, 1999), 150, n. 166.

55. Beauvoir, *The Second Sex*, 429.

56. cf. Merleau-Ponty *Phenomenology of Perception*, 154 ff., 317–20; Heinämaa, *Toward a Phenomenology of Sexual Difference*, 63, 67.

57. Merleau-Ponty, *Phenomenology of Perception*, 163–64.

58. Alakoski and Mogensen, *Fejkad orgasm*, 28.

59. This citation is not intended to imply that women's bodies are more complicated than men's bodies when it comes to the ability to experience pleasure. Rather, it means that in a culture where girls' bodies and body parts are the objects of shame earlier, more deeply and to a larger extent than are the bodies of boys (Haug, *Female Sexualization*), and where norms for sex are heteronormative and connected to the notion of penetration, for some this "fiddling" may have to be given some scope.

60. Alakoski and Mogensen, *Fejkad orgasm*, 138.

61. Ibid., 15.

62. cf. Lars Hertzberg, "On the Attitude of Trust," *Inquiry* 31 (1988): 307–22; Olli Lagerspetz, *Trust: The Tacit Demand*. Vol. 1, *Library of Ethics and Applied Philosophy* (Kluwer Academic Publishers, 1997); Kalman, *The Structure of Knowing*.

63. Merleau-Ponty, *Phenomenology of Perception*, 142.

64. Ibid., 143–44.

65. cf. Kalman, *The Structure of Knowing*, 102–9.

# BIBLIOGRAPHY

Alakoski, Susanna, and Amanda Mogensen, editors. *Fejkad orgasm* [*Faked Orgasm*]. Stockholm: Ordfront Förlag, 2008.

Andersson, Åsa. "Från fula gubbar och liderliga gummor till vitala casanovor och glada änkor: Om 1900-Talets förändrade synsätt på äldres sexualitet [From Dirty Old Men and Lascivious Old Women to Vigorous Casanovas and Merry Widows: On the Changed Perspectives on the Sexuality of Elderly During the 20th Century]." *Tidskrift för Genusvetenskap* 4 (2009): 47–71.

de Beauvoir, Simone. *The Second Sex*. New York: Alfred A. Knopf, 2010 [1949].

———. *Les Mandarins*. Paris: Gallimard, 1954.

Dahlén, Sandra. "Varför fejkar så många kvinnor orgasm [Why Do So Many Women Fake Orgasms]?" In *Fejkad orgasm* [*Faked Orgasm*], edited by Susanna Alakoski and Amanda Mogensen, 155–68. Stockholm: Ordfront Förlag, 2008.

Dworkin, Andrea. *Letters From a War Zone: Writings 1976-1989*. New York: Dutton, 1989.

———. *Pornography: Men Possessing Women*. London: Women's Press, 1981.

Elmerstig, Eva. *Painful Ideals: Young Swedish Women's Ideal Sexual Situations and Experiences of Pain During Vaginal Intercourse*. PhD diss., Linköping: Linköpings Universitet, 2009.

Elmerstig, Eva, Barbro Wijma, and Carine Berterö. "Why do Young Women Continue to Have Sexual Intercourse Despite Pain?" *The Journal of Adolescent*

*Health: Official Publication of The Society For Adolescent Medicine* 43, no. 4 (2008): 357–63.

Finlay, Sara-Jane, and Natalie Fenton. "'If You've Got a Vagina and an Attitude, That's a Deadly Combination': Sex and Heterosexuality in *Basic Instinct, Body of Evidence* and *Disclosure.*" *Sexualities* 8, no. 1 (2005): 49–74.

Haug, Frigga. *Female Sexualization: A Collective Work of Memory.* London: Verso, 1999.

Heider, Don, and Dustin Harp. "New Hope or Old Power: Democracy, Pornography and the Internet," *Howard Journal of Communications* 13, no. 4 (2002): 285–99.

Heinämaa, Sara. *Toward a Phenomenology of Sexual Difference: Husserl, Merleau-Ponty, Beauvoir.* Lanham: Rowman & Littlefield Publishers, 2003.

Hertzberg, Lars. "On the Attitude of Trust." *Inquiry* 31 (1988): 307–22.

Holmberg, Carin. *Det kallas kärlek: En socialpsykologisk studie om kvinnors underordning och mäns överordning bland unga jämställda part [It's Called Love: A Social Psychological Study of the Woman's Subordination and the Man's Superordination Among Young, Equal Couples].* Göteborg: Anamma Förlag, 1993.

Jónasdóttir, Anna G. *Love Power and Political Interests: Towards a Theory of Patriarchy in Contemporary Western Societies.* PhD diss., Göteborg: Universitet Örebro, 1991.

Kalman, Hildur. "Faking Orgasms and the Idea of Successful Sexuality." *Janus Head: Special Issue on Feminist Phenomenology*, 13, no. 1: 97–118.

———. "Njutning eller fejk?: En Filosofisk Betraktelse [Pleasure or Fake? A Philosophical Reflection]." In *Fejkad Orgasm [Faked orgasm]*, edited by Susanna Alakoski & Amanda Mogensen, 39–62. Stockholm: Ordfront Förlag, 2008.

———. *The Structure of Knowing: Existential Trust as an Epistemological Category.* PhD diss., Umeå: Universitet Umeå, 1999.

Keat, Russell, and John Urry. *Social Theory as Science.* London: Routledge & Kegan Paul, 1975.

Kinsey, Alfred C., Wardell B. Pomeroy, and Clyde E. Martin. *Sexual Behavior in the Human Male.* Philadelphia: Saunders, 1948.

Koedt, Anne. "The Myth of the Vaginal Orgasm." In *Radical Feminism*, edited by Anne Koedt, Ellen Levine, and Anita Rapone, 198–207. New York: Quadrangle, 1973.

Lagerspetz, Olli. *Trust: The Tacit Demand.* Vol. 1, *Library of Ethics and Applied Philosophy.* Kluwer Academic Publishers, 1997.

Lugones, María. "Playfulness, 'World'-Traveling, and Loving Perception." In *Women, Knowledge, and Reality*, 2nd edition, edited by Ann Garry and Marilyn Pearsall, 419–33. New York: Routledge, 1996.

MacKinnon, Catharine. *Feminism Unmodified: Discourses on Life and Law*, Cambridge: Harvard University Press, 1987.

———. *Only Words*, Cambridge: Harvard University Press, 1993.

Merleau-Ponty, Maurice. *Phenomenology of Perception.* London: Routledge, 1962 [1945].

Mufweba, Yolanda. "Corrective Rape Makes you an African Woman." *IOL: News for South Africa and the World* (November 2007). http://www.int.iol.co.za/index.php?click_id=139&art_id=ct20031107212728265P430805&set_id=1 (retrieved February 11th 2008).

NORDICOM, *Nordic Information Centre for Media and Communication Research*: http://www.nordicom.gu.se/eng.php - retrieved 2012-04-17

Pickett, Brent. "Homosexuality." In *The Stanford Encyclopedia of Philosophy (Spring 2011 Edition)*, edited by Edward N. Zalta, http://plato.stanford.edu/archives/spr2011/entries/homosexuality/.

Reddy, Vasu, Cheryl-Ann Potgieter, and Nonhlanhla Mkhize. "Cloud Over Rainbow Nation," *HSRC Review* vol. 5, no. 1 (March 2007). http://www.hsrc.ac.za/HSRC_Review_Article-51.phtml (retrieved February 11th 2008)

Rushkoff, Douglas. "Picture Perfect." In *What Makes a Man: 22 Writers Imagine the Future,* edited by Rebecca Walker, 54–66. New York: Riverhead Books, 2004.

Sandberg, Mattias. " 'Ta över Victoria': När alla skandaler briserade räddade hon familjens rykte ['Take over Victoria': When All the Scandals Exploded She Saved the Family Reputation]," *Aftonbladet* (Stockholm), 2010.

Saul, Jennifer. "Feminist Philosophy of Language." In *The Stanford Encyclopedia of Philosophy (Fall 2010 Edition)*, edited by Edward N. Zalta, http://plato.stanford.edu/archives/fall2010/entries/feminism-language/.

Sundén Jelmini, Maria. "Överlämningen en kompromiss [The Delivery a Compromise]," *Svenska Dagbladet* (Stockholm), 2010.

Ullholm, Pelle. "Visst fejkar män [Indeed—Men are Faking]!" In *Fejkad orgasm [Faked Orgasm]*, edited by Susanna Alakoski & Amanda Mogensen, 201–2. Stockholm: Ordfront Förlag, 2008.

World Economic Forum. The Global Gender Gap Report 2011: http://www.weforum.org/ - retrieved 2012-04-2.

Young, Iris Marion. *On Female Body Experience: "Throwing Like a Girl" and Other Essays.* Oxford: Oxford University Press, 2005.

# Index

between parents and adult children,
157–58. *See also* parent-child
relationship; love, parent-child
between partners, 117
between women, 7, 102
between women and men, 106
compared to love, 157
love prioritized over, 94
"with benefits," 92
within polyamorous
relationships, 93
Frye, Marilyn, 136, 137

gender, 7, 47–8, 55n49, 55n50,
129, 162n19, 174, 178, 191,
236–37, 260;
identity, 225
impact on of beliefs about on love,
7, 47–8
inequality, 236–37
and lived experience, 170–71,
177–78. *See also* phenomenology,
feminist
popular and cultural beliefs about, 7,
101, 103
roles, historical/traditional, 129, 237,
261, 263–65, 267.
*See also* male nonage; men; women
generosity. *See* gift/giving
Giddens, Anthony, 47, 55n48
gift/giving, 69, 73, 163n29, 259
Goffmann, Erving, 45, 173
Goldman, Emma, 125
grammar. *See* discourse
Greek language, ancient, 22
Guevara, Che, 129–30
Gutting, Gary, 103

happiness, 88
hate. *See* hatred
hatred, 126, 135. *See also* anger,
distinguished from hate
Heidegger, Martin, 18, 70, 71, 81n67
Heinämaa, Sara, 217

heteronormativity, 7, 62, 81n72,
264–67, 275n59. *See also*
homosexuality; gender, roles,
historical/traditional; sexuality,
normative/"normal"
*History of Sexuality*, 24
Hochschild, A.R., 43, 45
Homer, 19, 22. *See also* The Odyssey
homophobia, 176
homosexuality, 23–25, 175, 266–67;
historicity of concept of, 23, 24
pederastic paradigm, 32n47,
246, 248
hooks, bell, 106, 114
Husserl, Edmund, 65, 71, 79n31

ideal types, 86–87, 89, 95
identity. *See* gender, identity; self;
sexual identity
inauthenticity. *See* bad faith; love,
inauthentic
infidelity. *See* cheating
in-itself/for-itself, 68, 72, 222. *See also*
bad faith; objectification; self-other
relation
intersex, 169–70, 172, 174, 176–79,
180n2. *See also* Androgen
Insensitivity Syndrome (AIS)
intersubjectivity. *See* self-other
relation
intimacy, 95, 159, 197, 226, 270
Irigaray, Luce, 197

jealousy, 93–94;
between friends, 94
joy, 130–32, 137, 211, 269

Kahneman, Daniel, 112
Kant, Immanuel, 101
Kaufmann, J.C., 42, 49
*Kinsey Reports*, 266
Kristeva, Julia, 172–73
Kupfer, Joseph, 150–57,
162–63n28, 163n44

# About the Editors

**Sarah LaChance Adams** is associate professor of philosophy at the University of Wisconsin, Superior. Her previous publications include *Coming to Life: Philosophies of Pregnancy, Childbirth and Mothering* (coedited with Caroline R. Lundquist, 2013) and *Mad Mothers, Bad Mothers, and What a "Good" Mother Would Do: The Ethics of Ambivalence* (2014). She has published articles on Levinas, Merleau-Ponty, Beauvoir, Bataille, Sartre, Hegel, and care ethics. LaChance Adams works primarily in feminist philosophy, ethics, existential phenomenology, and nineteenth-century German philosophy.

**Christopher M. Davidson** is assistant professor at Ball State University. He focuses on Foucault's *The History of Sexuality* series, Spinoza's political and ethical thought, and Ancient philosophical practice as a way of life, as seen in his chapter "Spinoza as an Exemplar of Foucault's Spirituality and Technologies of the Self" (in the *Journal of Early Modern Studies*, Fall 2015) and "Foucault on *Askesis* in Epictetus: Freedom Through Determination" (in *Epictetus: His Continuing Influence and Contemporary Relevance*, 2014).

**Caroline R. Lundquist** is an instructor at Lane Community College and adjunct instructor at the University of Oregon in Eugene, Oregon. Her previous publications include *Coming to Life: Philosophies of Pregnancy, Childbirth and Mothering* (co-edited with Sarah LaChance Adams, 2013), and various articles in feminist philosophy and ethics. Her primary areas of research are ethics and critical thinking, and her recent work engages the themes of kindness, entitlement, and the design of educational institutions.

# About the Contributors

**Alain Beauclair** is assistant professor in the department of humanities at MacEwan University in Edmonton, Alberta. He works in the areas of phenomenology and American pragmatism, with a focus on the work of John Dewey and Hans-Georg Gadamer.

**Erik Jansson Boström** is a PhD candidate in philosophy at Uppsala University, Sweden. His dissertation is on Max Weber's philosophy of social science. He teaches theory of science and contemporary philosophy.

**Elena Clare Cuffari** is assistant professor of philosophy at Worcester State University, where she teaches courses on embodied cognition, philosophy of language, and philosophy of love and sex, among other topics. Previously, she investigated interdisciplinary approaches to social interaction and sense-making as a Marie Curie Experienced Research Fellow in the TESIS (Towards an Embodied Science of Intersubjectivity) Network. Her doctoral work on the rational contributions of conversational hand gestures to meaning construction was carried out at the University of Oregon.

**Phoebe Hart** is a writer, director, and producer of documentaries, and a film academic. Phoebe completed her PhD at the Queensland University of Technology (where she now lectures) in 2009. She is the creator of a multi-award-winning, long-form documentary film entitled *Orchids: My Intersex Adventure*.

**Fulden Ibrahimhakkioglu** is a feminist philosopher and an independent scholar. Her work focuses on social and political philosophy, philosophy of the body and affect, and continental philosophy. She holds a PhD from the

University of Oregon. She currently resides in Istanbul, where she plays with her riot grrrl band Secondhand Underpants.

**Hildur Kalman** is professor of social work, and associate professor in philosophy of Science, currently employed at the Department of Social Work, Umeå University, Sweden.

**Yong Dou (Michael) Kim** is a doctoral candidate in philosophy at Villanova University and currently teaches in Colorado. He works at the intersection of philosophy, criticism, and theory. His current work is on the first of a pair of twin projects entitled "Image and Phenomenon: For a Critique of Appearance" and "Form and Expression: For a Critique of Representation."

**Rebecca Kukla** is professor of philosophy and senior research scholar in the Kennedy Institute of Ethics at Georgetown University. Her publications include books and articles on methodological issues in the special sciences reproductive ethics, health communication, philosophy of language, and social epistemology, among other topics. She is the former coordinator of the Feminist Approaches to Bioethics Network, and the current editor-in-chief of the *Kennedy Institute of Ethics Journal*.

**Christine Overall** is professor emerita of philosophy and holds a University Research Chair at Queen's University, Kingston, Ontario. Her teaching and research are in the areas of bioethics, feminist philosophy, and philosophy of religion, in which fields she has published over 125 book chapters and journal articles. She is the editor or coeditor of five books and the author of six.

**Chiara Piazzesi** is professor of sociological theory at the Department of Sociology, Université du Québec à Montréal. Piazzesi has been working for several years on Nietzsche's philosophy and on classical and contemporary sociological theory. In addition, she has worked on the relationship between knowledge and belief—especially religious belief—in the thought of Pascal, Kierkegaard, and Wittgenstein. Her current research project focuses on the contemporary paradigms and forms of erotic and romantic love in Western societies.

**Louis A. Ruprecht Jr.** is the inaugural holder of the William M. Suttles Chair in Religious Studies, as well as director of the Center for Hellenic Studies at Georgia State University. His scholarship ranges from classical literature, history, and culture to modern ethics and politics. The author of ten books and over seventy articles, his latest books include *Classics at the Dawn of* *the Museum Era: The Life and Times of Antoine Chrysostome Quatremere de Quincy* (2014).

**Amy E. Taylor** is a clinical psychologist on the staff of The Austen Riggs Center. She holds a PhD in existential-phenomenological clinical psychology with certification in gender studies and qualitative research from Duquesne University. Her scholarship, teaching, and clinical interests are broadly about how embodied, sexed, and gendered identities develop within a network of overlapping interpersonal, cultural, and technological contexts.